COSTA BLANCA ROCK

Another winter's day and another deserted cliff!
Pete O'Donovan approaches Reconco for some sport

COSTA BLANCA ROCK

by
Chris Craggs

CICERONE PRESS
Milnthorpe, Cumbria

© Chris Craggs 1997
1st Edition 1990 (Costa Blanca Climbs)
2nd Revised Edition 1997
ISBN 1 85284 241 5
A catalogue record for this book is available from the British Library.

ACKNOWLEDGEMENTS

My thanks go out to the people I have climbed with on the Costa Blanca over the past ten years: the original team of adventurers (*motto:* nothing ventured, nothing broken!) of Dave Spencer and Mike Riddings, and all those who came later mentioned below; John and Oliver Addy, Colin Binks, Ian Clayton, Willie Jeffrey, Andy Nicholson, Graham Parkes, John 'JR' Robinson, Jim Rubery and Noel Williams. Special thanks again to Pete (POD) O'Donovan who managed to drag himself away from the delights of the Barcelona area and was suitably impressed with the Blanca; to Dave Gregory and his team of friends, Bruce Goodwin, John Street and Alan Lawson, who have explored some of the more out of the way spots for me; and to the many people who have sent me comments, grades, topos, etc. concerning the area. Special thanks as ever to Sherri Davy, who always handles the mundane tasks of organising flights, accommodation, car hire, shopping etc. and still finds the energy to do plenty of belaying, sunbathing and a few routes.

Finally, a special thank you to Walt Unsworth of Cicerone Press who gave the OK to the idea of a small climbing guide to the Costa Blanca in 1988. Who could have guessed what we started?

Advice to Readers

Readers are advised that whilst every effort is taken by the author to ensure the accuracy of this guidebook, changes can occur which may affect the contents. It is advisable to check locally on transport, accommodation, shops etc. but even rights-of-way can be altered and, more especially overseas, access paths can be eradicated by landslip, forest fires or changes of ownership.

The publisher would welcome notes of any such changes.

Front Cover: *A local climber enjoying NINA DE PORCELANA 6a+ at Gandia, currently the most popular cliff in the north of the area*

CONTENTS

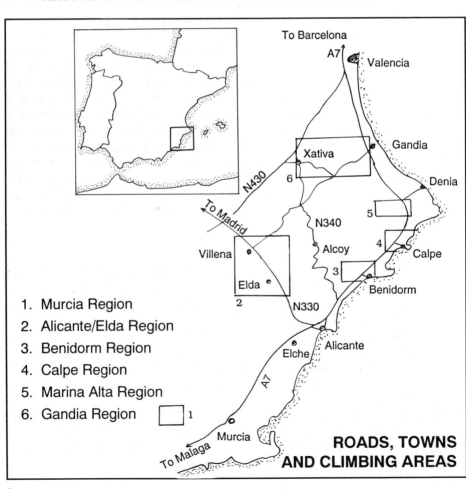

1. Murcia Region
2. Alicante/Elda Region
3. Benidorm Region
4. Calpe Region
5. Marina Alta Region
6. Gandia Region

ROADS, TOWNS AND CLIMBING AREAS

INTRODUCTION

The area of the Costa Blanca between Benidorm and Calpe has become known as one of the premier sun rock destinations for Britons (and Germans and Scandinavians) wanting to escape the rigours of our grim northern winters. The whole of the coast from Murcia right up to Valencia has much rock and many developed climbing areas. I have climbed extensively in Spain over the last ten years and the Costa Blanca still remains my favourite destination. The simple reason for this is the immense variety that is available both in the climbing and in the countryside. The coastal strip is heavily developed (though nothing like on the same scale as the Costa del Sol) and the cliffs tend to be rather urban. Inland are high mountains, the extensive and ever popular cliffs at Sella and Gandia, fruit and nut terraces by the million and considerable aridity. Further inland still the landscape changes again, with fortified towns, fertile farmland and plenty of rock, in the form of extensive scarps, isolated cliffs, and impressive mountains.

I first visited the Calpe area for a week's holiday at Christmas 1987 after reading an inspirational article in *Mountain* magazine by German climber Nico Milander (author of the first *Sun Rock* volume). We climbed on Dalle d'Ola, the Toix cliffs, Mascarat and did Diedro UBSA on the Peñon and Diedro Magicos on the Piug Campana. The range of climbing, from 10m roadside routes to high mountain classics, allied to very acceptable weather, was intoxicating and so the following year we were back for two weeks. By the end of that trip we felt we had almost worked the place out. How wrong can you be? During Easter 1996 I made my twelfth visit to the Costa Blanca. We climbed on a different crag every day (five of which were new to me) for two weeks and shared only one of them with other climbers (who were British!). I feel the area has a good few visits left in it yet, and if you feel the climbing potential is running out take a drive up the road from Benidorm to Alcoy via Guadalest - the rock goes on for ever!

THE GUIDE
My little original 1990 guide to the Costa Blanca contained information on about 200 routes on nine cliffs. Things have moved on apace since and the new volume includes over 1500 routes on over 50 cliffs (some of which are very extensive). Keeping up with this dramatic expansion has not been easy (It's a tough job but someone's got to do it!). I have presented as much information as I have been able to accumulate over the years. The cliffs I have climbed on regularly are given full coverage, and the more recent discoveries contain as much detail as possible. In all cases accurate approaches are included (surely the single most important piece of information about any crag), plus details of the best climbs across as broad a range of grades as possible.

I have finally dropped the use of UK grades as I feel most climbers now travel enough to have an understanding of the continental grading system. As a rough guide (and let's face it, that's all it can ever be) here is a comparative grades table built up from over 25 years of personal experience, and countless hours of discussion.

UK	French	Spanish	USA
Severe	4+	4	5.6
VS (4c)	5	4+	5.8
HVS (5a)	5+	5	5.9
E1 (5b)	6a	5+	5.10a
E2 (5c)	6b	6a	5.10c
E3 (6a)	6c	6b	5.11a
E4 (6a)	7a	6c+	5.11c
E5 (6b)	7a+	7a	5.12a
E6 (6b)	7b	7a+	5.12c
E6 (6c)	7c	7b	5.13a

If a route is known to be particularly tough (or soft touch) for the grade, I have mentioned this in the text and for the longer routes have offered a suggested UK grade where I feel this to be appropriate. As further help I have also given the cliffs a star rating from 1 to 5 to help you in the right direction. A ** cliff, eg. Dalle d'Olla or Chatsworth, is worth a visit if you are in the area and the crag offers the style of climbing you prefer. A *** crag, eg. Toix East or Cratcliffe, is worth visiting from afar if it offers your style of climbing. A ***** star cliff, eg. Sella or Stanage, is worth an extended visit by anybody. (See Contents.)

As an indication of the quality of the climbs, I have reduced the UK three star system to two symbols. ☺ indicates a climb considered to be one of the best on its cliff - do it and you won't be disappointed. A ♠ indicates a route considered to be one of the best in the area - do it if possible whatever grade you climb at!

LOGISTICS
Winter is the time to go, though there is enough shady and/or high altitude rock if you end up in the area in August. From October to April the climate is kind, the resorts are quiet and the prices are low.

Getting There
There are regular winter flights to Alicante from almost all regional airports. Currently, prices vary from knock down (less then £50 return) at quiet times to rather inflated (say £150+) during the school holidays. All inclusive packages can be good value, though self-catering accommodation of all classes abounds. Shop around! For flights only (the way we usually do it) check the teletext pages on commercial TV. Ignore red herrings such as 'flights from £9.95' and look for specific dates from your chosen airport. If all else fails it is worth considering a scheduled flight with Iberian airlines, though obviously more expensive. They fly direct from Heathrow, or from Manchester via Barcelona. At quiet times they do special 'two for the price of one' deals. Information from: London 0171 830 0011, Manchester 0161 436 6444, Glasgow 0141 248 6581.

Transport
A car is pretty much a necessity. Although the area has a reasonable transportation system

a number of the cliffs are remote, and the distances between the various centres make for difficult commuting. It would be possible to stay at Sella (in the refuge) or in Calpe and manage without a vehicle once you were established. For a number of years I have used Premier Car Hire, based in Harlow, who have always proved reliable and inexpensive. They offer a range of vehicles with current prices starting at about £85 a week in the winter (phone 01279 641040 for a brochure). A rep will meet you at the airport (don't forget your driving licence) and the car is normally delivered with a full tank of petrol. You leave it as empty as you dare at the end of the holiday.

A Base

Quite where you stay depends mainly on where you want to climb. Both Calpe and Benidorm have long been popular and are ideal centres with plenty of climbing within an hour's drive. If you want comfortable, cheap accommodation with easy shopping and some low-key nightlife you could do worse! Alternatively anywhere from Campello, just north of Alicante, to Gandia in the north of the region is acceptable.

A good percentage of the villa accommodation in the area is owned by Britons and it is usually possible to arrange to rent one before you leave home. The Sunday papers and magazines such as *Dalton's Weekly* or *Private Villas* have plenty of places to rent, usually with UK contact numbers. Another alternative is simply to turn up and look for signs showing 'apartments to rent' in any of the resorts. Prices can be as low as £10 a night for basic accommodation for four (cheaper than camping). Again the key is to shop around.

A PLEA

Despite the scale of the tourist industry on the Costa Blanca, much of the area away from the coast remains amazingly unspoilt (apart from the occasional river bed that doubles as a rubbish dump!). This applies specifically to many of the climbing areas; please treat them and the local inhabitants with due respect. More specifically, don't leave litter, be careful with fires, don't block access routes, avoid crossing cultivated land and don't taint water supplies. If you cannot organise your bodily functions to use the resort facilities, get WELL away from footpaths and climbing areas. (A group trowel might not be a bad idea!)

A WARNING

Crime here is a major problem. A small group of local disreputables check out the popular parking areas on a regular basis. There is a high possibility that anything left in the car will be stolen. So it makes good sense not to leave ANY valuables in your car. As an extra precaution I have always made a point of leaving the empty glovebox open, the boot empty and the parcel shelf out so as to discourage speculative break-ins.

Temperature

	Jan	Feb	Mar	Apr	May	Jun	Jul	Aug	Sep	Oct	Nov	Dec
Daily Max (C)	16	17	19	21	24	28	31	32	29	25	20	17
Daily Min (C)	6	6	8	11	13	17	20	20	18	14	10	8

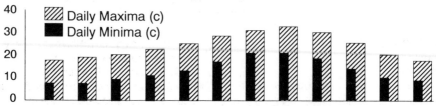

Sea Temperature

	Jan	Feb	Mar	Apr	May	Jun	Jul	Aug	Sep	Oct	Nov	Dec
	14	14	14	15	17	20	24	25	24	21	18	15

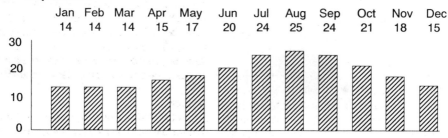

Hours of Sunshine

	Jan	Feb	Mar	Apr	May	Jun	Jul	Aug	Sep	Oct	Nov	Dec
	6	6	7	8	10	11	12	11	8	8	6	6

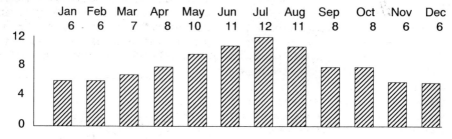

Precipitation (mm)

	Jan	Feb	Mar	Apr	May	Jun	Jul	Aug	Sep	Oct	Nov	Dec
	30	20	18	40	31	12	4	14	46	52	36	25

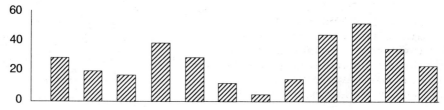

MURCIA REGION

LEIVA

Crag Facts

Star rating: *****
Aspect: south
Height: 12 to 180 metres
Spread of grades (individual pitches, not routes):

4	5	5+	6a	6b	6c	7a	7b	7c	8
6	2	13	35	28	18	18	10	5	5

Introduction

Although a long way south from the popular climbing areas around Benidorm and Calpe, Leiva is technically within the hinterland of the Costa Blanca, and as nothing about this superb cliff has appeared in English I felt it worth including some brief notes here. Leiva is a magnificent cliff of international significance. The main face is a 150m high south facing wall of excellent rock, not unlike the top half of the Falaise d'Escales in the French Verdon. The routes here were all done in traditional style originally, but in recent years there has been a substantial rebolting programme and a good number of the best climbs are now fully parabolted. All that is required for these is 15 quick-draws (some of the pitches are pretty big!), and double ropes for the abseil descent. If you prefer to travel even lighter and just use a single rope it is possible to walk off at the right side of the cliff, but can your feet take it?

To the right of and at a lower level than the main cliff are two (relatively) small crags with a good selection of single pitch climbs across a range of difficulty, all of which are fully bolted. These are the SECTOR DE LA CUEVA on the left and the SECTOR PERCERA on the right.

Leiva is a long day's outing from the Calpe area, though of course it is well worth the effort. A good option is to consider stopping over in the area for a couple of days. To this end there are several campsites passed on the way to the crag; there are rooms in Alhama de Murcia; and I have heard of people staying cheaply in the spooky sanatorium (rumoured to be a youth hostel) a short distance below the cliff (see map). In the usually settled weather here car-camping is also a possibility.

A camping area is set aside (See map below) in the pine forest (washing water only). Apply for permission from the Forest Warden at the Casa Forestal where drinking water is available. Finally there is a refuge some distance up the track, beyond the spot where cars are allowed. This is a small bothy with no facilities or water.

Access

Follow the toll-free motorway south from Alicante to Murcia (80km) then continue southwards for another 22km to a turn-off into the town of Alhama de Murcia. In the centre of the town is a right turn signed Sierra Espuna. 1.7km after the built up area is a left turn following the same sign. Follow this as it winds up into the hills, passing a wide water channel and a red snow barrier. After 10km there is an abrupt right turn

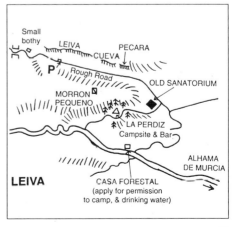

at a small roundabout and a large house - take this road. Follow this as it descends a little and then winds back northwards for 3km to a left turn onto a dirt road by three perched stones and opposite a picnic area. This is signed La Perdiz & Albergue Ven. 0.2km along the dirt road is a right turn by a sign with a house and the words Region de Murcia. 3.5km up this gradually deteriorating track is extensive parking, just before a terrace wall that crosses the valley, and a sign permitting foot and cycle passengers only. This is about 1½ hours from Alicante.

The foot of the main face is reached in 10-15 minutes up any one of a selection of steep scree paths.

The two smaller cliffs (Cuevas and Peceras) are reached by a steep track that starts 500m below the main parking area. Here there is parking on the left, and the cliffs are reached in less than 10 minutes.

The Main Face Climbs

The main section of the face is home to approximately 60 routes though research of the literature suggests that only about a third of these have been fully bolted up at the time of writing. Included here is a topo for a dozen routes up the central, most popular area. Many of the climbs have small metal plaques, inscribed with the name plus the grade of the hardest pitch on the climb, at their bases to aid identification. This should greatly reduce the chance of setting off up the wrong climb.

When you have done these 12 there are plenty more sections of the cliff to explore.

Descent

There are two normal ways off the cliff top. The least stressful way is to walk to the right edge of the crag, looking at the cliff, to locate a reasonable track that skirts round the edge of the rock and back under the main face - allow 30 minutes. Alternatively and potentially faster, there is an abseil line down the face to the right of the soaring crack line of the FISURA CARRILLO-VERA. This starts at a triple bolt belay on the cliff edge with tapes and an insitu karabiner. This point is marked by a couple of small cairns

set back from the cliff edge. There is a large flake 15m down with a gap down the back that has a habit of swallowing ropes, so throw them well out. Getting onto the first abseil is rather tricky because of the low anchors. A 45m abseil leads slightly leftwards (looking in) to a foothold stance with triple bolts and chain belay. From here two further 45m abseils lead to the foot of the cliff.

The dozen routes are listed from left to right. They are all 130m to 200m and several of them are named after the first ascent team. All are well worth doing.

1. CARRILLO-CANTABELLA 5+ 200m
P1, 4+ 40m. P2, 5+ 35m. P3, 4+ 35m. P4, 4+ 35m. P5, 5+ 40m. P6, 4+ 15m.
Takes a line up the disjointed grooves on the left side of the central section of the face.

2. GALLEGO-SEIQUER 6b 168m
P1, 5 38m. P2, 5+ 40m. P3, 6b 50m. P4, 5+ 10m. P5. 5+ 30m.
Finishes up the hanging corner on the right side of the great block overhang near the top of the cliff.

3. CARRILLO-DEL CAMPO 6b+ 153m
P1, 6a+ 35m. P2, 6a 38m. P3, 5+ 25m. P4, 6a 35m. P5, 6b+ 20m.
Tackles a series of corners and grooves to the left of the major crack system of FISURA CARRILLO-VERA.

4. CARABINA LARGA 6c 141m
P1, 6a 30m. P2, 6a 28m. P3, 6c 28m. P4, 6c 25m. P5, 6c 30m.
Climbs a series of cracks and wall to the left of the big crack line of FISURA CARRILLO-VERA.

5. FISURA CARRILLO-VERA 6b+ 133m
P1, 6a+ 40m. P2, 6b+ 38m. P3, 6a 55m.
The prominent long crack splitting the left side of the most continuous section of the wall.

6. EIGER 6c 163m
P1. 6a+ 10m. P2, 6c 35m. P3, 6a+ 35m. P4, A0&6b 30m. P5, 4 8m. P6, 6a 25m. The smooth-looking wall to the right of FISURA CARRILLO-

Leiva: Main Face

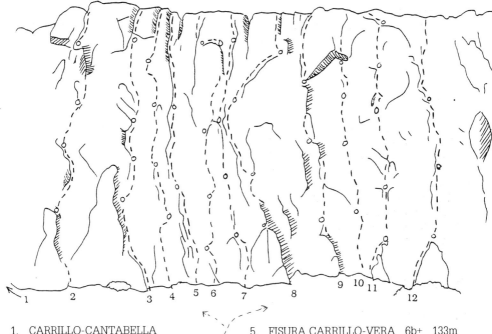

1. CARRILLO-CANTABELLA
   5+ 200m
2. GALLEGO-SEIQUER
   6b 168m
3. CARRILLO-DEL CAMPO
   6b+ 153m
4. CARABINA LARGA
   6c 141m

5. FISURA CARRILLO-VERA 6b+ 133m
6. EIGER 6c 163m
7. HISTORIA INTERMINABLE 6b+ 140m
8. GALLEGO-CARRILLO 6a+ 165m
9. CARNAVAL 6b 150m
10. YOSEMITE 7b 150m
11. LAVAREDO 7a 145m
12. CHOCHOS VOLADORES 6b+ 132m

VERA.
The direct finish is 6c 25m.

7. HISTORIA INTERMINABLE 6b+ 140m
P1, 6a+ 25m. P2, 6b 33m. P3, 6a+ 28m. P4, 6b+ 40m. P5, 6a 14m.
Grooves and crack just to the right, split by good stances.

8. GALLEGO-CARRILLO 6a+ 165m
P1, 6a 40m. P2, 6a+ 35m. P3, 6a 40m. P4, 5+ 35m. P5, 6a 15m.
Follows a great arc up the cliff starting in the groove on the right side of a large flake, and finishing up a large right-trending ramp.

9. CARNAVAL 6b 150m
P1, 6a 40m. P2, 6b 30m. P3, 5+ 40m. P4, 5+ 40m.
Takes a series of grooves that finish up the left side of the inverted Y overhang near the top of the cliff.

10. YOSEMITE 7b 150m
P1, 6c 35m. P2, 6c 35m. P3, 7a 30m. P4, 6b+ 25m. P5, 7b 25m.
A direct line to and through the right side of the inverted Y shaped overhang.
There is a variation first pitch to the right at 7a.

Leiva: Main Cliff
Colin Binks starting the crux middle pitch
of FISURA CARRILLO-VERA

11. LAVAREDO 7a 145m
P1, 6b 35m. P2, 6c 15m. P3, 6b+ 35m. P4, 7a 25m. P5, 6a 35m.
The wall and grooves just to the right.

12. CHOCHOS VOLADORES 6b+ 132m
P1, 6a 30m. P2, 6b 32m. P3, 6b+ 30m. P4, 6b 40m.
Start up the left side of a tower/flake and then continue direct.

Pared De Las Cuevas

A collection of over 50 single pitch routes from quite small to very large and from grade 4+ to 8b.

The routes here are listed from left to right - consult the topo for their exact locations.

There appear to be rather more routes on the left side of the face than even the most recent topo to the cliff shows, so some exploration may be needed. A very small number of the climbs have their names painted on the rock, helping with identification of other climbs in the area to a small degree.

The left side of the face is a series of leaning walls and grooves.

1. EL MOCO ASESINO 6b 15m
The left-hand line on the cliff, equipped with old bolts.

2. PUTAS FEVER ☺ 7b+ 18m

3. LANMAS EN LOS DEDOS ☺ 7a+ 18m

4. ERIK EL VIKINGO ☺ 7b 18m

5. CON TO LA RAJA AL AIRE ☺ 6c+ 20m

6. GNOMOS 6c 20m
One route with its name painted on the rock.

7. EL TRUCO DEL ALMENDRUCO 7b 20m

8. ESCAQUEO FINAL 7a 20m
A right-hand variant to the upper part of the previous climb.

9. A LA SOMBRE DEL PINO 6c 20m
The name tells you where to find it.

10. DESEO 6c+ 20m
Directly up the rib. A right-hand variant is of unknown grade.

12. THE GROOVE ☺ 6c 25m
The obvious leaning and heavily cleaned groove is excellent.

13. THE WALL 6b? 22m
The wall to the right, passing left of a prominent bush.

14. SALTAMONTES CAGON ☺ 7a+ 26m
Starts at some blocks on the ground.

To the right is a deep 10m high cave with two

long routes starting to its left and two short ones starting inside it.

15. LA CONTINUIDAD ME VA ☺ 7c 26m
The left edge of the cave and the line directly above it.

16. COPON DE REYES ☺ 7b+ 26m
Start as for the last route and take the right-hand line up the wall above.

17. CRUCIFISION 7a+ 10m
The short but butch line out of the back of the cave to a lower-off on the lip.

18. PELOTILLA 7a 10m
The line up the right wall of the cave.

To the right is the start of the major cave/hollow that is the main feature of all of the central part of the cliff. Above the left end of this are two impressive leaning grooves.

19. ESCALERAS AL CIELO ☺ 7a 22m
The left-hand line has substantial glue-in ring bolts and a tough start. The lower-off is on a ramp.

20. DIVINAS PALABRAS ☺ 7a+ 22m
The right-hand groove leads to the same lower-off or swing right below this onto the arete and continue up this in dramatic position ☺ 7b 30m.

Just inside the cave is:
21. SETAS IBERICAS 7a 12m
Start at the painted name and climb the leaning wall rightwards.

22. SUBE TU QUE A MI ME DE RISA ☺ 6b 15m
The right slanting traverse line under the roofs passing two sawn-off trees.

23. SOY UN CAGALINDRES 7a+ 14m
A steeper, more direct start to the above via a leaning rib.

24. PODER DE LA MENTE ☺ 8b 25m
Just to the right but crossing the traverse line

and the mass of overhangs above.

25. HUMENDO Y REBALOSO ☺ 7b+ 12m
A short pocketed line leads directly to a lower-off below the belay at the end of the traverse line, press on to reach it if required.

26. SI LA SIGUES LA CONSIGUES 8a 12m
A much harder right-hand variant to the same lower-off.

To the right are a couple of impressive routes up the steepest part of the back wall of the cave. On the left is a 25m 8a+ (or possibly still a project) that goes right through the roof and to its right is 28. PANK FLOUD 7b 15m.

To the right and beyond the steepest section of the wall the next obvious feature is a crack rising diagonally to the right:
29. HOSTIA ERNESTO ☺ 6b+ 20m
Follow the crack to the lower-off hanging from the impressive bulges above.

To the right and running to the same belay is:
30. SUBIENDO COMO LA ESPUMA ☺ 7a 18m
A tricky slab and thin pull gain the tufas and pockets, then easier climbing leads to the lower-off.

To the right are a series of red stepped bulges in the centre of the lower wall, two routes climb through these and share a lower-off:

31. LOS PICAPIEDRA ☺ 6c+ 18m
The thin left-hand line.

32. MONICA ATOMICA ☺ 6b 18m
The central, juggy, and rather polished line starting at the painted name.

Above the shared lower-off of the previous two climbs is
33. UN HOMBRE Y HORA ES POLI 20m 8a.

To the right the cliff becomes more slabby and there are several well bolted lines at an amenable grade.

Leiva: Pared De Las Cuevas

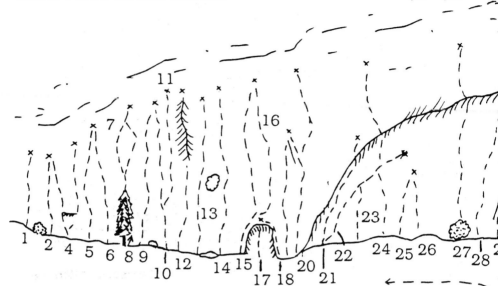

1. EL MOCO ASESINO 6b 15m
2. PUTAS FEVER ☺ 7b+ 18m
3. LANMAS EN LOS DEDOS ☺ 7a+ 18m
4. ERIK EL VIKINGO ☺ 7b 18m
5. CON TO LA RAJA AL AIRE ☺ 6c+
   20m
6. GNOMOS 6c 20m
7. EL TRUCO DEL ALMENDRUCO 7b
   20m
8. ESCAQUEO FINAL 7a 20m
9. A LA SOMBRE DEL PINO 6c 20m
10. DESEO 6c+ 20m
11. VARIANT ?
12. THE GROOVE ☺ 6c 25m
13. THE WALL 6b? 22m
14. SALTAMONTES CAGON ☺ 7a+ 26m
15. LA CONTINUIDAD ME VA ☺ 7c 26m
16. COPON DE REYES ☺ 7b+ 26m
17. CRUCIFISION 7a+ 10m
18. PELOTILLA 7a 10m
19. ESCALERAS AL CIELO ☺ 7a 22m
20. DIVINAS PALABRAS ☺ 7a+ 22m
21. SETAS IBERICAS 7a 12m
22. SUBE TU QUE A MI ME DE RISA ☺ 6b
    15m

23. SOY UN CAGALINDRES 7a+ 14m
24. PODER DE LA MENTE ☺ 8b 25m
25. HUMENDO Y REBALOSO ☺ 7b+ 12m
26. SI LA SIGUES LA CONSIGUES 8a 12m
27. PROJECT 8a+ 25m?
28. PANK FLOUD 7b 15m
29. HOSTIA ERNESTO ☺ 6b+ 20m
30. SUBIENDO COMO LA ESPUMA ☺ 7a
    18m
31. LOS PICAPIEDRA ☺ 6c+ 18m
32. MONICA ATOMICA ☺ 6b 18m
33. UN HOMBRE Y HORA ES POLI 8a 20m
34. CHUPAME LA MINGA DOMINGA 6c
    14m
35. YABADA BA DUUU 6b 14m
36. PUMUKY 6b+ 10m
37. MARABUNTA 4+ 10m
38. 4F QUE JOBIA 6a+ 14m
39. AQUI NO ME CAIGO ☺ 6a 14m
40. UN BESO O UNA FLOR ☺ 5+ 15m
41. DESPISTE ☺ 5+ 15m
42. PAJERO LOCO ☺ 6a+ 22m
43. CHITAS CATOLICAS ☺ 7a+ 22m
44. MAS TE VALE CAMARON ☺ 7b+
    22m

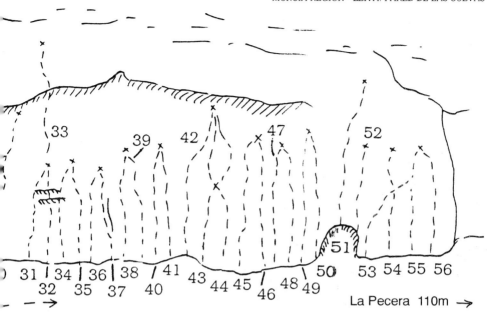

La Pecera 110m →

45. FLAKY DE MAKY ☺ 6c 20m
→ 46. SOLO UN SONRISA ☺ 6a 20m
47. CON PELOS EN LA LENGUA ☺ 6b+
    20m
→ 48. EL BESO NEGRO ☺ 6a+ 20m
→ 49. LA DOLOROSA ☺ 6b 20m
50. LA PINCHOSA ☺ 6c 20m
51. NO ES BROMA LO QUE DESPLOMA ☺
    8a+ 25m
52. CAGA SUPERFICIAL ☺ 7c+ 18m
53. CAGA HONDO 7a+ 20m
54. TIRA DE LA CADENA 7b 18m
55. HEMMORROIDES 7a+ 18m
56. CRISTINA VENTE A MI PISCINA 7a
    10m

---

34. CHUPAME LA MINGA DOMINGA 6c 14m
The next line through the right side of the red
bulges.

35. YABADA BA DUUU 6b 14m
Right again up easier angled rock and sharing
the lower-off.

36. PUMUKY 6b+ 10m
A short outing immediately left of the easy
central flake crack.

37. MARABUNTA 4+ 10m
The flaky groove in the centre of the slab is the
easiest route on the cliff.

38. 4F QUE JOBIA 6a+ 14m
The thin crack splitting the slab protected by
spaced bolts.

39. AQUI NO ME CAIGO ☺ 6a 14m
The line just to the right with twice as many
bolts.

To the right is an attractive slab with parallel
bolt lines.

40. UN BESO O UNA FLOR ☺ 5+ 15m
The left-hand line.

41. DESPISTE ☺ 5+ 15m
Just to the right, more of the same.

To the right are three longer pitches that run

17

right up to the bulges that crown the wall and have a communal lower-off.

42. PAJERO LOCO ☺ 6a+ 22m
The left-hand line trends gradually rightward up the steepening slab/wall.

43. CHITAS CATOLICAS ☺ 7a+ 22m
The almost direct line to the lower-offs, with a little loop out the right just below the top.

44. MAS TE VALE CAMARON ☺ 7b+ 22m
Start just to the right of the previous climb then cross it to finish direct to the lower-off.

Right again is another area of steep slabs bounded on the right by a deep cave (used as a bivvy cave by the locals. There are six good-looking pitches here that run up to three lower-offs in the steepening rock above. In each case an easier route is paired with a harder one, an ideal set up with a 'warm-up' and 'project' side by side and sharing the same belay.
The first pair are:
45. FLAKY DE MAKY ☺ 6c 20m
46. SOLO UN SONRISA ☺ 6a 20m

The second pair are:
47. CON PELOS EN LA LENGUA ☺ 6b+ 20m
48. EL BESO NEGRO ☺ 6a+ 20m

The final pair are:
49. LA DOLOROSA ☺ 6b 20m
50. LA PINCHOSA ☺ 6c 20m
The latter route starts up the left edge of the cave.

51. NO ES BROMA LO QUE DESPLOMA ☺ 8a+ 25m
The roof of the cave and the wall above.

52. CAGA SUPERFICIAL ☺ 7c+ 18m
The leaning right edge of the cave.

Around to the right of the cave is a steep wall with four tough climbs.
53. CAGA HONDO 7a+ 20m
Start on the left but follow the diagonal line away to the right to join and finish as for 'PILES'.

54. TIRA DE LA CADENA 7b 18m
The direct line just to the right.

55. HEMORROIDES 7a+ 18m
A potentially painful pitch on the right side of the wall.

56. CRISTINA VENTE A MI PISCINA 7a 18m
The last route on the steep section of the cliff.

Around to the right the cliff turns into an easy-angled grey slab with at least four lower grade climbs on it. They look to be about grade 3 or 4 and may be ideal for instructional purposes.

Sector La Pecera
110m right of the Sector de la Cuevas is a broad grey slab with 18 good climbs on it. Nearly all of these are 5+ to 6b and are well bolted. The cliff lacks the grandeur of the main face or the butch test pieces of the Cuevas but if south-facing, bolted rock of a less than vertical nature is your cup of tea a day or two spent here should fit the bill. The names of many of the routes suggests that there is something fishy going on around here!

1. DIEDRO BARRACUDA ☺ 6a 20m
The right facing groove that bounds the left side of the cliff entered directly and exited out to the right.

2. PEZ GLOBO ☺ 6a 20m
The direct line to the lower-off of the previous route.

3. TIBURON MARTILLO ☺ 6b 20m
The slab just to the right.

4. CONGRIO BELGA ☺ 6c 18m
A direct line to and through the tough roof high on the cliff.

5. EL BOQUERON ☺ 6b+ 18m
The slab to the right.

6. EL MERO ☺ 6b+ 18m
The right-hand line to the same lower-off.

Leiva: La Pecera

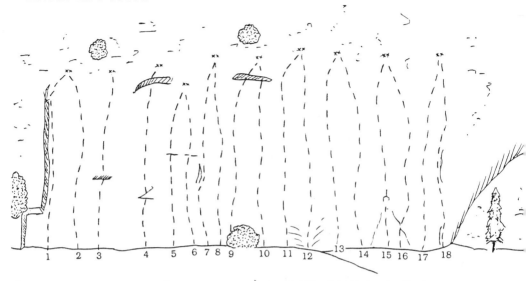

→1. DIEDRO BARRACUDA ☺ 6a 20m
→2. PEZ GLOBO ☺ 6a 20m
→3. TIBURON MARTILLO ☺ 6b 20m
4. CONGRIO BELGA ☺ 6c 18m
5. EL BOQUERON ☺ 6b+ 18m
6. EL MERO ☺ 6b+ 18m
7. NUDIBRANQUIO ☺ 6b+ 20m
8. EL ABADEJO 7b 20m
→9. PULPO ROQUERO ☺ 6b 20m

→10. LENGUAO BUELLERO ☺ 6a+ 20m
→11. LA MANTA RAY ☺ 6a 18m
→12. PASTINACA ☺ 6a 18m
→13. EL METILLON COLARO ☺ 6b 18m
→14. EL RASCACIO ☺ 6a 18m
→15. EL SARGO REAL ☺ 6a+ 18m
→16. LA BALLENA AZUL ☺ 6a+ 18m
→17. LA TORTUGA CAREY ☺ 6a 18m
→18. EL DELFIN ☺ 5 18m

---

7. NUDIBRANQUIO ☺ 6b+ 20m
The next line to the right passing through a niche early on.

8. EL ABADEJO 7b 20m
The route that climbs the smoothest rock around is obviously on the wrong cliff.

To the right is a bush at the base of the cliff and starting just to the left of this is:
9. PULPO ROQUERO ☺ 6b 20
Climb to the roof at 18m and pull rightwards through it.

10 LENGUAO BUELLERO ☺ 6a+ 20m
Start to the right of the bush and climb to and through the same roof as the previous climb, by leftwards manoeuvres.

11. LA MANTA RAY ☺ 6a 18m
The second line right of the bush, with a jig right at the top.

12. PASTINACA ☺ 6a 18m
Direct to the lower-off of the previous climb and starting up a shallow groove.

13. EL METILLON COLARO ☺ 6b 18m
The steep slab right again.

14. EL RASCACIO ☺ 6a 18m
A slightly easier line up the slab to the right, leading to the same lower-off.

15. EL SARGO REAL ☺ 6a+ 18m
Start up a low relief pillar, and press on through a hole and on to the lower-off.

16. LA BALLENA AZUL ☺ 6a+ 18m
The Blue Whale is a right-hand variant on the previous climb.

17. LA TORTUGA CAREY ☺ 6a 18m
A gradually rightward-trending line to the lower-off of the next climb.

18. EL DELFIN ☺ 5 18m
The last route before much steeper and grassier rock proves to be the easiest on the cliff.

Salinas: Sector Alto Don Pedro
The author on CEFALINPADUS 6b+, (p27) possibly the best route on the crag

ALICANTE/ELDA REGION

1. Sierra Magdalena *
2. Salinas ***
3. Marin ***
4. Sax ***
5. Penya del Corb ***
6. Peña Rubia ***

7. Forada *****
8. Reconco ****
9. Agujas Rojas ***
10, Ibi **
11. Alcoy **/***
12. Cabezon de Oro **

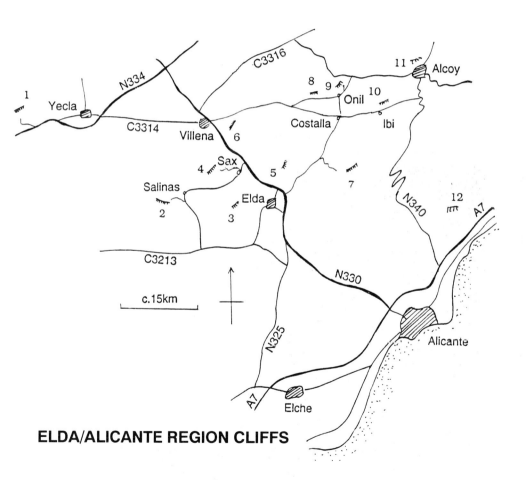

ELDA/ALICANTE REGION CLIFFS

SIERRA MAGDALENA

Crag Facts

Star rating: *
Aspect: south (3 cliffs), north (1 cliff), east (1 cliff)
Height: 10 to 20 metres
Spread of grades:

4	5	5+	6a	6b	6c	7a	7b	7c	8
/	9	9	17	6	6	4	4	1	/

Introduction

A small selection of routes in a slightly scruffy setting, the climbing here is not worth a visit from afar, but if you are in the area or passing through it may be worth calling in. Probably the best piece of rock here it the PARED NEGRA which has a pleasant collection of lower grade slab climbs in a sunny setting. The PARED ROJA has a selection of short fierce routes, worthwhile for those who like that kind of thing! Generally speaking the grades here are rather tough. The routes are presented in topo form.

Crag Geography

From the parking area four of the five climbing areas are visible (don't be **too** disappointed). Opposite the approach track is a rocky ridge and the largest tower on this is LOS VAGOS which is home to three very short climbs. Behind the ridge is the wide flat wall of the PARED DEL CHARCO with a dried-up water cascade in its centre. To the right of the LOS VAGOS tower is a steep gully and prominent at the top of this is the PARED ROJA with a tree in front of it, and to the left of this the end of the PARED NEGRA can just be seen. The final crag is the PARED DE SALTO which is reached in 10 minutes by walking up the good path that follows the main valley which runs to the right of the steep gully leading up to the PAREDES ROJA and NEGRA.

Access

From just south of Alicante follow the N330 Madrid road past Elda and Sax and onto Villena

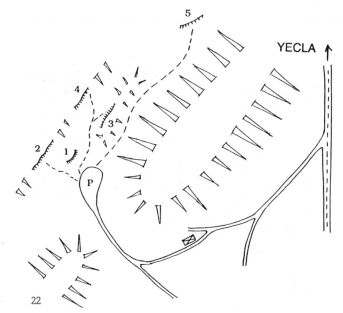

SIERRA DE LA MAGDALENA ACCESS & LAYOUT

1. Los Vagos
2. Pared del Charco
3. Pared Roja
4. Pared Negra
5. El Salto

(50km), the home of Boreal. Drive past the town, through a tunnel then turn right off the dual carriageway. To pass under it pick up signs for Yecla. Follow the ring road until the main C3314 road is joined then head cross-country to Yecla for 18km along straight roads. Almost in Yecla turn left onto the new ring road, and follow this until the road from the town comes in from the right. Just half a kilometre from here and opposite a scrap yard is a nondescript dirt track turning to the right. Follow this to a fork by a sunken water tower and take the right branch. Continue along this bearing left at a ruined house then right at a T junction. Follow the road through a low point in the ridge to an open parking area, 4km from the road. Please don't be too disappointed.

Los Vagos

Three tiny offerings share the same lower-off on the small tower just north of the car park. From left to right these are:
1. METEHE GOLES 6a 8m
2. SAMBA PA TI 6b+ 8m
3. GOZAS NEGRO 6a 8m

Pared Del Charco

Pass to the left of LOS VAGOS to find this sector scattered around either side of a normally dried up cascade. The setting is somewhat quarry-like.

The routes are listed from left to right.

High on the left are three short routes that climb through a prominent bulge.
1. GOLONDRINAS EN ESCABECHE 6a 10m
2. MUERTE A LAS GOLONDRINAS 6a 10m
3. TODA TULLA 7a+ 12m

To the right of the line of the waterfall are two climbs that start together. The left-hand one is LA FRONTERA with no known grade and the right-hand one has no name but is 20m and 6c.

Right again is an attractive slabby wall with routes that are harder than they look:
4. PEPA ESPAÑA 6a+ 20m
5. T'ASPERO EN CALIFORNIA 6b+ 18m
6. MAS SE PERDIDO EN CUBA 6a+ 18m
7. ? 7a 18m
8. PUTA NAVIDAD 6a+ 18m
  Up the slope to the right are the last three routes on this Sector.
9. NOTECORRAS EN MI POLLA QUE ME LA BOLLAS 6b 15m
10. ? 6b+ 15m
11. EL VIOLADOR DE CHOTAS 7b 15m

Pared Del Charco

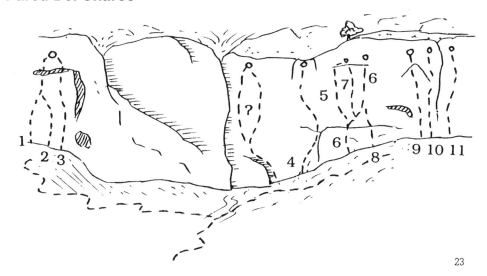

Pared Roja

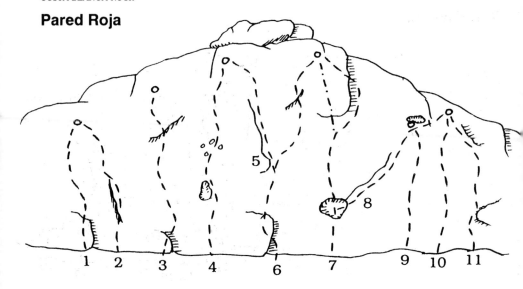

Pared Roja

Looking up the gully to the west of the parking is the conspicuous short wall of the PARED ROJA with a solitary tree standing in front of it. This crag is home to a small collection of fierce fingery routes. Some of the rock is a little dubious but the bolts are big and beefy to make up for this. The routes are listed from left to right.

1. PUE 6a 10m
2. MOLLUNGA GONGORINA 6c 10m
3. MASTURBACIONES CON SENSACIONES 7c 12m
4. REINE MATADORA 6c+ 14m
5. CORLEONE 7b 15m
6. VOLVER A EMPEZAR 6a+ 15m
7. SETA NEGRA 6c 14m (7a direct)
8. ES DOZ 6a 14m
9. SOY UN BORRACHO 6b+ 8m
10. CHINA BLUE 6c+ 10m
11. ? 6a+ 10m

Pared Negra

Arguably the best bit of rock in the area, the 'Black Wall' may be worth a visit if you are looking for a collection of low grade and low angle climbs that are well protected. Walk up the gully that contains the PARED ROJA and continue over the col. The PARED NEGRA is on the left. The routes are listed from left to right:

1. A PAN Y AGUA 5+ 20m
2. ULIMATUM 5+ 20m
3. CALIENTA MOTORES 5 15m
4. AL LORO CON EL CAZEROLO 5+ 15m
5. 36 6a 15m
6. JOVITO POCO 5 20m
7. ETIOPYN BOYS 5 20m
8. PAPA MATEO 5+ 20m
9. CAPFRUCITA ROJA 5 18m
10. RAMBLA MATXAKA 5 18m
11. CORNERED 5+ 18m
12. INOMINATA UNO 5- 15m
13. INOMINATA DOS 5- 15m
14. INOMINATA TRES 5+ 15m
15. INOMINATA QUATRO 5 15m
16. CASIOPER 5 20m
17. RAMBLIZO 5+ 20m
18. MESSALINA 5 20m
19. CALIGULA 6a+ 20m

Pared De Salto

The final cliff to be listed is the Pared De Salto which lies at the end of the dry valley to the right

Pared Negra

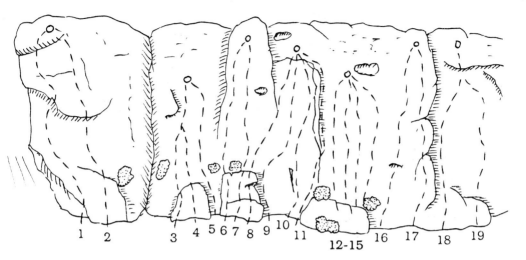

of the smaller valley that contains the Pared Roja and Negra, less than 10 minutes from the car. The routes are mostly hard and are approximately 15m long.

1. HOLA MAMONCETE 7a+
2. CURRAS MENOS QUE EL ANGEL DE LA GARDIA 7c
3. YANQUI BUENO YANQUI MUERTO 7b
4. NO ME TOQUES 7b+
5. EL SUEÑO DE LAS TORTUGAS AZULES 6a+
6. DE HAY PARRIVA PRURRR 6a+
7. JOSHUA TREE 6b+
8. 091 7a
9. GULA DE FIN DE AÑO 6b+
10. SACRILEG NAVIDENO 6a+

Pared De Salto

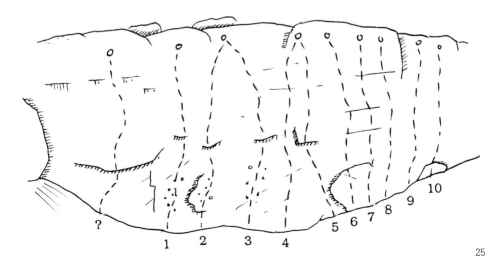

ALTO DON PEDRO
(SALINAS)

Crag Facts

Star rating: ***
Aspect: East-south-east facing
Height: up to 24 metres
Spread of grades:

4	5	5+	6a	6b	6c	7a	7b	7c	8
1	6	4	9	18	6	7	9	5	3

Introduction

A compact cliff with almost 70 routes in a sunny setting commanding expansive views over arid agricultural land and the salt flats of Salinas. The cliff was developed by Alicante climbers in 1991 but it has only recently been revealed to a wider audience (although one of the locals pointed me towards the place in 1992!). The broad spread of grades, pleasant aspect and varied climbing make it worth a visit by any team within striking distance and the cliff is especially suitable for lovers of steep, hard face climbing. The rock is good if somewhat rough and the fixed protection is perfect without exception. The Lower Cliff is steep on the right and slabbier to the left whereas the Upper Cliff is steep throughout its entire length.

NOTE: During March, April and May signs are posted forbidding climbing during these months.

Access

From Alicante turn inland and follow the N330 Madrid road to the prominent castle at the small town of Sax. Turn off here and follow signs to Salinas (10km). Turn left and follow the road for 1.5km to a right turn signed Fontanas & Finca Castillejos. Drive up the tarmaced road until an unsigned left turn (the second) can be taken. Follow this past two houses, up the hill until the road bears hard left and the cliff can be seen dead ahead. Parking is available on the right and one of two paths lead to the main areas, SECTOR PICARA VIBORITA on the right two minutes from the car and SECTORS RATOLI, ESPOLON MAGICO, LA HIGUERA and FINAL 10-15 minutes up the bank to the left. If you try to get closer to the cliff you will encounter a chain across the track (which actually leads to the small marble quarry visible to the left of the cliff). The routes are described from right to left as this is the usual direction of approach.

Down the slope to the right of the main Sectors are three small areas that face in the opposite direction to the rest of the cliff. These are the SECTORS CONTINUO, NORTE and DESPLOME. The first of these has three hard routes, from right to left IMPONE EL DESPLOME 7b, ROCA DE PANDORA 7b+ and TORTURA CONTINUA 8a. The second has three climbs close together on the right, LICOR AMARGO 7a+, ATACALE ☺ 6b and SELVA VERTICAL 6a+, and down the slope a short way is LA PRIMERA Y LA ULTIMA 6b+. Some distance down the slope, the final area is recognised by its very steep right-hand side. There are six bolt lines here, three of which are projects, two of which are very hard and one of which is very short!

Sector Picara Viborita

Returning to the main cliff, the right side is steeply bulging and abuts a low dry-stone wall.

1. DESTROYER 6c+ 12m
A short steep route up the right edge of the wall.

2. ALICANTORROCA ☺ 8a 18m
The steep bulges and hanging rib above give one of the hardest offerings here.

3. CHRIMOYA ☺ 7b+ 18m
The line of pockets through the bulges to the left gives a battle. Once through these trend left to join and finish as for the next climb.

4. SUBE GOLONDRINA ☺ 7a 18m
The initial bulge is tough (but avoidable), the upper bulge is not avoidable but not very tough either.

5. LA PUERTA DE ANUBIS ☺ 6a+ 18m
Climb the right edge of the shallow scoop then pull rightwards through the diagonal bulges to a lower-off.

6. MACHU QUE PICHU 6b+ 15m
The left side of the scoop, trending left to finish.

7. EL ABOMINABLE 6b 15m
Just left again pulling over a thin overlap early on.

8. CEFALINPADUS ♦ 6b+ 18m
The fine, pocketed wall has hard moves on sharp holds where the big jugs run out. The best route on the cliff?

9. CERNICALCUS 7a 12m
The short 'route-to-nowhere' just to the left.

10. LENIN ☺ 6c 18m
The orange streak and line of big pockets gives a good pitch, thin early on and then strenuous above.

To the left a long roof runs across the top of the cliff.
11. BOCADILLOS DE MICROBIOS ☺ 6b 20m
A line leading to the right edge of the roof at the top of the cliff, a tasty little number.

12. FLASH BEA 6b+ 20m
Just to the left similar climbing leads to the same lower-off.

13. ANDREA 6b+ 20m
A direct line to and through the widest part of the roof.

14. ASI HABLO PEPETRUSTA ☺ 5 18m
A pleasant pitch up the left bounding rib of the wall.

15. ME ESTOY MULTIPLICANDO ☺ 6b 20m
To the left is a grotty gully splitting the upper section of the cliff and left again is a shallow groove which gives a long fingery pitch.

To the left the cliff takes the form of a steep wall, becoming more easy angled as it rises up the slope. It is the best destination hereabouts for lower grade climbers.

16. LOLITUS 7a 18m
The first line is a tough fingery pitch, though a bit of 'ducking and diving' on the upper wall can lower the grade one notch.

17. EL CANTO DE LA ABUBILLA ☺ 6b+ 15m
The sustained and sharp line up the steep slab (or low angled wall) to the left.

18. ALI BABA Y LOS 40 MOSQUETONES ☺ 6b 15m
Just left again, more of the same passing a prominent pocket in the initial bulge.

19. SANCHO PANZA ☺ 6a 18m
A fingery bulge early on leads to easier climbing above, at last the routes are getting easier.

20. AMONITE ☺ 5+ 18m
Just left again this passes a couple of 'eye holes' and is pleasantly sustained above.

21. PERO YAYO ☺ 5 16m
Start beside a bush and climb through the centre of a scoop.

22. JARPICHUELA 5+ 18m
A line just to the left before things begin to deteriorate seriously.

Around the left of the pine trees are three bolt lines
23. PONTELO ☺ 5+ 18m
The first line has a tough bulge just below the lower-offs.

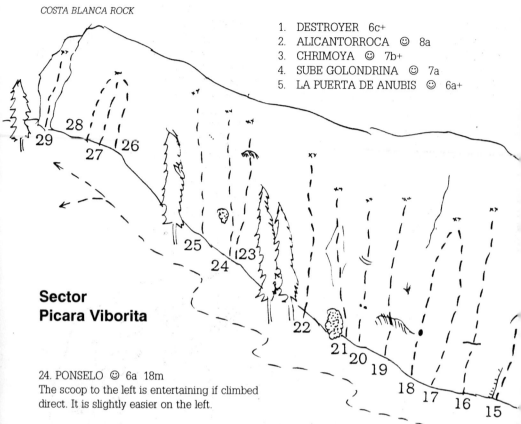

1. DESTROYER 6c+
2. ALICANTORROCA ☺ 8a
3. CHRIMOYA ☺ 7b+
4. SUBE GOLONDRINA ☺ 7a
5. LA PUERTA DE ANUBIS ☺ 6a+

Sector Picara Viborita

24. PONSELO ☺ 6a 18m
The scoop to the left is entertaining if climbed direct. It is slightly easier on the left.

25. NO TE LO PONGAS ☺ 4 18m
The third of the trio has an awkward start for the grade, the easiest route on the cliff.

Further up the slope are three shorter offerings sharing a lower-off. They are, of course:
26. ATOS 5 12m
The right line.

27. PORTOS 5 12m
The central line.

28. ARAMIS 5 12m
The other line!

Up the slope where the cliff swings round is their diminutive companion:
29. DARTAÑAN 6c 12m
Short sharp and sunny.

Sector Ratoli & Espolon Magico

Follow the path up below the SECTOR PICARA VIBORITA until a minor branch forks off to the left, descends slightly then arrives below an attractive steep wall. There are seven routes here that generally get harder (and better) the further left you go, so you know just where to start, if you think you're 'ard enough!
1. AVIORAZ EN PELOTAS ME VERAS 5+ 15m
The right-hand line is the poor relation hereabouts.

2. PAPRIKA 6b 15m
Just to the left and right of a scar on the wall, a fingery pitch passing through a small overlap.

3. CANGRENA 6c+ 15m
Just left again is another fingery offering trending slightly leftwards.

6. MACHU QUE PICHU 6b+
7. EL ABOMINABLE 6b
8. CEFALINPADUS ☙ 6b+
9. CERNICALCUS 7a
10. LENIN ☺ 6c
11. BOCADILLOS DE MICROBIOS ☺ 6b
12. FLASH BEA 6b+
13. ANDREA 6b+
14. ASI HABLO PEPETRUSTA ☺ 5 KST/EST 29/12/98
15. ME ESTOY MULTIPLICANDO ☺ 6b

16. LOLITUS 7a
17. EL CANTO DE LA ABUBILLA ☺ 6b+ EST/KST 29/12/98
18. ALI BABA Y LOS 40 MOSQUETONES ☺ 6b 29/12/98
19. SANCHO PANZA ☺ 6a EST/KST 29/12/98
20. AMONITE ☺ 5+ KST/EST 29/12/98
21. PERO YAYO ☺ 5 KST/EST 29/12/98
22. JARPICHUELA 5+
23. PONTELO ☺ 5+ KST/EST 29/12/98
24. PONSELO ☺ 6a EST/KST 29/12/98
25. NO TE LO PONGAS ☺ 4 KST 29/12/98
26. ATOS 5
27. PORTOS 5
28. ARAMIS 5
29. DARTAÑAN 6c

13 12 11 10 9 8 7 6 5 4 3 2 1

4. 7B EL PLUMERO ☺ 7a 18m
Straight up the wall passing to the right some flowstone lumps at 5m and pulling through a mid-height bulge.

5. AGARRATE DONDE PUERDAS ☺ 7b 16m
Hard climbing up the gently leaning wall, initially to the left of a flake crack.

6. MARCA PASOS ☺ 7a+ 20m
The longest and probably the best of the bunch, climbing the highest part of the wall.

7. LOS DEDOS DEL MONO ☺ 7b 18m
Just to the right of the cave is this sustained orange wall and overlap. Using the tree on the left is taboo at the grade.

Around to the left is a pointed tower the front face of which is the ESPOLON MAGICO. Unfortunately the piece of rock doesn't really live up to its name. There are three climbs here and they all start up the grotty crack below the tower and share a communal lower-off on its tip.

Sectors Ratoli, Espolon Magico & Higuera

1. AVIORAZ EN PELOTAS ME VERAS 5+
2. PAPRIKA 6b
3. CANGRENA 6c+
4. 7B EL PLUMERO ☺ 7a
5. AGARRATE DONDE PUERDAS ☺ 7b
6. MARCA PASOS ☺ 7a+
7. LOS DEDOS DEL MONO ☺ 7b

8. ESPOLON MAGICO 6b
9. PLACA MAGICA 6b+
10. FISURA MAGICA 6a+

11. PEPITO CONEJO ☺ 5
12. SALTIMBANQUI ☺ 6a
13. ROCA LOCA ☺ 6a
14. DIRECTISIMA ☺ 6b+
15. HAY CANTO 7b+
16. PAPA VEN EN TREN ☺ 7a+
17. PUERCOESPIN ☺ 7b+

18. AFRICA 7c
19. RIENA DE CORAZONES ☺ 8a
20. EL GRAND CANON ☺ 7b+
21. BABIECA ☺ 7b
22. PEQUENA Y JUGUETONA ☺ 6c+
23. LLOVIENDO SALE CORRIENDO 6a
24. SERRANO-MAGUI 6a

SECTOR RATOLI

SECTOR ESPOLON MAGICOLA

SECTOR LA HIGUERA

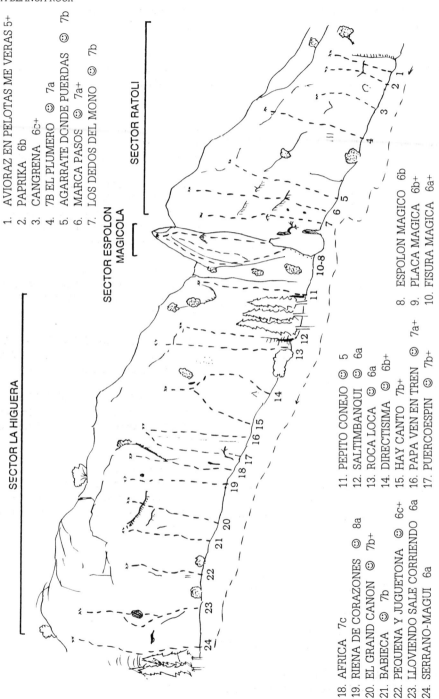

8. ESPOLON MAGICO 6b 22m
The initial crack and well positioned arete on the right is the best of the trio.

9. PLACA MAGICA 6b+ 22m
The initial crack and wall left of the arete feels 'squeezed in'.

10. FISURA MAGICA 6a+ 22m
The initial crack is followed almost to its end then the thinner continuation on the right leads to the summit.

Sector La Higuera
To the left of the tower of ESPOLON MAGICO is an easy gully and then a long flat wall with several orange streaks. There are some fine (and hard) face routes here.

11. PEPITO CONEJO ☺ 5 15m
Start just left of the gully and right of some pine trees and climb straight up the rib.

12. SALTIMBANQUI ☺ 6a 16m
Start left of the trees at a vertical slot and climb slabby rock eventually leading into a left-facing corner.

13. ROCA LOCA ☺ 6a 18m
Just left again is a sustained pitch straight up the wall.

14. DIRECTISIMA ☺ 6b+ 16m
Start left of some bushes and climb the tough lower wall passing a scar then trend left under a bush to reach the lower-off. No, it's not really very direct is it?

15. HAY CANTO 7b+ 15m
The next line left should have been called DIRECTISIMA, it shares the same lower-off.

16. PAPA VEN EN TREN ☺ 7a+ 20m
The next line left climbs straight up orange streaks, good climbing but hard for the grade!

17. PUERCOESPIN ☺ 7b+ 20m
Start behind the old tree and climb the wall right of the right-facing groove to the lower-off of the last climb.

18. AFRICA 7c 20m
The next route left climbs past a couple of elongated pockets, one low down, one near the top.

19. RIENA DE CORAZONES ☺ 8a 20m
The Queen of Hearts. Face routes don't come much harder. How are your tips feeling?

To the left is a wall capped by a horizontal roof.
20. EL GRAND CANON ☺ 7b+ 20m
Start on the left (as for the next route) but step right and climb the thin wall and pull over the centre of the roof above.

21. BABIECA ☺ 7b 18m
Start as for the last climb but head straight up the pocketed wall to a finish over the left edge of the roof.

22. PEQUENA Y JUGUETONA ☺ 6c+ 15m
The shorter wall to the left has a crucial rightward traverse and a drilled pocket to boot.

23. LLOVIENDO SALE CORRIENDO 6a 18m
Climb the ramp on the left then pull through the roof of the cave or skirt around it. Finish direct with some suspect rock.

24. SERRANO-MAGUI 6a 22m
Climb the wall and bulge to the right of a groove then continue more easily up slabbier rock above. Named (by me) after the first ascensionists.

Sector Final

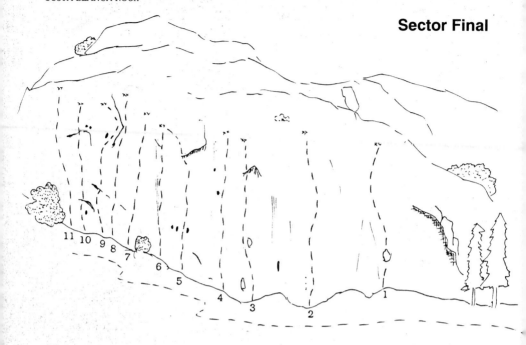

1. LA SILLA DE LA RIENA ☺ 6b
2. DONDE DICES QUE VAS ☺ 6a
3. LINEA MAESTRA ☺ 7b
4. METAMORFOSIS ☺ 7c
5. MATA-HARI ☺ 7a+
6. DANZA INTERRUMPIDA ☺ 7c
7. AHI VA LE LIEBRE ☺ 7c
8. CRUCIFIXION ☺ 7c
9. SERRANO-MAGUI 6b+
10. TERRANOVA 6c
11. MANZANITA VERDE ☺ 6b

Sector Final

The last area to be reached at the top of the bank is home to a fine collection of hard face routes. Unfortunately there is not a lot up here for normal mortals, though knowing at least that saves you having to walk up!

1. LA SILLA DE LA RIENA ☺ 6b 15m
Climb to a deep pocket and pull through the bulge above on indifferent holds; continue more easily.

2. DONDE DICES QUE VAS ☺ 6a 22m
The grey rib that bounds the right edge of the steeper wall is the best lower-grade route here, and has some good moves on pockets and 'gouttes'.

To the left the wall is unremittingly steep and is home to six hard face climbs, with barely a decent hold between them.

3. LINEA MAESTRA ☺ 7b 20m
The line of big beefy 'glue-ins' has a tough start passing a couple of large holes and offers fine sustained wall climbing above.

Leiva: Pared De Las Cuevas. The author on MONICA ATOMICA 6b
one of the many high quality single pitch routes here

4. METAMORFOSIS ☺ 7c 22m
The steep smooth wall just to the left is the first of the really hard routes.

5. MATA-HARI ☺ 7a+ 20m
Up the major orange streak that falls from the roof trending left then pull over the left side of the overhang. The warm-up for the area, and fortunately a high quality pitch as well.

6. DANZA INTERRUMPIDA ☺ 7c 20m
Starting right of a bush, the wall between the two streaks is chipped and tough.

7. AHI VA LE LIEBRE ☺ 7c 22m
The smooth wall to the left on 'tinies'.

8. CRUCIFIXION ☺ 7c 24m
Left again, more of the same, will it ever end?

9. SERRANO-MAGUI 6b+ 16m
Just to the left an easier offering at last. Follow the holds and not the bolts. I wish these guys would name their routes.

10. TERRANOVA 6c 18m
The penultimate line before the bushes encroach.

11. MANZANITA VERDE ☺ 6b 15m
The rib above the bushes to a final tricky move.

Penya del Corb: Colin Binks on the photogenic PIPONA 6b

MARIN

Crag Facts

Star rating: ***

Aspect: Just east of south, making it an ideal venue on hot afternoons

Height: Up to 52 metres

Spread of grades:

3	3+	4	4+	5	5+	6a	6b	6c	7
/	2	4	15	5	4	1	2	1	/

Introduction

To the west of the small town of Onil is a prominent dome of cream-coloured rock where a slabby crag sits on the crest of the hill high above the valley. Developed in the 1960s then rebolted in 1992 this is most definitely not a cliff for the hard-core. On the other hand climbers who operate at HVS and below and who feel they have been hard done by when it comes to sport climbing should find a visit here very rewarding.

This south-facing cliff is home to 20 pleasant low grade climbs of a respectable length. The routes are up to 60m high, are very well bolted and generally are less than vertical. Many of the climbs have their names and approximate grades painted at their foot in large ugly writing. Brief descriptions and quality assessments are included to aid identification and route choice. The crag can conveniently be combined with a visit to Peña del Corb which is only ten minutes drive away.

Access

Take the N330 Madrid road (recently upgraded to a toll-free motorway) north-west from Alicante for 32km to Elda/Petrel, pass the castle and then continue past the right turn at the sign 'Centro Commercial' used on the approach to Penya del Corb and Forada. After a Cepsa petrol station take the slip road off to the right signed 'Elda'

and 'Substacion H.E.' then loop back over the motorway and head back towards Elda. Go around a corner then bear right following signs to Sax. After 1km turn right at T junction (signed Sax) and drive over a col. The road descends under power-lines. On a long right-hand bend turn left immediately before some white gates set under an orange tiled roof (with a sign La Curva). Follow the track for 1.3km, turn left through some grey concrete gate posts with old rusty iron gates (avoid the main track heading straight on) and park 0.4km further on, at a bend on a broad col (1.7km from the road). A track starts on the col and ascends gradually rightwards up the slope overlooking Elda. The rocks are reached in less then 10 minutes from the parking.

The climbs are described from right to left as this is the direction of approach.

Descent

From the ramp that runs across the top of the cliff, either abseil back to base (two ropes or two abseils required) or scramble to the cliff top and then descend the awkward rocky gully that leads down the back of the cliff and around the left arete of the face.

1. CAPICUA ☺ 4,4+ 60m

The longest route on the cliff and worth doing for that reason alone. Start on the far right side of the main face where there is a scratched cross and the name plus a hopeful number '3' are painted in large green lettering. Climb easy white slabs then a brown streak up the right side of the open bay to a good stance on the ridge (30m). The second pitch trends leftwards back up the left side of the rib to eventually join the ramp that runs across the upper part of the main face. There is also an easier variation (3+) around to the right of the standard final pitch (30m).

Marin

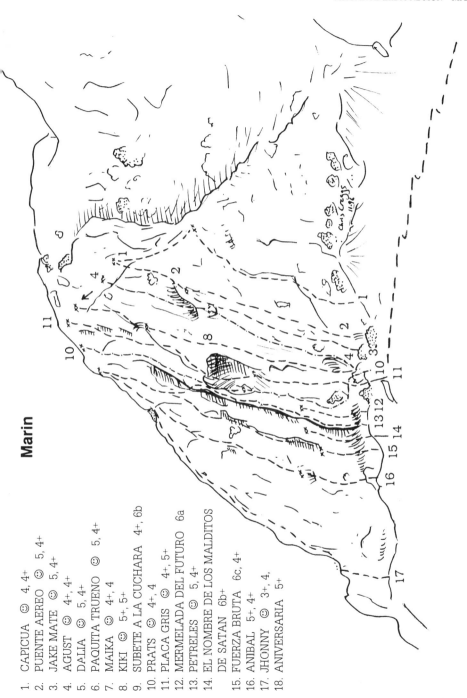

1. CAPICUA ☺ 4, 4+
2. PUENTE AEREO ☺ 5, 4+
3. JAKE MATE ☺ 5, 4+
4. AGUST ☺ 4+, 4+
5. DALIA ☺ 5, 4+
6. PAQUITA TRUENO ☺ 5, 4+
7. MAIKA ☺ 4+, 4
8. KIKI ☺ 5+, 5+
9. SUBETE A LA CUCHARA 4+, 6b
10. PRATS ☺ 4+, 4
11. PLACA GRIS ☺ 4+, 5+
12. MERMELADA DEL FUTURO 6a
13. PETRELES ☺ 5, 4+
14. EL NOMBRE DE LOS MALDITOS
    DE SATAN 6b+
15. FUERZA BRUTA 6c, 4+
16. ANIBAL 5+, 4+
17. JHONNY ☺ 3+, 4,
18. ANIVERSARIA 5+

35

*Marin: a local girl on MAIKA 4+, one of the
excellent training routes on this crag*

2. PUENTE AEREO ☺ 5,4+ 52m
The first route on the main section of the cliff.
Climb into a rounded hole and then press on
straight up the face on good holds to a stance
and belay below the right side of the roof high
above, 32m. The second pitch pulls around the
right edge of the roof and then trends easily
leftwards to the cliff top 20m.

3. JAKE MATE ☺ 5,4+ 52m
Start at the name painted in brown writing and
climb the smart sustained rib to the choice of a
stance on the routes to either side. Finish up the
appropriate bolt ladder from your chosen stance.

The next three climbs start out of a cave at the
base of the cliff:

4. AGUST ☺ 4+,4+ 52m
Start at the right side of a cave (name in
green writing) and climb out of this and
straight up the face above to a very
comfortable stance in a large solution
hollow (30m). Pull straight through the
bulges above the stance then continue
up easier rock to a belay on the ramp.

5. DALIA ☺ 5,4+ 52m
Climb out of the cave steeply then parallel
the previous route eventually moving
right to share its stance (30m). Move left
below the bulges then finish up the rib
above (22m).

6. PAQUITA TRUENO ☺ 5,4+ 52m
Climb out of the left side of the cave
(name in green writing) and climb straight
up the slab to a belay on twin ring bolts
in a little hollow (32m). Finish more easily,
in the same line (20m).

7. MAIKA ☺ 4+,4 50m
Start just left of the cave and head straight
up the slab, passing a series of flakes and
eventually pulling over the right side of
the line of red bulges high on the cliff
(35m). The lower part of this first pitch
has bolts every 1 metre, obviously a place for the
timid to see if lead climbing is for them. Above
the half-height twin bolts (possible stance) they
are spaced more normally to the proper stance.
Finish up the straightforward slab above (15m).

8. KIKI ☺ 5+,5+ 52m
Start at the name and arrow emblazoned in
green paint and squeeze between bushes to get
onto a ledge. Climb up a brown scoop heading
rightwards towards the prominent large cave
but bear right up its right edge to reach a stance
in a smaller red hollow a short distance below
the top of the cliff. Climb steeply out of the right
side of the hollow then finish more easily.

9. SUBETE A LA CUCHARA 4+,6b 48m
A wildly unbalanced route! Trend left above the
bush then climb straight up the slab following

the right side of a brown streak that leads to a stance in the large cave halfway up the cliff, chipped thread belay (25m). Climb the back wall of the cave by powerful moves then pull over the right edge of the overlap above (23m). A pitch that has been especially imported from Forada.

10. PRATS ☺ 4+,4 53m

A devious but excellent climb that follows the easiest line up the central part of the cliff. Start by the vague green name and trend left above the overhangs passing one bolt line (PLACA GRIS see below) then climb straight up the pleasant narrowing rib before stepping right to a stance on the left edge of the large cave in the upper section of the cliff (28m). Climb the left edge of the cave on convoluted rock then step left and finish up the continuation of the chimney of PETRELES (25m).

11. PLACA GRIS ☺ 4+,5+ 48m

An excellent direct route. Start under the right edge of the bulges that run along the base of the left side of the cliff at a triangular hole and climb straight up the slab keeping left of the brown streak to the stance in the cave (25m). Step right and climb the left side of the cave via a steep rib then step right and traverse into the exposed slanting groove that hangs over the cave. Climb this and then finish easily (25m).

12. MERMELADA DEL FUTURO 6a 10m

The steep wall to the right of the base of the steep chimney gives a short steep struggle, especially if you keep right of the bolts, 3 clips.

13. PETRELES ☺ 5,4+ 52m

The deep twisting chimney is the most conspicuous feature on the cliff and as such is a must. Enter the fissure steeply then continue up the groove and narrowing slab passing one potential stance to a stance and twin bolt belay (32m). From the belay either pull out left onto the rib (more exciting) or continue up the slab above (more logical) which leads directly to the cliff top (15m).

14. EL NOMBRE DE LOS MALDITOS DE SATAN 6b+ 12m

The bulges just left of the chimney give a short sharp struggle, three bolt runners lead to a chain lower-off.

15. FUERZA BRUTA 6c,4+ 50m

Another hopelessly unbalanced route. A short hard pitch leads to a stance in the base of groove (10m). Lower-off from here or continue (much) more easily (spaced gear) up the groove all the way to the cliff top (40m).

16. ANIBAL 5+,4+ 48m

Climb the bulge steeply (solitary bolt runner) on good holds to a not-in-situ thread and then into the cave, belay here (18m). Climb the right rib then step back left into the groove above the cave, climb this to the rib of JHONNY and finish up this in a fine position (30m).

17. JHONNY ☺ 3+,4 50m

The left arete of the cliff gives a well positioned climb, perhaps the best of the easier climbs here. Start at the green writing and scramble around to the left then step out right and climb the clean lower rib past some trees to a stance on a small tower (25m) before step left and continuing up the upper arete to the cliff top (25m). Excellent stuff.

18. ANIVERSARIO 5+ 45m

The final offering on the cliff is supposed to climb the steep rock above the scrambly start of the previous route. I failed to locate any bolts. Take care with some of the rock if you venture this way.

Ten minutes walk to the left is a steep red cliff that might be ideal if you are looking for a place to call your own!

CABRERAS (SAX)

Crag Facts

Star rating: ***
Aspect: south-east facing
Height: Up to 70 metres

Spread of grades:

4	5	5+	6a	6b	6c	7a	7b	7c	8
7	11	10	39	13	5	5	1	/	/

Introduction

The crenated ridge to the north of the small town of Sax has much exposed high quality rock. The main feature is the fine tall (70+m) triangular tower of the PEÑAS DEL REY (the King's Peak and nothing more Freudian), the summit of which commands expansive views out over the surrounding countryside. The main part of this cliff faces south-east and is in the sun until mid-afternoon; the right side of the face goes into the shade earlier. Running leftwards from the PEÑAS DEL REY the rock continues along the ridge to the ZONA DEL BUHO and then the rounded dome of the SECTOR CUMBRE at the high point of the range. Despite the comments in the local guide quite a number of the routes still haven't been rebolted, fortunately most of the best ones have! The date when this took place (after each route) gives you a pointer as to what kind of gear to expect.

Access

Drive west from Alicante towards Madrid along the N340 for about 30 minutes. Take the second turning into Sax, having passed the 'Desert Song' castle. Drive down towards the town then at the foot of the steep hill with the castle, turn sharp right onto a new by-pass that avoids all of the town centre. Follow this around the hill then as it re-enters the built up area look for a right turn onto either the Calle San Juan de la Cruz, or the Calle Maestro Granados. These soon unite and head south-west, aiming at a spot to the right of the prominent pointed crag.

Note: the only other tarmacked road heading in roughly this direction aims straight for the cliff but stops before the rocky ridge that lies in front of the main hills.

Follow the road (initially passing a blue-gated council depot on the left and a large 'Defende la Montana' sign on the right) for 1.2km and turn left, the main road displaying 40 (speed) and 10t signs at this point. Continue on tarmac for 1.2km and then turn left onto dirt. Follow this and take the obvious right turn at a 'Via Pecuaria' sign. When the track splits keep to the left; the right leads to the same place but is composed of deep soft sand. For the PEÑAS DEL REY bear right at the next junction then sharp right to cross the river bed and reach the foot of the path that leads up to the cliff in less than 10 minutes. It is possible to drive up the hill towards the cliff but the track soon fizzles out and turning round is difficult. It is 3.5km from the edge of town to the parking. For the other cliffs continue steeply straight up the hill past the right turn, to parking on the right directly below the dark rocky dome of the SECTOR CUMBRE.

The best routes on the more popular PEÑAS DEL REY are described briefly first from left to right. It is probably worth carrying a single rack of wires and a couple of slings when climbing the bolted routes here 'just in case'. Occasional red-painted numbers from a bygone age aid the location of many of the climbs.

Descent

From the belay bolts at the top of the routes scramble to the summit and then turn left (looking in) and scramble down to the col behind the tower. From here there is an easy walk off down open slabs at the left side of the cliff.

Sax - Peñas Del Rey

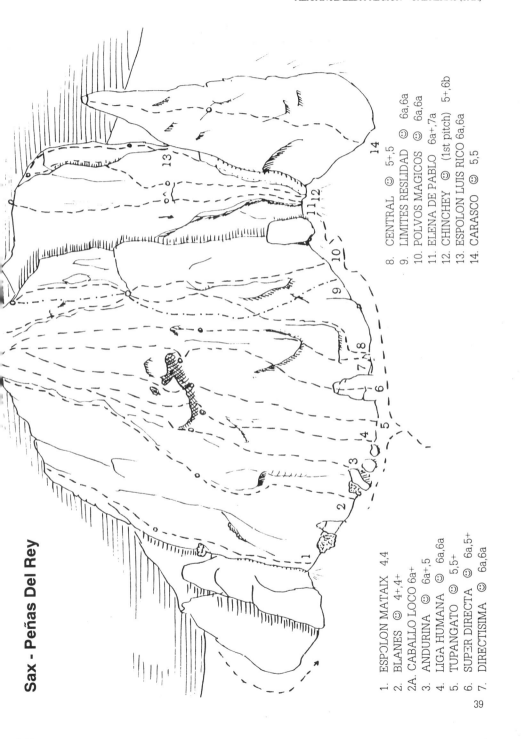

1. ESPOLON MATAIX 4,4
2. BLANES ☺ 4+,4+
2A. CABALLO LOCO 6a+
3. ANDURINA ☺ 6a+,5
4. LIGA HUMANA ☺ 6a,6a
5. TUPANGATO ☺ 5,5+
6. SUPER DIRECTA ☺ 6a,5+
7. DIRECTISIMA ☺ 6a,6a

8. CENTRAL ☺ 5+,5
9. LIMITES RESLIDAD ☺ 6a,6a
10. POLVOS MAGICOS ☺ 6a,6a
11. ELENA DE PABLO 6a+,7a
12. CHINCHEY ☺ (1st pitch) 5+,6b
13. ESPOLON LUIS RICO 6a,6a
14. CARASCO ☺ 5,5

The path from the car arrives at the toe of the main buttress. To the right of this is a deep recess containing some huge blocks and to the right of this is a prominent 'aiguille', the CARASCO. The first route is located up to the left, where a gully separates the main tower from a smaller one.

1. ESPOLON MATAIX 4,4 50m

This route starts at the foot of the left-slanting shrubby diedre and climbs the left arete of the tower in two pitches. Only the belays are fixed, so carry a rack.

2. BLANES ☺ 4+,4+ 60m

Start right of the corner at the letters 'FR' scratched on the rock and climb the pleasant rib passing left of a bulge at 15m to enter a crack, up this to a stance, 30m. Move right and climb a short white wall then follow the pleasant open groove all the way to the cliff top. Re-equipped 1990 so carry a light rack if you feel at all intimidated.

2A. CABALLO LOCO 6a+ 30m

The smooth shallow scoop to the right contains some old gear, plenty of vegetation and is not very popular. Lower off from the first stance of the previous route.

3. ANDURINA ☺ 6a,4+ 63m

Two metres right of the shallow scoop a line of new bolts runs straight up the steep, pocketed slab, through an alcove to reach a belay in a niche to the left of the central band of overhangs, offering superb climbing throughout, 33m. The second pitch (4+ in the local topo!) skirts the left side of the bulges by bridging then swings back right with difficulty to gain and finish up the easy rib in a fine position, 30m. Rebolted in 1992.

4. LIGA HUMANA ☺ 6a,6a 70m

Start behind some large blocks 5m right of the shallow scoop, where there is a small broken overlap at ground level. Head straight up the face then move slightly leftwards to pull over the centre of a small roof before pressing on to a stance below the main overhangs. From the

stance pull rightwards through the roof then climb the pillar above. Rebolted 1992.

5. TUPANGATO ☺ 5,5+ 70m

Start at a blunt rib to the right of the biggest fallen block and follow the oldish bolts up into a steep red groove containing a prominent big peg and then onto belay under the roof. Pull left then right through the centre of the roofs in spectacular fashion then continue in a direct line to the top. Rebolted 1990.

The next line to the right is MUERTA SABROSA 6b, a direct start to the previous climb that has not been re-equipped. A number '5', a ring bolt and an odd collection of tatty old threads mark the line if you feel the need.

6. SUPER DIRECTA ☺ 6a,5+ 75m

Start at the flat base of the cliff at a 6m high squat pillar with a faded number '4' painted on it in red. Climb the pillar then the wall into a hanging groove (threads) before moving out right and climbing a long juggy and gradually steepening rib before escaping out left to a stance under the right side of the central roofs, 45m. Step back out right and continue up the exposed and sustained rib above, gradually easing, 30m. Re-equipped 1992.

7. DIRECTISIMA ☺ 6a,6a 70m

To the right of the big pillar at the foot of the cliff is its little sister. Start by this and pull through the left side of a small, rather shattered overhang. Climb up passing a big hole and on up the smooth wall and scoops above to moves out left to belays in a shallow bay, 35m. The second pitch climbs straight up the steep arete and wall above the stance, 35m. Re-equipped 1994.

8. CENTRAL ☺ 5+,5 70m

Climb to the centre of the overlap and round its right side then up the rib to a small niche (possible stance and single bolt belay, better to continue). Exit steeply left from this to locate a better stance on a ramp, 40m. Step left and climb the slab to a short awkward wall, up this then follow the obvious left-trending line all the way to the final bulges and pull through the left edge of these to reach the crest, 30m. Rebolted 1990.

Around to the right is a right-facing flake and 3m to the right of this is a pair of blocks on the ground.

9. LIMITES RESLIDAD ☺ 6a,6a 70m
Start from the left-hand block, climb the slab passing a diagonal overlap and then join the previous climb and follow it to the stance, 40m. Finish up the bulging red wall directly above by good sustained climbing, 30m. Rebolted 1994.

Around the corner to the right is the great recess that splits the right-hand section of the cliff. It is a rather forbidding spot. The left trending overlap in the left wall here is the unequipped single pitch line of DIEDRO DINAMITA 6a 35m whilst right again is:

10. POLVOS MAGICOS ☺ 6a,6a 65m
Start at a 'ban-the-bomb' sign, climb through a small alcove, up the wall then trend left into a corner. Up this then keep right up the rib to a stance further up the ramp than the one used by CENTRAL, 40m. Continue up the left side of the final rib via a sustained shallow corner, 25m. Rebolted 1991.

The wall to the left of the huge club-shaped block is the sparsely equipped single pitch route of HOLLYWOOD 6a+ 35m.

A scramble through the cave/arch on the right reveals a pedestal holding up an immense boulder and whole different world (snakes, vampires, scorpions and things less mentionable). The front face of the aforementioned boulder is the first pitch of the circuitous expedition of NAVARRO 5+,5+,5+ 70m with a possible stance on its top. It then continues up the rib left of the big chimney and the wall above to the belay ledge of POLVOS MAGICOS, and finishes up the fine flying rib at the top of the cliff (rebolted 1993).

The huge soaring chimney line with '17' painted in it is the CHIMENEA GROEN-70 5,5 50m. I found no difficulty resisting the temptation to climb this immense spooky and clammy rift, but please feel free! The back wall of the bay has odd bits of aid gear scattered around it but on the right and just past a big left trending overhanging chimney line things improve again.

11. ELENA DE PABLO 6a+,7a 55m
The right arete of the chimney gives an excellent steep juggy pitch to a lower-off on the rim where the wall turns mean. The upper pitch is a whole different ball game. Rebolted P1 1993, P2 1990.

12. CHINCHEY ☺ (1st pitch) 5+,6b 50m
The rib just to the right again gives another steep and enjoyable pitch. A second bigger pitch spiralling up the rib and imposing flake crack above provide a harder (and possible not equipped) extension. P1 rebolted 1992.

13. ESPOLON LUIS RICO 6a,6a 55m
The corner immediately to the right leads to a stance above the col behind the pointed tower and the second pitch runs up the rib above. Rebolted 1992.

To the right is the elegantly pointed 'aiguille' that stands in front of the right side of the main face, its top ringed by a substantial wire cable which acts as an ideal abseil anchor. Its left wall (ie. the right bounding wall of the gully) is home to five climbs though the first four of these are poorly equipped at present. Fortunately the fifth one provides a great way to this unique summit.

RETRI 6a 40m
Start at the '16' painted on the face and climb direct in one long pitch (1990).

QE2 6a,6a 45m
Climbs the face to the right in two pitches (1993).

TECHO 7a+ 45m
Tackles the widest part of the roof and the wall above (1989).

CON CUARTO BASTA 6a+,5 45m
The left trending ramp on the right side of the face and the top pitch of the next climb (1988).

14. CARASCO ☺ 5,5 45m
Start left of the toe of the buttress (at a '14') and climb interesting rock to a stance and then on up the exposed arete above. The one to do if you want to tick the mini-summit, carry a light rack (1990).

The front face of the tower contains a couple of routes but the rock is poor and the fixed kit worse. If you are into summit ticking, across the prickly gully to the right is another smaller tower, the AIGUILLE ELISA-BELTRAN. The front face of this gives a pleasant route of the same name 4,4, 45m (1992).

The rest of the climbs at Sax are reached by continuing up the main track to a parking spot on a broad col. Away to the right is the ZONA DEL BUHO (Zone of the Owl) and directly above is the SECTOR CUMBRE (Summit Sector). Both are 15 or so minutes from the car and neither of these areas has proved popular with 'holiday rockers' in the past as most of the routes here were equipped from 1988 to 1990 and the fixed gear is somewhat old wave now. Despite this there is some good climbing here, especially on the compact walls of the SECTOR CUMBRE. The routes are presented here in topo format so that you can have a bit of an adventure! All the two pitch routes 'top-out', so take wires for the belay in case the belay bolts are missing. In keeping with the main cliff the routes here are listed from left to right.

Sector Cumbre

A fine cliff of very compact rock with some good face climbing. The 8mm bolts are mostly small and black and thus take some spotting from below, making for difficult route identification. The number of clips required for each route is listed here. A few climbs have their names painted at their base which may help sort things out.

On the far left there are five routes starting off a ramp, the first three sharing a communal lower-off:
1. MORENO MACHACON 7a+ 15m
Hard for the grade, five bolts.

2. ROMPE BRAGAS 6a+ 15m
The central line, four bolts.

3. POLLA ASESINATO 6c 15m
The left trending line passing holes and an overlap, five bolts.

4. HOMOCIDIO FRUSTRADO 6c+ 18m
The wall left of the groove is one of the most recent routes here (1991), six bolts.

5. ASESINATO PREMEDITATO 6b+ 18m
The shallow groove/crack line is more awkward than it appears from below, six bolts.

To the right the routes get longer:
6. INGRESO CADAVER 6b 22m
The wall right of the groove is devious, seven bolts and no lower-off, so top out.

7. PINCHA PANSIDA ☺ 6a 18m
The sustained slabby wall to the right, six bolts.

8. GORILERO 6a 18m
A delicate left trending line to the same lower-off, definitely misnamed, six bolts.

9. TAURO 6a 18m
The run-out line to the right, start at the name, five bolts.

10. TUBULAR BELLS ☺ 6b+,6b+ 30m
Start at the name, the first of several two pitch offerings. The second pitch jigs right then left, four spaced bolts plus four bolts.

11. ZOMBIS 6b 20m
A single pitch just to the right, six bolts.

12. FIESTA SALVAJE ☺ 6a+,6b+ 30m
A long first pitch up a thin pockety seam and a jug pulling pitch round the left edge of the roof, eight plus four bolts.

13. BUSQUE Y COMPARE ☺ 6a+,6a+ 30m
Another sustained face climb, start at the name and finish around the right side of the roof. Seven plus four bolts.

Sector Cumbre

1. MCRENO MACHACON 7a+
2. ROMPE BRAGAS 6a+
3. POLLA ASESINATO 6c
4. HOMOCIDIO FRUSTRADO 6c+
5. ASESINATO PREMEDITATO 6b+
6. INGRESO CADAVER 6b
7. PINCHA PANSIDA ☺ 6a

8. GORILERO 6a
9. TAURO 6a
10. TUBULAR BELLS ☺ 6b+,6b+
11. ZOMBIS 6b
12. FIESTA SALVAJE ☺ 6a+,6b+
13. BUSQUE Y COMPARE ☺ 6a+,6a+
14. DE PELICULA ☺ 6a+,6b+

15. TOREROS MUERTOS ☺ 6a+,6b+
16. DEMONIO CON FALDAS 6a+,7a
17. LUCECITAS DE COLORES ☺ 6a+,6a+
18. JABATO CON PI DE GATO 6a,6a+
19. GRINGO 6a+,6a+
20. CIVERA ☺ 5,5+
21. SENSACIONES AZULDAS 5+,6a+

43

14. DE PELICULA ☺ 6a+,6b+ 30m
Start just left of a flake and don't deviate. The best bolted route on the cliff! Six and ten bolts.

15. TOREROS MUERTOS ☺ 6a+,6b+ 30m
Start at the name and climb direct to a stance then on up the shallow groove in the same line, four and seven bolts.

16. DEMONIO CON FALDAS 6a+,7a 30m
The line to the right with an easy but poorly protected first pitch and hard but safe second one, four plus eight bolts.

17. LUCECITAS DE COLORES ☺ 6a+,6a+ 32m
Start up a ramp to the right and traverse left above a hollow, finish up the groove above, five plus seven bolts.

18. JABATO CON PI DE GATO 6a,6a+ 32m
Start at the name and climb straight up the wall, one long pitch, one short pitch. Seven and five bolt runners.

19. GRINGO 6a+,6a+ 32m
More sustained wall climbing just to the right, seven and six bolts.

20. CIVERA ☺ 5,5+ 30m
The pleasant groove leads to the left edge of the cave, move left to finish, six and six bolts.

21. SENSACIONES AZULDAS 5+,6a+ 30m
The last route climbs the rib on the right edge of the cliff and the bulges to the right of the cave, eight and six bolts.

Zona Del Buho

A hotchpotch of short walls and towers reached by a 15 minute diagonal ascent from the parking on the col. The routes are on four discrete sections of cliff.

To the left of a narrow pinnacle are three climbs on a triangular wall:
1. SUBE SI PUERDES 6c 15m
The left-hand line, short and sharp.

2. ASIGNATURA PENDIENTE 7b 20m
The centre of the wall, tough.

3. PRISIONERO ☺ 6c+ 20m
The right-hand line is the best on this Sector and is (just about) worth visiting the crag for if it's your grade.

On the front face of the pinnacle are:
4. ZIPI 5+ 10m
Short and unremarkable.

5. ZAPE 5+ 10m
Ditto!

Starting from a ledge around to the right reached by a scramble are three climbs, the right-hand pair sharing a lower-off:
6. MARIONETAS 6b+ 15m,
7. TITERS 6a+ 20m and
8. BANDOLERO 6b+ 20m.

To the right is the tallest buttress in the area, with a prominent cave halfway up the wall. This is home to a most odd collection of pitches:
9. ROMULO ☺ 5 15m
The left-hand line into the cave, pleasant.

10. REMO ☺ 5 15m
The right-hand line into the cave, also quite pleasant.

11. PERRO VERDE 7a 12m
From the belay above the last two routes hard climbing leads out of the cave to a stance/lower-off in the base of a groove. Above here are two more pitches.

12. CALIGULA 6b+ 12m
The rib on the left above PERRO VERDE.

13. NERON 6a 14m
The arete on the right above PERRO VERDE.

14. MATOJO DE LA BRUJA 6b+ 35m
The ridge on the right of the cave passing a potential belay at three-quarters height.

15. FUEGO SALVAJE 6c 22m
The last line on the cliff.

Zona Del Buho

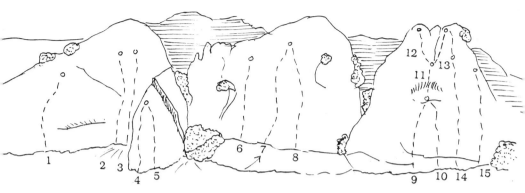

1. SUBE SI PUERDES 6c
2. ASIGNATURA PENDIENTE 7b
3. PRISIONERO ☺ 6c+
4. ZIPI 5+
5. ZAPE 5+
6. MARIONETAS 6b+
7. TITERS 6a+
8. BANDOLERO 6b+
9. ROMULO ☺ 5
10. REMO ☺ 5
11. PERRO VERDE 7a
12. CALIGULA 6b+
13. NERON 6a
14. MATOJO DE LA BRUJA 6b+
15. FUEGO SALVAJE 6c

*Cabreras: Peñas Del Rey,
the author on the first pitch of
the long classic ANDURINA 6a+*

PENYA DEL CORB

Crag Facts

Star rating: ***

Aspect: west

Height: Up to 30 metres

Spread of grades (pitches):

4	5	5+	6a	6b	6c	7a	7b	7c	8
8	4	/	8	4	5	/	/	/	/

Introduction

A short distance north of the centre of Petrel/
Elda is this illusive face of rock, 'the tower of the
raven', set high above the valley with a black
metal cross on its summit. This west-facing cliff
was the first to be developed in the area, initially
climbed on in the mid 1960s. The routes were re-
equiped in 1994 and now the place is home to 20
excellent and well protected face climbs several
of which are of a lower grade than is usual for
'sport' cliffs. The routes are up to 30m in length,
often of two pitches and are very well bolted.
The rock is generally less than vertical, and
many of the routes finish on a true summit. All
in all the place is well worth a day if you are in
the area and climb at the appropriate grade.

Access

Take the N330 Madrid road (recently upgraded
to a toll-free motorway) north-west from Alicante
for 32km to Elda/Petrer, pass the castle and turn
right at the sign 'Centro Commercial'. As the
slip road splits left and right, head straight
across onto a smaller road signed 'Aguarrios'.
Continue straight up this passing a tiny
crossroads and a tip, and after 0.4km the road
forks. Bear right gradually rising for another
0.5km until the tarmac ends; 0.2km further on is
parking on the right by a solitary tree. The path
starts here and zigzags up the grassy rib (two to
the right of the prominent cliff) until it contours
away to the left to arrive at the right edge of the
cliff, 20 minutes from the car.

Note: a direct ascent to the base of the cliff is
best avoided (speaking as one who knows) as
the slope is steep, loose and scrub covered.

Descent

For any of the routes that arrive at the cross it is
possible to abseil back down the front face (two
ropes required) or alternatively make a 12m
abseil down the back of the tower into the notch
from where there are two ways back to base.
Either scramble north (right, looking out) down
the steep scratchy gully passing under several
good climbs, or trend down and across the rocky
slope to the south (on the left, looking out) until
easy scrambling leads back to the foot of the
cliff. Avoid the direct descent of the south side
gully as it contains some steep steps.

The routes are described from right to left,
starting at the steep arete that bounds the right
edge of the main face of the cliff. The east-facing
leaning wall around to the right is the two pitch
aid route of PASCUAL SOLER at A2+; I don't
think it gets done much these days!

1. PASCUAL NAVARRA ☺ 6a+,5 30m
The right arete of the cliff gives an excellent
climb. Start in the gully around to the right and
scale a rounded bulge to get onto a ledge on the
arete itself. Step left and continue up the steep
face left of the arete on good holds to a stance
at the change in angle. The second pitch gives
easier climbing up the arete above until it is
possible to step into the gully on the left. Up this
to a two bolt belay just below the cliff top.

2. DIRECTISIMA FRANCISCO MOYA 6c,4+
30m
Start in a 'sentry-box' just left of the arete and
follow the steep pocketed seam up and slightly
leftwards to a stance in a bay. From here step
back right and follow the wide easy corner/
groove to a two bolt belay just below the cliff
top. A rather unbalanced climb.

Penya Del Corb

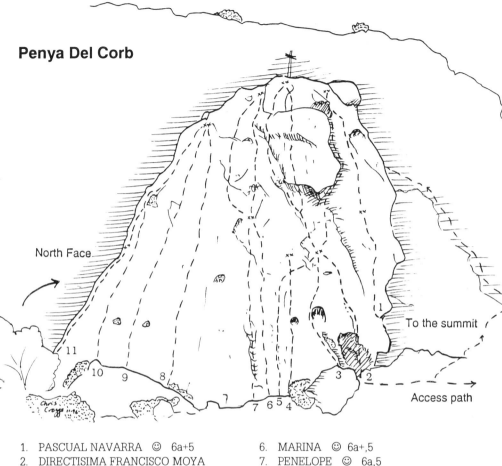

North Face

To the summit

Access path

1. PASCUAL NAVARRA ☺ 6a+5
2. DIRECTISIMA FRANCISCO MOYA
   6c,4+
3. ISABEL ☺ 6a,3
4. 9 D'OCTUBRE ☺ 6b
5. DANIEL ESTEVE ☺ 6c+,6c+

6. MARINA ☺ 6a+,5
7. PENELOPE ☺ 6a,5
8. PEDRO AYUSTE 6a+
9. NO SE SABE ☺ 6a
10. ESPOLON OESTE NORD OESTE 5 28m
11. LARGA ☺ 3,4 30m

---

3. ISABEL ☺ 6a,3 35m
The easiest climb up the central section of the cliff with only a couple of harder moves on the first pitch. Start on the left side of a 4m high hollow at a left-trending, bolt-spattered rib and climb this to reach some large pockets. Make steep moves back right then climb easily to reach the stance of the previous climb. From here follow the left-trending ramp to outflank the impressive double overhangs and finish easily.

4. 9 D'OCTUBRE ☺ 6b 15m
Just to the left at a head-high flake is this direct line with good climbing passing a large hole and a couple of tough moves just before the angle eases.

5. DANIEL ESTEVE ☺ 6c+,6c+ 35m

The hardest climb on the cliff, with two tough and contrasting pitches. Climb a thin pocketed seam in the wall with difficulty and when things ease traverse 3m to the right to the stance in a hollow used by the previous routes. Follow the ramp up to the left then power through the double overhangs following a cream and then red streak. The line through the biggest overhang directly above the stance is an unknown quantity.

6. MARINA ☺ 6a+,5 30m

Start at a 'man high' cave at ground level, climb the sharp pocketed crack up the right side of scoop to a comfortable stance. From here either step out onto the rib on left, 4, or more logically climb direct above the stance, pull through the left side of a bulge and then finish easily, 5.

7. PENELOPE ☺ 6a,5 30m

Start just right of the lowest point of the cliff and climb into the groove passing a moon-shaped flake. Exit from the groove using continuously surprising holds to reach the belay of the previous route. Take its direct finish to the cliff top.

To the left a ramp runs leftwards up the foot of the cliff and there is a line of rusty old bolts. Left again is a line of newer ones:

8. PEDRO AYUSTE 6a+ 28m

Start 8m up the ramp and climb the initial awkward steep wall then continue up much easier rock above. Pleasant climbing, though the start is appreciably harder then the rest of the route.

9. NO SE SABE ☺ 6a 28m

The next line up the ramp passes a large scar early on then climbs between two bushes before continuing in a direct line to the crest of the crag. Pleasantly sustained.

10. ESPOLON OESTE NORD OESTE 5 28m

The line just to the right of the left bounding rib of the cliff gives a long pleasant pitch easing as height is gained.

11. LARGA ☺ 3,4 30m

The left arete of the cliff is the easiest route hereabouts. It has a stance at 15m and from here there is a choice, 4 to the right of the crest and 4+ to the left.

The next routes are found around to the left in a steep gully colonised by some scratchy vegetation. The routes here face north (cool in the middle of the day) and are described as they are passed from right to left. The first route climbs an attractive grey slab:

SENDA PARA TUS DEDOS ☺ 6a+ 15m

The slab gives a nicely technical pitch with several sketchy moves until the angle eases. Lower-off the large ring bolt on the next ledge up.

GRETA 472 ☺ 6a 15m

The once-pegged thin crack with 'EJOR' scratched near its foot is good and is harder than it looks. Exit right at the top and lower-off as for the previous route.

ESTILO LIBRE 6b 14m

The line of bolts running up the slab to the left of the crack is rather tougher than it looks, especially the innocuous bulge at three-quarters height.

MA-MA 6c 14m

The steep line passing to the left of the prominent black streak near the top of the wall is hard, especially if you don't use the chipped holds when passing the bulge.

FUERZA FUTURA 6b+ 12m

The right side of the arete at the top of the gully has a couple of fierce moves early on (chipped pockets) and then eases dramatically.

PIPONA 6b 12m

The right arete of the short side of the tower gives a pleasant and photogenic pitch with a couple of long reaches between good holds. It is more than half a grade easier than its neighbour to the right.

CORTA 4+ 12m

The shortest way to the summit starts at the top of the slope behind the tower and climbs up to the top of the large fallen block and then continues up the short flake crack above.

TRIENTO Y UNO 3 18m

Down the slope to the left is the easiest way to the summit of the tower though it is sparingly bolted. Trend left across the undercut slab to reach the base of an open corner (DIEDRO DEL MECHERO 5 15m no fixed gear) then continue leftwards around a hanging arete to reach easy ground.

Penya Del Corb: John Addy on the excellent first pitch of
PASCUAL NAVARRA 6a+, one of the best climbs on the cliff

PEÑA RUBIA

Crag Facts

Star rating: ***

Aspect: north-west

Height: Up to 30 metres, though many of the routes are much less than this

Spread of grades:

4	5	5+	6a	6b	6c	7a	7b	7c	8
2	6	5	11	10	8	8	5	2	3

Introduction

A good set of easily accessible climbs on a series of steep cream and red walls in a pleasant wooded setting. The cliff is in the shade until mid afternoon and hence proves a haven when it gets really hot. The 50 odd routes here cover the spectrum from 4+ to 8a. The crag has been climbed on for many years and some of the routes here are rather polished. The proximity of the world famous Boreal factory (you can see it from the cliff if you know where to look) has meant that many of the planet's top climbers have exercised briefly here, though history doesn't report on what they thought of the place.

Access

The cliff is situated to the north-east of the centre of Villena on the left side of the hill ('the' Peña Rubia) with the conspicuous 'repetidor' (radio/TV mast).

When approaching from Alicante/Benidorm, about 10km after Sax, keep an eye out for the castle that stands in the centre of Villena. About 1km before this and just after the Campista gas station is a right-branching slip road signed Villena/Alcoy. Follow this then just before the town is an acute right turn signed 'Peña Rubia 5km'. Follow this road as it rises steadily aiming for the col on the hill dead ahead. Pass a strange-coloured building on the right and soon the road widens at an undeveloped 'urbanisacion' (ie.

impressive roads and streetlights but not much in the way of houses). Drive to the high point of this then turn left and park at the beginning of a sandy track. Don't be tempted to try and get 'just a little bit closer'. Three minutes up the sandy track and through bushes is the right end of the cliff. Most of the cliff is divided arbitrarily into SECTORS A to F though a few of these have 'proper' names.

All the routes are described from right to left (ie. generally trending leftwards up the hill) starting from the leaning wall entitled:

Sector Internacional ('A')

A short but very steep wall with a collection of tough climbs featuring chiselled holds, polished rock, hideously hard moves and a large white arrow painted on its left side (pointing the way to better things?).

1. MANTEQUILLA DE NAPOLES 6c+ 8m
Up the slope on the far right and starting just right of a big hole, follow the bulging crack out to the left, three clips.

2. ESTALACUS TOPUS 7a 8m
Start off perched blocks (name painted on the rock) and use tufas and an undercut pocket to levitate up the wall, two clips.

3. MEN OF STILL 6c 10m
Left of the block on the ground is a round yellow hole, climb leftwards through this, poor bolts, to a chain in a hollow.

4. HOMBRES DE PAJA 7a 10m
A tough direct on the last route passing a conspicuous hole with orange streaking below it. Three poor bolts.

5. POCKER DE BASSI 8a 14m
The left-trending line links natural pockets by using chipped (and then filled in?) finger holds.

6. LLUVIA DE ARAÑAS ? 10m
Despite being bolted and chipped the left-slanting line apparently remains unclimbed.

7. A BASSI LE FALTO ? 8m
The direct on the last, just right of the white arrow, also awaits a suitor.

8. AQUA FORCE 7c 8m
Just left of the edge of this sector and right of a tree is this short fierce route up a tufa, three clips.

To the left is a tree and just beyond this the pleasant slab of:

Sector 'B'
A single slabby buttress with some congenial though polished routes.
1. HUELSITOS KRAC 6b 12m
The right-hand line is a test of adhesion, five bolts protect it very well.

2. PLACA SOLAR ☺ 5+ 12m
The central line featuring flake cracks starts at a painted '3' and has a couple of slippery moves high up, five bolts.

3. VAMOS JOAQUIN 6c 12m
Climb a flake to the right of two sets of bushes then up the blunt rib above, lean right to use the lower-off of the previous routes.

4. MARIA 'A' ☺ 5+ 12m
Five metres left is this climb starting at the name painted on the rock in green writing and a '2'. The pleasant slab, 4 clips.

Just to the left is the start of what is probably the most worthwhile part of the cliff:

Sector 'C'
Just left of a purple arrow and '1' on the rock is the start of the first two routes
1. EN LA ESPERA TE ESQUINEO MASCANDO CHICLE 6a+ 10m
Start at a 'beehive-shaped' piece of rock at ground level and trend right then back left to chains on a ledge.

2. WARY WARY YEAH 7a+ 10m
Directly up the leaning wall to get to the same place. Originally given 7b+.

3. ROMPE PELOTAS ☺ 7a+,6c 12/24m
Just left and starting at the barely legible name climb up a steep bubbly crack passing a purple arrow to a lower-off then the slab and final bulge above. You choose, two short pitches or one longer one.

To the left is a white streaked wall pleasantly situated behind a stand of pine trees.
4. TXAVITO CLAVO UN CLAVITO 7c 14m
Start just right of the right-hand tree and climb the tough leaning wall rightwards almost to the initial lower-off of the previous route.

5. HAMBRE DE GAMBA 8a 14m
Start in the same place and climb the hideous wall leftwards.

6. EL AMPIRO CONTRA PACA ☺ 6c+ 24m
Start just behind the tree and climb the yellow wall to and through a large hole then on up the slab above, finishing over the left side of the roof high on the cliff.

7. LA IRA DEL TIEMPO ☺ 7a+ 20m
Start at the red painted name and climb the left side of the rib through a bulge to a belay on the slab above.

8. COCODRILO DIN DON ☺ 7b+ 20m
Four metres left and behind the left-hand of three trees is the name in green writing. Up the slab past a ledge then up the crack in the pocketed bulging wall to the lower-off of the previous climb.

9. ANDA TIE HUEVOS ☺ 7b 25m
Starting from a large block on the ground climb a slab, a small bulge and then a much larger bulge via a ragged pocketed crack. Pass a bush and press on to a lower-off at the top of the cliff.

10. VIVIENDO EN UNA SUPLICA ☺ 5+ 25m
A bubbly yellow groove gives one of the easier

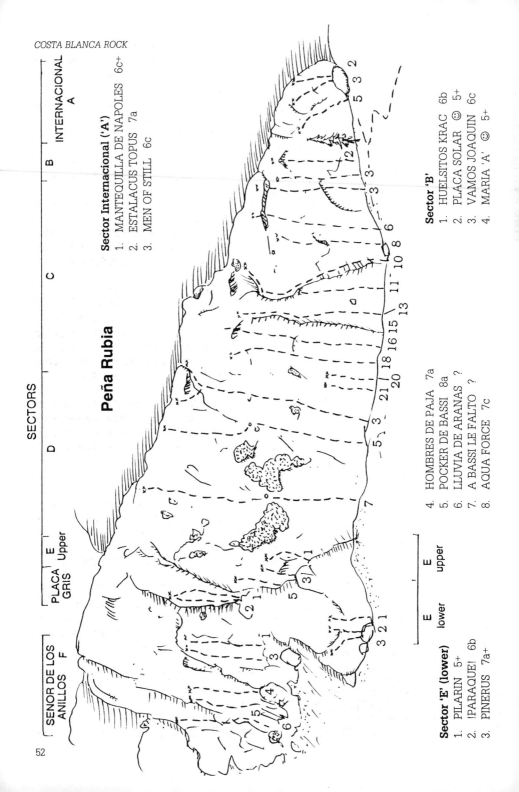

Peña Rubia

SECTORS

F	E	D	C	B	A
SENOR DE LOS ANILLOS	PLACA GRIS — Upper			INTERNACIONAL	

Sector Internacional ('A')

1. MANTEQUILLA DE NAPOLES   6c+
2. ESTALACUS TOPUS   7a
3. MEN OF STILL   6c

Sector 'B'

1. HUELSITOS KRAC   6b
2. PLACA SOLAR ☺   5+
3. VAMOS JOAQUIN   6c
4. MARIA 'A' ☺   5+

Sector 'E' (lower)

1. PILARIN   5+
2. ¡PARAQUE!   6b
3. PINERUS   7a+
4. HOMBRES DE PAJA   7a
5. POCKER DE BASSI   8a
6. LLUVIA DE ARANAS   ?
7. A BASSI LE FALTO   ?
8. AQUA FORCE   7c

52

Sector 'C'

1. EN LA ESPERA TE ESQUINEO MASC-ANDO CHICLE 6a+
2. WARY WARY YEAH 7a+
3. FOMPE PELOTAS ☺ 7a+,6c
4. TXAVITO CLAVO UN CLAVITO 7c
5. FAMBRE DE GAMBA 8a
6. EL AMPIRO CONTRA PACA ☺ 6c+
7. LA IRA DEL TIEMPO ☺ 7a+
8. C3CODRILO DIN DON ☺ 7b+
9. ANDA TIE HUEVOS ☺ 7b
10. VIVENDO EN UNA SUPLICA ☺ 5+
11. TE TIEMBLAN LAS PIEMBLAS ☺ 7a+
12. CLAVELES ☺ 6b
13. LA MUERTE DE LA HIGUERA ☺ 6b
14. ? ☺ 6a
15. VERAS QUE FUERTE TE PONES ☺ 5+
16. TE CUELGAN LOS CHURUMBELES ☺ 6b+
17. VACILANDO CON LOBOS ☺ 6a+
18. LOS 4 CHINETES DE LA POCA LECHE ☺ 6c+
19. KORTATU ☺ 6c+
20. TXAVO TU VALES MUCHO 8a
21. FARIDAKAR 7b+

Sector 'D'

1. MEDIO METRE ☺ 6a
2. SHARON PISTONES 7a
3. CARU ☺ 5
4. EL ULTIMO YECLANO ☺ 5
5. CHIMET ☺ 4+,4+
6. TAMPONES LEJANOS ☺ 6a+
7. EL VUELO DEL MONO 5,5

Sector Señor De Los Anillos ('F')

1. SAMSAGAZ ☺ 6b+
2. HELLS BELLS 6c
3. CONDON SIMON 6a+
4. SAURON ☺ 7a+
5. EL ESPEJO DE GALADRIEL 7b+
6. NO SABE 5

Sector 'E' (upper)

1. EL CHICO DEL LORE 5+
2. CINCO CONTRA EL CALVO 6a
3. PONTELO PONSELO 6a
4. POR SI EL SIDRA 6b+
5. SEMOS PELIGROSOS 6a+
6. VOLTAGE 6a+

Sector Placa Gris

1. GANDALF EL GRIS ☺ 6a+
2. SMAUG EL DORADO 6b+
3. ME DA LO MISMO ☺ 4+

classics of the cliff. Start at the name (green paint at knee level) and climb the groove, following it out to the left into a corner then traverse the slab back to the right to a lower-off just beyond the overhangs. A more direct version up the final slab is a delicate 6b+.

The hanging crack above the corner is the true finish to CLAVELES. This gives an alternative finish, though it is a bit of a nightmare.

To the left and behind a small Christmas tree is a smart yellow wall.

11. TE TIEMBLAN LAS PIEMBLAS ☺ 7a+ 15m
Climb through the beach-ball sized hole at 4m to a lower-off where the angle drops back.

12. CLAVELES ☺ 6b 15/25m
Start just left and climb past a tree in a hole and on up the fine pocketed wall. At the top of this either lean right to the lower-off of the previous climb (sensible but only two-thirds of a tick) or climb the corner and hanging crack above (puritanically correct but what a thrash).

13. LA MUERTE DE LA HIGUERA ☺ 6b 20m
Start at the name and passing to the left of the tree in the hole is this route up the grey then orange pillar. The final prow gives spectacularly positioned pocket pulling.

14. ? ☺ 6a 20m
To the left is a red groove running up to bulges high on the cliff. Start at the red painted name of the next climb, head straight up broken rock and then climb the left side of a bulge and a short crack in the arête on the right side of the groove.

15. VERAS QUE FUERTE TE PONES ☺ 5+ 20m
Start at the name then climb leftwards into the red groove which gives pleasantly steady climb to an awkward exit out right to reach the lower-off used by the previous climb.

16. TE CUELGAN LOS CHURUMBELES ☺ 6b+ 22m
The left wall of the red groove, there are two routes that utilise the same start. This one climbs through the bulges on the left then over

the large overhang that glowers over this section of cliff.

17. VACILANDO CON LOBOS ☺ 6a+ 22m
Start as for the previous route but eventually trend left to pull round the left edge of the final overhang.

18. LOS 4 CHINETES DE LA POCA LECHE ☺ 6c+ 22m
To the left is a fine steep slab with a '6' painted on it. Climb the right-hand line passing a bulge early on and continuing on sharp rock up a rib.

19. KORTATU ☺ 6c+ 20m
Start at the name and climb left of a small bush at 8m then straight up the steep slab (or easy-angled wall) to a lower-off.

20. TXAVO TU VALES MUCHO 8a 12m
Start just right of a tree growing close to the rock, climb the hard and sharp wall to a prominent large lower-off.

21. FARIDAKAR 7b+ 12m
Start up a pink scoop just left of the tree and climb the wall above.

To the right a longer route starting up a scoop is the first on:

Sector 'D'
1. MEDIO METRO ☺ 6a 25m
Interesting scoopy climbing. Start just to the left again at a name, climb the initial pockety groove then escape out right before trending generally left up slabs to a lower-off just to the right of a series of orange roofs.

2. SHARON PISTONES 7a 10m
Start just left at a head height hole and a strange 'spaceman' drawn on the rock. A short route up a bulging rib, four clips.

3. CARU ☺ 5 22/28m
Start at the name on the rock, climb straight up ambling slabby rock to steeper stuff and on to a lower-off under bulges. From here it is usual to move right to the lower-off of MEDIO METRO

though it is also possible to climb the bulges on the left to claim: VARIANTE MOCO DE PAVO 6b+

4. EL ULTIMO YECLANO ☺ 5 22m
Immediately left is another long pleasant slab climb. Follow new bolts up the slab and through a band of steeper rock to a lower-off below the overhangs at the top of the cliff.

5. CHIMET ☺ 4+,4+ 30m
Start at the name painted in green, climb the rib and slab pulling over or skirting around a couple of bulges to a large ledge. The second pitch trends leftwards passing the edge of an orange niche.

To the left is a clean grey rib sporting four shiny new bolts:
6. TAMPONES LEJANOS ☺ 6a+ 12m
Start up a broken groove then follow the line, short but good.

7. EL VUELO DEL MONO 5,5 28m
Six metres left is the start of a two pitch climb. Climb the left side of the open groove then step right across its closure to reach a broad grassy ledge. The second pitch passes a variety of fixed gear to finish just left of a block at the top of the cliff.

At this point a steep ramp runs leftwards up the cliff, and gives scrambling access to nine generally short routes of variable quality. Before this the routes around to the left of the base of the ramp are described briefly.
The first three of these are on the lower part of:

Sector 'E' (lower)
Fifteen metres left of the foot of the ramp is a pleasant clean rib and an alcove containing a big block.
1. PILARIN 5+ 12m
The front of the rib using a thin finger crack, the best of this diminutive trio.

2. ¡PARAQUE! 6b 10m
Around the corner and up the slope, the bulging wall in the back of the bay, short!

3. PINERUS 7a+ 10m
The left-trending bubbly wall, short and hard!

Continuing around to the left is another collection
of routes on a couple of fine grey faces, to the left
of a col at the top of the cliff. Unfortunately most
of them could do with being rebolted. This is
graced with the title:

Sector Señor De Los Anillos ('F')

The right-hand buttress has three climbs most
easily accessed via a 20m scramble from the left:
1. SAMSAGAZ ☺ 6b+ 18m
The crack and drainage streak on the right side
of the rounded buttress is the best hereabouts.

2. HELLS BELLS 6c 18m
The centre of the face sports rather old bolts.

3. CONDON SIMON 6a+ 18m
The left-hand line on the rounded buttress also
has older bolts and shares a lower-off with the
previous climb.

To the left is a prominent orange cave high on
the cliff and to the left of this is a fine grey face
reached by a short scramble.
4. SAURON ☺ 7a+ 14m
The right-hand line starts by some bushes and
crosses a small overlap then climbs the sustained
pockety face.

5. EL ESPEJO DE GALADRIEL 7b+ 14m
The centre of the face is climbed passing an
orange hole, to an orange painted lower-off.

6. NO SABE 5 22m
The groove on the left side of the face and the
buttress above are not really worth the effort
expended in the approach!

Returning to the base of the ramp that runs
leftwards up the cliff and gives slightly awkward
access to an odd collection of routes. This is the
upper part of:

Sector 'E' (upper)

Twenty metres up the ramp is an area of orange
rock. The short routes here have recently been
rebolted and may be worth visiting for that
reason alone.

1. EL CHICO DEL LORO 5+ 12m
Skirt the right edge of the orange rock then move
left to a lower-off.

2. CINCO CONTRA EL CALVO 6a 12m
The right side of the roof has a couple of
strenuous moves.

3. PONTELO PONSELO 6a 12m
Pull through the left side of the roof at a large
rounded hole.

4. POR SI EL SIDRA 6b+ 12m
The grey slab left of the cave is harder than it
looks, four bolt runners.

5. SEMOS PELIGROSOS 6a+ 14m
Continuing up the ramp to a left trending scoop
with a yellow dribbly tufa in its back, nicely
technical, five bolts.

6. VOLTAGE 6a+ 14m
Climb the very edge of the wall until it is possible
to swing right and finish as for the previous
climb.

The orange tower at the top of the ramp has the
best routes on this sector and may actually be
worth the effort of getting up to them (unlike
those lower down the ramp!). This is known as
the:

Sector Placa Gris

The base of the tower has a wire cable handline/
belay running round it.
1. GANDALF EL GRIS ☺ 6a+ 18m
The right arete of the tower on grey bubbly rock
is sustained and exposed.

2. SMAUG EL DORADO ☺ 6b+ 18m
The centre of the leaning tower is sustained,
sharp and worthwhile.

3. ME DA LO MISMO ☺ 4+ 22m
To the left a bolt-protected crack (tut tut) is
reached through bushes and followed as it
zigzags up the face. A good lower grade outing.

FORADA

Crag Facts

Star rating: *****
Aspect: north and south
Height: Up to 30 metres, though many of the routes are much less than this

Spread of grades:

4	5	5+	6a	6b	6c	7a	7b	7c	8
3	5	11	15	7	17	18	8	1	2

Introduction

A fine, varied cliff, with everything from sunny south-facing slabs to glowering bulging walls that rarely see the sun. Hot shots rave about the SECTOR SUPERHEROES though there is much more to the place than this. The cliff is at an altitude of 900m so the steeper north face can be cold in winter, though it offers superb shady climbing in high summer. The 80+ routes here offer a day or two's sport whatever grade you normally operate at. The routes are described from left to right, on the north cliff first, then the three small outlying buttresses that are passed on the right-hand path to the crag, then finally the south face (see map).

Note: the name of the cliff is pronounced in Spanish FOR-AH-DAR, accenting all syllables.

Access

Take the N330 Madrid road (recently upgraded to a motorway) from Alicante airport for 32km to Elda/Petrer, pass the castle and turn right at the sign 'Centro Commercial'. As the slip road splits, bear right to Xarret de Cati. Follow this rather tortuous road past a (dry) ford at 4.9km, bear left at 7km and pass over a col at 9.6km. At 11km when an extensive red roofed hotel with tennis courts can be seen ahead, bear right down a surfaced road marked by 'Coto Privado de Caza' and 'no fires' signs. A right turn-off by an elongated water trough soon turns to dirt and

is followed for 1.6km to a sharp left turn by an open flat area ('hermita' hidden in the trees on the right). At 2.2km the track suddenly starts to descend steeply, park on the left just before this point.

For climbers coming from the Calpe/Benidorm area a shorter approach is to come off the motorway at junction 70 (University) and then head towards Castalla for 25km. 2.2km beyond a half railway arch on the right, and immediately after a tiny bridge, is a left turn onto a white road. Follow this under an arch to a T junction (watching out for a particularly nasty dip at one point) and turn left. Follow the surprisingly steep road over a high col and down to the hotel, and just after this turn left onto the dirt road at the elongated water trough.

From the parking there are two ways to reach the cliff: for the left side of the north face descend the road for 100m and bear right along a good track (green flashes) that passes the toe of the cliff in 10 minutes; the route descriptions start here. If you can't wait to get at the SECTOR SUPERHEROES a direct approach from the green flashed trail is possible. For the right side of the north face and all of the south face climbs, follow the chained track that heads directly towards the right side of the cliff from the car, passing three minor sectors on the way (see below).

Sector Comic

The face just to the right of where (green-flashed) the track reaches the foot of the cliff offers vertical face climbing on sharp holds. The first route starts immediately to the right of a big pine tree:

1. EL PEQUENO FRANKENSTEIN 6c 12m
The leftmost line on the wall.

2. MUNDO MUTANTE 6c+ 15m
Just right again.

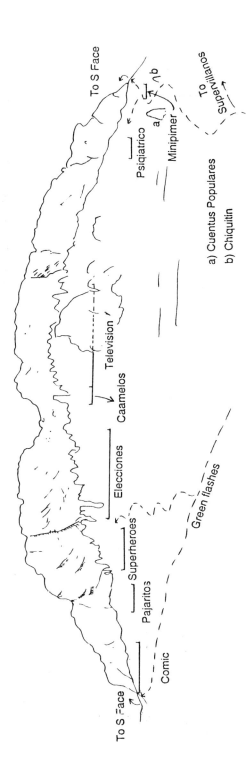

FORADA NORTE, SECTORS & APPROACHES FROM THE PARKING AREA

NORTH
1. Comic
2. Pajaritos
3. Superheroes
4. Elecciones
5. Caramelos
6. Television
7. Psiquiatrico
8. Minipimer
9. Cuentos Populares
10. Chiquitin

SOUTH
11. Petorri
12. Descote
13. Del Forat
14. Goteta

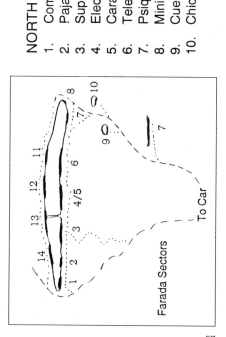

Sector Comic

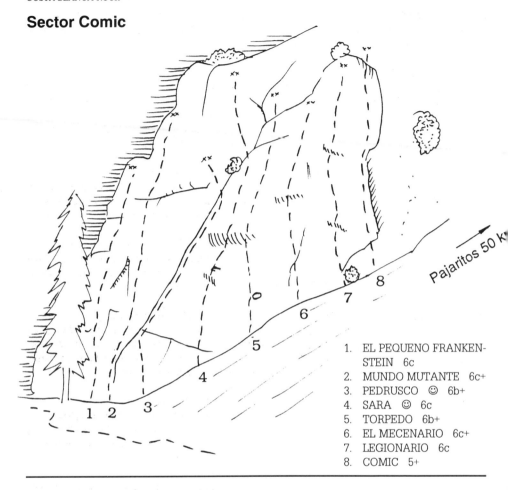

1. EL PEQUENO FRANKEN-
   STEIN 6c
2. MUNDO MUTANTE 6c+
3. PEDRUSCO ☺ 6b+
4. SARA ☺ 6c
5. TORPEDO 6b+
6. EL MECENARIO 6c+
7. LEGIONARIO 6c
8. COMIC 5+

---

3. PEDRUSCO ☺ 6b+ 14m
The thin right-slanting seam is followed across the face.

4. SARA ☺ 6c 18m
The wall and twin bulges just to the right.

5. TORPEDO 6b+ 16m
Start up the slope to the right, climb past a hole with a small bush and then the right side of the bulge of the previous climb.

6. EL MERCENARIO 6c+ 16m
The wall and bulge.

7. LEGIONARIO 6c 16m
The wall and then overlaps immediately to the left of a left-facing flake.

8. COMIC 5+ 15m
The left-facing flake and rather totty wall above are no laughing matter.

Fifty metres further up the slope is a short triangular white slab to the right of an orange alcove, and below some huge undeveloped roofs:

58

Sector Pajaritos

There are four pleasant though unspectacular climbs here in the Birds Sector, all at reasonable grades.

1. GORRION 6a+ 12m
The left-hand line leads through an overlap to a lower-off just below bushes.

The next three climbs to the right share a common lower-off:

2. GOLONDRINAS 6a 14m
Climb up to and through a bulge then step right.

3. CUCU ☺ 6a 12m
The centre of the slab.

4. PERIQUITO 5+ 14m
The right side of the slab trending left.

Nine metres right is the start of series of hugely impressive orange bulges that characterise the:

Sector Superheroes

An impressive 'orange' bulging wall, filled with pockets and offering ten excellent steep routes. A true 'superhero' would tick the sector in a day; the best effort I have heard of is seven of the 'easier' climbs! On the left side of this section of the cliff is a gnarled tree growing from below the biggest bulges. Passing to the left of this is:

1. TUNDRA ♦ 8a+ 32m
A huge expedition of a pitch up the barely explored wastelands of the left side of the bulges.

2. BATMAN ☺ 7b+ 24m
A powerful route through the bulges and substantial roof (tough clip near the lip), bat-suckers will be required by most mortals.

3. MUSCULMAN ♦ 7b 24m
The overhanging groove and juggy pockets with a tough sequence just below easy ground. The name says it all.

4. ROCK'N ROLL EXPRESS ☺ 8a 24m
A line just to the right linking the two prominent deep pockets via radical moves and finishing as for the previous route.

5. RADICALES LIBRES possibly 8b? 32m
A monumental-looking line up the rib left of the slanting groove of:

6. THOR ♦ 7b+ 26m
The slanting groove and bulges above are well endowed with jugs. The final steepening and wall to the lower-off are not! The line of bolted-on holds above the lower-off may become a PLASTICMAN one day.

7. ELIOS ♦ 7a+ 28m
A stunner. Climb the obvious thin crack and tough bulge above then follow the (easier!) scoopy groove all the way to the lower-off.

8. GUERRERO DE ANTIFAZ ☺ 7b+ 28m
The continuously-leaning wall to the right of the thin crack on holds that tend to be a disappointment.

9. SPIDERMAN ☺ 6c+ 24m
The broad rib on the right is climbed on good pockets until you thought it in the bag, and then there is a horribly precarious move to reach easy ground. Tough at the grade.

10. STARMAN ☺ 7a 24m
The broad rib before the major diagonal break gives an excellent pitch of pocket pulling, easing after half height. Despite the grade this route is easier than SPIDERMAN!

The diagonal break offers an awkward way through the cliff via the tunnel of the AGUJERO for those not frightened of the dark. It arrives a short way up DEL FORAT (5+) on the SECTOR DEL FORAT on the South Face and is not really recommended because of its slippery nature and quite awkward climbing. Mind you, it might be better than walking all the way around!

To the right of the huge diagonal chimney line is the:

Sector Elecciones

Recognised by a steep lower section and large undeveloped orange bulges hanging high above.

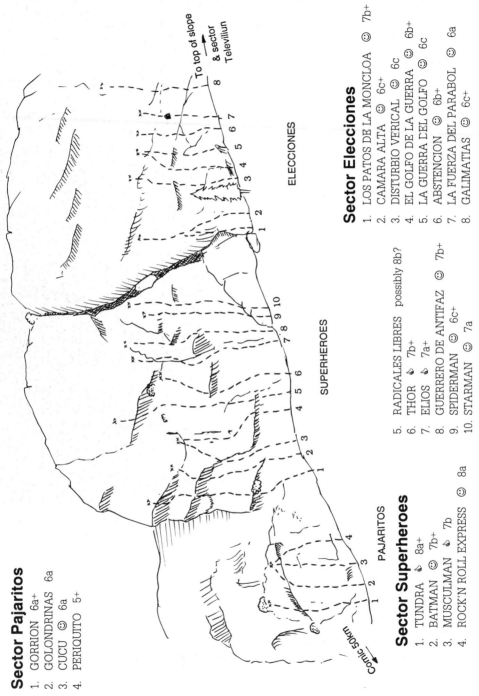

To top of slope & sector Televiliun

ELECCIONES

SUPERHEROES

PAJARITOS

Comic 500m

Sector Pajaritos

1. GORRION 6a+
2. GOLONDRINAS 6a
3. CUCU ☺ 6a
4. PERIQUITO 5+

Sector Superheroes

1. TUNDRA ☚ 8a+
2. BATMAN ☺ 7b+
3. MUSCULMAN ☚ 7b
4. ROCK'N ROLL EXPRESS ☺ 8a
5. RADICALES LIBRES possibly 8b?
6. THOR ☚ 7b+
7. ELIOS ☚ 7a+
8. GUERRERO DE ANTIFAZ ☺ 7b+
9. SPIDERMAN ☺ 6c+
10. STARMAN ☺ 7a

Sector Elecciones

1. LOS PATOS DE LA MONCLOA ☺ 7b+
2. CAMARA ALTA ☺ 6c+
3. DISTURBIO VERICAL ☺ 6c
4. EL GOLFO DE LA GUERRA ☺ 6b+
5. LA GUERRA DEL GOLFO ☺ 6c
6. ABSTENCION ☺ 6b+
7. LA FUERZA DEL PARABOL ☺ 6a
8. GALIMATIAS ☺ 6c+

1. LOS PATOS DE LA MONCLOA ☺ 7b+ 22m
Start just right of the huge slanting break, climb
the lower wall then make difficult fingery moves
on small holds where the rock turns white.
Climb the slab above to finish.

2. CAMARA ALTA ☺ 6c+ 22m
Just to the right a steep start leads to the finish
of the previous climb, an excellent long pitch
and mild at the grade.

3. DISTURBIO VERTICAL ☺ 6c 24m
Just to the right of the tree, tackle the wall and
bulges above, more pleasantly strenuous sport.

4. EL GOLFO DE LA GUERRA ☺ 6b+ 22m
Five metres up the slope to the right is this line.

5. LA GUERRA DEL GOLFO ☺ 6c 20m
Just right again and climbing through a red
groove and on over the bulges above.

6. ABSTENCION ☺ 6b+ 18m
Attack the steep lower wall, crux, and crinkly
slab above.

7. LA FUERZA DEL PARABOL ☺ 6a 16m
Start directly below a small red hole at 12m;
passing this is the crux.

Ten metres to the right is the last route in this
Sector, the long:
8. GALIMATIAS ☺ 6c+ 32m
A slippery, slabby, lower section leads to a
series of bulges climbed on sharp holds and
leading to a spectacular finish high on the arête.
Note the length of the pitch.

Ten metres right is a grey slab with two lines of
attractive gold bolts running up it. This is the
tiny:

Sector Caramelos
PICTOLIN 6a 15m
Pull onto a ledge and through a rickety bulge to
reach a flake, exit to the right over another
bulge. Reminiscent of some of Wildcat's better
offerings!

*Forada: Pete O'Donovan on the crucial bulge
of the super classic Èlios 7a+*

SUGUS 6a+ 15m
The right-hand line is precarious low down and
eases with height. Again the rock is not the
best!

To the right at the high point of the slope is a tall
grey wall with a ramp and a large pine tree at its
left side. This is the left side of the wide:

Sector Television

There are three routes on the grey wall, from left to right:

LA CALLE DEL RITMO ☺ 6c+ 20m
The good left-hand line starts from the tip of the ramp, pulls through a bulge, and ends up on the right of recess near the top of the cliff.

WAKU-WAKU ☺ 6c 20m
The central line passing a bulge low down is also worthwhile.

SESION DE TARDE ☺ 6c 20m
The right-hand line starting just to the right of a small tree gives more of the same.

On the right is a hanging mass of ivy and beyond this a tall pine tree growing close to the rock and the rest of the SECTOR TELEVISION. To the right of the tree is a roof low down with two hard routes crossing it.

EL ULTIMO MOHICAN 7c 20m
The left-hand line with reassuringly chunky ring bolts and depressingly fierce moves.

QUIERES QUE ME COMA EL TIGRE 7b+ 20m
The line just to the right is easier, but only just.

BUM-BUM 7a+ 20m
Just around the corner is this line with a boulder problem start through the bulges and some sloping holds above.

Behind two trees is a crack/groove protected by white bolts.
NEW ROUTE 7a? 18m
The route looks about 7a, but don't quote me.

EL PRECIO JUSTO ☺ 7a 16m
Right again is another crack/groove system; this is sustained and sports an awkward third clip.

CARTA DE AJUSTE ☺ 7a 24m
The right-hand climb in this Sector has a technical central bulge, and a delicate finish past a dodgy-feeling flake.

A hundred metres down the slope to the right is a wall bounded on the left by vegetation and with a deep horizontal slot at one-third height. This is the:

Sector Psiquiatrico

CARNE DE PSIQUIATRICO 7a 12m
Climb the orange lower wall to the slot, pull through the bulge with difficulty, and continue to the lower-off.

BLOQUEO MENTAL 7b 12m
Climb a tufa to the right edge of the slot and the grey wall above passing another bulge.

Down the slope to the right is the final area of FORADA NORTE:

Sector Minipimer

This is a north-west facing wall split by deep horizontal fissures and home to three bolt lines.
TERMOMIX 7b 15m
The left-hand line.

PICADORA MULINEX ☺ 7a+ 15m
The central line initially passing a diagonal crack.

MINIPIMER 7a+ 15m
The right-hand line up an orange face.

Before passing around to the delights of FORADA SOUTH there is the small matter of a couple of diminutive Sectors that are passed if the right-hand approach to the cliff is used.

Sector Villanos

To the right of the approach path (see map) is a low wall with seven short sharp routes. They are all about 10m high and their starts are marked with white painted squares, though no names are displayed at present. As might be expected with such short routes, they are quite tough for the grade. If you like short, hard, well protected ticks, look no further.
From left to right these are:
JOKER 7a 10m
The crimpy wall on the left.

Forada Sur, Sector Goteta: Colin Binks climbing superb rock on PANCHUFLAS 5+

PANCHO VILLA 7a+ 10m
The bulge and wall just right.

DOCTORO NO 7a 10m
The thin crack.

LUTOR 6c+ 10m
The overlaps right of the crack.

ESQUELOTOR 6c+ 10m
The overlap right again.

PHANTOMAS 7a+ 10m
The (at present) penultimate route crosses the
right edge of the bulges.

BARRABAS 6c 10m
The last offering starts where the overlaps
disappear into the ground.

Continuing along the path to the right side of the
cliff are two towers, on the left of the path is the
25m high:

Sector Cuentos Populars
The north face has some worthwhile pitches.
From left to right (ie. starting at the top of the
slope) these are:
TRES CERDITOS ☺ 6c 20m
The steep face just right of the arete.

CUENTOS POPULARES ☺ 7a 22m
The centre of the highest part of the face passing
right of a bush early on.

DUMBO 7a+ 14m
The short wall and small bulges just to the right.

PINOCHIO 6b+ 15m
The warm up for the face.

JUAN SIN MIEDO 7a 15m
A direct line to the lower-off of the previous
route passing the left edge of an overlap at half
height.

The south face has one line:

LAS BOTAS DE SIETE LEGUAS ☺ 7a 15m
Plough up the enticing tufas.

To the right of the path the boulder of the
SECTOR CHIQUITIN has one short offering:
CHIQUITIN 6b+ 10m, the bolted slab with a
steep start.

The next area to be described is FORADA SUR,
the broad sweep of cream-coloured slabs looking
out over high farmland, catching any sun that is
going and with many excellent low grade climbs.
This can be approached around either end of the
'cockscomb' of the cliff with the right-hand
(western) path being marginally the easier. With
this being the case the routes are described from
left to right.

Sector Petorri
The first area of note is a zone of pleasant tan-
coloured slabs near the high point of the base of
the cliff. A set of cracks forming an X near the
centre of the foot of the wall is a useful
distinguishing feature.
1. BON DIA 5 12m
The left-most line on the cliff contains a solitary
fixed peg. Climb a left-sloping ramp and a
bulging rib then move right to the lower-off of
the next climb, all very traditional.

2. CURSILANA ☺ 4 12m
The easiest route on the cliff and an excellent
beginner's climb. Start just right of a large bush
and pull over an overlap then pass left of a tufa
streak to reach the lower-off.

To the right is a new line of five big bolts that
stop at the bulges that cross the wall. At present
it is necessary to move right and join the next
route to finish, ☺ 5+, though it may eventually
be extended upwards.

3. FAM DE GOS ☺ 5+ 15m
A tricky start up the blunt rib left of the X leads
to easier climbing, then continue up the slab

Sella: Pete O'Donovan dwarfed by the first pitch of the majestic YA SOMOS OLIMPICOS 7b+

and pull awkwardly over the right edge of the bulges that cap the wall.

The next three routes are rather 'squeezed-in' but do offer good climbing.

4. PILAR ☺ 5 15m
The best in this sector is the direct line starting at the left edge of the X and pressing up superb rock above.

5. NOCHE GOLFA 6a 15m
Climb through the right side of the X then directly up the slab (blinkers!) before moving left to join the last climb. It is also possible to trend right to join the next route.

6. PAULA ☺ 5+ 18m
Start up a right slanting crack to reach holes and a flake then head on up the pleasantly sustained slab slightly rightwards to chains set above a bulge.

7. TIBURON 5+ 18m
Right again start at a wide crack leading to a break containing a small bush and climb to the same lower-off as the previous route via a mid height bulge, then a slab and a final groove.

OTRA RUTA 5 20m
Start up yellow broken rock then climb a wall and a yellow bulge before moving right to a lower-off below a bulge. Better than it looks.

To the right is the low point in the crest of the ridge and based around here is the:

Sector Descote
1. CABALLARI ☺ 4,4+ 30m
Start up a right-facing corner (peg) to reach a stance and two peg belay on the left. Continue up the slab then a right-trending groove before moving right to a belay/lower-off just short of the ridge. Carry a rack to supplement the sparse

fixed gear. A good route if you don't mind using those fiddly nut things!

The grey slab to the right has three excellent pitches:
2. MARISOL ☺ 6a 16m
The left side of the slab right of the corner is climbed direct and unlike its immediate partner is well equipped with shiny silver bolts. There is a thin bulge early on and then it proves to be 'jug-city'.

3. FRIERE SIN ACEITE ☺ 6a+ 18m
The centre of the slab gives a good pitch with a 'bloc' move passing the small slab at two-thirds height, a line of black bolts marking the way.

4. MUJER FURTIVA ☺ 6a+ 20m
The right side of the slab offers a pleasantly sustained pitch that proves to be quite intricate and mild at the grade.

5. COSME 5+ 18m
Beyond a long broken corner is a rib that starts at the foot of a blocky ramp. Follow this throughout with two cruxes, a delicate one early on and a strenuous one higher up.

A short distance down the slope to the right is the next developed area, centred around the through cave. This is the:

Sector Del Forat
Note: despite what you might have read elsewhere the through cave is not a good way of getting to the north face. At the far end there is slippery rock and a large drop - be warned!

The left side of the face has four routes based around a grey rib.
1. LA GOLONDRINA ☺ 6a+ 15m
The left-hand line up a fine flake gives sustained climbing and has gold-coloured bolts and a thin move at two-thirds height.

Puig Campana: Colin Binks on the first pitch of the mountain's great classic DIEDROS MAGICOS 5. The crucial overhang 6a+, can be seen above

Sector Petorri

1. BON DIA 5
2. CURSILANA ☺ 4 *KST/EST 28/12/98*
3. FAM DE GOS ☺ 5+ *EST/KST 28/12/98*
4. PILAR ☺ 5 *KST/EST 28/12/98*
5. NOCHE GOLFA 6a *EST/KST 28/12/98*
6. PAULA ☺ 5+ *EST/KST 28/12/98*
7. TIBURON 5+

Sector Descote

1. CABALLARI ☺ 4,4+
2. MARISOL ☺ 6a *EST/KST 28/12/98*
3. FRIERE SIN ACEITE ☺ 6a+
4. MUJER FURTIVA ☺ 6a+
5. COSME 5+

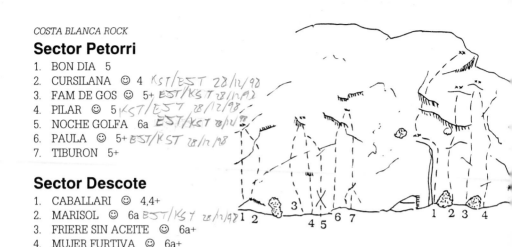

PETORRI   DESCOTE

Sector Del Forat

1. LA GOLONDRINA ☺ 6a+
2. MAMA UKRI ☺ 6b
3. CHORRO SIN AGUA ☺ 6a *EST/KST 21/12/98*
4. SUBE QUE ES GRATIS ☺ 6a+ *28/12/98*
5. ANA A2,5+
6. DEL FORAT 5+
7. JAVIER MUNOZ 6a+
8. PLUTGA 5+

---

2. MAMA UKRI ☺ 6b 15m
Sustained face climbing just to the right, passing a crucial bulge near the top on poor pockets, silver bolts protect.

3. CHORRO SIN AGUA ☺ 6a 15m
The central line to the shared lower-off starts just to the right of a flake with a small bush growing from it and again proves quite sustained. Avoid the use of the flake for the full effect.

4. SUBE QUE ES GRATIS ☺ 6a+ 15m
The right-hand line climbs the steep face to the right using good pockets and one move on crimps, excellent climbing.

5. ANA A2,5+ 30m
Aid up the bolt ladder on the leaning wall to the left of the ramp to a small stance then pull over the bulge and free climb to the top. All very archaic.

6. DEL FORAT 5+ 22m
The ramp passing the through cave is followed rightwards, and presents good climbing and a dearth of fixed gear.

7. JAVIER MUNOZ 6a+ 12m
The short steep wall to the right is climbed centrally and proves to be tough cookie; the old bolts are a bit of a worry.

8. PLUTGA 5+ 25m
The bulging ramp that runs up to the right is followed to its end then trend back left to the belay at the top of DEL FORAT. The route contains no fixed gear.

Just to the right is a zone characterised by a large orange roof (yet to be developed) hanging over it, the:

Sector Goteta
This area features fine slab climbing on rock of exceptional quality and roughness. On the left is:

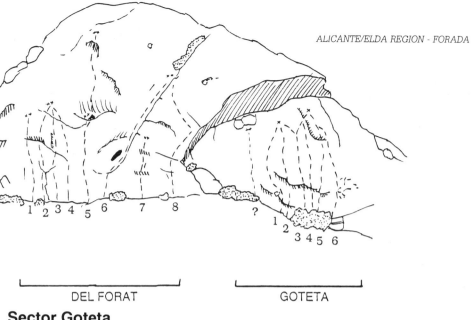

DEL FORAT   GOTETA

Sector Goteta

1. MAYAYA ☺ 5 KST/EST 28/12/98
2. LLEI DELS MALEANS ☺ 6a
3. MCFLAY ☺ 5

4. PANCHUFLAS ☺ 5+
5. CRISTINA ☺ 5+
6. LIGERO DE EQUIPAJE 5

---

1. MAYAYA ☺ 5 20m
Pull over an overlap early on (old first bolt) then pass round the left edge of another by steep moves and continuing on sharp holds. Tough at the grade.

2. LLEI DELS MALEANS ☺ 6a 20m
The line just to the right has a steep start up a crack (stand on the loose block) and a crucial bulge, wire thread, at half height. The finish is prickly.

The next three routes share the same initial bolt reached from a ledge behind bushes.

3. MCFLAY ☺ 5 20/24m
From the ledge behind a tree climb left of the bolt then pass the overlap and gain the slab before trending slightly left to a large lower-off.

4. PANCHUFLAS ☺ 5+ 20m
From the ledge follow the central bolt line with sustained (and sharp) interest until it is possible to pull rightwards across an overlap to reach the lower-off.

5. CRISTINA ☺ 5+ 20m
The final equipped route off the ledge proves to be the best route here, initially passing right of the first bolt and with thin moves into and out of the scoop at half height.

6. LIGERO DE EQUIPAJE 5 20m
Start on the right and pass poor rock early on then follow (or don't bother) the poorly equipped line throughout. A pretty poor offering for the final route on such a fine cliff!

RECONCO

Crag Facts

Star rating: ****
Aspect: Due south!
Height: Up to 52 metres
Spread of grades (pitches):

4	5	5+	6a	6b	6c	7a	7b	7c	8
4	3	2	12	11	4	6	/	/	/

Introduction

To the west of the small town of Onil is a prominent cream-coloured dome-shaped slabby crag set high above the valley. This south facing cliff is home to 30 excellent and well protected face climbs the majority of which are in the ever popular 'middle grades'. The routes are up to 52m in length, are very well bolted and generally are less than vertical. Many of the climbs have a metal tag with the name and grade of the route stamped on it attached to the first bolt. The identity of the few that don't can easily be extrapolated. Brief descriptions and quality assessments are included to aid identification and route choice. Have no doubt you will enjoy this place.

Access

Drive to Onil. The easiest approach is as for the alternative route to Forada, but continue through Castalla to reach Onil. The cliff is reached via a steep and rough dirt track that starts just before a house with 'wagon wheel' fences (not the concrete track a little further west) 3.5km west of the central roundabout on the Onil bypass. This is not to be confused with the large new Biar to Ibi road a little further to the south. The track is steep and rough and proves to be a bit of a challenge for small front wheel drive cars. Either park early on at a side branch on the left or take a run at it and if your ascent is a success, park at a flat turning area where the track ends amongst the terraces. The cliff is a steep 15

minutes away from the highest parking, 25 minutes from the main road. On the far left the crag is slabby, it steepens up towards the centre above a solitary almond tree (shade when the heat is on) and then becomes slabby again away on the right. A small number of the routes are two pitches, the rest are long single rope lengths. On the far right the easy lower pitches of some of the longer routes make excellent introductions to sport climbing.

Warning: If you are using a 50m rope be aware that many of the single pitch climbs are longer than 25m. Knot the end if in doubt. A spare rope will be needed to effect a descent. For routes that end up on the cliff top, abseiling from the many ring bolts is preferable to walking off.

The routes are described from left to right, many of them have large pale blue or white squares at their bases where it appears names and grades have been painted out. On the far left the first routes start at a flat, rather battered area where there is a white square painted on the rock.

1. CHINO-CHANO ☺ 6b 25m
Climb the lower slab then pull through bulges on better holds trending leftwards to a lower-off by a bush just below the top of the cliff.

2. CHINO-CHANO VARIANT 6c 25m
Three metres to the right is a variation start that passes behind a bush; it is short and sharp, joining the regular route after 8m.

3. PATA CHULA ☺ 5+ 25m
An excellent outing.

Start at an attractive grey tufa streak, dribbling out of a thin crack. Climb both these features (well bolted) then move out left awkwardly and continue up a rib to pass to the left of a tree to the lower-off used by the first two climbs. Thirteen bolts protect.

4. EL REY DEL SIS A 6a+ 18m
Start on a rounded rib above the ubiquitous prickly bush and climb the hard rib (the King of 6a indeed!!) then on rightwards through an area of broken rock to a lower-off on the slab above.

5. CORBELLA 6b 18m
Start in an orange scoop and climb straight up this on pockets and on past shrubbery to a steep bubbly wall that leads to the lower-off of the last climb.

6. PA EN CUBITOS 6a+ 20m
Climb out of the right side of the scoop mentioned above and trend slightly rightwards to a lower-off at the level of some ledges, shared with the next route.

7. GORBACHOV 6a 20m
Climb past the tagged bolt which is situated just down and right of a conspicuous tennis-ball-sized hole and follow small sharp holds then jugs as things steepen to a lower-off at the change in angle.

8. TACHER ☺ 6b+ 20m
Climb to and straight up the brown streak to the hole at its apex. The lower-off is just a little higher, sharp and sustained.

9. DESCONEGUDA ♦ 5,5 37m
The first two-pitch climb on the cliff and possibly the best lower-grade route here, though the second pitch isn't up to much. Start at the painted name and arrow and climb straight up pocketed rock passing a bush then loop right and left to reach the rather small stance (25m) 10 bolt runners. The second pitch climbs a shallow groove and then the slab on its right (12m) though it is rarely worth the effort, 2 bolt runners.

10. SEXTA ☺ 6a,6a+ 44m
An excellent long climb with a particularly good second pitch. Climb flakes and cracks up a grey streak then past a white scar to a belay in a niche (24m). The second pitch follows a diagonal bubbly weakness away to the right and gives fine sustained climbing with the bolts in just the right place (20m). Users of a short rope might have become aware of a problem on reaching the lower-off! Hint: lower to the stance on DIRECTA and then abseil from here to the ground.

11. PARIS - TEXAS ☺ 6a+ 28m
Start at the blue-painted name and climb the white rib passing a 'thread' and then some ledges to a lower-off in a bay.

12. CANAL ☺ 6a 26m
To the right are two small trees at the foot of the face. Above the right-hand of these climb a series of scoops then up the left edge of a large bay to a lower-off where the rock blanks out.

13. SEVINA ☺ 6b+ 28m
Start at a 'V' feature and climb the back of the main scoop initially and then the right side higher up to reach the chains where the rock turns blank.

14. DIRECTA ☺ 6b, 6a+ 40m
Start at the scratched name and climb the right rib of the scoops to a small ledge (28m). A shorter pitch leads up and left to a belay almost on the cliff top (12m).

15. DIT-LASER ☺ 6a+ 28m
Start at the foot of a crack that rises diagonally up to the right and climb the broad front of the buttress to chains a short way below the overlap that cuts across the top of the face.

16. LLENGUA FREE 6b¹ 25m
A good lower section climbs through a break in the diagonal overlap then sustained face climbing leads to a final perplexing move to reach the lower-off. Unfortunately it is easier to step left and use the belay of the previous route.

17. LA PERLA DEL CARIBE ☺ 6c 30m
Two squares left of the tree, climb to a bolt below the overlap then pull through this and press on up the sustained grey face on rock as good as you could wish for.

Reconco

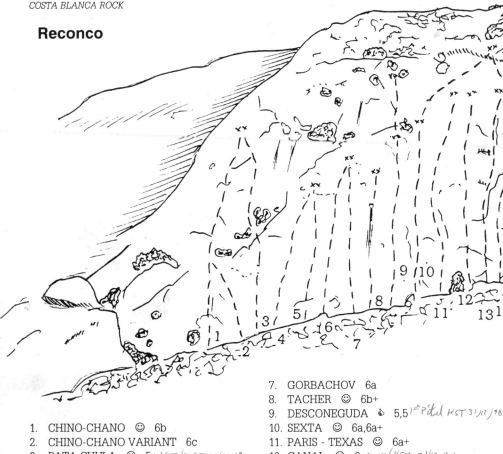

7.   GORBACHOV 6a
8.   TACHER ☺ 6b+
9.   DESCONEGUDA ♦ 5,5 1ᵉʳ *Petd* KST 31/12/98

1.   CHINO-CHANO ☺ 6b
2.   CHINO-CHANO VARIANT 6c
3.   PATA CHULA ☺ 5+ KST/EST 31/12/98
4.   EL REY DEL SIS A 6a+
5.   CORBELLA 6b
6.   PA EN CUBITOS 6a+

10. SEXTA ☺ 6a,6a+
11. PARIS - TEXAS ☺ 6a+
12. CANAL ☺ 6a EST/KST 31/12/98
13. SEVINA ☺ 6b+
14. DIRECTA ☺ 6b,6a+
15. DIT-LASER ☺ 6a+ EST/KST 31/12/98

To the right is the almond tree and on the steep rock behind this are a collection of four of the hardest routes on the cliff. Climbers who enjoy aping up leaning jug encrusted tufas will not enjoy these highly technical face climbs:

18. CHUNAY - FREE ☺ 7a 28m
Start left of the tree and climb steepening rock into a scoop. The leftward exit from this proves to be the crux and the lower-off is in the bay a short distance higher.

19. GEMMA BOOM ☺ 7a 30m
Start behind the tree and climb the left side of the pale grey streak by a fiercely sharp and sustained pitch.

20. EN BUSCA DEL POSETS ☺ 7a+ 28m
Behind the right edge of the tree this climb begins amenably enough and then gives more sustained climbing trending slightly leftwards up the steep cream coloured wall, ouch!

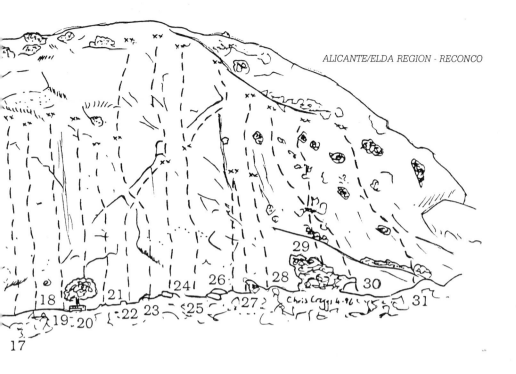

16. LLENGUA FREE 6b+	24. RUDA ☙ 6b,6b
17. LA PERLA DEL CARIBE ☺ 6c	25. LA LLAGRIMA ☙ 6a,6b/7a 1ˢᵗ Pitch EST /
18. CHUNAY - FREE ☺ 7a	26. LA PILMA 5+ KST/EST 31/12/98 KST
19. GEMMA BOOM ☺ 7a	27. SENSE POR 5 KST/EST 31/12/98 31/12/98
20. EN BUSCA DEL POSETS ☺ 7a+	28. FAM DE FIGA ☺ 4+,7a
21. NO SES TAN GUAY ☺ 7a+	29. SUPER ALI ☺ 4,6c
22. CENTRAL ☺ 6a+	30. TEDI - MAN ☺ 4,7a
23. CHICA DE MODA ☙ 6a+,6b+	31. SUPER - FACIL 4

---

21. NO SES TAN GUAY ☺ 7a+ 25m
Two routes right of the tree climb the wall
passing the left edge of the prominent overlap
then head up the steep sharp wall to a lower-off
by a tree in a bay high on the face.

22. CENTRAL ☺ 6a+ 24m
Start right of the tree, climb the large left-facing
flake to the diagonal overlap and then follow this
up to the right to the lower-off at the top of the
first pitch of RUDA.

To the right is a trio of superb two pitch outings
up the tallest buttress on the cliff. The first of

these is:

23. CHICA DE MODA ☙ 6a+,6b+ 52m
The initial pitch (26m) climbs the buttress right
of the flake crack then pulls through the centre
of the overlap to reach a tiny stance. The second
(26m) pitch heads up the steeper wall and then
climbs a delectable 'blank' slab to easy ground.

24. RUDA ☙ 6b,6b 52m
Climb the centre of the slab, sustained and
crimpy with crucial moves at half height, using
a couple of thin pockets to reach a poor stance
just below a bulge (22m). Pass the bulge by
crafty moves out left then back right (crux) then

71

continue on consistently surprising finger holds through another bulge to eventually reach easy ground (30m).

25. LA LLAGRIMA 🔾 6a, 6b/7a 52/55m
Climb the right side of the slab via a long pitch (30m), pleasantly sustained to a cramped stance where the cliff bulges.

Pull left through the bulge then climb up into the large conspicuous hole ('the teardrop'), the exit from which is the crux of the route (hint: bail out blindly to the right), 24m. The spectacular right-hand variation follows a series of undercut flakes out to the right then finishes up the bulging rib. This is much harder and just as good, 25m.

To the right are two shorter climbs that share a lower-off at the point where the rock becomes steeper:

26. LA PILMA 5+ 18m
Tackle the left-hand line keeping left of the vegetated rock then move slightly right to the belay.

27. SENSE POR 5 18m
Climb into the bay and then follow a pleasant flake up leftwards to the communal belay.

The main, rounded, right arête of the cliff and the east-facing side wall are home to three fierce routes on very compact rock. All of them have easy fully bolted lower pitches that may be of interest to those in search of low-angled low grade climbs.

28. FAM DE FIGA ☺ 4+,7a 45m
Climb the lower wall passing some large spiky bushes to a stance just below and overlap. From here head straight up smooth rib, passing left of a small bush. Hard.

29. SUPER ALI ☺ 4,6c 37m
Two metres to the right a shrubby lower pitch leads to a stance shared with the next climb (12m). From here climb the steep wall immediately right of the black streak and on up the orange flake above with just one especially thin section (25m).

Colin Binks following the first pitch of RUDA 6b on limestone as good as it gets

30. TEDI - MAN ☺ 4,7a 35m
Start from white ledges and climb pleasant white slabs to a small stance (15m). The smooth wall above and right of the stance is a whole different ball game (20m).

31. SUPER - FACIL 4 25m
Twenty-five metres beyond the last route, at the right edge of the main face, is a scrubby apron of rock that steepens as it rises. There is only one route here starting 6m left of an orange rubble-filled bay. Follow the line of bolts as it weaves between the vegetation to a lower-off just above the crest of the wall.

On the far right side of the crag is a flat-floored cave with obvious potential for some very hard routes. A single set of chains high above the right side of this is the only sign of development here at present.

AGUJAS ROJAS

Crag Facts
Star rating: ***
Aspect: Mostly westish
Height: Up to 32 metres, though most of the routes are half this height

Spread of grades:

4	5	5+	6a	6b	6c	7a	7b	7c	8
2	/	1	5	4	3	5	6	5	1

Introduction
A recently developed set of climbs on a series of red towers in a pleasant wooded setting. The 30 or so routes cover the spectrum from 4+ to 8a. Many of the routes have their names and grades stamped on the first hanger.

Access
The cliff is situated 1.5km north-east of the centre of Onil. Take the Baneres road for 0.8km, passing a right turn to Ibi. A left turn (at a large sign: 'Red Decaminos de Montana') leads past a couple of houses on the left, round some bends to parking on the left 100m beyond the rather small-looking towers of the cliff (1.3km from the left turn) that stick out of the trees. All the routes are described from right to left (ie. generally trending leftwards up the hill) starting from the roadside tower of the:

Sector La Esfinge
On the far right is a grey slab.
1. PEQUEÑECOS 4+ 10m
The thoroughly bolted slab on the far right gives a pleasant, well protected intro. to sport climbing.

2. RUFO 5+ 10m
The centre of the slab leads to the belay of the previous climb. It contains no fixed gear so top rope it, or solo it and claim a 'proper' E2 5b.

3. GONSO 4+ 10m
The rib on the left of the grey slab has an awkward start on strange 'stuck-on' holds and is much easier above.

4. NAMELESS 6c+ 18m
The next line left has a sharp, undercut start then trends left up the face above.

5. BESUGU ☺ 7c+ 18m
The steepest part of the wall is tackled by this beast; the bolt-on holds make it just possible rather than easier.

6. LA TUFONA ☺ 7b 20m
The line to the right of the large, painted, red cross features red bubbly rock, some hard climbing and at least one very long reach.

7. ESCUPE CUBATAS ☺ 6b+ 20m
Start where the crag swings round and climb the lower wall on good holds, step left and make a thin pull to easier angled rock. Finish precariously, up the steepening slab and shallow groove.

Up the slope to the left is a steep arete climbed by:
8. ROMPE TECHOS 7b 15m
Climb the steep arete!

9. CLIP-CLAP 7b 15m
The line up the left side of the arete.

On the 'back wall' of the tower is:
10. A LA SOMBRE ☺ 6a 12m
Climb delicately to the flake and swing right to finish.

To the left are three new routes up the steep grey slab. No grades or names known.
Behind the tower is the shady and slabby block of the:

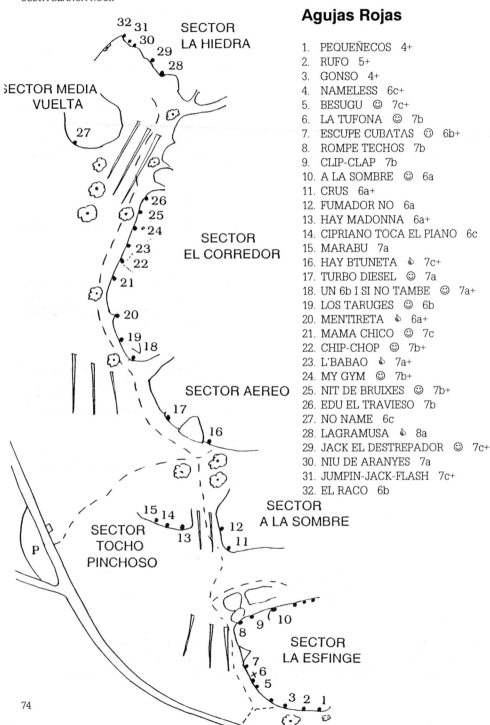

Agujas Rojas

1. PEQUEÑECOS 4+
2. RUFO 5+
3. GONSO 4+
4. NAMELESS 6c+
5. BESUGU ☺ 7c+
6. LA TUFONA ☺ 7b
7. ESCUPE CUBATAS ☺ 6b+
8. ROMPE TECHOS 7b
9. CLIP-CLAP 7b
10. A LA SOMBRE ☺ 6a
11. CRUS 6a+
12. FUMADOR NO 6a
13. HAY MADONNA 6a+
14. CIPRIANO TOCA EL PIANO 6c
15. MARABU 7a
16. HAY BTUNETA ♦ 7c+
17. TURBO DIESEL ☺ 7a
18. UN 6b I SI NO TAMBE ☺ 7a+
19. LOS TARUGES ☺ 6b
20. MENTIRETA ♦ 6a+
21. MAMA CHICO ☺ 7c
22. CHIP-CHOP ☺ 7b+
23. L'BABAO ♦ 7a+
24. MY GYM ☺ 7b+
25. NIT DE BRUIXES ☺ 7b+
26. EDU EL TRAVIESO 7b
27. NO NAME 6c
28. LAGRAMUSA ♦ 8a
29. JACK EL DESTREPADOR ☺ 7c+
30. NIU DE ARANYES 7a
31. JUMPIN-JACK-FLASH 7c+
32. EL RACO 6b

SECTOR LA HIEDRA

SECTOR MEDIA VUELTA

SECTOR EL CORREDOR

SECTOR AEREO

SECTOR A LA SOMBRE

SECTOR TOCHO PINCHOSO

SECTOR LA ESFINGE

Sector A La Sombre

On the right side is a slab with some evidence of old routes. The sharp arete of the boulder is:
11. CRUS 6a+ 12m
The arête has a tricky start and midway bulge.

12. FUMADOR NO 6a 12m
The flake and slab just to the left; no smoking up this one!

Across the gully is the short red tower of:

Sector Tocho Pinchoso

There are three short lines on the front face here.
13. HAY MADONNA 6a+ 12m
The right-hand line up the wall and flake crack.

14. CIPRIANO TOCA EL PIANO 6c 12m
The central line through a bulge and with some suspect rock.

15. MARABU 7a 14m
The left-hand line.

The next tower up the slope features a steeply tilted front face with a prominent hand crack on its left. This is the:

Sector Aereo

16. HAY BTUNETA ♦ 7c+ 28m
The centre of the leaning wall via the big beckoning pockets is a stunner.

17. TURBO DIESEL ☺ 7a 32m
The crack and hanging prow above is another corker, though lovers of elegant face climbing won't enjoy the start!

To the left and past an easy break is a slabby face with an overlap 3m from the ground.
18. UN 6b I SI NO TAMBE ☺ 7a+ 22m
The right side of the face starting by a flake and leading to some very sketchy face climbing on the grey slab above.

19. LOS TARUGES ☺ 6b 22m
Pull through the centre of the overlap and then climb the flake and the face above to the lower-off of the previous route.

20. MENTIRETA ♦ 6a+ 24m
The shallow slanting groove on the left side of the face is a corker giving sustained climbing to a final 'blank' face.

Around to the left is a fine high wall running up the side of a gully. The most conspicuous feature of this is the thin pocketed seam followed in part by L'BABAO that runs across it from right to left.

Sector El Corredor

21. MAMA CHICO ☺ 7b 15m
The right-hand line on the wall is steep, sharp and hard.

22. CHIP-CHOP ☺ 7b+ 18m
Climb the snappy wall above a sawn stump then make hard moves into and out of the big pocket on the left. Just when you thought it was all over the wall above provides the crux!

23. L'BABAO ♦ 7a+ 22m
Starting from a block climb up to the pocketed seam and follow it away to the left with sustained difficulties before blasting up the superb head-wall on a continually surprising set of holds.

24. MY GYM ☺ 7b+ 18m
Effectively a hard direct start to the upper section of the previous route via the big prominent hole.

25. NIT DE BRUIXES ☺ 7b+ 16m
The sustained rib just left again.

26. EDU EL TRAVIESO 7b 15m
The last route on this section of wall.

In front of the last area is a block with a solitary route.

Sector Media Vuelta

27. NO NAME 6c 15m
The central line on the downhill face.

Up the slope to the left of the SECTOR EL CORREDOR is a maze of narrow canyons and wide chimneys and then a flat-floored area behind the block that forms the previous sector. There are five bolted lines in this secluded setting.

Sector La Hiedra

28. LAGRAMUSA � 8a 32m
A superb climb up the scooped wall on the right side of the face, starting between the ivy streaks and heading ever upwards.

29. JACK EL DESTREPADOR ☺ 7c+ 30m
Start below an elongated pocket and pass this to climb the crinkly 'water streak' issuing from a large hole high on the face. Finish directly above this.

30. NIU DE ARANYES 7a 20m
Begin right of a bricked up recess and climb the wall directly and then leftwards.

31. JUMPIN-JACK-FLASH 7c+ 20m
Fierce climbing up the wall just to the left.

32. EL RACO 6b 15m
The final short offering just to the right of a hanging dry-stone wall.

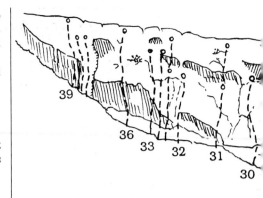

Crag Facts

Star rating: **

Aspect: west facing

Height: Up to 25 metres, though many are shorter

Spread of grades:

4	5	5+	6a	6b	6c	7a	7b	7c	8
/	3	4	7	6	9	6	5	/	1

Introduction

A closely packed set of well bolted routes running steeply up the side of a 'barranco' or ravine. The routes are well protected and tend to be steep and strenuous. Some of the rock is rather suspect. The cliff faces north-west and thus only gets the sun late in the day. It can be a rather cool venue in the winter. The grades here veer towards being on the harsh side. Climbers who operate in the sixes and low sevens and who enjoy fingery climbing should find a good day's sport here.

Access

In the centre of Ibi take the Baneres (A200) road to a right turn just before the second bridge and just beyond a 'no overtaking' sign (c. 1km from the edge of town). Drive down the track past a red 'probihut fer foc' sign and park on the right after 100m. Leave nothing in the car. Walk to the mill and climb steps just in front of it to reach the base of the crag.

BARRANCO DE LOS MOLINOS (IBI)

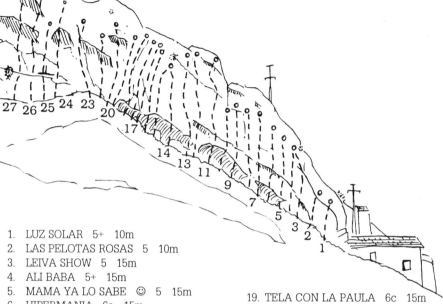

1. LUZ SOLAR 5+ 10m
2. LAS PELOTAS ROSAS 5 10m
3. LEIVA SHOW 5 15m
4. ALI BABA 5+ 15m
5. MAMA YA LO SABE ☺ 5 15m
6. HIPERMANIA 6a 15m
7. TAIFONS S2 ☺ 6a+ 18m
8. HOLE MI BELEN 5+ 15m
9. H.M.T. 6b 15m
10. CAPULLOS EN FLOR 6a 14m
11. CHORIZO BAILARIN ☺ 6a+ 22m
12. SHOW DE YEMAS ☺ 6b+ 22m
13. UHELE A BACALAO ☺ 6b 20m
14. NO TE INQUIETES ESTO NO ES UN 7 6b+ 15m
15. LINDA BONITA 6b 16m
16. MALDITA HEPATITIS ☺ 6b+ 16m
17. LICENCIA PARA MATAR 6c+ 16m
18. ARTURO NO SEAS DURO 7a 16m

19. TELA CON LA PAULA 6c 15m
20. VALLA MARRON 6c 14m
21. FIGUERETA 6a 15m
22. QUE POTITO 6c+ 12m
23. PICONETA 6a+ 20m
24. VIRAL OS ☺ 22m
25. PARANOIA 6c 15m
26. INTRON 'A' ☺ 7a 25m
27. BON PROFIL ☺ 7b 25m
28. LA CAGASTE BURLAN CASTER 8a 15m
29. ? 7a+ 15m
30. PONTECT 6c 18m
31. LA CHICA YEYE ☺ 7a+,7b+ 25m
32. ? 7a 12m
33. ELVIRA ☺ 6c,7b 22m
34. BACALAO DE BILBAO 7a+ 18m
35. MEDITERRANEO FREE 6c+ 18m
36. ROMPEDEDOS 7b 20m
37. CARLO Y BRUNA 7b 12m
38. CHINTO FANO 6a+ 12m
39. BUHO 5 15m

The routes are listed as they are passed walking up the steep slope, from right to left. Many of the climbs have their names painted on the rock or stamped on the first bolt bracket. Further description is superfluous, pick a line and go for it!

ALCOY

Crag Facts

Star rating: ** if you climb to 6b, *** if you climb above 6c

Aspect: south-east facing

Height: Up to 30 metres

Spread of grades:

4	5	5+	6a	6b	6c	7a	7b	7c	8
/	/	5	8	4	4	5	3	2	3

Introduction

Behind the large crowded town (small city?) of Alcoy is a wealth of rock and as is so often the case in Spain the local climbers have chosen to develop a small section of this as the local 'escuela', largely ignoring the rest of the cliffs nearby. The cliff runs diagonally up a steep hillside, is well bolted, is a sun trap and is characterised by steep, hard climbing and harsh grades. Whether the cliff is worth the long haul from the coast is debatable, though if you are after 'way-hard, severely-overhanging, pocket-pulling', get to it! Climbers of lesser ambition should enjoy the fine grey slab on the left side of the main face.

On the right is a vertical face which run leftwards into steeply leaning tufa-encrusted walls rising above a steep ramp and home to a bunch of test pieces. At the top of this is a pleasant grey slab, most easily reached via the gully right under the cliff or by an awkward scramble up the slabby rib a little further out from the face.

Access (see map p21)

From junction 67 on the A7 (10km north of Alicante) follow the recently upgraded N340 past Jijona (Xixona) and over the 1024m high pass of the Puerto de la Carrasqueta to Alcoy

(46km). Drive through the congested town towards Cocentaina (ie. keep heading north) until a large bridge over the gorge is crossed. A little further on and immediately after another smaller bridge is a left turn, just before a large church, onto the Carrer Esponeeda. Drive up this (the crag is dead ahead) until obliged to turn left then go straight across at each junction until you can drive up a narrow road with high walls on both sides. As this starts to descend there is limited (3 cars) parking under a tree opposite a house called MARI-SARI (no 25) where steps lead steeply past graffiti of various standards to the foot of the cliff. The routes are described from right to left and as mentioned in the introduction many of the grades here are particularly severe. The first routes are on a short flat wall at the right side of the face just above where the path arrives at the cliff. This is bounded on its left by a hanging corner. Some of the names are painted on the rock.

1. LOS CHINOS 6a+ 10m
Start at the name by some bushes and climb the short tower by a gently leaning rib to chains on the left. A good introduction to the grades here!

2. GRIPTORQUIDEA 6a 10m
Start at a painted white square and climb a short leaning wall then easier-angled rock to the lower-off of the previous route.

3. TENTACULOS 5+ 16m
Start at the name and climb the grey wall, a flake and the vague rib above. The easiest route on the cliff; now you know what you are up against.

4. VENTANA ELECTRONICA 6b+ 16m
Start at the name at the right edge of the graffiti

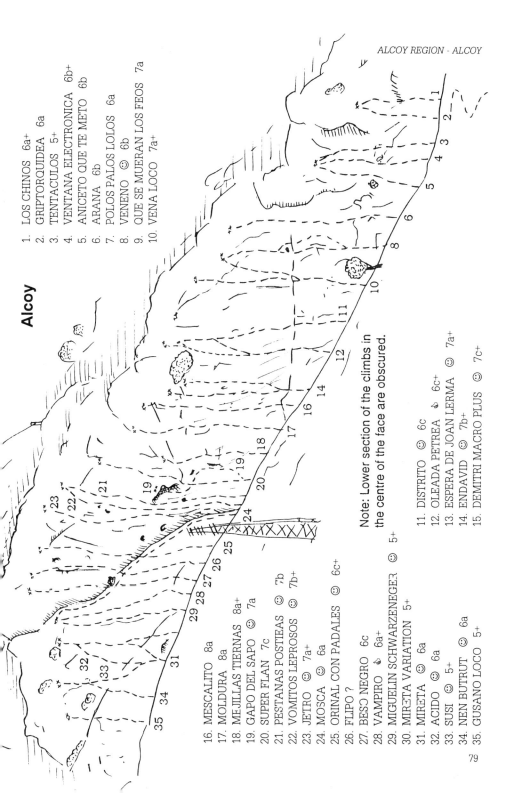

Alcoy

1. LOS CHINOS 6a+
2. GRIPTORQUIDEA 6a
3. TENTACULOS 5+
4. VENTANA ELECTRONICA 6b+
5. ANICETO QUE TE METO 6b
6. ARANA 6b
7. POLOS PALOS LOLOS 6a
8. VENENO ☺ 6b
9. QUE SE MUERAN LOS FEOS 7a
10. VENA LOCO 7a+

11. DISTRITO ☺ 6c
12. OLEADA PETREA ♦ 6c+
13. ESPERA DE JOAN LERMA ☺ 7a+
14. ENDAVID ☺ 7b+
15. DEMITRI MACRO PLUS ☺ 7c+

Note: Lower section of the climbs in the centre of the face are obscured.

16. MESCALITO 8a
17. MOLDURA 8a
18. MEJILLAS TIERNAS 8a+
19. GAPO DEL SAPO ☺ 7a
20. SUPER FLAN 7c
21. PESTANAS POSTIEAS ☺ 7b
22. VOMITOS LEPROSOS ☺ 7b+
23. JETRO ☺ 7a+
24. MOSCA ☺ 6a
25. ORINAL CON PADALES ☺ 6c+
26. FLIPO ?
27. BESO NEGRO 6c
28. VAMPIRO ♦ 6a+
29. MIGUELIN SCHWARZENEGER ☺ 5+
30. MIRETA VARIATION 5+
31. MIRETA ☺ 6a
32. ACIDO ☺ 6a
33. SUSI ☺ 5+
34. NEN BUTRUT ☺ 6a
35. GUSANO LOCO 5+

79

and climb past a bush then on up the wall to the previous route's lower-off.

5. ANICETO QUE TE METO 6b 16m
Start at the name which is almost obliterated by graffiti, and climb past a rounded blob of rock and on up a bulging rib before trending right to the lower-off used by the last two climbs.

To the left is a steep, open (and unclimbed) crack/corner and beyond this the face steepens up and becomes more impressive.

6. ARANA 6b 20m
Start at horizontal break (name) and climb with difficulty up a ragged crack and the shallow groove above it.

7. POLOS PALOS LOLOS 6a 20m
Start at a pair of names and climb the wall passing a glued flake (gripper first clip) then take the right-hand line where the bolts split eventually rejoining the 'true' line at a beach-ball-sized hole in an overlap. Continue to the lower-offs. Good value!

8. VENENO ☺ 6b 20m
Start in same place and pass the glued flake before climbing directly to the hole with considerable difficulty via a shallow niche. Finish more easily.

9. QUE SE MUERAN LOS FEOS 7a 20m
This is basically an easier right-hand exit to the next climb finishing at the lower-off of the previous route.

10. VENA LOCO 7a+ 22m
A steep fingery wall climb, passing to the right of a prominent tufa high on the wall.

11. DISTRITO ☺ 6c 28m
Climb straight up the wall passing left of the prominent tufa mentioned above to gain the base of an open scoop. Finish elegantly up this.

12. OLEADA PETREA ♦ 6c+ 26m
Perhaps the best route on the cliff, steep, strenuous and of course under-graded. Start at

the name and jug haul through the bulges, pass the horizontal break then trend left up a grey corner before swinging steeply right into the final shallow groove of the previous climb.

13. ESPERA DE JOAN LERMA ☺ 7a+ 25m
The 'true finish' to the previous route is harder again.

14. ENDAVID ☺ 7b+ 22m
Start at and follow the next bolt line up the ramp until it splits then take the soft option of the right-hand line up the head wall.

15. DEMITRI MACRO PLUS ☺ 7c+ 25m
The direct version of the last route is certainly harder and some say better.

16. MESCALITO ☺ 8a 20m
Start at the name on the rock, the first and best of a trio of well chipped 'eighth grade' routes.

17. MOLDURA 8a 22m
Start up the orange streak one metre left and do battle with the leaning tufas if you are up to it.

18. MEJILLAS TIERNAS 8a+ 18m
Start just right of a ring bolt and climb past two large eye-holes. Above these the route keeps to the right edge of the grey rock.

19. GAPO DEL SAPO ☺ 7a 18m
Start at the left side of the grey rock and loop strenuously out right then back left crossing the previous route to reach the prominent belay chain on the lip of the cave roof. Good beefy sport and the easiest climb in this area.

20. SUPER FLAN 7c 22m
Start to the left and climb the wall passing the right edge of the cave (there are twinned bolts early on) and on up the shallow technical scoop above.

21. PESTANAS POSTIEAS ☺ 7b 30m
Climb the pocket wall to the left side of a large cave with conspicuous chains on its lip then continue in the same line up the long rib above.

22. VOMITOS LEPROSOS ☺ 7b+ 30m
Start 3m right of the major diagonal line at the top of the ramp (just left of a painted white square), cross the crevasse then head up the steep pocketed wall that appears to go on for ever and ever.

23. JETRO ☺ 7a+ 25m
The bulging wall above the base of the long diagonal corner gives a good powerful pitch following a set of mostly big holes via some strenuous 'monkey business'.

24. MOSCA ♦ 6a 30m
The long slanting corner that forms the boundary between the tilted wall and the slab is the best 'reasonably' graded route here. Climb steeply into the corner then make tricky moves (crux) to get out left onto more open rock. Sneak below the in-situ tree then continue up into the final steepening corner to reach a lower-off out on the slab to the left.

To the left is a fine grey slab. There are three hard routes that start up this and cross the break of MOSCA to scale the steep wall above and there are another eight routes that stick to the slab. As elsewhere on the cliff the grades are tough.

26. ORINAL CON PADALES ☺ 6c+ 25m
Start 3m left of the base of the corner and climb steeply onto the slab. Cross the break and head up the wall passing a hole with conspicuous threads then on up large, though spaced, holds to a chain.

The line to the left, up the slab, passing right of the bush and then climbing steep rock and a red streak is FLIPO, quite probably still a project.

27. BESO NEGRO 6c 25m
The third line out from the corner climbs straight up to the bush on the ramp, pass this then head up the steep rib above.

To the right are a series of good slab routes that avoid that nasty steep stuff that makes up so much of the cliff. Unfortunately the grades are harsh. Add one full grade if you feel you are getting demoralised!

28. VAMPIRO ♦ 6a+ 22m
Start at the foot of a small left slanting ramp (white square) and climb the sustained rib on bubbly rock (protected by difficult-to-spot black bolts) directly to the lower-off at the end of the ramp of MOSCA, sharp.

29. MIGUELIN SCHWARZENEGER ☺ 5+ 22m
Start below a shallow groove in the centre of the slab and enter it directly with difficulty (5+??). Continue more easily on good holds until it is possible to lean right to clip the lower-off used by the previous route.

30. MIRETA VARIATION 5+ 22m
Start just right of an overlap at the base of the cliff then trend left to join and finish as for the parent route (see below).

31. MIRETA ☺ 6a 22m
Start at the name and a pair of spectacles painted on the rock and trend slightly rightwards up the pleasantly sustained slab.

32. ACIDO ☺ 6a 22m
Immediately left of the name and starting by some bushes, keep right of the grassy rock to eventually step out right and join the upper section of the previous two climbs.

33. SUSI ☺ 5+ 22m
Start as for the previous climb but follow the line of least resistance that trends continuously away to the left.

34. NEN BUTRUT ☺ 6a 20m
Start left of the bushes and climb the grey slab following the line of nice new bolts to join the upper section of the previous climb.

35. GUSANO LOCO 5+ 15m
The last route on the cliff is unremarkable unless you are looking for just one more undergraded 5+!

CABEZON DE ORO

Introduction

Travelling north from Alicante the first mountain of any significance passed on the left is the Cabezon de Oro. The mountain is most famous for the show caves of the Cuevas de Canalobre, and although the seaward side of the hill looks fairly tame the western face features extensive sheets of rock with many traditional climbs. Information is difficult to come by and only one route is described here in detail, the long traditional classic of Via Gene.

Access

From the N332 to the north of Alicante follow signs to Busot and the Cuevas de Canalobre. Before the caves are reached there is a red and white control barrier across the road. Shortly before this is a right-hand bend and just before this three tracks branch off to the left. Take the first of these and follow it for 3km, passing one tricky section, to parking (sensibly please) by the first house on the left. The path to the cliff starts directly opposite the house and zigzags up a series of old terraces with pine trees to arrive just to the right of where VIA GENE is scratched on the rock.

VIA GENE ☺ 5 (UK VS 4c) 275m

A good route following a strong natural line up this extensive face. The climb is rather slow to get going but has a fine climax high on the face. The descent route is off the back of the face and is not a very comfortable proposition in rock shoes. The whole thing can be managed on a single rope. Start at the groove where the name is scratched. Take a rack of gear.

1. 30m 4+ Climb the vegetated groove, to its cleaner continuation and then climb this to a belay on a tree.

1a. 25m 4+ A better option is to start 18m to the left and climb the clean groove in the blunt arete (peg, bolt and bush) to join the original pitch near its top.

2. 25m 4 Traverse diagonally right to a tree and continue past a pair of bolts to a belay on a pair of pegs.

3. 45m 4+ Move right into a groove with a bush at its base and climb it (bolt and peg) using a tortured crack. At the top of the groove move right up slabs, past bushes to a stance on a huge ledge, peg and bolt belay.

4. 55m 4+ Scramble up right to a left-slanting break (possible belay), and climb this to get onto a long ridge. Climb this to the top of a pillar where a two bolt belay is located in a corner.

5. 35m 5- Move up and left into a groove which is seamed with black rock. Move left into a smoother groove and climb this passing two old pegs to an exit on the left which reaches comfortable ledges and a three peg belay.

6. 45m 5- Continue up the ridge passing three pegs to reach a ledge just below the crest, single peg belay.

7. 45m 3 Move up right onto the ridge and traverse its crest (or stay below it) rightwards to reach the first deep notch in the ridge, and a triple bolt belay with wire cable. The descent starts here.

Descent

A single 50m rope can be used to reach the ground in four abseils; the last of these requires threading the rope through two bolt hangers. With double ropes the ground can be reached in two long abseils, the second of these from a monster shackle on a wire cable around a tree. From the foot of the abseils descend scree to the foot of the face and then contour around the end of the cliff to get back to the start of the route.

Sella: El Divino, how much adventure can you cope with?

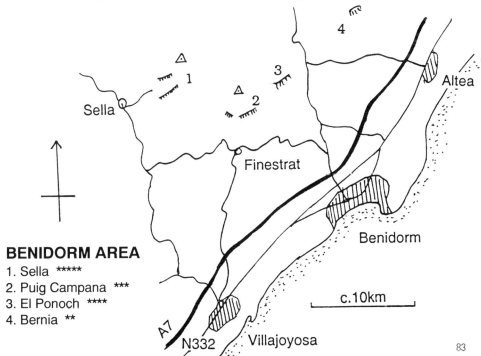

BENIDORM AREA

1. Sella *****
2. Puig Campana ***
3. El Ponoch ****
4. Bernia **

c.10km

83

SELLA

Crag Facts

Star rating: *****
Aspect: Mostly south and north facing
Height: 20 to 150 metres
Spread of grades:

4	5	5+	6a	6b	6c	7a	7b	7c	8
18	12	13	34	36	26	33	26	20	23

Introduction

This remote-feeling though easily accessible valley lies only a short distance inland from the bustling resort of Benidorm. The Sella valley contains a wealth of rock, much of it south-facing. There has been a great deal of development here in recent years and this continues apace with new routes appearing between the existing ones. The rock is invariably superb, much of the climbing being on classic finger pockets known as 'gouttes d'eaux' (drops of water). All the routes are equipped with substantial and closely spaced bolts as well as lowering chains. An immensely popular area, and with good reason! At the moment there is not a lot on the main cliff to attract the 'top notch hot shot' but for climbers operating in the lower and middle E grades a good time is assured. When you have done all the routes do them all again - it is better than freezing your rocks off back home. For those who feel the need for tougher deeds a visit to the SECTORS WILD SIDE and EL ELEFANTE should provide food for thought. As in the rest of the guide Spanish grades are used throughout.

Note: Camping below the cliffs is discouraged nowadays, chiefly because of problems of sanitation. There are some flat areas opposite the refuge that are used regularly - enquire within!

Crag Geography

The cliffs are scattered along both sides of the valley and on a rocky ridge which protrudes into its centre. The cliffs can loosely be grouped into

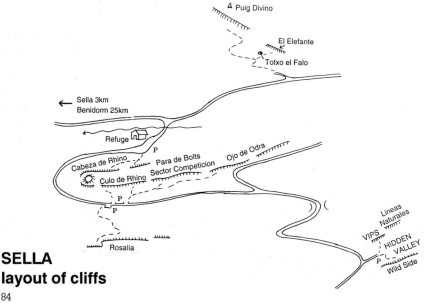

SELLA
layout of cliffs

84

four main areas (see map). Under the lower rocks of the majestic Puig Divino are the Sectors TOTXO EL FALO, LA SARTEN, and EL ELEFANTE. On either side of the rocky ridge that splits the valley is the shady Sector CABEZA DE RHINO, and the ever popular (and ever sunny) Sectors CULO DE RHINO, COMPETICION, and OJO DE ODRA. Opposite these are the large walls of the PARED DE ROSALIA. Finally the dirt road leads over a col to the Valle Oculto (Hidden Valley) where the Sectors WILD SIDE, VIPS and LINEAS NATURALES are located.

Access

The Sella valley runs north-east from the superbly situated town of the same name. This is most easily reached by driving inland for 12km from the Villajoyosa exit on the A7 motorway. If coming from Calpe it is also possible to take the Benidorm exit and drive through Finestrat, a bit shorter but also a bit slower. As the road rises into Sella there is a right turn leading to the conspicuous cemetery on the hill. Take this recently tarmacked road for 3km up the ever more impressive valley. At the point that the road turns into a dirt track and forks there is a rock ridge (the Rhino) splitting the valley. The SECTORS TOTXO EL FALO, LA SARTEN, and EL ELEFANTE are up the left fork (see below). The rest of the cliffs are reached by crossing the seasonal stream. The large building on the right is the refuge where the latest topo can be bought. Almost opposite here the short steep northern wall CABEZA DE RHINO, is reached in 30 seconds from the car. The rest of the climbs on the Rhino are round on the southern face reached by a bumpy 5 minute ride up the dirt track and a slightly longer (one minute) walk. Opposite these are the grand walls of the PARED DE ROSALIA, reached by a spiky 15 minute bushwhack, and over the col is the Hidden Valley.

Fifty minutes from Calpe, thirty from Benidorm.

The various areas are described in clockwise fashion starting at the Divino and ending with the Hidden Valley, see map.

PUIG DIVINO & ASSOCIATED CLIFFS

I have only done a relatively small amount of climbing on the cliffs around the impressive Puig Divino and so do not feel qualified to describe the routes here in detail. Instead here are brief notes on the smaller cliffs and accurate descriptions of three of the longer outings, just to whet your appetite. If you feel suitably inspired get a copy of the local guide and take care!

El Elefante, CP10M, Totxo El Falo & La Sarten

There are three sparsely developed areas around the lower slopes of the impressive peak of the Puig Divino. Two are home to many recent hard routes while a third of these appear to have been developed some time ago, judging by the state of their bolts. From in front of the refuge a dirt road branches to the left and runs up into the hills. After 1.2km there is a track on the left that doubles back sharply and there is restricted parking on the right; do not block access. Follow the track and then a poorly marked path that winds up through abandoned terraces. Wearers of designer sandals and short shorts beware: much of the vegetation is man-eating! The impressive smooth cliff of EL ELEFANTE is reached first by a path that branches across to the base of the deep gully that splits the wall, 15 minutes from the car. To its left is the shorter but still impressive wall of CP10M. The main path continues to the obvious red tower of TOTXO EL FALO, and just up the bank behind this is the start of the impressive walls of the Puig Divino.

CP10M & El Elefante

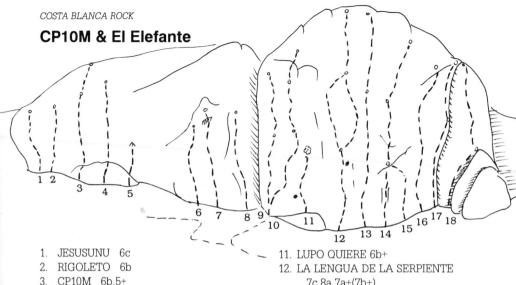

1. JESUSUNU 6c
2. RIGOLETO 6b
3. CP10M 6b,5+
4. TRAMONTANA TREMENS 7c+
5. A project
6. HOSTIA SUCCIDANEA 7c
7. PONTIFEX MAXIMUM 7a+
8. THE SHAME 4+
9. CANDYMAN 6b+,6a
10. SCORPION 7a, 7c

11. LUPO QUIERE 6b+
12. LA LENGUA DE LA SERPIENTE
    7c,8a,7a+(7b+)
13. A project or possibly an 8a,7a+
14. DIVING INSPIRATION 7b+,7c,7a+
15. EL ARUSPICE 7b+
16. A project
17. GRAN FISSURA 6b+
18. NAKED EDGE 5,6c+

CP10M & El Elefante

The recently developed EL ELEFANTE and CP10M have smooth flanks that are home to some of the area's hardest climbs. The two faces are divided left of centre by a deep gully. To the right of this the cliff soars up for 80m in a most spectacular fashion. Unfortunately much of the rock here is hideously spiky, and on some of the routes the bolts are very spaced or are missing altogether. I have only done one route here and that turned out to be under-graded and overrated. If you are interested the local topo lists the routes on the wall.

Totxo El Falo

The conspicuous red tower is home to three climbs and although they are quite pleasant it is questionable whether they are really worth the walk up. Some of the fixed gear is antiquated. From right to left the three routes are:

ESCALERA DE COLOR ☺ 7b 12m
The very steep right arete.
MORFIGREY 6b+ 10m
PENETRADOS 6c 10m

La Sarten

Behind the red tower is a short grey wall, with a series of equally short routes, which are generally poorly equipped. Again they are most definitely not worth the walk up. Consult the local topo if you must!

Puig Divino

The impressive triangular peak that dominates the head of the valley is home to twenty or so routes up to 14 pitches in length. These are mostly traditional climbs (the locals have designated the crag a bolt-free zone) with little fixed kit and apparently much low grade mixed (ie. free and aid) climbing. Some of the hard new offerings point to the considerable potential on

Puig Divino

1. ESPONOL PEMBERTA 4+ 295m
2. IGNASI HERNADEZ/AMOUR DE ODIO ☺ 6a 385m
3. PLACAS SOLARES 5 535m

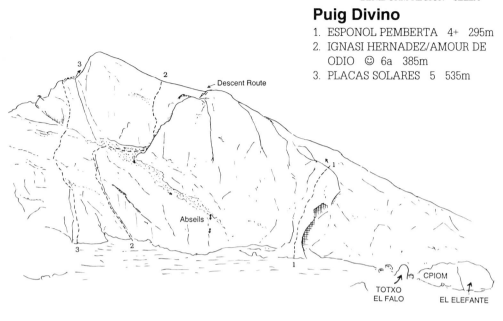

this mountain. It is a venue where double ropes, a sizeable rack and a helmet are all advisable. The length of the routes and the fact that they are in the sun for much of the day makes an early start a good idea and the carrying of water a sensible precaution if the weather is at all hot.

Access

From the red tower of TOTXO EL FALO vague paths run leftwards under the face, passing the rounded buttress of ESPOLON PEMBERTA (see below), to reach a wide grassy ramp that runs leftwards up the wall. This ramp gives access to the upper part of the face and is also used as the normal descent route from the mountain. The upper continuation of the ramp is followed by LA ZAPATILLA 4,4,5,4,4, though I have heard reports that this is mostly grassy scrambling.

The three routes described here are listed from right to left as this is the direction of approach.

The first climb described starts to the left of a huge cave/alcove where a rounded buttress

effectively forms the right side of the main face.

1. ESPOLON PEMBERTA 4+ 295m

Not a particularly outstanding route though it does have the advantage of being one of the easiest climbs on the Divino (about UK VS 4c) and so it gives you a chance to have a good look without getting too committed.

1. 45m 3 Start at the foot of the buttress and climb direct (loose in places) to a ledge with a single bolt (+ threads) belay.
2. 45m 4+ Climb the face above the stance via cracks and pockets to a bleached thread then continue straight up the wall to another single bolt (+ thread) belay.
3. 40m 4 Continue more easily in the same line to yet another single bolt belay at a good ledge.
4. 40m 4 From the ledge climb up and left into a groove and follow this to its end and then move diagonally rightwards to a peg in a slabby scoop. From here climb up and left to a stance and belay (no fixed gear) on blocks on the ridge.

5. 45m 4 Move up and left climbing a slab via a black crack, then continuing in the same line to reach a bay that has twin belay pegs in its right side.

6 & 7. 80m 3 Two rope lengths lead rightwards over stone strewn ledges and through patchy vegetation, to reach the small ridge on the right, below the final walls. There is a variation finish up the steep slabs on the left (Grade 5) but the easiest way off is to trend right to reach a small left-facing corner and climb this to reach the open slopes beyond.

Descent

Walk UP the slope until you can see both:
a)   the tip of the summit high above, and
b)   a small projecting buttress down and left.

Head down towards the buttress and then enter a small gully. Descend this then continue down the ramp (slings in situ for two short abseils if needed) to reach the main ramp. From here a vague track zigzags down to reach some in-situ slings. A short abseil from these reaches yet more slings from where a full length abseil reaches the ground.

2. IGNASI HERNADEZ/AMOR DE ODIO ☺ 6a (UK E2 5b/c) 385m

A huge expedition of a route up the centre of the face. The combination uses the easiest halves of two routes to create a logical way up the cliff. Despite this the climb is still a little unbalanced with a long easy lower section (plus a few hard moves) on the lower ramp then a steep and excellent section on the upper wall. This upper part of the route is sustained, there is little fixed gear and the route finding is difficult, so start early and take a full rack. Approach as for the previous route but continue leftwards passing the foot of the broad ramp used for the descent to reach an obvious ramp in an orange-walled bay just left of a white '14' painted on the rock. It makes sense to leave sacks etc. here and collect them on the descent.

1. 30m 3 Climb the ramp until it is necessary to move left below some loose-looking blocks to enter a groove where there is a single bolt belay.

2. 20m 4 Continue up the slab to a bolt then climb leftwards up cracked blocks to a good stance in a yellow corner.

3. 25m 4 Go up the yellow corner and the crozzly slab above to reach a stance and a rather odd home-made bolt belay.

4. 35m 6a Climb the crozzly shallow groove to a bolt and make awkward moves to a second bolt before climbing the corner above to reach the final difficult section passing two more bolts, with a twin bolt belay a short distance above.

5. 25m 5 Follow the corner crack above and then move left through spiky vegetation to a stance at the foot of another yellow groove.

6. 40m 5 Continue up the groove avoiding the first spiky bush on the left (possible wire thread) then continue until it is possible to avoid the second bush via a difficult leftwards traverse (possible wire thread). Continue up the grey rib to nut and thread belays.

7. 40m Scramble easily up until below a short water worn scoop, nut belays.

8. 15m 4 Climb the left side of the first scoop and then the right side of the next one before moving carefully over rubble to a belay in the shade of a bush. (This is the last shade on the route, enjoy it while you can!)

9. 3 Scramble right across stone-strewn, vegetated ledges to the short gully that is part of the descent route and scramble up this passing abseil tat before moving up and right to a point where there is a chipped arrow on the wall on the left of the gully.

10. 25m 5+ Climb up the wall above the arrow, deviating left and right as the rock dictates, to reach a bolt and nut belay.

11. 25m 5+ Trend up and left to pass an overlap (bolt) then traverse left passing in-situ threads before climbing straight up to an in situ thread by a niche. Belay here. Friends or nuts back up the in-situ thread.

12. 30m 5+ Move up and left to clip a thread and then step down and follow a traverse line out to below blocks and a small bush. Climb past the blocks (care required) then trend first left to peg then back right to a narrow ledge and another peg. Continue for

8m to some peg scars then move awkwardly left onto a slab to reach bolt and peg belays.

13. 30m 5 Continue trending left, now on easier rock, to reach a large block and thread belay at the foot of the final steep cracked wall.

14. 45m 6a Move diagonally right then follow flakes and cracks to a peg (possible stance) then continue up the wall and move left to flakes. Continue to some welcome holes, pull up on these and make a long reach left for flake holds and one more fingery pull which gains easier rock and the top. Belay a few feet back.

Descent

Head down the slope to the right to reach the narrow gully mentioned in the descent for the previous route. Follow this description throughout.

3. PLACAS SOLARES 5 (UK HVS 5a) 535m
Another massive expedition of a route that makes the most of the rock on the left side of the mountain. The climbing is not of a particularly outstanding quality but the route is the longest on the mountain and it does visit the summit. Approach as for the previous climb but continue past the orange-walled bay to reach a large grassy slab and a rounded rib with a grassy groove to its left. There is an arrow chipped on the rock to the left of the groove.

1. 45m 4+ From the arrow climb the rib, passing a potential stance at half-height, to reach a ledge and thread belays just above a 'pruned' bush. Another arrow indicates the way on.

2. 45m 5 Follow the direction indicator to a possible stance at 25m then climb steeper rock past another chipped arrow, before trending left into a groove and climbing this to a belay at an in situ thread and yet another chipped arrow.

3. 50m 4 Continue up the slab, eventually passing to the left of a cracked overhang to reach a stance, nut and Friend belays.

4 & 5. 70m Two pitches of easy scrambling and walking lead to the foot of the next steep section at a chipped arrow and a substantial thread belay.

6. 30m 5 Follow the line diagonally, gradually steepening up to arrive at a vegetated ledge and various (not in-situ) belays. From here on there are no more arrows, so it is a matter of following your nose.

7. 40m 5 Head straight up the slab to a left-facing corner and climb this until the angle falls back and it is possible to belay below some cracked blocks.

8. 35m Scramble up to a vegetated terrace and then move right to the base of the upper buttress.

9. 45m 4+ Start 15m right of an obvious right-facing corner and climb a slabby rib and steeper rock to gain a right-slanting ramp. Climb this then move around right onto the face and climb this diagonally rightwards passing an in-situ thread to enter and climb a blocky corner to reach a belay on a bush.

10. 40m 5 Climb easily to a pillar then follow the crack on its right side. Continue in the same line and then move left and belay below some wide cracks.

11. 40m 4+ From the left end of the ledge follow slabby ribs and grooves, then trend right on easier ground to nut belays 6m left of a prominent palm tree.

12. 25m 4 Move diagonally left to a small overhang split by twin cracks, climb these and continue in the same line to the crest of the ridge.

13 & 14. 70m Follow the crest of the ridge rightwards to easy ground, where it is possible to unrope safely.

Scramble towards a huge bay up and to the right, go into the back of this and then scramble up the corner to arrive just below the summit. The DESCENT lies down the ridge to the right until a small rock face running down and right comes into view. A footpath develops below this and this runs into the narrow gully described in the descent for the earlier routes. Follow this throughout.

SELLA
An overview of
the Rhino

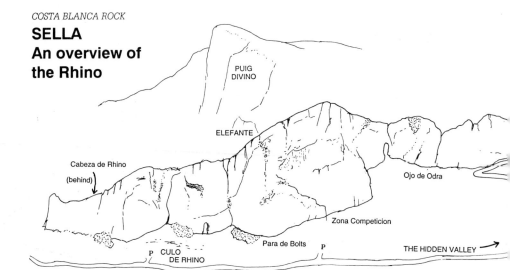

Returning to the main area where there is some 'proper climbing' the first section to be described is:

Derecha De Cabeza De Rhino

The short steep wall that faces the refugio is home to a small number of steep routes. Most of the routes here are butch with a capital B, ideal for thugs or when it's raining!!

At the left side of the leaning wall is a Gruyere-like buttress leading to steeper rock, and on the left side of this and rising from 'the toilet' is:

1. L'EURA 6a+ 15m

The most left-hand offering involves a strenuous pull up the lower wall then the pleasant slab above, keeping right of the floribunda.

2. CHAPO EL SEGUNDO Y ME BAJO 6a 14m

Climb the pillar and the leaning wall above on good holds. The warm up for the area.

3. MENESTREL PESCANOVA ☺ 7b+ 15m

To the right of the supporting pillar a line of bolts leads up and then left passing a spot where a good hold used to be with difficulty, to reach buckets. Continue steeply to the top.

4. SINDROME DEL BETUN ☺ 7a+ 20m

Start just to the right of the previous route and head up the steep wall using pockets and finger jams until a difficult traverse left can be made on more pockets to the belay of the previous route.

5. PROXIMA BAUTIZO ☺ 7a+ 20m

The next feature to the right is three cracks springing from a common point 7m up. This route takes the central one shooting straight up the wall, a blind flake with a tricky exit.

6. COMTITAPEL ☺ 7a 20m

Climb up to where the cracks divide then swing right for a couple of moves before heading up the tilted wall by powerful moves on excellent pockets. The easiest of the offerings in this section.

7. LE DIAGONAL ♦ 7a+ 25m

The best route on the wall. Follow the rightward slanting crack throughout, on mostly good holds to a tricky exit. Big and butch.

8. HOMBRES DE POCA FE ☺ 8a 22m

The direct start is harder (about three grades).

9. MULTIGRADO ☺ 7c 20m

To the right a finger crack leads to bulges. Up the crack with difficulty (and a little pain) then battle with the bulges above. More butch than delicate.

Cabeza De Rhino

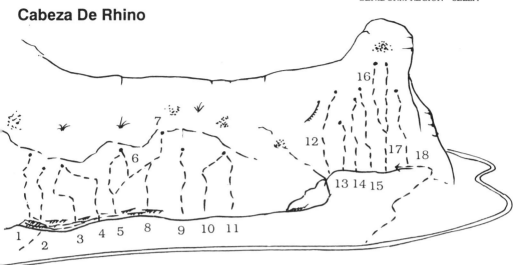

1. L'EURA 6a+
2. CHAPO EL SEGUNDO Y ME BAJO 6a
3. MENESTREL PESCANOVA ☺ 7b+
4. SINDROME DEL BETUN ☺ 7a+
5. PROXIMA BAUTIZO ☺ 7a+
6. COMTITAPEL ☺ 7a
7. LE DIAGONAL ❧ 7a+
8. HOMBRES DE POCA FE ☺ 8a
9. MULTIGRADO ☺ 7c

10. JULIO CEASAR ☺ 6c+
11. CHULERIAS DE LA ALBANILERIA 6b+
12. PENQUEÑECOS ☺ 3+
13. LA TINA DE TURNER ☺ 5+
14. TAIS TOS TOLAIS 6b
15. FRUSTRACION AGRICOLA 4+
16. QUISIERA SER UN OCTAVO ☺ 4
17. VERGLAS QUE SI? 5
18. REGISTRO SANITARIO 6b+

10. JULIO CEASAR ☺ 6c+ 18m
At the right side of the wall climb onto an overhung ledge and climb the leaning wall on surprising holds. Just when you think it is in the bag the route turns mean. Continue left then right with 'interest'.

11. CHULERIAS DE LA ALBANILERIA 6b+ 15m
The most right-hand line weaves up the leaning arête, more arm exercise though on rather poor rock.

CABEZA DE RHINO

The next feature to the right is a flat topped pinnacle that forms the Rhino's Horn. This is reached by a short track from the road. The northern side of the Horn has a series of pleasant though short and rather crowded pitches that can be of use when it is too hot around the corner. The bolt ladders are listed from left to right and several of them have their names painted at the bottom. Descriptions have been kept brief.

12. PENQUEÑECOS ☺ 3+ 15m
The leftmost line starts by stepping off a block and gives well bolted climbing.

13. LA TINA DE TURNER ☺ 5+ 12m
Start at a white patch and climb direct on great rock and with some surprising holds.

14. TAIS TOS TOLAIS 6b 15m
Start just left of a bush and climb to a stiff couple

of moves past the second bolt. The upper rib is easier and maintains the interest.

15. FRUSTRACION AGRICOLA 4+ 15m
Start just right of the bush and climb a short wall into a groove which is followed until it is possible to exit left to the belay of the previous climb.

16. QUISIERA SER UN OCTAVO ☺ 4 18m
From the left side of a niche climb a thin crack (keep to its right) and a shallow groove (keep to its left).

17. VERGLAS QUE SI? 5 15m
From the right side of the niche climb direct on flaky rock with sustained difficulty.

18. REGISTRO SANITARIO 6b+ 15m
Start at the narrowest point of the path and climb the smooth slab to easier but sustained climbing above. Passing the second bolt is very thin but is also avoidable on the left, reducing the grade to 6a.

The south side of the Rhino's Horn contains three short routes worth ticking if you have a few minutes to spare. The area is known as IQZUIERDA CABEZA DE RHINO.

TODO POR LA PUTA PATRIA 7b 10m
The left-hand line, three bolts protect.

AQUI NO PINTA NADIE NADA 5+ 10m
The central line, again with three bolts.

FACILE TODA-VIA 4+ 12m
The right-hand and most worthwhile line.

All the next 70 or so routes described lie on the south facing slopes of the Rhino. As mentioned in the APPROACHES SECTION all of the rock is within a couple of minutes of the car. Follow the dirt road up around a long bend to find parking on a flat area in front of a red wall containing an impressive overhang at three-quarters height.

This area is known as the CULO DE RHINO (politely translated as the Rhino's Flanks) and

the climbing is concentrated in three areas. Dead ahead is the large wall and big overhang of CULO DE RHINO 3 (or TECHO DEL RHINO), rather to the left is the clean wall of CULO DE RHINO 2, whilst further to the left hidden from the car park are two walls flanking a vegetated corner. This is CULO DE RHINO 1. Again the routes are described from left to right.

Some of the names are painted on the rock, and occasionally the hanger of the first bolt has the name and grade of the route stamped on it.

Culo De Rhino 1
To the left of the grotty corner is a red, rounded buttress containing two short but sweet routes.

1. TIMATIRITICON 5+ 15m
A pleasant pitch up the slabby left-hand side of the buttress.

2. CHUSMANIATICA 6a 15m
The right side of the buttress gives an interesting exercise with a difficult bulge taken on spiky holds.

To the right of the gully is a fine grey wall 30m high with prominent roof in its centre at three-quarters height.

3. OTIGOFRENICA ☺ 7c 20
The smooth wall to the right of the grotty gully has a desperate section of climbing where everything 'blanks out'. Talent and/or a very long reach are required.

To the right are three long and excellent pitches.

4. CONDENOMINO CION DE ORIGEN ♦ 6a 25m
Trend left up the sustained white wall with thin moves off a small tufa at 15m. L BST 8/5/00 Excellent

5. CAMILO EL REY DE LOS KUMBAYAYAS ♦ 6a+ 24m
A classical pitch on great rock up the centre of the wall to the right of the corner. Passing the central bulges requires a degree of lateral thinking.

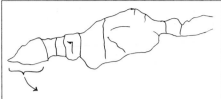

Culo De Rhino 1 & 2

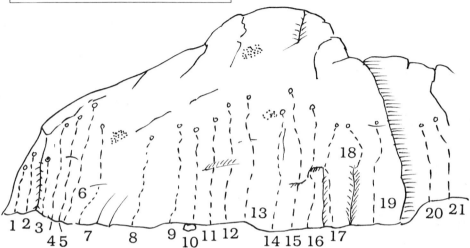

1. TIMATIRITICON 5+
2. CHUSMANIATICA 6a
3. OTIGOFRENICA ☺ 7c
4. CONDENOMINO CION DE ORIGEN ♦ 6a
5. CAMILO EL REY DE LOS KUMBAYAYAS
   ♦ 6a+
6. VALO Y CORAGE ♦ 6a
7. MARTILLAZOS DE MAICONA ☺ 6b
8. LOS REFUGIADOS ☺ 5
9. VIA DEL INDIO 5+
10. DIVINOS CHAPUZAS 6a
11. TU DIRAS ☺ 6a+

12. VINO DU OPORTO ♦ 6b+
13. GUIJA LOCAL ♦ 6c
14. KINA BORREDEGA ☺ 7b
15. NO FRENES MIS INSTINTOS ☺ 7a
16. SUSPIROS DE DOLOR ♦ 7a
17. LA COSA 7a
18. A GOLPE DE PECHO ☺ 7a
19. CON LAS MANOS EN LA COSA ☺ 6c
20. DIAS DE LLUVIA ☺ 6a+
21. DIME DIME ☺ 3+
22. CON MALA A Y A LOCO ☺ 3+

---

6. VALO Y CORAGE ♦ 6a 28m
The third of this excellent trio. Trend right up the wall to reach parallel flakes and continue to a lower-off below the capping roof. Owners of 50m ropes should note the length of the route.
Exellet, Spaced bolts L: EJT 8/3/00

7. MARTILLAZOS DE MAICONA ☺ 6b 30m
The rightmost line on the wall is reached by a diagonal ascent from the left over rather scruffy rock. The bolt ladder gives sustained interest

with a tough crux move past 3.

Thirty metres to the right is a groove which is supposed to be SENJE NOVETAL, 6a+ but it did not appear to have been completed on my last visit. Take a rack of nuts if you must.

Ten metres right again is
8. LOS REFUGIADOS ☺ 5 20m L KST 8/3/99 Good
Start at the painted name and climb the delicate

93

slabby wall above the diagonal break, with interest.

Thirty metres right again is the start of:

Culo De Rhino 2

On the left side of the section and just beyond a large fallen block are two recently added lower-grade routes.

9. VIA DEL INDIO 5+ 20m
Climb the wall passing between the bushes and taking care with the occasional loose block.
ᒃ KST 8/3/00 Good

10. DIVINOS CHAPUZAS 6a 22m
Start at the name and climb the wall leftwards past a scar. A rather run-out section leads up flakes to the lower-off.

To the right the quality and height of the rock increases, and there is a fine collection of face pitches.

11. TU DIRAS ☺ 6a+ 22m
The leftmost line on the smooth section of the wall. From a big flat block trend left then back right. The upper section is taken on the left.

12. VINO DU OPORTO ⚲ 6b+ 22m
The next line in gives fine sustained climbing passing round the left side of a small overhang. The climbing is deliciously varied as delicate and strenuous moves alternate.

13. GUIJA LOCAL ⚲ 6c 22m
Begin below and right of a flake at 3m. A desperate starting sequence to pass the first bolt (avoidable on the right but you wouldn't, would you?) gives access to the fine sustained upper wall.

14. KINA BORREDEGA ☺ 7b 22m
Starting behind a white block climb sporadic tufas to reach a thin seam high on the wall. Follow this with escalating interest. Tough!

15. NO FRENES MIS INSTINTOS ☺ 7a 20m
The smooth looking wall just to the right is climbed passing to the right of a shrubby flake and gives sustained moves up the 'plonk-on' wall.

Sella: Colin Binks on the superb grey limestone of CAMILO EL REY DE LOS KUMBAYAYAS 6a+, typical of the routes on the south face of the Rhino

16. SUSPIROS DE DOLOR ⚲ 7a 22m
From a 2m-high fallen flake climb rightward then awkwardly up the wall to a hidden jug. The crux section is taken left then right and locating the discreet drilled holds is not easy.

17. LA COSA 7a 22m
The attractive-looking groove is a bit of a nightmare, being climbed on prickly rock, initially via the right rib and then trending right through the bulges to the belay on the next route. Originally graded a miserly 6c.

18. A GOLPE DE PECHO ☺ 7a 22m
The ever-steepening wall to the right of the corner is climbed starting on the right and trending to the left. The lower part is pleasant but the bulging section has a 'bloc' move on small drilled holds and a tricky clip. Jugs above lead to the lower-off. Recently uprated into the seventh grade.

19. CON LAS MANOS EN LA COSA ☺ 6c 22m
Another spiky groove with hard moves at its closure swinging up to the right. No pushover at the grade.

Right again is a line up the right side of the rib, just before the cliff swings round into a large bay:
20. DIAS DE LLUVIA ☺ 6a+ 20m
Follow the bolts up the wall then away rightwards to the lowering point.

Around to the right is an amenably angled slab containing two bolt lines (Haskett-Smith will be turning in his grave).
21 (1). DIME DIME ☺ 3+ 15m
The left line gives a pleasant piece of exercise (Climb 1 on topo p96).

22 (2). CON MALA A Y A LOCO ☺ 3+ 15m
More fun in the Costa Blanca sun.
(Climb 2 on topo p96)

Culo De Rhino 3

Directly in front of the car park is a fine wall with an excellent collection of pitches across a broad range of difficulty. The left side of the wall is quite low and consists of slabby rock to the left of a large shrubby corner. This contains two pleasant routes.

3. PEQUEÑECOS 2 ☺ 4 18m
The left line (up the centre of the bay) gives a reasonable and very safe pitch.

4. PEQUEÑECOS 3 ☺ 4+ 30m
The right line offers more of the same fare, though being twice as long is almost twice as

worthwhile. Sadly the top pitch is a bit disappointing.

To the right of the corner is a smooth scooped wall containing a line of black bolts.
5. VARIENTE PORKO 7a 24m
Follow the black bolts but where they bear away right continue straight up the scooped wall above.

6. PORKO NIENTE LIRE ☺ 7a 20m
The lower section is straightforward, the upper less so; smoke or struggle up it, the choice is yours.

7. CUIDAD CON MI SOMBRERO ☺ 6b 15m
The obvious line up the groove starting at a low cave just as the bushes encroach on the base of the cliff.

To the right behind bushes is a short wall with bolts. Starting from a split flake is:

8. FULANITA Y SUS MENGANAS 6b 12m
A pitch of greater technical interest than appears from below.

Twelve metres to the right again is a shallow corner with bolts spattered on both side of it.

9. ZIG ZAG ATOMICO 5+ 12m
A pleasant but short-lived affair, starting at the name painted on the rock.

A major groove bounds the left side of the impressive main wall of the crag. This is taken by:
10. TWO NIGHT OF LOVE ☺ 5+ 30m
Recently extended into a two-pitch route though the second is not up to much. Slant right into the corner and follow it to a belay in the right wall of the gully. Cross the gully and climb the slab to escape onto the open rib beyond. Belay above from where it is possible to reach the ground in one long abseil.

To the right of the fall line from the big roof high overhead is a flat area backed by a fine grey wall.

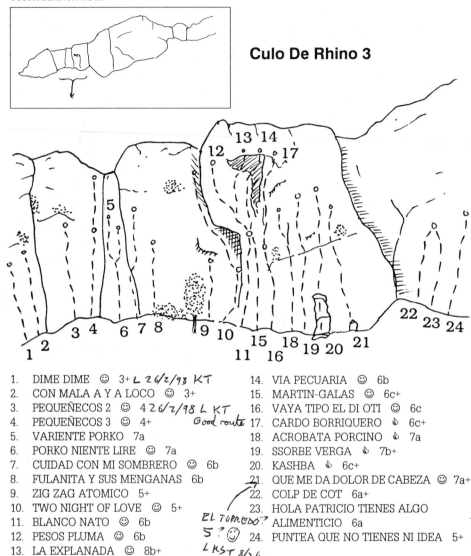

Culo De Rhino 3

1. DIME DIME ☺ 3+ *L 26/2/98 KT*
2. CON MALA A Y A LOCO ☺ 3+
3. PEQUEÑECOS 2 ☺ 4 *26/2/98 L KT*
4. PEQUEÑECOS 3 ☺ 4+ *Good route*
5. VARIENTE PORKO 7a
6. PORKO NIENTE LIRE ☺ 7a
7. CUIDAD CON MI SOMBRERO ☺ 6b
8. FULANITA Y SUS MENGANAS 6b
9. ZIG ZAG ATOMICO 5+
10. TWO NIGHT OF LOVE ☺ 5+
11. BLANCO NATO ☺ 6b
12. PESOS PLUMA ☺ 6b
13. LA EXPLANADA ☺ 8b+
14. VIA PECUARIA ☺ 6b
15. MARTIN-GALAS ☺ 6c+
16. VAYA TIPO EL DI OTI ☺ 6c
17. CARDO BORRIQUERO ♦ 6c+
18. ACROBATA PORCINO ♦ 7a
19. SSORBE VERGA ♦ 7b+
20. KASHBA ♦ 6c+
21. QUE ME DA DOLOR DE CABEZA ☺ 7a+
22. COLP DE COT 6a+
23. HOLA PATRICIO TIENES ALGO ALIMENTICIO 6a
24. PUNTEA QUE NO TIENES NI IDEA 5+

EL TORREDO? 5 ? ☺ L KST 8/3/00

The left edge of the wall below the overhangs is taken by:

11. BLANCO NATO ☺ 6b 22m
Follow the edge of the wall starting up an awkward crack with sustained interest. Lower off from the belays, or bring your second up and have a go at any of the next three climbs.

12. PESOS PLUMA ☺ 6b 20m
Trend left to outflank the great roof by precarious climbing on 'sticky' rock.

13. LA EXPLANADA ☺ 8b+ 12m
The line of bolts that runs across the roof was originally done with a bolt on hold and then without; the best of British to you.

14. VIA PECUARIA ☺ 6b 15m
The groove that runs up to the right side of the big roof with the lower-off right on the lip (close your eyes before you let go).

15. MARTIN-GALAS ☺ 6c 20m
Start at the name painted on the rock. A fine sustained wall climb following the line of bolts up grey then yellow rock passing a big flake on the way.
Above the lower-off it is possible to climb the steep groove of VIA PECUARIA 6b+ (see above) or the stunning arete of CARDO BORRIQUERO 6c+ (see below).

Right again is a shield of rock with a bolt ladder up its centre passing to the left of a bush at 10m.
16. VAYA TIPO EL DE OTI ☺ 6c 20m
An easy lower section on sharp rock leads to steeper climbing above, the crux being the last couple of moves to the chains.

Above this pitch are the obvious continuations of VIA PECUARIA 6b (see above) and:
17. CARDO BORRIQUERO ♦ 6c+ 20m
Tackles the superb leaning arete. The climbing is brilliant, even if some of the holds are not. Climb the left side of the arete until forced round the exposed corner to the right, out of the frying pan....

To the right is a leaning, red wall with four routes up it, and with a large fallen block at its base. These offer climbing that is steeper than normal for this part of the cliff.
18. ACROBATA PORCINO ♦ 7a 22m
Start left of the block and follow easy rock to the base of the steep wall. Good flowstone layaways and undercuts allow for rapid progress to a point not too far (or just too far) from the chains. Levitate up this last section, and if all else fails jump (and pigs might fly).

19. SSORBE VERGA ♦ 7b+ 25m
From the top of the pedestal follow the slab then line up the leaning wall. Steep and sustained with a fiercely technical crux sequence passing the bulge on razor edges.

20. KASHBA ♦ 6c+ 25m
Start just right of the pedestal and climb a tricky slab to the base of the shallow groove on the right. This has an awkward entry and increases in difficulty until a rest on the right can be reached. The final section to the chains is taken on flat holds and is distinctly pumpy. Quite generously graded by local standards!

21. QUE ME DA DOLOR DE CABEZA ☺ 7a+ 22m
The right-hand line on the wall starts on top of stacked flakes and gives a steep pitch on mostly good but spaced holds with a highly technical wall just before the angle eases. The local topo grades it 6c+!

To the right the rock deteriorates until a clean bowl of white rock containing three short lines is reached. These all appear rather trivial from below but are quite worthwhile.

22. COLP DE COT 6a+ 15m
An easy start leads to a scoop. Exiting from this provides the fun.

23. HOLA PATRICIO TIENES ALGO ALIMENTICIO 6a 18m
The central line on the wall is taken via an 'interesting' set of holds.

24. PUNTEA QUE NO TIENES NI IDEA 5+ 20m
The bolts are very close together (all nine of them) and the route is quite precarious.

The wall to the right is supposed to be home to ROSALIND SUTTON though close inspection has revealed no fixed gear.
1. ROSALIND SUTTON ☺ 5+ 25m
A good first pitch, but there is no top pitch despite local topo.

The remainder of the described routes are to the right of Culo de Rhino 3, and are described as they are approached from left to right. The first bolt ladder is found in the back of a groove 60m right of the last routes.

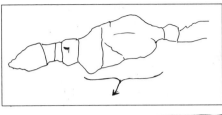

Para De Bolts & Zona Competicion

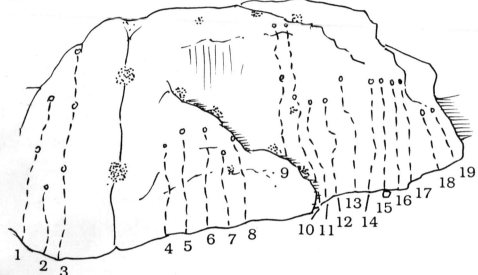

1.	ROSALIND SUTTON ☺ 5+	
2.	MISTER PI, EL REY DEL PORNO ☺ 5+	
3.	MARION ♦ 5	
4.	EL GRAN COSCORRON ♦ 6a+	
5.	NIDO DE PIRATAS ♦ 6b	
6.	TU QUIEN ERAS ♦ 6a	
7.	DESBLOQUEA QUE NO ES TANTO ☺ 5	
8.	PERLETERA ☺ 5+	
9.	WASP FACTORY ☺ 6a,6c+	
10.	RATITO DE GLORIA ☺ 6a+,7a+	

11.	MARX A D'ACI ♦ 5+
12.	DINGO BOINGO EL CULO TE LA INCO ☺ 6c
13.	PEDRO ESTAS INSPIRADO ♦ 7c+
14.	SOPA DE MARSOPA ♦ 6b+
15.	ADIOS LOS DOMINGOS ♦ 6c+
16.	TECHNOCRATAS ♦ 6b+
17.	EL VUELO DE LA MAQUINA ♦ 6a+
18.	ALMORRANAS SALVAJES ♦ 4
19.	ALIBABA Y LOS 40 KOMANDOS ☺ 4

---

2. MISTER PI, EL REY DEL PORNO ☺ 5+ 22m
Bridge up the groove then follow the bolts passing most of them on the left.

Round to the right of a rounded buttress is the start of the longest route on the cliff.
3. MARION ♦ 5 68m

1. 24m 4 Climb the initial bulges awkwardly then trend left up the wall past 'plenty bolts' to a small stance.

2. 22m 4+ Continue in the same vein to another stance.

3. 22m 5 The groove above is gained and followed with sustained interest to a small bulge (crux) and a little higher the summit.

The DESCENT is most easily effected by two or three abseils down the line of the route. Alternatively bushwhack down the back to gain the track then walk back round the Rhino. Or go right along the ridge and scramble down left into, then through the cave of the Ojo de Odra.

To the right rising behind some wiry bushes is an area known as the PARED DE BOLTS. This contains five fine routes, as well equipped as you could wish for.

4. EL GRAN COSCORRON ♦ 6a+ 22m
The leftmost line gives a great pitch, sustained but never desperate and with exemplary protection, 10 bolts.

5. NIDO DE PIRATAS ♦ 6b 22m
The second line gives steady climbing to a line of bulges where the holds are rather scant. Once past this minor obstacle romp to the belay. 11 clips.

6. TU QUIEN ERAS ♦ 6a 22m
Another fine pitch with sustained moves, great protection and holds to match. 10 clippity clips.

7. DESBLOQUEA QUE NO ES TANTO ☺ 5 20m
Right again, excellent rock and climbing, though just a bit short lived.

8. PERLETERA ☺ 5+ 18m
The rightmost line is the shortest of the bunch, though it is still well worthwhile.
The bulge at two-thirds height may prove problematical for shorter climbers.

To the right is a fine smooth wall sprouting a conspicuous small tree at 25m and a whole bunch of lines of bolts. This is the ZONA COMPETICION. A 60m rope may be needed to effect a retreat from the longest of these routes.

9. WASP FACTORY ☺ 6a,6c+ 50m
A two-pitch climb started by scrambling up the left-slanting ramp line to a twin-bolt belay. The initial pitch is on occasional patches of soft rock and the bolts are rather spaced approaching the stance (25m 3). The upper pitch starts delicately,

has tough precarious moves to reach the tufa and is then just strenuous.

10. RATITO DE GLORIA ☺ 6a+7a+, 55m
Another long route stating at the foot of the ramp. The first pitch is superb in its own right (30m ♦), whereas the second has a taxing sequence around the prominent roof where holds used to be!

11. MARX A D'ACI ♦ 5+ 22m
The leftmost line on this main section of wall is a classic (as they all are). Climb straight up the wall on continuously surprising holds until forced rightwards into a groove. Bridge this to chains just above.

12. DINGO BOINGO EL CULO TE LA INCO ☺ 6c 24m
The leftmost line, steep, smooth and excellent. Entering the scoop above the third clip is the crux, though the interest is well maintained!

13. PEDRO ESTAS INSPIRADO ♦ 7c+ 28m
Start at the name painted on the rock and follow the line passing to the left of the tree up the smoothest part of the wall. 8a in some topos.

14. SOPA DE MARSOPA ♦ 6b+ 30m
Start below and left of a large white scar then follow a line trending slightly rightwards. The crux is at half height, gaining and leaving a small pillar, and the pitch is quite tough for the grade.

15. ADIOS LOS DOMINGOS ♦ 6c+ 28m
Step off the fallen flake and make very thin moves up to the scar (crux) Continuo in the same line with sustained and sharp climbing.

16. TECHNOCRATAS ♦ 6b+ 28m
Just to the right of the scar climb straight up the steep wall by magic climbing, very sustained and very sharp with the crux climbing the shallow corner.

17. EL VUELO DE LA MAQUINA ♦ 6a+ 28m
The rightmost line takes the ever steepening wall, great climbing on great holds, generally to

the right of the bolt line and with a tricky finale up a steep wall. Tough for the grade.

Further up to the right are two lines on slabby rock between vegetation before the cliff swings round into a bay. These are:

18. ALMORRANAS SALVAJES ✪ 4 25m
The left-hand line easing as height is gained; enjoy. (Climb 1 on topo p98)

19. ALIBABA Y LOS 40 KOMANDOS ☺ 4 28m
The right-hand line, more of the same. (Climb 2 on topo p98)

The final area that has been developed lies further up to the right where there is a curious through cave. There is a dirt road below the cliff here and this forks left of the main track, though parking below the cliff is discouraged. The best approach is to park below the main area and walk up below the cliff, 10 minutes. This is the

Sector Ojo De Odra
There are several routes here that are well worth seeking out if the main areas are crowded. The first climbs are in a bay of rock well to the left of the dirt road. (Routes 1 & 2 see 18 & 19 above)

3. KAMIKAZE ✪ 7a+ 22m
Start behind a bush and climb slabby rock passing left of a detached grey flake at 4m then on up steeper terrain to a couple of taxing moves to better holds. Trend right (crux) then back left (difficult clip) to easier ground.

4. BUMBLIES 6b 22m
Start at a head-height cave/hole and climb straight up the steepening wall passing some suspect rock until it is possible to trend left to the lower-off used by the previous climb.

5. FISURA CON FINURA ✪ 6a 22m
The long crack line gives a very pleasant pitch with a stiff little layback as the crux about halfway to the belays.

6. ROBERTO ALCAZAR Y MERIN ☺ 6a 20m
A steep pitch up the red wall to the right of the

crack line. The lower section is tough and then things ease until the final bulge is passed rightward by tricky moves.

7. SPIRITU DE SATUR 6b 15m
To the left of the through cave is a short route with a tough lower wall and much easier climbing above.

8. EL OJO DE ODRA ☺ 6b+ 15m
This route takes the line up the left side of the prominent tunnel entrance starting well inside it. The holds are mostly huge (bucket city) but the angle is quite ridiculous, especially in the central section. Very photogenic.

9. LOS COREANOS 6b+ 15m
The right rib of the cave then trend left to the lower-off of the previous climb.

Close to the bend in the dirt road is the final selection of climbs, across a spread of grades and in a quieter setting than the CULO DE RHINO.

On the far left are two very well bolted low-grade climbs.
10. LA VERGUENZA ☺ 3+ 15m
The left-hand line.

11. LA VERGUENZA 2 ☺ 3+ 18m
The right-hand line with 11 bolts!

The final climbs are above the parking area on the bend, with the first three routes on the fine clean buttress just left of the road.
12. SPEEDY GONZALEZ ☺ 5 16m
The bolt ladder on the left side of the buttress is approached from the right (or more easily from the left), and climbed via a tricky little groove. Trend right at the top to reach the belays.

13. EL PITXOCET ✪ 6a 18m
A great pitch starting atop the dirt heap. Climb onto a flake then take a line up the centre of the buttress on superb rock and with exemplary protection, brilliant.

Ojo De Odra

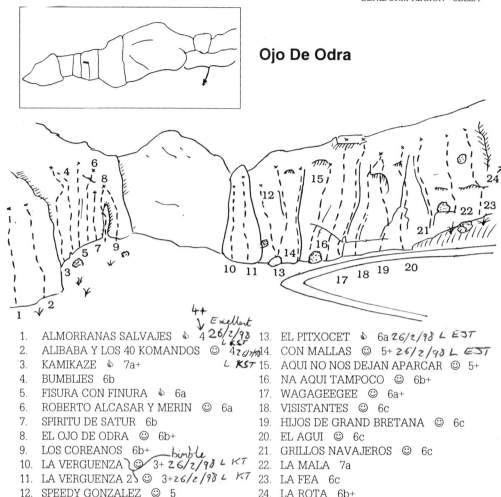

1. ALMORRANAS SALVAJES   4 *26/2/98* 4+ Exellent L KST
2. ALIBABA Y LOS 40 KOMANDOS ☺ 4? (7/99)
3. KAMIKAZE   7a+   L KST
4. BUMBLIES 6b
5. FISURA CON FINURA   6a
6. ROBERTO ALCASAR Y MERIN ☺ 6a
7. SPIRITU DE SATUR 6b
8. EL OJO DE ODRA ☺ 6b+
9. LOS COREANOS 6b+ — bimble
10. LA VERGUENZA ☺ 3+ *26/2/98* L KT
11. LA VERGUENZA 2 ☺ 3+*26/2/98* L KT
12. SPEEDY GONZALEZ ☺ 5
13. EL PITXOCET   6a *26/2/98* L EST
14. CON MALLAS ☺ 5+ *26/2/98* L EST
15. AQUI NO NOS DEJAN APARCAR ☺ 5+
16. NA AQUI TAMPOCO ☺ 6b+
17. WAGAGEEGEE ☺ 6a+
18. VISISTANTES ☺ 6c
19. HIJOS DE GRAND BRETANA ☺ 6c
20. EL AGUI ☺ 6c
21. GRILLOS NAVAJEROS ☺ 6c
22. LA MALA 7a
23. LA FEA 6c
24. LA ROTA 6b+

---

14. CON MALLAS. ☺ 5+ 18m
The groove that separates the two buttresses is followed throughout.

15. AQUI NO NOS DEJAN APARCAR ☺ 5+ 20m
Start left of the lowest point of the buttress. A thin lower section (Hint: keep left) leads to a steep fingery rib and above this a much easier groove.

16. NA AQUI TAMPOCO ☺ 6b+ 22m
The fine clean lower rib leads to a block overhang requiring a powerful lock-off and with the belays just above. Originally given a more sensible 7a+!

17. WAGAGEEGEE ☺ 6a+ 22m
The open corner that bounds this section of wall on the right is approached via a tricky slab and climbed bypassing a bush early on and a bulge near the top to a lower-off on the right. Generous for the grade.

101

To the right is a steep buttress right over the road, home to a series of hard high quality pitches.

18. VISISTANTES ☺ 6c 20m
The left-hand line follows a pockety seam on very rough rock, and passes the bulges on the left. The bolts are rather spaced. Single bolt lower-off.

19. HIJOS DE GRAND BRETANA ☺ 6c 20m
The second line climbs a steep 'crinkly' wall in to the base of a shallow groove then trends left via a continuously interesting set of moves to the single bolt lower-off of the previous climb.

20. EL AGUI ☺ 6c 20m
Immediately to the right is a shallow groove running the full height of the cliff. This is entered with difficulty, followed with interest and exited with more difficulty.

21. GRILLOS NAVAJEROS ☺ 6c 20m
To the right is the final route before the bank as the foot of the cliff rises up from the road. Climb a steep 'spiky' slab leftwards to its apex then swing onto the steep wall and sprint up this to the chains.

To the right there are three more bolted lines behind the trees. The left one climbs a steep slab passing to the left of prominent green bush high on the cliff: **22. LA MALA 7a**. To the right is a line pulling through a bulge: **23. LA FEA 6c**, and the final line tackles the rounded buttress to the right: **24. LA ROTA 6b+** possibly with some loose rock.

Pared Rosalia

A good path leads through heinous vegetation to arrive below the centre of the cliff. This starts at the corner of the last cultivated land on the southern side of the track, 50m below a small dug out parking area with a colourful hand-drawn sign: SEPRUNA SERV. PROTECC. NATUR. Other tracks lead off into the vegetation but invariably arrive at bits of tissue paper and small smelly piles. If the correct path is located it rises steeply, makes a couple of zigzags then

tacks away to the right to arrive at the foot of the cliff just to the right of SOURISA VERTICAL. Away to the left is a conspicuous smooth face with two lines on it: **1. ESCALERA DE COLOR** on the left is 8b and **2. EL BUROCRATA** on the right may be 8a+.

From left to right the routes are:

3. LUNA ☺ 6b+, 6b, 6b+, 7a 100m
The left-hand route on the main face, fully bolted and with all pitches 25m in length.

4. LEJOS DE LA MULTITUD ☺ 4, 6c, 7a 70m
A line through the big red bay, fully bolted.

5. VENUS ERYCINA 4, 6c, 7b, A2 70m
A right-hand variant on the previous route, carry a rack.

6. TANIT ☺ 6b, 5, 6a+, 6b 80m
A line running all the way to the cliff top, mostly bolted, carry a rack.

7. SOURISA VERTICAL ☺ 6b+, 7a, 6b 78m
Start at the painted name, a short distance left of where the path arrives at the cliff, fully bolted.

8. CALFAMUSCULS ☺ 6a+ 20m
The short left-hand bolt ladder above the path.

9. CALEIDOSCOPIO ☺ 6a 20m
The right-hand line.

Well to the right is a scooped groove with some in-situ threads, no name or grade known, and well right again a right-trending bolt line that could be either -
10. SIN COMENTARIOS 7b, 6b, or **11. ROSA DE PIEDRA 7a**, though the local guide shows four routes in this area.

12. LA VERGONYA 5 28m
A long but rather scruffy pitch just right of where the cliff swings round, 11 bolt runners.

Around to the right is a flat, streaked wall that was home to a competition a few years ago. There are four excellent pitches here, almost always in the shade, and on more featured rock than is usual at Sella. On the left is a deep cave and on the right wall of this is a short (six bolt) route that looks about 6c. The left-side of the wall has an open attractive scoop, with steeper rock leading into it.

13. INDECISA ☺ 6c 28m
The lower wall is hard for the grade though the rest is about par for Sella face routes. A long sustained pitch with 13 clips.

Behind the flat area at the base of the wall are two excellent routes.

14. QUITA LA MUSICA, MACARRA ☺ 7a+ 22m
Climb the juggy orange lower wall, then jig right and back left to pass the crux section, 9 clips.

15. FINAL D'ESTIU ☺ 7b 22m
The lower third of the climb is juggy, the rest

devious and sustained, though mostly on good holds, 10 clips.

Right again a couple of old ring bolts mark an abandoned project and to the right and up a small step is:

16. LOS AVUTARDOS 7b+ 22m
Climb the red flake to a couple of desperate moves up and left to reach more accommodating tufas that are followed right to finish.

The rock extends rightwards for miles!

1. ESCALERA DE COLOR 8b
2. EL BUROCRATA 8a+?
3. LUNA ☺ 6b+,6b,6b+,7a
4. LEJOS DE LA MULTITUD ☺ 4,6c,7a
5. VENUS ERYCINA 4,6c,7b,A2
6. TANIT ☺ 6b,5,6a+,6b
7. SOURISA VERTICAL ☺ 6b+,7a,6b
8. CALFAMUSCULUS ☺ 6a+

9. CALEIDOSCOPIO ☺ 6a
10. SIN COMENTARIOS? 7b,6b
11. ROSA DE PIEDRA? 7a
12. LA VERGONYA 5
13. INDECISA ☺ 6c
14. QUITA LA MUSICA, MACARRA ☺ 7a+
15. FINAL D'ESTIU ☺ 7b
16. LOS AVUTARDOS 7b+

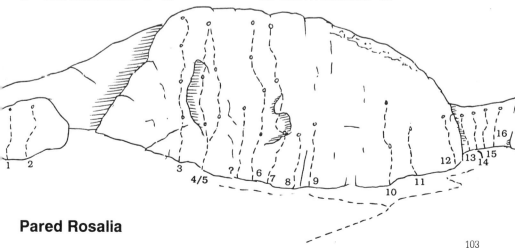

Pared Rosalia

SELLA'S HIDDEN VALLEY

Introduction

The 'Hidden Valley' is where much of the recent development at Sella has been occurring, though most of the climbing here at present is very tough. Two cliffs VIPS and WILD SIDE have seen the most development and LINEAS NATURALES has a small collection of longer climbs that require carrying a rack. The two best developed cliffs are usually in the shade and so form a great retreat in hot weather.

It is worth noting that here is scope for easier routes on scattered cliffs throughout the valley; if you fancy exploring go to it, though there is a good chance Joe Brown will have been there first! The impressive leaning tower further up the valley has a Bhuddist retreat at its foot and apparently they don't welcome intruders - pity!

Access

From the main area continue up the dirt road for 0.5km to a col. The road then descends around a series of bends for 1.5km to a right-hand bend where a narrow, rough track branches to the left. Drive up this passing a branch to the left until the road bends hard left and parking is possible on the right. All three areas can be reached from here in a few minutes.

SECTOR VIPS Continue up the road (best on foot!) to reach the obvious steeply tilted wall, 5 minutes from the car.

SECTOR LINEAS NATURALES is reached by a short scramble up to the right from SECTOR VIPS.

SECTOR WILD SIDE From the car scramble up the bank and follow a track to the right through the trees. After a short distance a knotted rope is found which leads leftwards up easy rock to the foot of the face.

Sector Vips

A short wall of severely tilted rock. The dozen or

so routes here should occupy those in search of short sport the wrong side of vertical. All of the routes are less than 15m long. From left to right they are:

1. LA INVASION DE LAS MORCAS 7b+
The short left-hand line.

2. ??? 6c
A direct on the above.

3. HASLOO AHORA 8b+
Chippity chip.

4. JUMPING MACHA FLASH 8a
Chip chippity.

5. DESERT STORM ☺ 7c+
The best of the hard routes.

6. EJECUCION RADICAL (project)

7. MARK OF THE BEAST ☺ 8a
Chippity chop.

The tiny groove in the front of the squat pillar under the centre of the cliff has some stuck on pebble holds. It is supposed to be 6b+.

8. BULLARENQUE 8c
Directly behind the pillar, chips with everything.

9. LA GENERACION DEL YOGUR ☺ 7a+
The slab and groove is the best of the (2) easier routes.

10. LA FUERZA DE LA COSTUMBRE ☺ 7c

11. ESTRATEGO ☺ 7c

12. COPACABANA 7b+

13. EL MEJOR MATARIFE 6c+
A right-hand finish to the above.

Sector VIPS

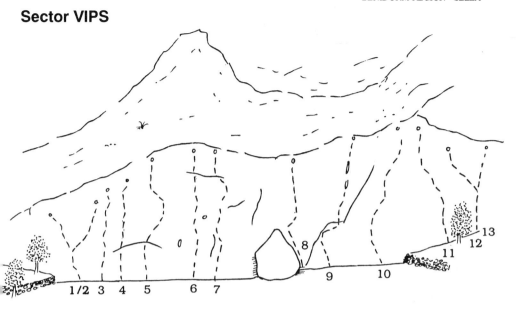

1. LA INVASION DE LA MORCAS 7b+
2. ??? 6c
3. HASLOO AHORA 8b+
4. JUMPING MACHA FLASH 8a
5. DESERT STORM ☺ 7c+
6. EJECUCION RADICAL (project)
7. MARK OF THE BEAST ☺ 8a
8. BULLARENQUE 8c
9. LA GENERACION DEL YOGUR ☺ 7a+
10. LA FUERZA DE LA COSTUMBRE ☺ 7c
11. ESTRATEGO ☺ 7c
12. COPACABANA 7b+
13. EL MEJOR MATARIFE 6c+

Lineas Naturales

Home to three major crack lines all of which require gear and are therefore unlikely to prove popular. From left to right these are:
ENTRANCE EXAM 6a+,7c+,6c
MIDDLE EXAM 5+,6c,7a+
FINAL EXAM 6b+,6c

Sector Wild Side

An impressively steep cliff that is always in the shade and which has only seen limited development at the present time. Despite this it is well worth a visit if you operate in the mid 7's and don't enjoy all the poncy slab climbing on the main section of the cliff.

The first route is located 10m left of the end of the knotted access rope.

1. SI TE DICEN QUE CAI ☺ 7a 25m
A steep start leads to a blank open groove high on the face, climbed using the right arete.

2. TODOS LOS CAMINOS CONDUCEN AL ROMO 7b 25m
Start in same place but trend left up the wall to reach a slightly unstable finish.

Thirty metres left along ledges two routes start up a grey streak:
3. CELIA 8a 30m
This one goes rightwards up the wall and then continues right passing some long in situ slings.

4. LA FORQUETA DE DIABLO 7c+ 30m
Straight up the wall using the right-hand of three prominent tufas 20m up cliff.

Sector Wild Side

1. SI TE DICEN QUE CAI ☺ 7a
2. TODOS LOS CAMINOS CONDUCEN AL ROMO 7b
3. CELIA 8a
4. LA FORQUETA DE DIABLO 7c+

5. EL GREMIO 7b+
6. NIDO AMOROSO ☺ 7b(8a)
7. ERGOMETRIA ☺ 8a
8. DOSIS 8b
9. CUESTION DE ESTILO ☺ 7b

10. EL USURPADOR 7c,7a
11. YA SOMOS OLIMPICOS ♦ 7b+,7a+
12. WATERMARK ☺ 8a+

Somewhere before the next climb is 5. EL GREMIO 7b+.

35m left of LA FORQUETA DE DIABLO and starting at flat grassy area is:
6. NIDO AMOROSO ☺ 7b (8a) 30m
Climb the wall trending leftwards through bulges then trending back right above bulges to a choice of finishes. Good but chipped.

To the left the bank starts to rise up steeply. 20m up the bank a tree grows from a hole in the wall.
7. ERGOMETRIA ☺ 8a 30m
To the right of the tree this route climbs tufas and series of holes to reach more tufas and then on to a belay at the base of a crack system.

8. DOSIS 8b 22m
Left of the tree growing from a hole is this hard offering up grey tufa marked with white bolts. Another 'well hammered' route.

9. CUESTION DE ESTILO ☺ 7b 15m
3m left the first of two diagonal crack systems leads to a lower-off in the right wall. The start is especially steep.

10. EL USURPADOR 7c 30m
The left-hand crack system. The crux is where the crack closes at 10m. A second pitch is available at 7a.

Beyond some vegetation is the route of the cliff, the two pitch offering of:
11. YA SOMOS OLIMPICOS ♦ 7b+, 7a+ 45m
Outrageously steep with an optional belay in a recess. Start direct or more easily to the right.

10m further left by bush on the wall is:
12. WATERMARK ☺ 8a+ 40m
The stunning pocketed wall though with some chips. Also called EUROCANCER on some topos.

PUIG CAMPANA 1406m

Crag Facts

Star rating: ***

Aspect: Due south but much variation on different faces

Height: 200+ (sometimes + a lot) metres

Spread of grades described here (pitches not routes):

4	5	5+	6a	6b	6c	7a	7b	7c	8
21	7	9	4	2	1	/	/	/	/

Introduction

As you travel northwards on the motorway from Alicante the Puig Campana is the first of the larger mountains that appears on your left. It is instantly recognisable because of the great square notch missing from the summit ridge. The giant Roldan kicked a chunk out of here in a fit of pique and it now resides in the sea off Benidorm, or so the story goes.

The lower flanks of this fine rocky peak are home to some great routes on great limestone. They are in a dramatic high mountain setting, despite only being 5 minutes (as the crow flies!) from the black hole of Benidorm. The routes described are to be found on the south face of the mountain. They are generally not of a great level of difficulty, in the range 4 to 6c, but are a respectable length (mostly 4 to 12 pitches) and are in a remote setting - certainly not a sensible place to have an accident. There is rather a dearth of fixed gear in many of the routes so carry a light to average UK rack, depending on your level of confidence. A few tapes and old karabiners may be worth taking along in case an epic ensues, and double ropes are a good idea!

There is no doubt that the approach walk will deter many but the climbing is worth the slight effort involved and the mountain offers something a little different to the roadside cragging that is common in these parts. The chances are that you will have the mountain to yourself. A water bottle, at least at the start of the climbs, makes good sense.

Note: A recent Spanish guidebook to the mountains, *Guía de Escalada del Puig Campana* by Carlos Fudela, lists over 50 routes on all faces of the mountain. Rumours have it that the topos are 'moderately accurate', so if you enjoy exploring get a copy and go have an adventure.

Access

The walk-in starts at Finestrat which is reached by turning inland from the complex Benidorm exit on the motorway. The village is reached in 8km. Once in Finestrat follow signs to the impressive fountain/spring of the Font de Moli. 150m past here take a left turn and follow this road until it is possible to park on a bend a short distance past a bridge over a usually dry river bed. From here a gravel track leads northwards towards the mountain. The red paint flecks mark the walking route to the summit via the great gully in the south face - a worthwhile day out. This path is followed, initially out onto the ridge to the right of the lower section of the gully, and then follows it until it is possible to walk leftwards underneath the south face, the approach taking 50-75 minutes depending upon calf and rucksack sizes. More direct routes are harder work as they cross many abandoned terraces.

The routes are described from right to left as this is the usual direction of approach and some of the climbs have their names painted discreetly at the foot of the route.

Puig Campana: at the start of the approach path to the mountain

Puig Campana - South Face

1. VIA ESPOLON ELEGANTE 5 & A0, or 5+
   or 6b+
2. VIA ROMPEDEDOS ⚜ 6c
3. VIA ASESINA A TU VECINA ☺ 6b
4. DIEDROS MAGICOS ⚜ 6a+
5. VIA DIEDROS GALLEGO ☺ 6a
6. VIA JULIA ☺ 5+
7. DIRECTISIMA ESPOLON CENTRAL ☺ 6a
8. ESPERO SUR CENTRAL ⚜ 4+
   (a) Traditional approach to (8)
   (b) Descent from (8)

1. VIA ESPOLON ELEGANTE 5 & A0, or 5+ or 6b+ 130/175m

A route with a great name and some good climbing up the ridge that bounds the right side of the most continuous part of the face. Start at a chipped arrow below two bushy grooves.

1. 20m 4- Follow the rib to the right of the grooves, then step left into the right-hand groove and climb it to ledges with blocks.
2. 30m Above is leaning rib with grooves to either side. There are two ways on: either climb the right-hand groove (with a beckoning tree at its top) A0 & 5 pulling on the odd nut, or free at 6b+. Alternatively trend left and enter the sustained prickly left-hand groove and climb this (5+) to a ledge and two peg belay.
3. 35m 4+ Step right and climb grooves and cracks to a good ledge with large tree belay just above.
4. 45m 5 Climb past the belay and another tree to below a tough-looking orange groove. Move right into an easier groove (extend those runners) and follow it to a blunt pinnacle with old peg above. Climb left past the peg and enter another groove that soon leads to chain (and other) belays at the top of pitch 3 of ROMPEDEDOS.

Either abseil from here or:

5. 25m 4+ Move right around the corner and climb a chimney to a good stance.
6. 20m 4 Continue up easier climbing to find the abseil point at the top of DIEDRO MAGICOS on the left. The route continues for three more pitches of 4- to eventually join the final section of ESPERO SUR CENTRAL, though as it is much easier than the climbing below most teams call it a day here.

2. VIA ROMPEDEDOS ✿ 6c 139m

A very fine climb with an outstanding first pitch. The climb has recently been rebolted apart from the final pitch. The new bolts have been drilled close to the original placements to 'maintain the integrity of the climb' and you can guess what that means. Start below the centre of the broad face, 7m to the right of the prominent groove of

DIEDROS MAGICOS, where a large chipped arrow points up and a smaller one points down. Take Rocks 1-9 for pitches 2-4.

1. 45m 6c Climb easy rock and then a small bulge followed by the fine face until a tough sequence leads to a 'left-handed' finger flake and more hard moves (crux) gain a good ledge and possible belay. Enter the shallow groove above (hard for the short) and follow this past spaced bolts to a small stance, 11 bolt runners.
2. 30m 6b+ Climb up then left to the top of the large perched flake (old thread) then climb the wall passing a useful tree (peg and bolts) until harder climbing and then one very thin

Puig Campana: Graham Parkes on the tough first pitch of the excellent VIA ROMPEDEDOS ('break your fingers') 6c

move gains easier terrain with a stance to the right.

3. 34m 5+ Follow the groove (loose blocks to the left) behind the stance passing a bulge (bolt) before trending right then back left (old peg) over a small bulge to a short smooth groove to reach stance on the left. Abseil from here or:

4. 30m 6a Move right to a ledge and follow the old bolts up the wall to a new bolt. Lower from this or follow easier rock to the belay at the top of DIEDROS MAGICOS. Abseil descent down the line of the route.

3. VIA ASESINA A TU VECINA ☺ 6b 30m

A good but harrowing pitch on great rock. 3m right of the groove of DIEDROS MAGICOS is a short right facing flake at 6m. Climb to the flake then continue up the sustained face passing a small bulge to twin bolt lower-off, five bolt runners. It should be obvious that 30m divided by 5 bolt runners means that this is a 'sporting' climb, rather than a sport climb, be warned!

4. DIEDROS MAGICOS ↟ 6a+ (E1 5c) 180m

An excellent route giving sustained climbing up a fine line with the crux high off the ground. Start at a groove in the face which holds a thin 10m high pillar in its back and with a chipped arrow above '4' prominently displayed. Take a rack.

1. 30m 5 Climb the right side of the rib then follow the shallow groove to a cave stance.

2. 25m 5+ Continue in the same vein until the groove narrows and becomes a slanting crack.

3. 30m 5+ The crack starts off amenably enough but gets harder as height is gained. At 25m a ledge is reached (tat up to the left in the vegetated continuation of the groove) then traverse the slab rightwards to a small stance and substantial belay on the descent line.

4. 30m 5 Clip a bolt on the right then trend left up flakes and shallow corners to regain the groove line at a red bolt belay.

5. 25m 5 Continue up the groove to a stance 6m below the overhang on 5 pegs (and nuts

if you really must).

5. 40m 6a+ The pitch you have been waiting for. Climb the groove and do battle with the roof crack that splits the right side of the overhang. A narrow groove gives more hard climbing then 15m of easier climbing leads to a narrow ledge. Belay here (no fixed gear nearby) or continue for 10m to a large ledge with bolts and chain anchor away to the right.

Descent

From the belay anchor that allows the first of four long (45m, 35m, 30m, 45m) abseils back to the base of the route. The end of the second abseil ends up on the stance above pitch three of the route. From here continue directly to the ground in two rope lengths.

5. VIA DIEDRO GALLEGO ☺ 6a 190m

This route takes the striking deep groove line that soars up the centre of the south face. The crux pitch is appreciably harder than the rest of the route.

1. 45m A left-trending ramp leads easily (solo?) into the lower section of the groove to a stance below where the line steepens and deepens.

2. 40m 5+ Continue up the back of the corner, rather a grovel in places, to a stance below a deep chimney. Bolt belays.

3. 45m 6a Climb the chimney. At its termination traverse left to gain the bottom of a corner, which leads to a possible stance on the left. A steep wall on the right (pegs) gives difficult climbing until the situation eases and a rightward rising traverse leads to a good ledge.

4. 30m 5 The all too obvious chimney gives some 'classic' climbing to a small stance (peg belays).

5. 30m 4+ The chimney continues, thankfully in a lighter vein, to join the arete at a prominent tower.

Descent

Cross the ridge on to the south-west face, a short descent leads to abseil anchors. Two 25m abseils (or one of 50m) lead to a large tree. A 25m abseil from this joins the descent route from VIA JULIA at the ledge after the first abseil. Continue down as for this descent.

6. VIA JULIA ☺ 5+ (E1 5b) 150m

One of the shortest routes on the face offering varied climbing. It takes the centre of the face bounded on the left by the south ridge and on the right by the great groove line of DIEDRO GALLEGO. Start midway between the arete and the groove line where the name is chipped in the rock. Take a rack.

1. 38m 4 Climb straight up the slabby rock to a groove and a two peg belay.
2. 40m 5+ Climb up and slightly left to a rust coloured groove. Climb the flake/groove above then take the continuation passing two pegs. Move left to peg belays. A strenuous pitch that requires a reasonable rack of gear.
3. 38m 5 Move left then climb directly up the corner groove with harder moves over a bulge (old peg). Trend left into a corner which deepens above. Two peg and single bolt belay.
4. 34m 5+ Follow the corner by bridging and jamming (medium and large Friends useful) to reach large ledges with two ring pegs and a bolt around the arete to the left.

Gird your loins and head up ESPOLON SUR CENTRAL (see below) or:

Descent

1. Abseil 8m from the bolt to a tree.
2. Abseil 30m to large ledges to find abseil anchors then follow chipped arrows to the right (looking out) to find a wire cable belay.
3. Abseil to rock strewn ledges.
4. Walk left to a tree and abseil from this to a block with slings.
5. Abseil to the ground.

Note: the normal descent does 1,2 & 3 and then walks right and scrambles tediously down a series of broken ledges.

7. DIRECTISIMA ESPOLON CENTRAL ☺ 6a (E2 5c) 174m

A good route up the crest of the buttress with a
112

tough third pitch. Take a rack!
Start at a left-slanting ramp (chipped arrow) 15m left of where VIA JULIA is chipped on the rock. ◄

1. 30m 4- Follow the ramp leftwards into a corner and climb this to a bolt and peg belay.
2. 30m 5+ Climb the corner then move left to a peg and then an old thread. Follow blocks (care!) then continue up the wall trending rightwards to enter a groove. Follow this up and right to a flake then cross the steep wall rightwards to 'El Nicho'. Thread peg and Friend 2 belay.
3. 45m 6a Climb out of the right side of the cave into a red groove (poor protection) and follow this until it is possible to get out right. Trend up and right to a big thread in a hole then continue up the wall towards an overhang with small tree on the right. The corner above leads to a good stance and large tree belay.

It is possible to continue up the ridge for three pitches (5,4+,4) though this is rumoured to be artificial and on indifferent rock. As an alternative try:

4. 35m 4 From the tree climb up and right to an orange bulge, cross a slab to enter a groove and follow this to where it deepens. Belay on two pegs and a bolt (junction with VIA JULIA).
5. 34m 5+ Follow the corner by bridging and jamming (medium and large Friends useful) to reach large ledges with two ring pegs and a bolt around the arete to the left.

7A. DIRECTISIMA ESPOLON CENTRAL/VIA JULIA COMBO ☺ 5+ (E1 5b) 202m

An excellent long combination for climbers who are looking for a climb sustained at 5+ or thereabouts.
Start at as for DIRECTISIMA ESPOLON CENTRAL, see above.

1. 30m 4- Follow the ramp leftwards into a corner and climb this to a bolt and peg belay.
2. 30m 5+ Climb the corner then move left to a peg and then an old thread. Follow blocks (care!) then continue up the wall trending rightwards to enter a groove. Follow this up and right to a flake then cross the steep wall rightwards to El Nicho. Thread peg and Friend 2 belay.

3. 30m 4 Move right from the niche (peg) and climb to the top of a ramp which descends to the right. Follow this (large thread above) then move down the belay at the top of the first pitch of VIA JULIA.

4. 40m 5+ Climb up and slightly left to a rust-coloured groove. Climb the flake/groove above then take the continuation. Move left to peg belays.

5. 38m 5 Move left then climb directly up the corner groove with harder moves over a bulge (old peg). Trend left into a corner which deepens above. Two peg and single bolt belay.

6. 34m 5+ Follow the corner by bridging and jamming (medium and large Friends useful) to reach large ledges with two ring pegs and a bolt around the arete to the left.

Descent

As for VIA JULIA, see p112.

To reach the last route described continue along below the face until below an obvious oval 'shield' of smooth rock. Start just to the left of this

8. ESPERO SUR CENTRAL ♦ 4+ (UK Grade MVS 4b) c.400m

A magnificent long classic route following a fine mountain feature, the long time, long classic of the area. Technical difficulties are generally low so the situations can be enjoyed to the full, though route finding problems and the length of the climb can be wearing. There have been epics (and deaths) on this route. If you have doubts about your ability to climb quickly for a long period of time start at sun-up. A 62 year old acquaintance did the route with a lady partner who had never climbed outdoors before. Their 6 hours car-to-car time is your target! *Note:* all rope lengths are approximate! The addition of the direct start has removed the need for the long loop at the beginning by the addition of some fairly nondescript climbing. If you have doubts about your ability to complete the route in daylight it might be worth considering using the traditional start, thus saving 1 to 2 hours. For the 'Direct' start at the name in large red lettering, below and left of the conspicuous oval

of smooth rock, 'el escudo', the shield.

Note: for the traditional start traverse left below the face to a large cairn and scramble left up slabby rock to get into the bay under the south-west face of the mountain. Scramble up to the top right corner of this then climb easy (exposed) rock to gain a series of broad ledges. Follow these rightward to the tree belay at the end of third pitch of the direct version.

1. 30m 3 Climb above the name then trend right up a ramp to reach the base of 'the shield' then follow this up and left to a nut belay in the base of the prominent corner.

2. 25m 4+ Climb the corner to a fixed peg at the point where it steepens then step out left into the rib (small chipped arrow indicates the direction) then climb this on excellent rock, passing another peg, to reach ledges and nut belays.

3. 35m 4 Move right and climb a groove to the top of a small tower (peg to the left) then climb straight up the slab to a large tree. Move 5m left and belay on another tree, at the point where the regular route comes in from the left.

4. 40m 4 Climb excellent rock trending slightly right to pass a tree (red arrow), then trend right and climb an awkward slabby corner to reach a good ledge. Move right to thread belays.

5. 25m 3 Climb up and right, then follow grooves to a tree (situ sling) then continue a short distance to a small ledge right on the arete.

6. 25m 4 This groove leads to an open belay on the ridge crest. Good views across the south face.

7. 40m 4 Follow the exposed crest of the ridge on wonderful rock to a belay on a small ledge, a superb pitch.

8. 45m 4+ Move a few feet left of the ridge into a long open corner, at its top climb up and right to a good ledge back on the crest. Another great pitch.

9. 40m 4+ Again traverse up and left to gain access to a corner which leads to a break in the ridge. This and the next pitch are deemed the crux by most parties.

10. 40m 4+ Above lies another groove on the crest, with perhaps a move or two of UK 4b.
11. 30m 4 Continue up the ridge, now easier angled until a steep step leads to an open corner.
12. 30m 3 The climbing now eases as height is gained and scrambling indicates the end of the technical rock climbing.

For the **Descent** continue up the easy angled ridge for a short distance, heading towards where it steepens up in an obvious headwall, and keeping a sharp eye open for a large red paint spot near the right side of the ridge. Traverse to the right (occasional cairns and paint) passing a series of ridges and going around the back of a small tower. Descend into a broad gully and cross this to regain the path on its far side. This soon leads into the main gully 50-90 minutes from the end of the climbing.

Note: there are other lines of cairns that trend uphill; don't be tempted by these, and more importantly don't try to descend at any point before the **main** gully that leads to and from the mountain's summit.

Around to the left of the south face is the extensive and extremely complex west face. The present Tudela guide to the cliff lists many routes including some of the longest on the mountain, up to an almost interminable 900m in length. The lower right side of the face is the home of the **Aguja Encantada or Enchanted Spire**. The Edwards family have developed a series of steep and generally hard climbs on this face many of which they rate highly. I have only done one of these (supposedly amongst the best) and this is described in full below. Get a copy of the local guide if you want to check out the rest.

Approach

Drive past the normal parking place for the south face and continue for 0.6km to a pull-off on the right where a good track (red and yellow paint marks) heads towards the mountain. Follow this for about 20 minutes to the second track branching off to the right (cairn). This leads steeply to the foot of the face in another 10 minutes.

EL DIAMANTE ☺ 6b 175m
A fine climb up the right edge of the face. There is fixed gear where it is needed most though climbers used to designer clip-ups down by the coast may find the home made bolt hangers and do-it-yourself welded rings on the belays an eye-opener! Carry a light rack, the route can be done up and down (just) on a 60m rope, otherwise double ropes will be needed to effect a retreat.

Start at a man-sized pedestal at the left side of the flat foot of the face.
1. 5+ 45m Trend right up floral rock (solitary peg runner) to enter a series of grooves which are climbed to the base of a leaning corner. Jam this steeply to gain its crest then traverse right to a single bolt and descend 6m to an uncomfortable twin bolt stance in a groove.
2. 6a+ 25m Climb back to the bolt (loose blocks) then make steep moves through a bulge (two bolts) before climbing the easier wall into a shallow groove. Up this (two bolts) then layback strenuously out left to a good stance in the base of the continuation groove.
3. 6b 25m Climb the groove (two bolts) then head up the wall trending left (thread and two pegs) to reach the crux moves. Rather illogically keep climbing leftwards until the second of two bolts can be clipped then traverse easily to the right into a groove and on to a stance on top of some flakes.
4. 6a 20m Climb the fine grey slab above the stance (thread and bolt) then continue up the scoop above, exiting from its left side to a twin bolt belay on the left rib.
5. 5+ 18m Climb directly above the stance (huge thread) and pull through the diagonal bulge at a mini-thread handhold, trend right across easy ground to a stance by a pinnacle.
6. 6a 32m Climb up and right, then back left across a ramp (bolt and two pegs) to get into the groove above the stance. Follow this more easily to where it steepens then move out right and continue to abseil anchors a short distance below the top of the tower. Abseil back down the line in five rope lengths.

EL PONOCH

Crag Facts

Star rating: ****
Aspect: South-facing
Height: Up to 400 metres

No table of grades is given but suffice to say there are over 35 routes on the three interconnected cliffs here that run up to 500m and 16 pitches in length.

Introduction

As you drive northwards past Benidorm on the motorway the shapely peak of the Puig Campana catches the eye of any climber worth his salt. As this slips behind, a glance over your left shoulder reveals a truly huge wall of rock a couple of kilometres wide and up to 400m high hidden behind the Campana. This is the combined wall formed from summits of (from right to left) El Ponoch, the Torre de Murcia and the Tozal de Levante, rising above the small town of Polop. Only two routes are described here, the fully equipped sport route of GORILAS EN LA NIEBLA, and a complete contrast, the old classic of (yet another) VIA VALENCIANOS. There are plenty of other fine-looking routes here though information is not easy to come by. A *Desnivel* magazine of a few years ago had topos of the faces and this is the only original material I have ever seen. A copy of part of the section dealing with El Ponoch also appeared in the German publication *Sun Rock Band 1*.

Access

From Benidorm or Altea drive up to and through La Nucia and on around some sweeping bends into Polop, 10-12km from the A7. Soon the rather discreet Laboratorie Polop is passed on the left (look out for the Fuji film sign) then take the next left turn just before a bridge (Se Vende Chalet Sign here in 1997). Drive up this, keeping left through the houses and follow the narrow tarmacked road uphill, bearing right at a Y

junction by a high wall and then continue until the tarmac runs out, 1.5km from the main road. Good parking is available on the left after 100m or 100m further on, by a drive with a chain and two cartwheels. Walk up the drive for 100m then branch slightly right and follow a broad gravel path up the river bed. Continue up here until a discreet blue painted arrow on a rock on the right marks the start of a path that leads up through steep terraces (blue spots) to a 30m high pinnacle on the right-hand side of the main section of cliff, at the junction of the south and east faces, 25 minutes from the car.

Running left from the pinnacle is a broad steep wall that contains various pieces of fixed equipment scattered about it, and two lines of parabolts that run for at least a hundred or more metres up the cliff. It is possible that the right-hand of these is PUTON VERBENERO 6b,6c,6a,5+, 150m and that the left-hand line is ESTADO EMOCIONAL, 6c,6a+,5+,5,6b,5, c250m or 400m if followed all the way to the cliff top.

Further to the left past a leaning wall is a rough grey slab up which starts the classic route of:

GORILAS EN LA NIEBLA ♦ 6c+ 220m
A great climb, varied and direct up the centre of the most continuous part of this huge face. The gear is all fixed and although some of the bolts are old, there are always good gear when it really matters. Start about 150m left of the 30m tower where an apron of slabby grey rock (new bolts visible 10m up) offers a way through between steeper rock to left and right.

1. 6a 48m Climb the easy slab to its apex then continue up steeper rock moving left to reach ledges and a tricky bulge. Above this easier climbing leads past vegetated ledges to a stance (nut belay) below a shallow groove with rock scars and a scratched 'X'

on its left wall.

2. 6b+ 44m Climb the left wall of the groove (chain link first bolt) then continue to enter the shallow groove on the right. Climb the continuation of this then trend right up a ramp before climbing straight up to a stance in a hollow. A sustained and sharp pitch on great rock.

3. 6c+ 38m Climb the slab above the stance (a fair way to the first bolt) then attack the crucial leaning wall above, difficult to start, then better holds lead to the base of a shallow leaning groove. Again this is hard and leads to slabbier rock and eventually a good stance in a shallow cave.

4. 6a+ 30m Move right a couple of metres then climb straight up awkward rock to reach the first bolt on the slab above (loose blocks to the right). From here step out left and climb the rib and then the sustained slab to a bulge just above which is another stance in a bay.

5. 6b 25m Step left and climb carefully into a loose bay. Step right and pull though the bulges on pockets then head up the sustained wall by glorious jug pulling to reach a small stance just above the point where the angle drops back.

6. 6b+ 35m Step left and climb the steep slab to ledges then move right and pull steeply into a shallow groove on hidden holds. Trend left (avoid loose rock further left) then climb straight up the juggy wall to a final sharp slab and a three bolt belay at the end of all things.

Descend by 5 abseils to the Valencianos ramp then scramble down and left to a wire cable belay that allows a 40m abseil back to the ground.

To the left of the start of GORILAS EN LA NIEBLA is a wall of quality rock that contains some single pitch climbs from 15-40m in length. Several of them have new bolts and look to be 6a -6c and well worthwhile.

The long groove that bounds the left side of the pillar of GORILAS EN LA NIEBLA is the classic 400m route of FISSURA GALLEGO,

116

5,3,4,3,5+,5+&A0,5+&A1,4,4,5,5 an excellent looking route following a strong natural line and going to the top of the cliff. If you choose this one take a full rack.

A short distance around to the left is a scratched arrow pointing up and rightwards, to the lower end of the broad grass ledge that runs across the lower part of the face. This is the start of the:

VIA VALENCIANOS ☺ 6b (or 5&A0) c500m A classic route, the first (1972) on the cliff, following a strong natural line up the centre of this huge face. There is not much hard climbing on the route and the amount of fixed gear means that it can be climbed 'alpine style' if required. The length of the routes dictates an early start or the ability to move rapidly over easy ground.

1. 3+ 25m From the scratched arrow climb the rock band trending rightwards to get onto the ramp and then move right to a belay.

2. 3- 30m Continue along the ramp with the occasional tricky step to a good stance and a belay on a wire cable and substantial bolts.

3. 1 60m Amble along the grass ledge to a thread belay at the point where the ramp starts to rise up the face in a more determined fashion.

4. 2+ 40m Climb the ramp passing the odd piece of fixed gear to a mish-mash of a belay.

5. 2+ 40m Continue up the ramp with a jig right at mid-height to reach a stance below more imposing terrain.

6. 4+ 50m Climb the steep slab passing occasional bolts and other relics until it is possible to move right a few metres, continue in the same line to a small exposed stance below a steep wall.

7. 6b or 5 & A0 25m Climb the wall either free, clipping into everything, or by pulling on the occasional piece of fixed kit to bring the climbing down to a reasonable level.

8. 6a or 5 & A0 35m As the way on is now blocked and retreat is not an inviting option embark on the crucial link pitch. Traverse left following the line of fixed gear,

descending a short distance at one point and then reascending before climbing diagonally leftwards to a stance in the base of an open groove.

9. 4+ 30m Climb the groove to its exit then continue leftwards up easier rock to bolt belays on a ledge and an escape from the big drop.
10. 4 35m Climb the wall above zigzagging right and then back left (thread and pegs) to arrive on a major ledge system.
11. 3- 40m Move left a short distance then climb straight up to reach a larger ledge system that cuts right across the upper part of the face.
12. 1 50m Walk right along the ledge to a stance below an open groove.
13. 4 30m Climb the groove (pegs) to a stance on another ledge system, salvation is now just around the corner!

Escape Walk right along the ledge and descend a short awkward step (steps of 2 & 3) passing pegs to reach a tree. From here continue rightwards on ledges for several hundred metres until it is possible to descend into the broad gully in the left side of the east face (this is clearly visible on the approach to cliff, check it out). Descend this carefully as there is a big drop below, until a tree allows a 20m abseil to ledges from where another abseil of 40m leads back to easy ground.

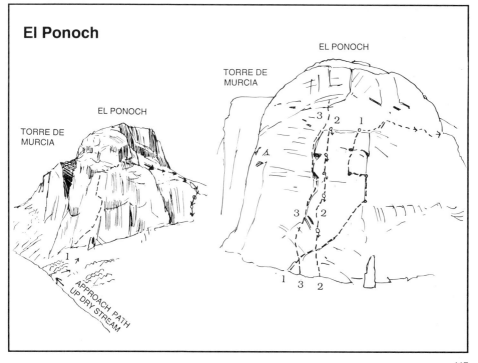

El Ponoch

BERNIA

Crag Facts

Star rating: **

Aspect: South-facing

Height: Up to 60 metres, though all the routes except two are half this height or less

Spread of grades:

4	5	5+	6a	6b	6c	7a	7b	7c	8
/	/	/	3	1	3	2	2	/	3

Introduction

Approaching Calpe from the south, the impressive rocky ridge of the Sierra Bernia is the Cuillin-like crest that blocks the way north and forces the coastal road to detour through the Mascarat Gorge. It is obvious from many miles away that there is a vast amount of rock available on this extensive hillside, though at present the development has been absolutely minimal with the Dalle d'Olla on the far right and the cliff described here on the far left. This second area is visible from the main road, if you know where to look, as two areas of reddish rock above and left of a tiny collection of white houses situated three-quarters of the way up the hillside. There are only a dozen or so pitches here and unfortunately these are generally very hard. Added to this is the very unpleasant vegetation that encroaches right up to the foot of the cliff, making moving about a prickly pain. Quality assessments are given for the few routes that I have concrete information about.

Access

From the N332 2km south of the Mascarat Gorge turn inland at Olla de Altea to reach Altea la Vieja (recently renamed as Altea Vella). Drive through the town then continue along the winding road as far as a tarmacked right turn just before a right-hand bend with chevrons. This junction is marked by a small concrete (gas or water?) box with the word 'Pirri' and an arrow spray painted on it in black lettering and is 1.8km from the sign indicating that you are leaving the town. Follow the narrow road through a farm then continue steeply uphill for 5km, passing one impressive undeveloped cliff, until the road begins to level out and there is a right turn to a parking and picnic area. Park on the roadside here and walk back along the terraces below the casitas to reach their end. Scramble up a short dirty gully and escape out left onto slabs. Follow these up and left to some large blocks then head straight for the cliff arriving close to the impressive prow tackled by SPHINX. From here a hacked-out path leads leftwards through the vegetation to the main area of development around a steep grey slab that runs into an overhanging wall. The safest way back to the car is to reverse the approach route; shortcuts are fraught with problems.

All the routes are described briefly, from left to right, starting at the very end of the path just right of a large barrel-shaped buttress.

1. IMMACULATE ARETE   8a   25m
Climb the black ramp and then trend out left onto the orange wall and climb this on small holds to reach a short hanging flake, this leaving a short runout to the belays. Apparently superb.

The right is a grey slab with several bolt lines running up it.

2. JANE'S PROJECT ☺   6c   25m
The left side of the sharp lower slab and then a short steep crack leads into a short blocky corner and above this are ledges with twin rings.

3. PARADISE LOST ☺   7a   25m
The right side of the slab leads to the leaning wall again which is longer at this

point. Climb it by a red crack and some strenuous pocket pulling to a lower-off on the rim.

The centre of the wall is home to two projects approached from either side of the prominent shrubby hollow.

The right side of the wall is a tough route (8b?) passing right of a big flake then 70m further right are two cracks that diverge slightly as they rise. These have been climbed using traditional gear and are included here for completeness but are unlikely to prove popular, being wide, sharp and unsavoury. Apparently there is a lower-off hidden on the bush-infested ledge above the cracks.

5. LEFT CRACK 6a+ 20m
The wide, red, left-hand crack.

6. RIGHT CRACK 6a+ 20m
The slightly narrower grey right-hand one.

Four hundred metres to the right is the spectacular hanging arête of the SPHINX and below it is one route worth the trip up here to do.

7. THE MAGIC FLUTE ♦ 7b+ 25m
Excellent pocket-pulling and tufa-pinching leads to a lower-off where the angle falls back.

Above and right of THE MAGIC FLUTE and using this climb as a 'warm-up' pitch is the spectacular hanging prow tackled by 8. SPHINX 7b,8a,6c+ c60m. Right again is a deep corner, the 9. GRAND DIEDRE 6c,6b+, c55m; be sure to take a full rack.

Several hundred metres further right is another impressive smooth wall with a line of bolts up its right side. It is likely that this is 12. MARK IN TIME 8b, whilst the crack to its left is 11. DIAGONAL 6c and the slab left again is 10. SECRETS 7a+. Again the need to carry a rack almost certainly resigns these latter two to obscurity.

There is reportedly another small collection of traditional routes further right but I failed to locate them. Maybe you will have more luck.

1. IMMACULATE ARÊTE 8a
2. JANE'S PROJECT ☺ 6c
3. PARADISE LOST ☺ 7a
4. ? 8b?
5. LEFT CRACK 6a+
6. RIGHT CRACK 6a+

7. THE MAGIC FLUTE ♦ 7b+
8. SPHINX 7b,8a,6c+
9. GRAND DIEDRE 6c,6b+
10. SECRETS 7a+
11. DIAGONAL 6a
12. MARK IN TIME 8a

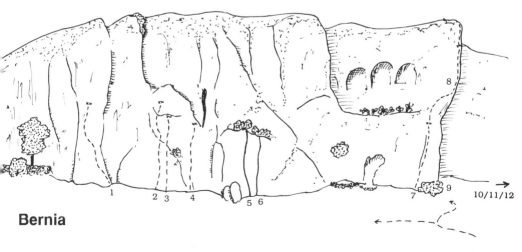

Bernia

10/11/12

CALPE REGION

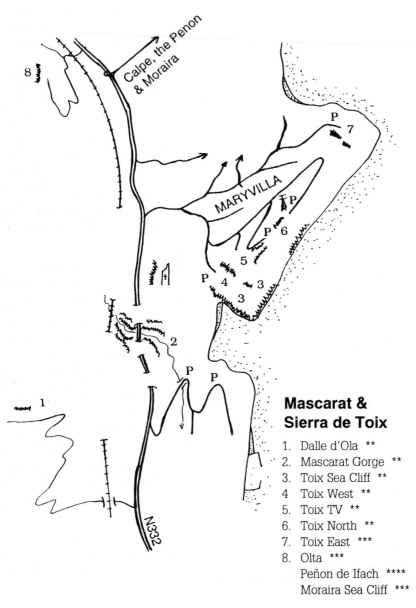

**Mascarat &
Sierra de Toix**

1. Dalle d'Ola **
2. Mascarat Gorge **
3. Toix Sea Cliff **
4 Toix West **
5. Toix TV **
6. Toix North **
7. Toix East ***
8. Olta ***
   Peñon de Ifach ****
   Moraira Sea Cliff ***

DALLE D'OLA

Crag Facts

Star rating: **

Aspect: south west facing

Height: 40 metres

Spread of grades:

4	5	5+	6a	6b	6c	7a	7b	7c	8
		2	3	3	2	2			

Introduction

A compact wall of perfect if occasionally polished rock, equipped with plenty of big beefy (and brightly coloured) bolts, and only seconds from the car. The cliff faces south-west from the lower slopes of the Bernia range (high point 1128m) and affords magnificent views out over the coastal plain. The tower blocks of the 'Black Hole of Benidorm' can be seen shimmering in the distance and beyond lie range upon range of unknown hills. The crag gets the sun from midday until it sets. Although only a minor cliff I still remember my first visit here in the late eighties and being well pleased, climbing in the sun at Christmas. The crag remains well worth at least one visit if you are in the area.

For the rock hungry the southern slopes of Bernia, stretching away to the left of the crag, contain enough rock to last several lifetimes, but can you afford the bolts?

Note: the local climbers call the cliff CANYELLES, though its better known name was first used by the German climber who placed the bolts. He named the place after his dog: OLA'S WALL.

Crag Geography

The cliff is basically a broad flat wall with a small subsidiary buttress to the left.

Approaches

From Calpe drive south on the N332 through the tunnels and bridges of the Mascarat Gorge. Take the first right turn, signed Marina Greenwich (1¹/₂km after the gorge), or the much grander second right signed Altea Hills (2km). Follow the road up over the motorway to a large flat area containing a complex junction/roundabout. Turn right and follow a tarmacked road which winds uphill, through villas. Eventually it levels out and deteriorates into a gravel track; the crag is 400m down this and it is possible to park right under it. It is also possible to continue straight on at the complex junction and take a rough gravel road that approaches the cliff from the other direction. This is only to be recommended for owners of four wheel drive vehicles or donkeys.

Note: There is still much construction activity in this area. Access details may change with time.

Descent

It is possible to climb down a rib to the left (looking in) of the main section of the crag, but this is exposed and has one short steep section near the bottom: care required. At the right side of the crag, 3m below the edge and beside some blocks, is a bolt/chain anchor which allows a 35m abseil back to base. It may be worth taking a spare rope if you intend to do several routes here and leaving it in place. Of course any of the single bolt belays at the top of the routes can be used as abseil anchors, it is all a matter of confidence - how long are they anyway?

The routes do not have names as such but are known by their appropriate (fading) colour. Colour blind climbers will have to seek help from their normal sighted friends. Descriptions are from left to right, and as all the climbs are 30-35m in length this information has been omitted from the text.

To the left of the main wall of the crag and the slanting rake is a subsidiary buttress split by a red groove; the first three routes are found on this buttress.

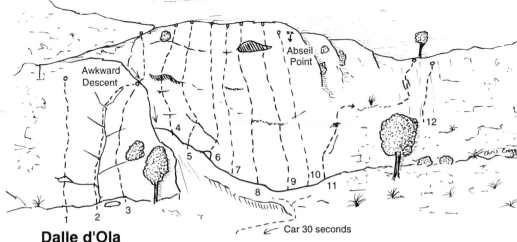

Dalle d'Ola

1. PUNTOS AZULES IZQUIERDA ☺ 5+
2. PUNTOS ROSAS IZQUIERDA ☺ 5
3. PUNTOS AMARILLOS IZQUIERDA ☺ 5+
4. PUNTOS NEGROS ☺ 6b
5. PUNTOS NARANJAS ♦ 6a
6. PUNTOS VERDES ♦ 6a+
7. PUNTOS AMARILLOS ☺ 5+
8. PUNTOS BLANCOS ♦ 6b
9. PUNTOS AZULES ☺ 6a
10. PUNTOS ROSAS ☺ 5+
11. PUNTOS ROJAS ☺ 6b/c
12. FIREZA ☺ 6c

---

1. PUNTOS AZULES IZQUIERDA (LEFT-HAND BLUE BOLTS) ☺ 5+
On the far left climb the pleasant slabby wall passing six bolt runners.

The rock to the right of the red corner is taken by
2. PUNTOS ROSAS IZQUIERDA (LEFT-HAND RED BOLTS) ☺ 5
Start to the right of the red corner at a flattened area.
Climb up and left following a thin crack which soon steepens up and curves to the right. Above these steeper moves a bolt belay is to be found on the rake. Cross this and finish up the steep wall behind, two bolt runners.

3. PUNTOS AMARILLOS IZQUIERDA (THE LEFT YELLOW BOLTS) ☺ 5+
Follow the right-hand bolt line, this being rather more difficult than its near neighbour, to a belay on the sloping rake. Finish as for the previous climb.

The rest of the climbs are on the main sheet of rock, the first four being reached by scrambling up a shrubby ramp to the left from the base of the crag.

4. PUNTOS NEGROS (BLACK BOLTS) ☺ 6b
A rather unbalanced climb with the crux low down.
The steep lower wall is taken on small painful holds until below the bulge. A rest on the flakes on the left at this point is possible. After passing the bulge with a long reach for a good jug the upper slab proves to be a bit of an anticlimax. The bulge can also be crossed further to the right by another black bolt, but this is a bit of a cop-out.

5. PUNTOS NARANJAS (ORANGE (or PINK!) BOLTS) ♦ 6a
Sustained climbing and spaced bolts make this an entertaining pitch.
Pull steeply on to the wall and climb leftwards passing a thread to clip the first bolt. The

bulging wall above is well furnished with jugs so press on to the second bolt. Once this is clipped relax and enjoy the rest of the route.

6. PUNTOS VERDES (GREEN BOLTS) 🗝 6a+

A sustained pitch, perhaps the best on the cliff with inspiring protection. Start from a large block.

Make difficult moves in a position of some safety to reach the first break. Continue steeply until the holds run out, a small side pull on a black "slug" to the left provides the key to gaining access to the interesting upper slab.

7. PUNTOS AMARILLOS (YELLOW BOLTS) ☺ 5+

A good climb, quite stiff for the grade.
The lower section is the most difficult but as the angle eases the bolts become more spaced and the climbing is much easier. Pass the upper bulge by the easy groove on its left.

8. PUNTOS BLANCOS (WHITE (or SILVER) BOLTS) 🗝 6b

Another gem. Steep fingery and sustained climbing with "bomber gear" leads to the slab. Saunter up this to the upper bulge which is taken at its left edge by a stiff pull. Once established over the roof step up and left to finish easily.

9. PUNTOS AZULES (BLUE BOLTS) ☺ 6a

A steady lower section leads to an awkward bulge at the top of the crag. The lower wall has good holds and the slab above leads easily to the final bulge. This is taken centrally; unfortunately the expected jug does not materialise so a little cunning is required to gain the top.

10. PUNTOS ROSAS (PINK BOLTS) ☺ 5+

Probably the easiest climb on the main section of the cliff, and a good introduction to the place.

The bolts are rather spaced on the lower wall but the holds are generally good. The slab above is interesting and should be tackled on the left. For those who are finding the whole experience a bit harrowing it is possible to trend right up easier rock directly to the abseil point.

11. PUNTOS ROJAS (RED BOLTS) ☺ 6b/c

A disjointed route with the upper pitch giving some of the hardest climbing on the crag. A must for thugs.

Follow the right-hand line on the lower wall. This looks innocuous enough but has a couple of distinctly delicate moves. At the arrow walk right to a belay below the crack. The bolts above can be clipped by leaning in from the left, but are passed on the right by powerful undercutting and laybacking (with the odd jump) to reach the jugs above. A stout tree provides a suitable belay/lowering off point.

12. FUREZA ☺ 6c

The only route on the cliff graced with a proper name! A short stiff pitch located to the right of the top pitch of the previous climb gives the hardest moves hereabouts.

The opportunity exists for a dozen or more rainbow coloured girdles and diagonal eliminates. Double ropes and a complete disregard for folk doing the 'up and down' lines would appear to be a prerequisite for such ascents.

BARRANCO DE MASCARAT
(MASCARAT GORGE)

Crag Facts

Star rating: **

Aspect: south and north facing

Height: 10 to 240 metres

Spread of grades:

4	5	5+	6a	6b	6c	7a	7b	7c	8
	4	3	5	4	1	1	5	2	

Introduction

Just to the south of Calpe lies what has always been one of the major physical obstacles to north - south travel along the coastal plain, the combined ranges of the Sierra Bernia and Sierra de Toix. This almost continuous ridge of rocky limestone hills runs out into the sea forming a series of impressive cliffs. Cutting through this range of hills is the spectacular 300m deep ravine of the Barranco de Mascarat. The various generations of engineers have crossed this magnificent feature with three impressive bridges, the lower two of which are the site of the now famous bridge jumping escapades.

AN ASIDE: If the prospect of completing the jump ('Los Pantalones Repleto' or 'the full trousers' as the locals refer to it) appeals to you the usual approach is thus: pass one end of a rope through a descendeur which is attached to the centre of the lowest (old) bridge. Meanwhile the prospective jumper is attached to the other end at the centre of the new road bridge (black arrow painted on the path). The jumper climbs over the railings and the team takes the rope in through the descendeur as tight as possible because the distance between the bridges is only slightly less than the distance to the ground! When suitably fired up it is just a matter of letting go, though it is traditional to lose your voice because of the screaming on the initial 25m free fall (didn't I mention that the bridge

you jump off is higher than the one the rope is attached to?). Finally the gibbering heap on the end of the rope can be lowered the short distance to the ground.

You are supposed to get a licence for this shenanigan from the police in Alicante, but it appears that the majority of people don't bother. Those with any sense take one look at the scale of the jump and run a mile. Be warned: if you try the bridge jump without the paperwork there is a high probability you will be moved on by the police. Perhaps you should consider doing it at the dead of night!

Crag Geography

There is a wide variety of styles of climbing in this rather grim setting. In the base of the gorge is a series of one pitch climbs. Shady desperate test pieces on the south side contrast with slabby, sunny, and much easier fare on the north side. At the level of the bridges are some short hard climbs and the lower pitches of some longer "semi-alpine" routes, that run all the way to the top of the mountain.

WARNINGS

1. By Sod's Law any material dropped off the upper pitches of the longer routes will land on the road. Either take great care or have adequate third party insurance.

2. Cars left on the road bridge are liable to be broken into, towed away, or both. See below for the solution.

Approaches

These unmistakable cliffs lie 10 minutes' drive south of Calpe on the N332. As mentioned above parking is something of a problem. If someone cannot be left to look after the vehicle

Barranco de Mascarat

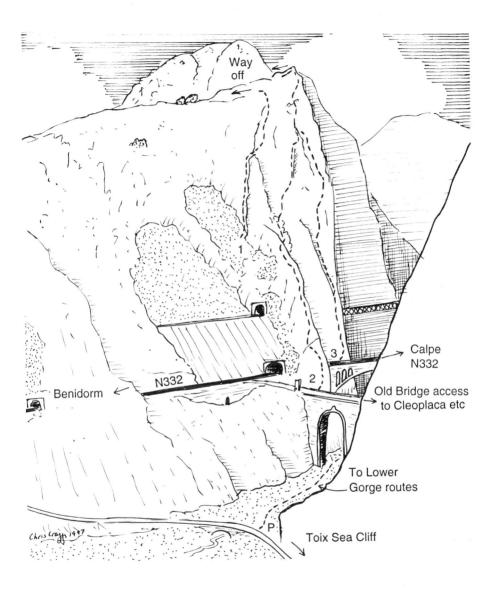

1. LA TETAS DE MI NOVIA   ☺ 6b
2. VIA U.P.S.A ☺ 5 (VS 5a)
3. VIA SULFADA ♨ 6b

then either get dropped of by the sunbathing team after arranging a suitable rendezvous, or continue southwards and take the first tarmacked left turn (1km) signed Pueblo Mascarat and Sol Ingrid. This leads back leftwards to a bridge crossing the dried up stream bed that issues from the ravine, where there are a variety of parking spaces. Leave nothing in the car. The climbing is 5 minutes' rough walking from here, up the stream bed.

The climbs at and above road level are described first.

1. LAS TETAS DE MI NOVIA ☺ 6b 150m

An interesting climb on good rock that takes the poorly defined buttress on the walls above the southern end of the central road tunnel. Reach the start by scrambling up from the downhill end of this tunnel. Cross the railway line and continue up a vague path in an open gully. This breaks out right past a small rock barrier. The start of the climb lies up and right and is marked by a cross and two circles scratched on the rock. The Spanish grades don't appear to be too accurate as we thought the first two pitches were UK 5c,5b!

1. 40m 5+ Follow the right-hand line of fixed gear up the front of the buttress to reach ledges below a bulge. Move left to climb a slippery flowstone wall protected by a couple of archaic bolts. Belay in the groove above.
2. 45m 6b Climb the groove until forced leftwards into another groove. Up this and the slabby wall above, where difficult moves right gain a crack (pegs) which leads to a stance.
3. 20m 5+ Traverse right to a short awkward wall, up this (pegs) to a belay on the edge of the buttress.
4. 45m 4 Climb the corner system on the right to easy ground.

Descent

The summit of the mountain lies some distance above; only ardent peak baggers will bother to visit it. Therefore follow a terrace to the left (southwards) and climb a 5m wall (2) on to the open hillside. Turn left and descend eastwards

in to a gully then cross the railway line to eventually reach the road. Do not be tempted to turn before the rock step as there is a line of cliffs below.

The right side of the pillar taken by LAS TETAS DE MI NOVIA is climbed in three long pitches by ESPERMACIO 5+,6a,5+, 150m. It looks worthwhile.

2. VIA U.P.S.A. ☺ 5 (VS 5a) 225m

A long and interesting route at an amenable grade, passing through some impressive rock scenery. The climb links the noisy world of the Mascarat Gorge with the aromatic limestone wilderness of the Sierra Bernia. For a short time the route was fully bolted. Only the belay bolts remain. Take a rack.

Start from the southern end of the old road bridge.

1. 30m 3 Easy rock leads past a variety of manmade objects to a peg belay on top of the first pillar.
2. 30m 4 A short awkward wall leads to easier rock and a belay where the angle falls back.
3. 45m 4 Generally easy climbing up the crest of the ridge leads to vegetated terraces that are followed leftwards until it is possible to move right to below a groove in the more impressive upper section of the route.
4. 30m 4+ Climb up into the groove then make a couple of moves right before climbing straight up the wall to ledges. A traverse is then made to a stance on the right.
5. 35m 5 Above and right is the crux groove. This is gained and followed by pleasantly sustained moves (or pulling on the pegs if you are an alpinist) until easier climbing leads to a stance on the right.
6. 25m 4+ Step left and climb straight up to a good thread, from which easier climbing leads to a stance with bolt belays.
7. 30m 4 Move up to a peg in a diagonal crack then swing right around the arete to gain a corner which eases as height is gained and leads to a shoulder above all difficulties.

Descent

Regain the mountain by traversing the narrow

ridge (a stroll for the confident, an 'a cheval' grovel for the more timid). Mountaineers can continue up the ridge for a couple of hundred feet of grade 3 climbing on good rock to reach the summit of the Mascarat Superior followed by a descent to the south. Ordinary mortals, especially those with sore feet, can follow the terrace to the left to join the descent of the previous route.

3. VIA SULFADA ♦ 6b 240m

An excellent outing on superb rock in a dramatic setting. Start at the uphill end of the middle road tunnel. The first two easy pitches can be soloed but the scenario in the event of a slip is all too obvious. A light rack might be required on pitches 6 & 7.

1. 25m Climb over the railings then up right over vegetated rock to a ledge. Follow the easy groove above past a thin thread until the line leads left to a ledge and two bolt belay.
2. 30m Step right then plough up the herbal gully (thread) before moving right to a peg and thread belay below a groove in steeper rock. Things now begin to improve.
3. 40m 5+ Climb the groove to two bolts, which are passed by steep bridging. Step right then continue in the same line past pegs and bolts to enter a groove. Up this to an exit left then climb diagonally left to a small stance and three bolt belay. The downward views are most photogenic.
4. 30m 6a Step right then climb straight up for 10m. Now traverse to the right to enter a hidden groove which is followed past several pegs (some of which stick out rather a long way) to another excellent stance.
5. 25m 6b Up the steep wall behind the stance to gain access to a slabby groove. Up this to its end then straight up the crack above until a traverse left brings you to another fine stance.
6. 45m 5+ Climb the red corner behind the belay, it contains no fixed gear so a couple of large Rocks might prove useful. At its top step out left on to some large flakes (peg) then follow easier cracks to a comfy ledge.
7. 45m 5 It is possible to finish up the top pitch of the previous route (4+). Alternatively trend left into a groove which is followed until it steepens, then either cop out by traversing left, or climb the strenuous jamming crack past the bush (runners required) to the top.

Descent is as for the previous route.

The impressive and very exposed buttress to the right of the previous route is home to the spectacular VUELO DEL AGUILA, reached by a grade 3 traverse, and graded 6a,6a,6b,5,4,5+. It looks well worthwhile.

The next routes that are described are reached by crossing the old road bridge. The wall to the right of the tunnel door contains some manmade finger pockets. Prospective suitors of CLEOPLACA should spend some time hanging off these to get warmed up (if you need to use the footholds you are in for a hard time). Scramble up left to a ledge with two bolts. The small tunnel to the left is worth a visit by those with an exploratory bent to their nature.

The obvious slanting groove containing several pegs is pitch 3 of VIA BOULDER which starts from the gorge bed (see below). The wall to the right of the groove is the site of three fine climbs reached by scrambling carefully up quarried rock past cactuses (a very un-British hazard). The wall gets the sun after mid-day.

4. CLEOPLACA ♦ 7b 50m

A breathtaking pitch tackling the centre of the stunning diamond shaped brown wall. The spacing and position of the bolts means that double ropes might not go amiss. Start at a single bolt belay just to the right of the slabby groove. The initial wall gives a taste of things to come and is climbed first left then back right. Above this an easier section leads past a huge 'ringing' flake. The upper wall is sustained and the route finding is intricate with only just enough bolt protection and little in the way of rests. The crux involves three successive 'mono' moves. Peg and bolt belay/abseil anchor.

Mascarat Gorge: a view into the narrowing gorge with the wall of CLEOPLACA prominent above the old bridge

5. VIA AURORA ☺ 5+ 55m

A good climb in a spooky setting, though overshadowed by its immediate neighbours. Begin below a weakness with a peg in it to the right of the bolt belay of CLEOPLACA.

1. 30m 5+ A couple of tricky moves are needed to get started, thread. Improving holds lead up on to a ramp which is followed up to the right past good but spaced peg runners. A final difficult few moves (hint: stay low) lead to a well endowed stance. The direct start running straight up the steep wall to the stance is La Caravela 6c.
2. 25m 5+ The slanting groove is followed past bolts and pegs and gives sustained climbing until the bolt belay on CLEOPLACA is reached. The route continues for some distance but the climbing does not compare with that below and is loose so a 45m abseil back to safety is the best idea.

6. BRIDGE OF SPIES ☙ 7c 30m

This route takes the grossly leaning prow to the right, above the top end of the gully to the right of the start of CLEOPLACA. Start at the top of the gully on the right side of the wall, below the direct start to AURORA. Follow the bolts to gain a large black 'caterpillar' containing two threads. Climb this (or ride it!) and then make desperate moves up and right to gain a flake hidden from below. Easier climbing now leads to twin bolts.

7. SPINACH PLEASE OLIVE 7b 10m

A well named route to delight the connoisseurs of the tough but trivial. Takes the wall just to the right of the tunnel entrance with two bolt runners and a hideous move using the obvious quarryman's mono doigt. Just remember tendons have feelings too.

To the right is a concaved wall with two routes, access requires care.

8. TO BE IN ENGLAND ☺ 7b 25m

The left-hand and more worthwhile line. From twin thread belays climb the wall generally trending rightwards passing five bolts and a thread to the lower-off.

9. CRAZY INGLESE 6a+ 20m

The right-hand line containing a peg and a thread!

The rest of the routes here start from the bed of the gorge, reached either by walking up the stream bed, see APPROACHES, or by a 45m abseil from the paired bolts below CLEOPLACA.

The base of the gorge is an interesting but sinister spot with traffic thundering by far above. Scattered around are huge boulders brought down by flash floods and the remnants of wall safes 'borrowed' from nearby villas and dumped off the bridge! It is worth a short walk upstream to where the walls close in and the atmosphere is even more impressive (or should it be oppressive). Certainly not a place to be when the region's rare flash floods are forecast.

The routes are described on the north side of the gorge first, from left to right and starting with a climb that reascends the line of the abseil and then weaves its way up the buttress above.

10. VIA BOULDER ☺ 5+ 230m

A long route which takes a devious line up the great buttress above the upper road tunnel, visiting some interesting spots 'en route'. It contains a variety of fixed gear, a light rack might be a sensible idea.

Start between the two road bridges at an attractive light coloured slab with a well trodden area at its base.

1. 40m 5+ Climb leftwards into the centre of the wall and then head straight on up (avoiding easier ground to the left). At 25m a couple of trickier moves up a flake give access to easier rock and a little higher is a small stance and peg belay on the right.
2. 15m 5+ Move left to below a shallow groove which is entered from the left by a tough little move. A short distance above is the terrace and an escape for those who have had enough. The next objective is the slanting groove above. Do not try to get at it from below (dangerously loose) but move right and up to the bolt belay below CLEOPLACA.
3. 30m 5+ Step into the groove and follow it delicately to steeper moves on better holds.

Pass a perfect 'bivi-site' to reach an exposed stance on the left.

4. 20m 5+ Gain the well pegged crack directly or more easily from the left, and follow it with sustained interest until it becomes possible to swing right onto easier rock. A small stance lies a short distance above.

5. 35m 4 Cross the slab on the left to its far corner, then climb diagonally across the steep left wall to gain access to easy rock. Traverse easily leftwards until a belay can be taken below a massive red corner with a prominent bolt in its left wall.

6. 30m 5 The corner is steep and imposing but it is less difficult than appearances might suggest. The mean looking wide crack in the upper section is outflanked on the left, and a slab leads to a stance.

7. 30m 4- The easy slab on the left is crossed and the corner above is entered past a "pothole". The giant flakes are climbed most easily and safely on the left and lead to a comfortable grass ledge.

8. 30m 4 The steep crack on the right is awkward to enter, but once gained leads more easily to a rather sudden finish.

Descent

Follow the rocky ridge northwards until it runs out into open hillside. Continue up to the ruin on the summit, from where a rough track leads north-east to the villas below Toix West.

The next climbs are a series of short bolt protected pitches which lie to the right (south-west) of the old road bridge on a steep grey wall which contains a prominent vertical cave to the right of the smoothest section. Some of the names of the climbs are of dubious origin and may not be correct.

To the left of the elongated cave is a large hole halfway up the smoothest section of rock. This is visited briefly by:

11. MUJER CONTRA MUJER ☺ 6b 25m
Enter the hole by climbing past a bolt and a thread then exit rightwards passing a bolt peg and two threads to a lower-off shared with the next climb.

12. MARICA EL ULTIMO (BLACK ORCHID) ☺ 6a+ 25m
Begin below and left of the cave entrance. Climb up to the right until it is possible to pull left to the first bolt. The crux lies just above and involves strenuous use of an undercut pocket. A few more steep moves lead on to a slab which is climbed keeping to the left of the bolts to a lowering point.

13. AUNTY BOLT ☺ 6a+ 25m
Basically a slightly easier right-hand version of the previous climb. Get up into the cave (optional thread on the left, not in situ) and bridge up to the first bolt. The steep wall has a selection of good holds but is strenuous, until the angle eases. Climb the slab keeping to the right of some rather familiar bolts to the belay.

14. SOFT ROCK ☺ 5 45m
A route that takes a line to the right of the cave and which improves as height is gained. It contains many in situ threads.

Head up to the right by some surprisingly awkward moves until it is possible to climb straight up passing some man-sized holes. The smart grey slab above leads to a single bolt belay. Abseil off this or walk to the left to the twin bolts below CLEOPLACA.

A few paces to the right is a short grey slab that has three slight but pleasant fillers in.

15. LEFT ROUTE 6a 20m
The left-hand climb proves to be hardest of the collection. Trend slightly rightwards avoiding easy ground just to the left.

16. BROTHER WOLF 5 20m
The central line climbs up a groove and over a bulge passing a substantial thread. Above this trend slightly right to a lowering bolt.

17. SISTER MOON 5 20m
Start to the right at the lowest point of the wall and take a direct line (or weave about a bit if you want) to the abseil anchor.

The final routes described in the gorge are on

the impressive leaning wall peppered with pockets that lies almost directly below the new road bridge. The wall catches the sun for a couple of hours around midday, at other times it can provide a welcome shady retreat. The names of the climbs were originally painted very elegantly on the rock, though these have now faded. All the pitches can be done to the belays and back to the ground on a 50m rope though they feel much much bigger than this. The routes could do with being rebolted, as the original ones are now rather old.

18. EL SHERRIF COCO ♦ 7b 25m
At the left side of the wall is a line of closely spaced bolts shooting skywards. These are the starting point of a brilliant and butch pitch.

The line of bolts is followed up the leaning wall using a variety of painful finger pockets and slippery footholds until jugs are reached. Move up and right on better holds then back left to below the more impressive upper section. The holds are mostly good but the angle is steep until a few final difficult moves gain the slab above and twin lowering bolts.

19. HAMBRE DE MUJER ♦ 6c+ 25m
The easiest of the bunch but quite a tough cookie. It takes the shallow sinuous groove up the middle of the wall.
  Begin in the centre of the wall from the leftmost of a series of blocks. A steep start leads to better but spaced holds which are followed up and right to a large hole (threads). Continue leftwards up the slightly easier angled wall until (bolt with long sling) the groove steepens up and some harrowing bridging is required to reach the sanctuary of a cave. It is possible to hide a while in here but glory lies only a short distance away around to the left. Don't worry about falling off - you won't hit anything.

20. QUE DIOS REPARTE SUERTE ☺ 7c 25m
A mighty pitch up the smoothest part of the wall, well protected but with a desperate starting sequence. Fierce moves on pinch grips pockets and the odd chopped dink lead up the leaning

lower wall to a big bolt on the easier angled 'slab' above. Lower off this or continue by easier quality pocket climbing until a belay on the slab above can be reached.

21. LUBRICANTE VAGINAL EN UNO 7a 15m
A delightfully named piece of climbing that takes the obscenely angled wall to the right followed by the butch layback above. Start below and left of the base of the flake crack at a rightward rising line of bolts. A couple of desperate moves (or a large cairn, 6b) using the feature the route is named after lead to ledges and then to the first decent pocket. The rest of the route is just plain hard work. Follow the bolts strenuously to the base of the flake. Continue up this until it is possible to swing right to a lowering bolt.

The final route in this area lies 100m further into the dragon's lair where the walls close in and a slabby rib on the left (just below a huge chockstone) gives a way through the initial barrier of overhangs.

22. ABDUL ♦ 7b 25m
A route with an impact considerably greater than its length might suggest. Climb the slabby rib then move slightly right to reach a pockety crack leading leftwards. From the end of this a swine of a move gains the slab on the left and a rest. When suitably recovered swing around the undercut corner on to a leaning pocketed wall which is climbed leftward to another difficult exit onto another slab. The final obstacle is the 3m roof with the belays dangling tantalisingly from the lip. Go for it.

High on the wall opposite ABDUL is an obvious but inaccessible bolt protected layback crack, which may be 6b+, and to the left of this is a long groove that runs up to the final section of VIA BOULDER. This is GEDE 5+. No further details are known.

SIERRA DE TOIX

The Sierra de Toix is the long rocky ridge that runs eastwards from the low point of the gorge of the Barranco de Mascarat, to disappear into the sea as the rocky headland of Toix East. The northern side of the ridge is the site of the Maryvilla complex, an extensive sprawl of impressive white walled villas that are scattered over almost every available piece of land, irrespective of angle. Attempted pronunciation of 'Toix' has caused some amusement to the local Spaniards - it turns out not to be a north country sounding 'Twax' or a French sounding Twaah, but is in fact a very Spanish 'Toysch', so now you know!

Character

Five cliffs are described, with Toix East and West offering short, open and well-protected routes that are easy of access and often of a reasonable grade on perfect rough rock. The Toix Sea Cliff/South are rather more serious and a little trickier of access, but they are well worth the effort. Toix North is a shady retreat from the searing sun. It contains some short sharp pitches by the road and some sterner stuff on the smooth white walls of the upper crag. Toix TV is the open south facing bowl of rock close to the antennae on the highest point of the hill. It offers generally hard climbs in a sunny setting. On the Sierra de Toix climbing can be enjoyed in the sun at any time of the day with just a little forethought. Access is described separately for each cliff.

TOIX SEA CLIFF/SOUTH FACE
(RACO DEL CORV & CANDELABROS DEL SOL)

Crag Facts

Star Rating: **

Aspect: south and west facing

Height: Up to 55 metres

Spread of grades:

4	5	5+	6a	6b	6c	7a	7b	7c	8
	1		5	1	3	1	2		1

Introduction

A large impressive crag that rises as the name suggests straight from the sea. Some of the rock is a rather strange red/brown colour and looks dangerously loose. It is mostly well-cemented and the cliff gives some impressive pitches. In atmosphere and angle it is somewhat similar to the 'gentleman's side' of Huntsman's Leap.

The south face gets the sun all day whereas the west face is in the sun from shortly after midday until sunset. It is a beautiful place to spend the evening, but make sure you are back down the abseils before darkness finally falls.

Crag Geography

The cliff is divided into two faces by the spectacular arete of MISSING LINK. The extensive south facing cliff rises straight from the sea and is approached from above whereas the west facing wall overlooking the bay is approached from the beach.

Access

There are two ways of getting to the boulder beach that allows access to the left end of the crag.

Firstly it is possible to walk from the parking place below Toix West by following the track down the hillside. As this peters out head to the right (facing the sea) across old quarried terraces until rough scrambling leads to the beach.

Secondly and more easily drive south on the N332 through the tunnels of the Mascarat Gorge and take the first tarmacked left turn, signed Pueblo Mascarat and Sol Ingrid (1km from the tunnels). Follow the road down the hill and over a dried up stream bed (the parking for the Mascarat Gorge) to a junction. Turn left and park on the left after a couple of hundred metres. From the parking place cross the "boulder field" and follow a rough track down across old terraces to the boulder beach and the foot of the cliff.

Descent

Most of the climbs finish on the conspicuous slanting rake that runs across the top of the crag. This can be followed up to the left to escape onto easy ground above the crag, but this is exposed and a little loose - not recommended. It is also possible to climb straight up from several points on the terrace to reach the top of the crag (easy but no fixed gear). The best and safest option is to abseil back to the beach from the rake. Almost directly above the beach is a bunch of threads on the rake; a 30m abseil from these leads over an overhang to the end of a ledge. Move left (looking in) to more anchors that allow a 35m abseil back to the beach.

The routes are described from left to right.

SOMBRA ☺ 7b 55m
A superb thin crack forms the main substance of this route though it is unfortunately somewhat hacked around. Carry a few small wires if you are feeling less than bold as the bolts are relatively spaced.

1. 25m 3 From the beach traverse to the right a short distance above the water to a rounded crack (bolt). Go up this then continue the traverse (bolt) to gain a good ledge and triple bolt belay.
2. 30m 7b To the left of the stance a thin crack soars up the smooth wall. This gives superb sustained finger jamming and laybacking on near frictionless rock. Eventually it is possible to swing left on better holds where the rock starts to bulge and strenuous jug pulling leads eventually to a two bolt lower-off.

MUNE ☺ 7b 75m
Directly above the stance at the end of pitch one of SOMBRE is a smooth leaning wall with a line of bolts up it.

1. 25m 3 As for the previous climb.
2. 30m 7b Trend left up the wall following the line of flakes by sustained strenuous climbing then head straight up to eventually reach the lower-off on the previous route.

ELDORADO 1 ♦ 6a+ 77m
A magnificent intimidating line, strenuous but well protected up the red chimney crack in the centre of the face. Fully equipped, though some of the gear is now rather old.

1. 25m 3 As for pitch one of SOMBRA to the triple bolt belay.
2. 30m 6a+ Climb up to the right to reach the first bolt that is passed awkwardly on the right by steep moves to gain a niche in the base of the chimney proper. The overhanging section above is bridged with ample protection from bolts and threads until a few strenuous pulls on good but "funny" hold lead to a gripping hanging stance on two large threads and a couple of pegs.
3. 22m 5+ From the stance climb steeply leftwards on sloping holds to a peg and slightly higher an obvious thread. Now climb up the centre of the fine grey slab above, a great contrast to the butch goings on below. A peg and thread belay are reached on the rake.

ELDORADO 2 ☺ 6a 75m
The bulging wall to the right of the chimney

crack of ELDORADO gives a strenuous piece of climbing, with good protection and good but often spaced holds.

1. 25m 3 As for pitch one of SOMBRA to the three bolt stance. If this is crowded it is possible to belay 10m further to the right directly below the line of the route, at the end of an old fixed rope that runs out to the arete.

2. 30m 6a From the start of the fixed rope climb up the steep wall to ledges below a line of bulges. Either climb straight over these, butch, or bear out right then back left, marginally less butch, to reach a hanging stance 5m right of ELDORADO 1. Although this pitch is given a lower grade than that of its nearby parent it is in fact a considerably tougher pitch!

3. 20m 5+ The obvious line leading steeply rightwards leads strenuously to the rake, no fixed gear. Alternately traverse horizontally left to join and finish up the parent route.

At the time of writing the impressive wall to the right is inviolate, though there is plenty of scope.

The impressive arete of the cliff is home to two exciting climbs:

VIA MISSING LINK ♦ 6a+ 95m

An atmospheric pitch with a long approach up the impressive arete of the crag gives a superb expedition very reminiscent of Gogarth adventure climbs. Carry a few medium nuts and Friends, a UK grade of E3 5c is about right.

1. 25m 3 As for pitch one of SOMBRA to the three bolt stance.

2. 35m 5 Descend the rock fall scar (where a large flake used to be) to the right of the belay until just above the water line (peg) then traverse easily on good holds but without much protection until things get a little tougher. Awkward moves up to the right lead to a descending line of jugs that are followed to a hanging stance on two rusty bolts. A fall from this pitch by leader or second may not prove fatal but will certainly 'dampen their enthusiasm' for the rest of the

route.

The tatty fixed rope at the stance is useful for keeping the climbing ropes out of the water and provides a scary escape route if problems arise.

3. 45m 6a+ Climb the slabby wall above the stance to steeper rock and some insubstantial threads. Continue up a flake crack just to the right of the arete until it is possible to pull back leftwards onto the very prow. Now follow a line just to the right of the arete (threads) into the final groove which is bridged to the rake. A superb pitch but don't look down.

From the stance on the rake it is possible to climb the flake above in three pitches 4,4,5 (see LUCES NOCTURNAS below) or traverse to the left up the rake for 100m to get back to the beach as described under DESCENT. A third option is to descend the narrow rake (keeping the rope on) to the right for 30m to a bolt belay at the foot a wall that is taken by LE GALLEON 6a (see below) thus giving an excellent five or six pitch tour of the crag.

LUCES NOCTURNAS ☺ 6a 165m

Another major expedition that (sensibly?) avoids the very arete of the cliff by heading out onto the right wall. Carry a light rack. Retreat would involve a wetting after pitch 2.

1&2. 59m As for MISSING LINK to the belay by the arete of the cliff.

3. 25m 5 Climb the slabby wall above the stance to steeper rock and some insubstantial threads then move round the corner and climb the wall trending rightwards passing occasional pieces of fixed kit to reach a shallow cave stance. Retreat is now problematical!

4. 25m 6a Exit rightwards from the cave then climb the wall above to reach the rake. It is also possible to exit leftwards from the cave and trend to the left to join the spectacular upper section of MISSING LINK.

Escape up the rake to the left followed by the abseil to the beach is possible from here. Alternatively:

5. 20m 4 Climb the flake crack that runs up the right side of the arete to ledges.
6. 20m 4 Continue in the same line to a belay at the top of the flake system.
7. 15m 5 The corner is climbed to the cliff top passing a short steepening 'en route'.

Descent
Scramble up and left then loop round old terraces to get back to the parking area.

Toix South is the kilometre of rock that runs from the great arete of MISSING LINK to Toix East. It bears a resemblance to Great Zawn on the Little Orme but unlike its Welsh counterpart this crag gets the sun all day. Much of it is undercut at the base and development is still in its infancy.

The top of the cliff is most easily reached by walking down the track from the parking place below Toix West. Access to the routes is by abseil from above where the names and the length of rope required are painted on the rock. Top roping the climbs is an obvious possibility.

The first route described is reached by a 40m abseil from a point about 30m to the left of the arete (looking out to sea) using anchors in a slab just below the cliff edge. Look for the name on the rock.

LE GALLEON ☺ 6a 35m
Climb straight back up the grey wall on exceptionally rough rock following the line of bolts and threads and the occasional chiselled hold to a horizontal break. Continue up easier angled smoother rock avoiding easier ground on both sides. It is possible to split the pitch at half height on a large flake to the right, bolt and large thread belay.

To the left (looking out) are two further routes, the right one is 6b and the left one is 6c though no further details are known.

There has been some development in the centre of the south face of the Sea Cliff where a series of old fishermen's ladders (or more sensibly an abseil) allows access to ledges well above the sea. There is a lot of scope here though some of the rock is a bit unusual.

Approaches
From the car park for Toix West follow the track to its end then pick up a line of cairns and a vague track that descends gently eastwards across the hillside. After crossing a shallow valley the path zigzags down then continues in the same direction to a point by some large blocks and below the centre of a scooped yellow cliff. There are two reinforcing rods in the rock here that provide the anchors for a series of old fishermen's ladders. Abseil descent advised. About 15 minutes from the car.

To the left of the foot of the ladders are three climbs about which I have no details. These are from right to left the impressive tufa encrusted overhanging groove of CANDELABROS DEL SOL 8a (two pitches), the wall and arete of THE FLAME 7a+ (two pitches) and the wall of RAPTURED DREAMS 6c. The state of the in situ gear on these routes is not known.

MAGICAL MYSTERY TOUR ☺ 5 180m for the round trip.
A bizarre but engaging trip into some wild and wonderful places. The climbing is technically reasonable but the fixed protection is sparse and some of the rock is slightly 'unfriendly', thus a UK grade of E1 5a might be felt appropriate. Take a few wires, a lot of care and a strong sense of adventure.

1. 35m Abseil or get top roped down the line of rotting wood and free hanging rusting iron ladders to large ledges above sea level. If you solo down the ladders award yourself an E6 tick and a visit to a therapist.
2. 75m Traverse easily left facing the cliff, below a lot of impressive scenery. An 'exposed rib' is passed and eventually a 5m high corner is reached. Bridge up this and move left to a bay. Nut and thread belays in the back of this. If you have not already put the ropes on, now is the time.
3. 20m 5 Traverse left past two old pegs to round 'a more exposed rib' and gain a bay (bolt). Continue traversing a little way until a larger bay and two bolt belay can be gained by a steep pull.

4. 25m 5 Trend up and right past a bolt to an 'even more exposed rib' which is climbed awkwardly to easier ground and another bolt. Continue up and right below steeper rock to a single bolt belay in a cosy bay.

5. 25m 5 Step left onto the 'wildly exposed rib' (bolt) and climb steeply to a bay. Head up and right into a shallow corner with a jammed block and exit right onto the 'ridiculous exposed rib'. The cliff top is just above and there are thread belays in a big boulder 15m back.

TOIX WEST

Crag Facts

Star rating: **

Aspect: west facing

Height: Up to 100 metres

Spread of grades:

4	5	5+	6a	6b	6c	7a	7b	7c	8
8	8	5	3	2	1		1		

Introduction

An easy accessible cliff that provides an excellent selection of routes some of which are of quite a respectable length. The left side of the cliff provides steeper pitches while around to the right the angle is rather more amenable. Quality climbs can be found throughout. The rock is perfect and bolts abound. The right side of the crag gets the sun from midday whereas the left side is only in the sun in the evening, so you can get scorched or climb in the shade according to personal preference and prevailing weather conditions. Since first describing these routes in 1990 no names have come to light so the vast majority of the climbs are still recognised by the colour of the bolts. This makes for easy route recognition but boring pub talk.

Crag Geography

The cliff is basically a broad rib of rock, easy angled on the right but becoming steeper around to the left where it rears up into an impressive orange bay. The main section of the cliff is bound on the right by a gully and across this is a recently developed wall with a selection of short easy routes, ideal for the newcomer to sport climbing.

Access

The cliff is reached from the Maryvilla complex that is at the southern end of the bay at Calpe. From Calpe go out on to the N332 and head south towards Alicante for about 1km. Just as the road begins to descend into the Mascarat Gorge, at a right-hand bend, turn left into the villa complex (signed Urbanisacion Maryvilla) through an impressive archway. Coming from the south it is the first right turn after the Mascarat Gorge, situated where the road begins to flatten out. It is easy to overshoot the junction from this direction.

Once in the complex take the first three right turns. The narrow road leads steeply uphill and over a brow to an adequate parking space at the end of the tarmac. Please do not block access to any of the properties. The cliff is an obvious two minutes away.

The routes are described from left to right. Descents are described after each route.

1. THE YELLOW ROUTE 5- 100m

A long climb that leads to the top of the cliff though it can be abandoned at several points on route. It contains little fixed kit and some of the climbing has a very bold feel about it on rock that is not perfect. Carry a rack and take care! Start at the left edge of the cliff.

1. 25m 4 Climb the steep lower section to easier angled rock that is taken left then right to a good ledge and belay.

2. 25m 5- The steep wall behind the stance is taken direct on (mostly) good holds to a ledge and single bolt belay. The crux over and done with the ground can be reached by a 45m abseil, but true mountaineers will

Toix West

1. THE YELLOW ROUTE 5-
2. THE SILVER ROUTE ☺ 5+
3. THE GREEN ROUTE ☺ 6a
4. BACK ROUTE ☺ 7a+
5. RED ROUTE DIRECT ☺ 6c
6. THE RED ROUTE ✍ 6a+
7. THE BLACK ROUTE ☺ 6b
8. ANOTHER GREEN ROUTE ☺ 5
9. A NEW ROUTE ☺ 4+
10. THE SLABBY RED ROUTE ☺ 5
11. THE BLUE ROUTE ☺ 5+
12. DIRE STRAITS ☺ 5+

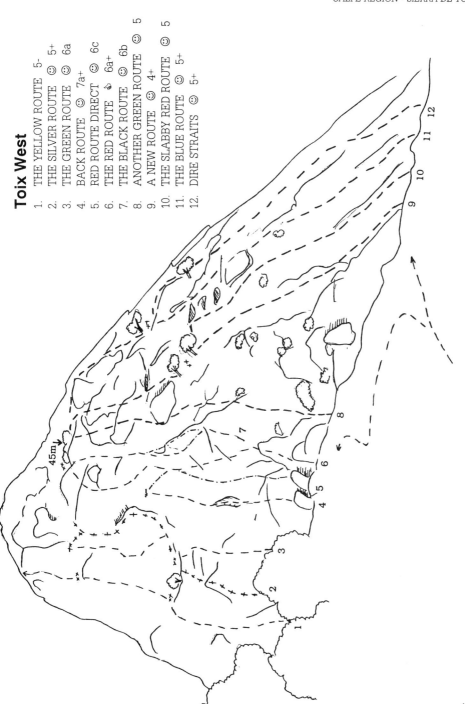

want to press on.

3. 20m 4 Move out to the left to find the easiest line which is followed up and then back to the right to another excellent stance. A more direct version of the pitch is 5.
4. 30m 3 Follow the crest of the ridge easily to the top.

Descent

Either abseil 40m down the north side of the ridge or easier on the brain and harder on the feet follow the crest of the ridge to the east until easy scrambling leads down to the right (south) and back below the cliff.

The next five routes take the walls of the steep bowl that form the left side of the main cliff.

2. THE SILVER ROUTE ☺ 5+ 45m

A rather devious climb that takes the easiest line up a steep piece of rock.

Start in the back left corner of the bay below a niche.

1. 20m 5+ Make a couple of steep moves in to the niche and pull quickly out rightward (crux, UK 5c?). Follow steep rock up to the left past bolts and a peg over a small roof, avoiding the easy corner on the left. At the tree move right to a small stance and multi-bolt belay.
2. 25m 5+ Trend up and right to gain the conspicuous leftward leaning corner that is followed awkwardly to an easy groove. This leads to a good stance and single bolt belay.

Descent

Either abseil 45m directly to the ground from the belay, or more safely traverse 15m to the right to the tree and belays above THE RED ROUTE from where a 45m abseil leads back to the ground.

3. THE GREEN ROUTE ☺ 6a 45m

Two excellent steep pitches with "bomber gear" allowing the experience to be enjoyed to the full.

Start at a short rightward rising ramp in the back of the bay.

1. 20m 6a From the top of the ramp (often wet) swing awkwardly up to the left to gain a series of flakes that rise to the right. These lead steeply to a semi-rest at a break. Pull rightward onto the steep wall and follow improving holds to below a bulge. Despite appearances to the contrary good holds do exist on the wall above allowing a swing left to be made to the stance on the SILVER ROUTE.
2. 25m 6a Step right and attack the steep wall above. A difficult swing left on tiny holds allows access to good flakes that are followed to the steep but easy groove above. This leads to a large stance and bolt belay.

Descent

As for the SILVER ROUTE.

4. BACK ROUTE ☺ 7a+ 25m

A good route, the hardest on the cliff. Start in the back of the bay, from the tip of a flake where a line of new bolts runs straight up a red scoop. Climb tufas into the scoop, bridge up this then climb the wall with escalating difficulty using a sequence of tiny undercuts followed by a final tricky section to reach a lower-off in a hollow.

5. RED ROUTE DIRECT ☺ 6c 25/45m

Starting from the flake again, the steep wall to the right of the shallow groove is climbed with difficulty in its central section, then follow a thin flake crack to join the next route. Finish more easily up this, or lower off as for the previous climb.

6. THE RED ROUTE ☙ 6a+ 45m

A magnificent varied pitch up the right edge of the bay. Quite hard for the grade but with exemplary protection, 15 quick draws should suffice but watch the rope drag. The lower-off recently established above BACK ROUTE (see above) can be reached from above the crux of the climb, and the ground reached from here, though it is much more satisfying to press on!

Start at the right toe of the bay at a 6m high pillar just right of two large fallen flakes.

Climb the pillar and continue (BLACK bolt

on the right if required) to the first red bolt, difficult moves into and out of the niche above may be the crux for many. The steeper flake above leads to a thin move where the angle changes as does the style of climbing. Teeter up the ramp to the left until all appears lost. Extemporise 1m left to a jug then head up to the right crossing the "blank" slab on a well-hidden slot to easier but steep climbing. A good ledge above has a bolt and thread belay.

Descent
One long or two short abseils lead back to the ground.

7. THE BLACK ROUTE ☺ 6b 45m
A good route rather spoilt by the out of character nature of the crux section. This can be avoided by the groove to its right which makes the overall grade a more balanced ☺ 6a. Start as for THE RED ROUTE.

Climb the pillar as for THE RED ROUTE, then continue slightly rightward up the steep wall to an easier angled section. Step left onto the smooth face and make fingery and committing moves up and left to a bolt. Step back to the right then climb straight up easier angled rock, passing a small scar (small scare?) with difficulty. Continue in a direct line via more thin moves passing to the right of a big detached block to arrive at the tree and belay of THE RED ROUTE. Descend as for THE RED ROUTE.

8. ANOTHER GREEN ROUTE ☺ 5 50m
An excellent pitch recently equipped with new bolts but still containing some interesting relics from the Iron Age. Start at a rounded groove just to the right of the pillar at the start of the RED and BLACK routes.

Climb the right side of the groove and the thin crack above to reach the base of a superb slab. Up this to its apex then follow the diagonal crack to its top. Possible belay to the right. Make a difficult move onto the wall then trend right to the huge flake system up which the route finishes. The difficult wall can be avoided by climbing the wide crack, containing two large wedges, farther to the right.

DESCENT is by a 45m abseil from a bolt and large thread.

The next routes lie at the lowest point of the crag where the rock is much slabbier.
RUTA DIEZ 4 45m
A pleasant route though with no fixed gear. Carry a rack.
Start just around the rib below a long detached pillar about 7m up.
1. 20m 3 Climb to the left of the pillar and move right into a white groove. Up this to a belay on a huge block.
2. 25m 4 Continue up the line of the groove to ledges and the belay at the top of the RIGHT-HAND RED ROUTE. Descend around to the right or by abseil.

9. A NEW ROUTE ☺ 4+ 20m
Start at the left side of the slab tackled by the next climb where there is a groove with well-disguised bolts to its right. Climb the slab by sustained moves to a tree belay, labelled R1. Lower from here, or belay and continue up the next route.

10. THE SLABBY RED ROUTE ☺ 5 50m
An interesting lower pitch leads to easier exposed climbing above. Start at the bottom of the slab at a line of red spots, hoping they are not contagious.
1. 20m 5 Follow the line as closely as possible; it is rather easier to the right of the bolts, passing the occasional "red herring" to a juggy bulge and a good stance. (R1).
2. 30m 5 Step left and plod up the open corner to a large detached flake. Step gingerly over this and move left into a bulging corner which leads to easy ground. The abseil point for the RED and BLACK ROUTES lies 10m to the left.

11. THE BLUE ROUTE ☺ 5+ 50m
Rather tougher than its near neighbours.
1. 20m 5+ Straight up the slabby wall following the appropriate colour coded bolts over a bulge to a stance slightly above that of the previous route.

2. 30m 5+ Above lies a bulging corner crack whose bark is worse than its bite, though it is no pushover. Romp up this to a swing round the final obstacle to easy ledges. The DESCENT is as for the previous route.

12. DIRE STRAITS ☺ 5+ 20m

Distinguished from the other routes in this area by having a name but not by much else. The start is rather obvious.

Climb up to the right to pass the Bonsai tree. The steep section above is easier than it looks, just tear up the dotted line. Traverse left to the belay of the previous route and abseil from here or continue up the BLUE ROUTE.

ANOTHER NEW ROUTE ☺ 4 60m

1. 30m 4 Start at lowest point of the right side of the cliff and climb rib to first bolt just right of the DIRE STRAITS tree. Pull over the bulge from the left and continue up walls and a groove to a stance.
2. 30m 3+ A corner above the stance leads to easier ground. Abseil descent or scramble up then walk off to the right.

The next climbs described lie around to the right and up the bank slightly in a bowl, a real sun trap in the afternoon and evening.

THE RIGHT-HAND RED ROUTE ☺ 5+ 20m

This route climbs a thin crack in a rib and gives pleasant if somewhat brief exercise. Start below the crack. Gain the crack via a couple of thin moves (or by the indirect start just to the right 5c) and follow it past several peg runners with surprising difficulty, until the rib on the right can be gained. This leads easily to a lowering point.

The final climbs in this area are located in the back of the bowl shaped area.

THE GREEN ROUTE ☺ 5+ 45m

Start at a pedestal/flake below a groove. A pleasantly delicate exercise, with a rather poorly protected left-hand top pitch (carry a few middle to large Rocks).

1. 25m 5+ From the top of the pedestal climb

thinly rightwards to get into the groove. Continue passing several pegs to gain and follow a crack that leads to the stance in a small niche, peg and bolt belay.

2. 20m Either, 5, in contrast to the pitch below climb the chimney groove above the stance (pegs) to a bolt belay,

or, 5+ in keeping with the pitch below move left and climb the delicate face to reach the same stance.

Descent

A 45m abseil from the belay will take you back to the ground.

EL MENU DEL DIA ☺ 6b or 5 45m

Slabby climbing on perfect rock with an element of choice.

Start at a deep rounded groove with a line of faded pink (very twee) bolts. Follow the groove until it steepens and things begin to look rather grim (at the last chain link bolt). Holiday makers and those in search of an easy time should make unobvious moves out right into a groove that is followed back left. Hot shots should continue left and make thin moves to a finger jug before swinging back right to regain the previous variation. From the meeting of the ways easier climbing leads up the rib to a good stance on the left reached by a short traverse.

Descent

A 40m abseil, or an awkward scramble up and then down to the right. The former is preferable except for those who suffer from a fear of heights.

THE BLACK ROUTE ☺ 5 35m

A rather sombre colour for a very pleasant pitch. Start up the slabby rib to the right of the bowl. Easy angled climbing past a possible stance at 15m leads up the crest of the ridge passing a second potential stance into a corner until a traverse leads left to the belay and a descent as for the previous climb. If the route is done in one pitch 12 quick-draws plus belay gear are needed.

Some distance up the hillside to the right of the

main crag is a conspicuous grey slab of perfect rock reached by an arduous 10 minute scramble. It contains two short routes that are worth seeking out if the main crag is crowded.

LEFT LINE 6a 20m
Climb up to the prominent bolt in the centre of the slab and pass it with difficulty. Continue in the same line to another bolt and a little higher a lowering station.

RIGHT LINE 5 20m
Follow a curving undercut flake up to the right to the bolt on its lip. Keep heading in the same direction to gain a slanting crack that leads back to the left (threads) to a belay.

TOIX FAR WEST

To the right of the main cliff and the gully used to reach the above two routes is a low wall of quality rock. This appears to have been used for top roping some years ago and there are still the numbers 1 to 6 painted in faded orange writing along its base. Recently the best looking lines have been bolted with 10mm 'Fixe' parabolts and the area now offers some quality lower grade routes that provide an excellent introduction to the clipping game. I have taken the liberty of making up the names of the routes.
LA ROJA UNA 3 15m
Start by the number '1' painted on the rock and climb the rib on excellent rock past seven bolt runners.

ASOMBROSO ☺ 3 15m
Four metres to the right of and slightly lower than the red '1' climb the amazingly fluted slab. Seven bolt runners.

COSTILLA 4 17m
Three metres right again follow rather less convoluted rock to a tricky move just below the chains. Six bolt runners.

LA ROJA DOS 4 17m
Start by the red '2' and climb straight up above this following the line of least resistance. Seven bolt runners.

BELLA RUTA ☺ 4+ 18m
Start 2m right of the red '2' and climb directly up the steep slab. Seven bolts and possibly the best of the bunch.

OCHO FIXE ☺ 4+ 18m
Start just left of a corner and climb direct passing eight bolt runners.

Ten metres to the right a red '3' is painted on a small flat topped pillar below a steeper shield of rock.

LA ROJA TRES 5 15m
Climb to peg in an indefinite crack and make a reachy pull leftwards past a thread to a ring-peg in a scoop. Continue past another peg and a bolt to twin bolt lower-off.

Seven metres to the right is a red '4' painted on the rock, though the line is not equipped. Traditionalists can form a queue here. Twenty metres right again is a large rock leaning against the face with a red '5' painted on it. Again the line is not equipped so if you are bored with waiting for '4' this may be the one for you. To the right is a cave/gully with slabby right wall. On its left side is a line of four bolts climbing past a small elephant's head, and not equipped with a lower-off. No grade known.
On the slabby right wall is a red '6' painted on the rock and starting at this is:
LA ROJA SEIS 5 10m
Climb the slab past bolts and pegs to a missing lower-off where a belay on a flake can be taken. Abseil descent from this, leave a sling.

TOIX NORTH

Crag Facts

Star rating: ** (for the Upper Cliff!)
Aspect: north east facing
Height: 10 to 28 metres
Spread of grades:

4	5	5+	6a	6b	6c	7a	7b	7c	8
				2	3	4		1	

Introduction

The smart white walls that overlook the Maryvilla complex are largely undeveloped. The exception to this is the tall white wall (PARED BLANCA) high on the right and a shorter cliff (PARED DE LA TUBERIA) directly below and rising straight from the tarmac of a minor road. A crag that is in the shade for most of the day and as such can prove useful 'when the heat is on.' Those who want to do these routes while they are in the sun will have, to get up early in the morning. The climbs on the lower cliff are short, on rough rock, and some of the bolts are rather elderly. Those on the upper cliff are longer, are on much smoother rock and the bolts here are sometimes a bit spaced. These climbs can be done to the belays and back to the ground on a 50m rope, but only just.

Crag Geography

Rising from the road is the short wide PARED DE LA TUBERIA, whilst directly above this is the steep smooth PARED BLANCA.

Access

The routes are to be found on and near the conspicuous large white wall at the right end of the long line of rock that fringes the upper edge of the whole of the north side of the Sierra de Toix. The highest villa on stilts is also a landmark. From the entrance to the Maryvilla complex take the first two right turns (as for Toix West) and bear left at the third junction. The road is followed, passing a right turn to a fork; follow the right branch and take the next right turn. The road contours back along the hillside and

then bends sharply back to the left before ending by the previously mentioned villa. There is room to turn and park here or on the apex of the last bend. The PARED DE LA TUBERIA is the bulging red wall you have just driven past, the PARED BLANCA is the big white face directly above and is reached in two minutes by a small diagonal path from the left. The PARED DE LA TUBERIA is described first, from left to right.

WARNING

Along the foot of the crag runs a water pipe that supplies the villas below. Unfortunately all of the routes use it to get started, please treat it gently.

Pared De La Tuberia

LA NINA 6b+ 10m
Starting to the left of the undercut base of the crag pass the first bolt by some difficult moves to reach a diagonal crack. Using finger jams in this, rock out right to reach much easier climbing and the 'hook' lower-off.

LA NOVIA 6b 10m
Start directly below the belay bolts. Climb into a depression and exit from it slightly rightwards using a good but discrete side-pull. A couple more tricky moves lead to the anchor.

LA VIULA 6c 10m
The right-hand line has an awkward undercut start requiring a short sharp pull on short sharp holds. The scoop above is trivial by comparison.

PINON 7a 12m
This route starts by ascending to the prominent large hole, lean left from this and launch onto the wall. Good but spaced holds lead to the last protection bolt, from here levitate to the belay.

The other two routes on the lower crag are found a short distance down the road to the right at an undercut scoop that has a back wall covered in flowstone. Names have not been forthcoming.

RIGHT ROUTE LEFT 7a+ 20m
Start at the left side of the scoop and pull rightwards over the bulge. Continue with difficulty to reach a hole then follow a wiggling crack to much better holds at the break. The upper bulges are passed on exceptionally sharp holds. For those with thick skin the belay is not far away!

RIGHT ROUTE RIGHT 7a 20m
The right-hand line of bolts is followed on good but spaced jugs until a difficult move up a scoop leads to the break. The steep upper section is taken leftwards to the lowering bolts.

Pared Blanca

The upper crag contains four routes, three of which now have rather old bolts. A fixed caving rope runs along top of wall linking all the lower-offs and providing a gripping way of fixing top ropes on the various routes.

LEFT WALL 7a+ 25m
A slabby start passing an in situ sling leads to tough white wall, then on through bulges to a lower-off at the left end of the fixed rope.

POR QUIEN DOBLON LAS ESQUINES ☺ 7b+ 25m
A steep tough pitch that starts at the name painted in neat green lettering. Trend slightly rightwards up the wall following old black bolts on up a slab to a flake. Above this is the desperately smooth crux white wall and beyond here more flakes to the lower-off.

CENTRAL WALL ♦ 7a 27m
The intimidating line up the steepest section of the wall, fortunately it has been rebolted with 10mm parabolts. This route is worth a special visit to the crag. Climb a shrubby slab and hidden flake (unprotected but straightforward) to reach the first bolt, then climb steeper rock to a hole. Continue with more difficulty (crux) before trending slightly left then back right to jugs. A final few reachy moves to the left gain the lowering bolts.

To the right is a brown streaked groove that bears a passing resemblance to the ORIGINAL ROUTE at High Tor. It is unclimbed.

S.S. ☺ 7a 25m
Another excellent pitch that takes the thin pockety seam to the right of the central groove line. Gain the bulge at the bottom of the seam by climbing past a prominent peg. A couple of fierce pulls through the bulge gains better holds, above this the crack gives fine sustained climbing until it is possible to swing left to easier rock. The belays are just above.

To the right is more undeveloped rock that could provide several worthwhile climbs at an amenable grade and beyond this is the left bounding arete of Toix West.

TOIX TV

Crag Facts

Star rating: ***
Aspect: south facing
Height: Up to 50 metres
Spread of grades:

4	5	5+	6a	6b	6c	7a	7b	7c	8
6	3	4	7	3	3	5	2	2	1

Introduction

High up the hillside above the gully to the right of Toix West is a steep sided south facing bowl of red rock flanked to left and right by areas of pleasant grey slabs. The whole area can be a real furnace in the middle of the day and is perhaps best visited in the cool of evening. It contains a

Toix TV

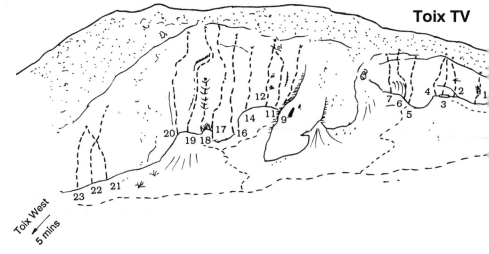

number of impressive routes in the main bowl and some lesser fare on the grey slabby walls that run away to both sides.

Access

The cliff can be reached from Toix West in about 15 minutes via the gully and scrubby slopes to its right. Alternatively and somewhat more pleasantly follow the directions to Toix West to the third junction. Keep left and follow the road to a fork. The right branch leads out to the headland (superb views) and then round to a small parking space by the antennae on top of the hill. Leave nothing in the car. The main section of the crag is just out of sight 5 minutes' scramble (descend a short distance first) away over rough ground, following vague tracks and

occasional cairns. The right-hand section of the cliff can be reached more directly by following painted red circles and cairns along a rough rocky band, all the routes are described from right to left. The first eight climbs look rather inconsequential but the best of these are worth doing:

1. BANANA JOE 6b+ 15m
The short sharp line on the far right, climb the wall passing a bolt to the base of a hanging corner then follow the arrow passing a thread to the lower-off.

2. DEAR RENATE 6a 22m
To the left start at the base of a ramp, climb through a zone of pockets (peg) and on up the

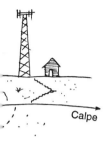

slab above passing three well spaced bolts and a big loose flake to a single bolt lower-off.

3. TROPICAL DREAMS ☺ 6a 22m
The clean slab above the 'art-work' is climbed rightwards with an awkward start (peg) and spaced bolts. At the top move blindly right or do a more difficult (6a+) direct finish to a double lower-off on a ledge below the ridge crest.

4. UB 40 ☺ 5+ 22m
The left side of the clean slab is climbed passing a thread, a red peg and a couple of bolts. If in doubt follow the arrows.

To the left is perhaps the area's best feature, the 'wellcome' sun-bathing slab then a short scramble down leads to a bay with four harder climbs:

5. GAUDI MAX ☺ 6b 20m
Follow the line of five bolts slightly right at first and the direct up the right side of the face.

6. SALIDA ☺ 7a 22m
Start just to the left and climb right then trend strenuously left and up to slab. This is still hard but is thankfully at least delicate. Seven bolts protect.

7. FOLLOW ME ☺ 7a+ 20m
Left again pulling through the overhangs with difficulty then on up the steep rock above, a fine strenuous pitch.

8. TERMINATOR 6c+ 25m
Start on the left and climb past a couple of bolts to a horizontal crack (thread). Continue up the steep slab then trend right all the way to the lower-off above SALIDA.

The next routes are around to the left in the red large bay and are reached by descending to pass a rocky rib (climbed by the unprepossessing BLACK ADDER 5) and then scrambling back into the bay.

9. CHUNKIES 5 18m
The rightmost bolt line in the top corner of the bay has closely spaced home made bolts and a big thread.

10. NUT ROUTE 5+ (E2 5b) 20m
In back right corner of bay climb up into the well cleaned groove. At its top go left then right to fixed belays; wires will be required if you want to make the route's second ascent!

11. CHAIN LANE ☺ 6a 20m
To the left is a line of spaced chain link bolt runners, follow these via intricate climbing (the big new 'proper' bolt by the crux is very welcome) then trend up and left towards the lower-offs which are reached over an awkward shrubby bulge.

12. GRIPPER ☺ 6a+ 20m
The direct version of the above through the scoops is quite a lot harder though just as good (and the bolts are better), the crucial central bulge can be tackled to left or right.

To the left is a smooth grey slab with some very thin routes, OK if you like that kind of thing!

13. DYNOSAURUS ☺ 7a+ 18m
The right-hand line, devious and reachy.

14. MONGOOSE ☺ 7b 20m
Central line is tackled direct from a bolt belay, gives fiercely fingery climbing.

15. MAX HEADROOM 7c 20m
The left-hand of three smooth lines in back of bay is apparently possible, though it doesn't look it!

To the left in the centre of the bay is a dusty hollow, two good routes start here.

16. PAINTED WALL ☺ 6c 30m
Step out right and climb the rough slab (no protection but not very hard) to a possible stance at the change of angle), then follow the right-hand line up the steep wall, passing right of the bulges to a lower-off on a ledge.

17. MONKEY WALL ♦ 7a 40m
1. 20m 6c Bridge up the back of the hollow to a thread then swing right to a couple of bolts. Make one difficult pull on spiky holds to gain the rugged slab, amble up this to a thread and bolt belay, or press on.
2. 20m 7a Step right and pull back left in to a hollow, before climbing steeply up and then right to reach a flowstone pillar. Move up and right on a horn and cross the bulge on spaced finger jugs. Easier climbing leads to the final steep crack which can be avoided (lower-off below it) but should be included for the full tick.

18. OMBRA ☺ 5+ 23m
A pleasant pitch up left side of bay directly below largest overhang gives steep sustained climbing.

19. COBRA ♦ 7b,7c,8a 50m
The 'super route' up the back left corner of the bay is apparently as good as it is hard. The first pitch is worth doing in its own right, ☺ 15m.

20. SCORPION 6b,7a+ 45m
The tall flake near the left edge of the bay and the long rib above leads to belay. Traverse right into steep groove to find the sting in the tail. A little loose and not too well bolted.

Around the rib to the left are two long climbs that have never proved popular: on the right is BALDRICK 6a,5+ 45m, whilst to the left is BLACK AND WHITE 4+,4+,4+.

Down the slope to the left is a fine grey slab with several lines only four of which are fully equipped at present. There are a variety of names and grades painted at the foot of the cliff, perhaps best used as a place to escape the crowds. On the right are HOVA 3 and HAFA 4+, both of

Toix TV: Dave Spencer on the excellent OMBRA 5+

which contain little in the way of fixed equipment. To the left is ALADDIN 6c following spaced bolts up a blunt rib and then steeper rock up the right side of a bay. The bolted blunt rib down the slope is FANTASIA 6a?

21. SEMI DULCE ☺ 6a 25m
Follow the spaced bolts up the clean slab (easier variations are inferior) and then trend left to the single bolt and fixed karabiner belay.

22. HETI ☺ 4 28m
Follow the line of a dozen (well irradiated) threads just to the left directly up the slab, crossing the previous route to reach ledges above with thread belays. Abseil descent.

23. JOHANNA ☺ 5 25m
Left again start at the name and climb directly up the slab before trending right to the lower-off used by SEMI DULCE.

Down the slope to the left are three partially equipped routes in the 6a/6c range on very compact rock. Carry a rack of wires if you must do them or better still buy some bolts and get them equipped properly!

TOIX EAST

Crag Facts

Star rating: ***
Aspect: south east
Height: 10 to 40 metres
Spread of grades:

4	5	5+	6a	6b	6c	7a	7b	7c	8
5	5	4	3	6	3	1	2		1

Introduction

A very popular and easily accessible crag (these two facts may not be totally unrelated) with a good selection of quality climbs across a broad range of difficulty. The routes are universally well protected by substantial home-made chain link or 10mm 'Fixe' bolts, and apart from quick draws the only equipment worth carrying may be one or two slings to replace missing threads on some of the easier climbs. Double ropes are required for abseil descents from the longer pitches. The rock is very rough and a sustained period of climbing here requires either skin like a pachyderm or a high resistance to pain. The crag gets the sun from dawn until a couple of hours after mid-day and it can be at its most pleasant in the cool of early morning. The outlook over Calpe and the Penon de Ifach is superb with the Mediterranean stretching away into the wide blue yonder. The crag can get rather busy at times when parking can be a problem (as can turning round); a little forethought and consideration for others might save inflaming those of a Latin temperament. Although belaying from the car seat with the stereo at full blast might be deemed 'cool' it can also be seen as antisocial - have a little consideration for other crag users

Crag Geography

The cliff basically consists of two broad buttresses, one rising from the road, and a taller one some distance up the bank to the left. The climbing is generally less than vertical.

Access

Follow the directions for Toix West into the main entrance to the Maryvilla complex (at the first entrance when approaching from the south and the second from the north). At the first junction turn left (right leads up to Toix West), at the second junction fork right. The next junction is a triple one, take the central road. At the fourth junction turn left and at the fifth turn right. The road dips down into a minor valley and then rises around a bend to arrive very suddenly at the cliff. Beware of traffic coming the other way on this final narrow section. It is possible to turn round a couple of hundred metres beyond the cliff at a slight widening in the road, but there is a considerable drop to the left; nervous passengers might like to disembark before the driver attempts this manoeuvre.

The routes are described from right to left starting at a short quarried wall that rises directly from the tarmac.

On the far right the cliff is very low and here there are some painted names on routes that would not be out of place on some of Cheedale's lesser cliffs, being both tiny and trivial. They are listed here purely out of completeness. On the far right is EL GATA LOCO ☹ 4 6m, and to its left is THE CATS ARE BACK ☹ 5- 8m. Neither route contains any fixed gear. To the left is the line of CAFE TOIX 6b 8m with two bolt runners and a maillon lower-off, and starting further left and finishing in the same place is the unprotected

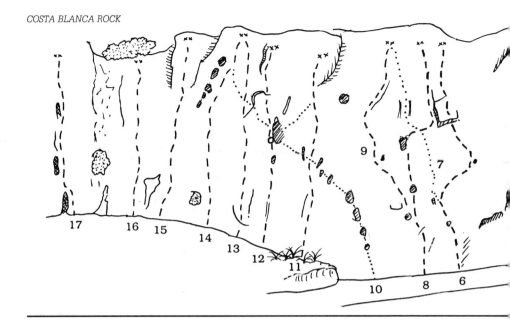

LOS TRES RATONES CIEGOS ⊗ 10m 5+.
Immediately to the left is the unprotected and
ungraded EL GATO GUAPO.

1. THE YELLOW ROUTE 4 12m
A more worthwhile climb than those to the right
(not too difficult, is it!). Start at the left side of the
wall below a curious twisting groove with yellow
painted bolts.

Follow the groove using advanced bridging
techniques until a couple of delicate steps lead
to the final bolt (the one with a big arrow painted
next to it!). Lower off this.

Directly across the road a pair of big ring bolts
allow abseil access to ADIOS DALI, a steep
slippery and quarried 8a+. Send your second
down first to sort the belays out or top-rope the
route!

To the left of the YELLOW ROUTE is more
quarried rock with two bolt lines protecting a
wall and a bulge of uninspiring looking rock
(some people must be desperate), both rumoured
to be 7a.

2. GRAPHIC WHORE 6c 15m
Climbs the steep blunt arete by a sustained
series of moves. It is quite photogenic but
polished and otherwise unremarkable. The name
is usually (but not always) painted on the rock.
Difficult delicate climbing leads to a small roof.
Layback round this to gain a big pocket, then
continue up to the right to the lower-off just
below the top of the cliff.

3. GOING SOLO 7a 12m
A good choice for your first 7a (ie. it is over-
graded!). Start a couple of metres left of the arete
of GRAPHIC WHORE, at a line of four bolts.

A problem start to a letter box gives way to
sustained face climbing on polished edges and
side-pulls leading to a pair of lowering bolts.

The next feature to the left is a right slanting bay
in the cliff face formed by a series of shallow
sandy caves filled with grotesque flowstone. A
line of green painted bolts climbs steep rock to
the left of this and a more recent climb tackles
the groove on the right.
4. LA RAMUNA ARENOSA ☺ 5+ 20m
A slippery start leads to pleasant romping above

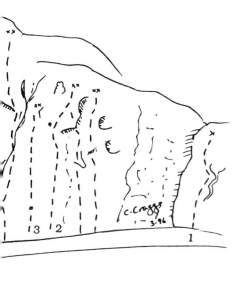

Toix East - Right side

1. THE YELLOW ROUTE   4
2. GRAPHIC WHORE   6c
3. GOING SOLO   7a
4. LA RAMUNA ARENOSA   ☺   5+
5. THE GREEN ROUTE   ☺   5+
6. EL OSO Y EL MADRONO   ☀   6a
7. KING CUCUDRULU   ☀   7b
8. VIA YOYOBA   ☀   6a+
9. SOL Y BON TEMPS   ☀   6b+
10. VIA PYRAMIDE   ☺   5
11. THE SILVER ROUTE   ☺   6a
12. LA FINA   ☺   4+
13. THE THIN CRACK   ☺   5
14. THE GREEN ROUTE   ☺   5
15. WINTER   ☺   5
16. SPOLLI   ☺   5+
17. THE PURPLE ROUTE   ☺   4+

which a final bulge and short tricky wall lead to the lower-off.

5. THE GREEN ROUTE ☺ 5+ 20m
Start as for the previous route and make a couple of tough moves to easier climbing leftwards into the caves (slippery rock and an optional thread), or start direct with more difficulty. Climb steeply up the crack above, with strenuous moves where it bulges. Pull out left on to easier angled rock that leads to the top and the lowering bolts.

To the left is a large hole/cave with an odd protuberance sticking from it. Beyond this is a steep brown pockety wall that gives some of the best pitches on the cliff, though blinkers might be needed on some of the lower sections. The first route starts at a thin crack that rises steeply to the right and contains a couple of old nails/pegs.

6. EL OSO Y EL MADRONO ☀ 6a 25m
A good pitch on unusual holds. It is rather easier than initial appearances might suggest.
Make a couple of moves up the thin crack then step left onto the wall and climb up to a large

pocket. A little higher trend diagonally to the right (crux) until a long step to the right leads to a large, well hidden hole. Now climb straight up on flowstone "snappies" until it is possible to step left to below a huge hanging flake from where there are two possibilities. If you are feeling lucky and the flake is still attached pull over the roof and continue direct. Otherwise step left into the groove and finish up VIA YOYOBA.

7. KING CUCUDRULU ☀ 7b 25m
A good challenging pitch that starts as for the previous route then forges straight up the wall past two big black bolts, using some tiny holds. Cross the traverse of VIA YOYOBA and continue up the spiky wall above to eventually reach the lower-off of SOL I BON TEMPS.

8. VIA YOYOBA ☀ 6a+ 25m
A fine pitch that gives steep climbing on mostly good holds. Start left of centre of the wall directly below a vertical keyhole shaped pocket at 15m.
Mantleshelf awkwardly onto a thin finger ledge and climb to the first bolt. Step left into a shallow

149

scoop and make a couple of tricky moves up this to easier rock. Now step right and climb steeply to the 'keyhole pocket'. From here traverse to the right, until a blind reach gains a huge hidden jug. Pull up then follow the much easier groove to the top.

9. SOL Y BON TEMPS ♦ 6b+ 25m

A worthwhile pitch that makes good use of the left side of the wall. The climbing is sustained, with a fierce fingery crux.

Start just left of the thin finger ledge that marks the start of VIA YOYOBA and below a solitary bolt in the slab.

Climb straight up to the bolt and pass it with difficulty to join YOYOBA at its easy section. Continue up and left to a round hole, then make difficult moves on painful pockets up and left again to easier ground. Amble up the ramp on the right to a final couple of steep moves to a lowering-station on the edge of the wall.

The next feature to the left is one of the major ones of the cliff, a prominent diagonal line of large pockets and holes rising leftwards to a conspicuous cave. This is the line of:

10. VIA PYRAMIDE ☺ 5 42m

Start at the foot of the diagonal line just to the right of the point where the base of the cliff steps up from the road.

1. 22m 4 Follow the line of large holes, all rather floral at first, with intermittent protection from assorted pegs and threads. The climbing involves making awkward moves between vast jugs until respite is possible at the cave stance. Bolt and thread belays.
2. 20m 5 Make a few difficult moves above the stance until it is possible to move left onto the exposed face (bolt runner on the GREEN ROUTE), and continue leftwards to finish up the edge of the wall in a fine position. The easier and inferior groove around to the left can also be followed.
2a. VARIATION 4 20m
   An easier finish can be had by crossing the rugged slab on the right of the belay, before heading for the cliff top.

Descent

Up and right of the top of the climb is an abseil anchor allowing a 40m abseil back to base. Beware of people climbing below.

The next routes in this area are reached by scrambling up the earth step to get to the foot of an attractive grey slab.

11. THE SILVER ROUTE ☺ 6a 25m

A route with some difficult but well protected moves on the right side of vertical, the name is a throwback to the days when the bolts were new and were sprayed with silver paint.

Start below the first line of bolts above the step.

The lower section of the climb gives sustained moves on small sharp holds until the diagonal break on PYRAMIDE is reached. From here step right on to the steeper wall and climb this to the lower-offs.

12. LA FINA ☺ 4+ 40m

In the centre of the grey slab is a vague scoop running up the rippled slab. Start below this.

1. 4 20m Climb up the centre of the scoop with sustained interest to a thread and bolt belay in the cave.
2. 4+ 20m Above the stance is a corner which the route finishes up. Gain this by a difficult move using a monodoigt (on a 4+!). Once entered the corner gives steep but steady moves to the summit. Move left to a belay and abseil anchor.

13. THE THIN CRACK ☺ 5 35m

Start below a sinuous crack that wriggles up the steep slab and follow this to an overlap. Step left and climb steeper rock on generous holds to the lower-off.

14. THE GREEN ROUTE ☺ 5 30m

Follow the line of paired bolts (clip the new ones!) up the steep slab. As they become more spaced the climbing gets easier despite appearances to the contrary. Continue up ever steepening rock on ever improving holds to reach a stance on top of the wall with bolt belays. Descent is by abseil.

15. WINTER ☺ 5 30m
Start immediately to the right of a large flake and climb the slab then steepening rock above, satisfying stuff.

16. SPOLLI ☺ 5+ 30m
Another 'spotty' climb, at a quite amenable grade. Big bolts and big holds make for a pleasant experience.

To the left, and immediately right of a vegetated gully is the ill-equipped and rather scruffy rib climbed by VIA SONIA. It's a pity the poor girl didn't have a better route named after her!

The other section of rock that contains routes at TOIX EAST is the impressively smooth piece of rock a couple of hundred metres up the hillside from the roadside crag. It is approached by walking along the road until a small path winds up through the undergrowth to arrive at a shallow cave/alcove below the wall, or by following a tortuous and spiky path from the routes described above.

The routes are described from right to left again. **Descent** from most of the routes is by abseil or lowering off if you own a longer than usual rope.

The first climb starts some distance to the right of the cave, at a smaller orifice. The colour of the bolts aids identification.

17. THE PURPLE ROUTE ☺ 4+ 28m
Start just to the left of the cave and follow the purple spots in a leftwards direction by pleasantly sustained climbing.

The next route starts a short distance to the right of the large rounded cave, behind some spiky bushes.

HANNAH (THE GREY RIB) ☺ 6b+ 28m
Follow the rib directly, with thin moves low down (no sneaking out right). A bulge is passed on excellent small finger holds above which more reasonable moves lead to a small bay. One awkward move gives access to jugs allowing a quick pull up to the chains. A recent Spanish

topo graded this 5+, but I don't think so!

VIA DE LOS FAKIROS ☺ 6b+ 23m
A fingery pitch, unfortunately the bolts are now rather old and could do with being replaced.

Climb the crack that springs from the right side of the cave past a prominent peg, until it is possible to swing left and mantel onto a pedestal. Move up to clip a bolt on the wall above (distinctly harrowing for shorties) and pass it on the right to a second bolt. Trend left then up past two more bolts to reach the long awaited jug with a lower off just above.

LA TONTA DEL BOTE 6c+ 23m
A tough climb with some hard though rather artificial moves. Start as for the previous route but swing out left and make difficult moves over the roof trending left to enter the shallow corner. From the ledge climb the very thin wall to a lower-off at the change in angle.

VIA VERDE 6c+ 23m
A line up the slab just to the left of the cave has some pathetic attempts at chipped holds, join the previous or the next route to finish.

BORO El TORO ☺ 7b 28m
The left side of the smooth slab is climbed with great difficulty (on chipped holds) to reach easier moves up the black streak and the headwall above, testing stuff.

Further to the left is a vertical elongated pocket a short distance up the wall; this is gained by the next two routes.
These were put up in 1987 and the bolts and the fixed threads are now rather old.

FLUID CONNECTION (a.k.a. LISA) ♦ 6b 28m
Another fine piece of climbing with a steep lower section giving way to open slab climbing above. From the starting block sprint up the lower wall, past threads and a bolt to gain the recess above. Move delicately right at one of two levels into a shallow groove and climb this steeply on its left side (crux) to a resting place at the foot of the upper slab. This gives excellent

climbing up its centre with rather spaced protection, leading to a final easy groove. Abseil off the in-situ threads or leave a karabiner!

FLUID CONNECTION LEFT ☺ 6b 18/28m
Rather harder and a little less satisfying than the original.

Follow the previous route in to the recess. Now climb the small red pillar on the left to its top. The bulge above is passed by swinging right on to the wall and back left a couple of moves higher passing a thread to reach several threads with fixed karabiner. Either lower off this or step right into the centre of the slab to join and follow the parent route to the top.

To the left is a line with a painted name (SOLAR POWER) but to my knowledge it has never been equipped. To the left again is the last offering on the cliff:
SOLI ☺ 1 40m
Start at a block and follow the obvious line of 14 fixed threads to easier ground and the belays. You shouldn't get lost on this one.

Olta: Graham Parkes on the leaning SUPER-TUFA GROOVE 6b+, the classic of the cliff

OLTA

Crag Facts

Star rating: ***
Aspect: south east facing
Height: Up to 28 metres
Spread of grades:

4	5	5+	6a	6b	6c	7a	7b	7c	8
/	/	3	1	2	5	1	1	1	

Introduction

A recently developed crag (thanks to the Germans) in a superb setting, positioned high above Calpe, well bolted and on excellent rock. There are only fifteen climbs here at present, though there is some scope for further development.

Access

From the N332, just north of the road into Calpe, turn uphill towards the station (signed Estacion f.c.). Pass this, cross the railway line and 100m further on take a turn left (0.7km from N332). Bear right past a line of post boxes, pass a phone box, then bear right at the next junction, left being a dead end. At Casa Andrea (1.2km from the N332) the road turns to dirt. From here head uphill always sticking with the best track. Another kilometre leads to a col. Pass a tall 'electricity house' and continue uphill until the track bears horizontally right to a parking place at its end, a steep 5 minutes from the cliff. The routes are described from left to right and many of the climbs end at a single bolt lower-off, often marked with a down pointing chipped or painted arrow. Most climbs have their names painted on the rock.

On the left side of the cliff is a recessed bay with a smooth bulging back wall bounded on the right by a leaning white groove:

1. SUPER-TUFA GROOVE ♦ 6b+ 28m
Follow the superb tilted groove throughout, sustained climbing with the crux at half-height, 10 bolts protect. Undoubtedly the route of the cliff.

The grey wall to the right has two worthwhile routes:

2. WINGS OF FREEDOM ☺ 7a+ 18m
Cross the initial bulge with difficulty then continue up the sustained wall above. 6 clips

3. KI ☺ 6c 18m
From atop blocks a tough start leads to deep pockets. Step left onto the wall before looping left then back right to a final steepening.

4. TAI CHI ♦ 6b+ 18m
The arete of the cliff gives a good pitch on great rock starting at a flake, with the crux at half height and a steep finish on jugs, 6 clips.

5. SPANISH EYES ☺ 6c 18m
Right of the arête easy rock leads to a bulge, passed leftwards with difficulty. Easier cracks lead to the lowering bolt, 5 clips.

6. FANTASIA ENCANTO 7b+ 20m
From blocks climb to a 'crimpy' slab then on up the technical and chipped wall above (inverted mono obligatory). Tough!

7. NINJA ☺ 7c 20m
Climb to and up the big white tufa then tackle the leaning wall above on poor holds. Very tough!

8. PROJECT To the left of the central cave is a line of bolts and the occasional peg, at present it finishes at half height.

To the right of the deep central cave is an unclimbed bulging buttress (some scope) then a deep crack, and then another buttress climbed by:

Olta

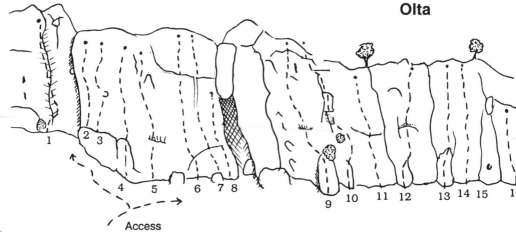

/ **Access**

1. SUPER-TUFA GROOVE 🖐 6b+
2. WINGS OF FREEDOM ☺ 7a+
3. KI ☺ 6c
4. TAI CHI 🖐 6b+
5. SPANISH EYES ☺ 6c
6. FANTASIA ENCANTO 7b+
7. NINJA ☺ 7c
8. PROJECT

9. HILLSIDE AVENUE ☺ 6c
10. HALT MICH 6c+
11. HOLA OLTA ☺ 6c+
12. BEST OF 95 ☺ 5+
13. DUD AFEST 🖐 5+
14. TURRON ☺ 5+
15. NO NAME 4
16. CHRISTMAS DREAMS ☺ 6a

9. HILLSIDE AVENUE ☺ 6c 20m
Climb the side wall of the lower rib then a step left and pull through a bulge. Continue up the rib and final pocketed bulging wall.

10. HALT MICH 6c+ 20m
A rather unbalanced route with a tough finale. Climb past a thin in-situ thread then trend left into a groove (drilled thread) before attacking the crux bulging wall.

11. HOLA OLTA ☺ 6c+ 20m
The gradually steepening slab and wall that crowns it gives good but sharp pitch.

To the right are some clean grey slabs riven by a series of cracks. The slabs have been climbed by a series of worthwhile routes, whereas most of the cracks await a homesick traditionalist.

12. BEST OF 95 ☺ 5+ 20m
The first line of big beefy bolts is well worth
154

doing despite the occasional scrappy ledge.

13. DUD AFEST 🖐 5+ 22m
Start at the name and climb past a thin in situ thread then follow the big bolts up the steep stab to another thread, and on to the lower-off. Excellent.

14. TURRON ☺ 5+ 22m
The next line to the right has an odd assortment of bolts with every one being different. Join the previous climb at the second thread and finish as for it.

The next crack to the right is:
15. NO NAME 4, gear required.

16. CHRISTMAS DREAMS ☺ 6a 12m
The last line a short but quality offering on great rock. 4 clips.

PEÑON DE IFACH
329m (1079ft)

Crag Facts

Star rating: ****
Aspect: south and north west facing
Height: Up to 300 metres
Spread of grades: routes (pitches)

4	5	5+	6a	6b	6c	7a	7b	7c	8
2	/	8	2	12	8	/	3	/	/
(74)	(30)	(36)	(22)	(37)	(12)	(1)	(3)		

Introduction

The "Peñon" is the huge unmistakable lump of rock that sticks out of the sea between the two beaches at Calpe, towering above the harbour. It looks for all the world like a volcanic plug, and indeed is described as such in some travel guides, but in fact the rock is coralline limestone of variable quality. The summit is a worthy objective for an afternoon's stroll, taking an easy hour from the harbour. There is a well made path throughout and the scenery is excellent with good views of the north face climbs, of the excellent beach of the Playa Levante, and of the alluring mountains inland. The summit offers a fine panorama in all directions and has several comfortable if graffiti-ridden picnic sites. Bivouacing on the top is now illegal so those who would like to see the sun rise out of the Mediterranean will have to get up early! Spectacular Brocken Spectres are not an uncommon phenomenon when a sea mist is blowing on to the land.

Recently the whole of the Peñon has been made into a nature reserve and some work has been done to limit the human impact on the area, most specifically the tidying of the footpaths that run up to the tunnel through the north face. Signs and fences have been erected encouraging people to stick to the footpaths and avoid cutting corners as this has led to considerable erosion. A word to the wise should be enough. The north face is closed when birds are nesting (usually February to June), though the south face is unaffected. All sides of the Peñon are rocky, but the climbing is concentrated in two main areas. These are very different in character and are described separately.

The South Face

This is a vast wall of rock over a 300m high, riddled with cave systems and with colossal overhangs crossing large sections of the cliff.

The left side of the face is flanked by a huge barrel shaped buttress that awaits development. This runs rightwards to form a relatively easy angled slab, buttressing the main face and providing a remarkably reasonable route, the VIA VALENCIANOS, up this imposing cliff. A short distance further to the right a conspicuous shallow twisting groove and flake system runs almost the full height of the cliff. This is taken by the classic DIEDRO U.B.S.A. Further right still the cliff becomes a complex mass of ramps, walls and overhangs through which a variety of routes weave their way, some using the odd bit of aid (tut tut). Beyond this, the cliff continues for a considerable distance rising straight from the sea.

The rock on this face is very variable though it is mostly solid on the routes described. On the traditional routes the in situ gear is often not as good as you may have come to expect in Spain, so it is worth carrying a comprehensive rack. For the newly bolted lines, a single rope and 15 quick-draws are all that is needed if you have the courage to go for a rapid ascent. A helmet is definitely a good idea, especially on VIA VALENCIANOS as the lower section of this has loose material on some of the ledges and acts as a bit of a funnel for stuff knocked down from above - be warned.

Any of the routes described here can be done comfortably in an afternoon by a competent party but bivouacs are not an uncommon experience, and winter nights here can get pretty cool. The message is clear, if in doubt start early. A leisurely afternoon on the beach is vastly more pleasant than an epic high on the face in the gathering gloom.

Despite these rather grim warnings the south face of the Peñon brings a different aspect to the climbing hereabouts and any visitor should sample at least one of the routes at the appropriate grade. You should enjoy it, and if not at least you will have ticked the experience. Of the great classics VIA VALENCIANOS weighs in at about VS 5a; for something a little harder DIEDRO U.B.S.A. is HVS 5b, and GOMEZ-CANO about E2 5b. For avid bolt clippers VIA COSTA BLANCA 6c+, EL NAVIGANTE 6c and LINEA MAGICA 6c are all 'must do's'.

Access

Drive to the harbour in Calpe (you can't miss it, it is just below that big rock!) then continue along the road until it bends right and runs out onto the sea wall, park here and leave nothing in the car. A dirt track continues out to below the face, the first close up views of which are impressive - many teams get no closer!

For VIA SAME and the most direct approach to the left side of the face scramble straight up to the foot of the barrel shaped buttress following a good track that starts a couple of hundred metres along the track opposite some large blocks on the right. For many years the start of this was marked by an abandoned glass fibre hull, but as soon as I mentioned it in writing someone removed it! If you reach a '20' painted on the right side of the main track you have overshot this approach to the cliff by 20m. For the easiest approach to all the other routes, go almost to the end of the dirt track to find a faint path that goes up loose earth and rock (just before the quarried section of the wall) until

Peñon de Ifach: Colin Binks following the fine layback of POLVOS MAGICOS 5+

right under the cliff. Here it improves and ascends steeply leftwards under all the routes. At an easing in the gradient there is a conspicuous diagonal crack rising to the right; this is the start of VIAS ANGLADA-GALLEGO and GOMEZ-CANO. A little further left is a steep flowstone wall sprouting a line of big rusty bolts; the first pitch of VIA MANUEL. Left again is the well trodden area directly below the flake of DIEDRO U.B.S.A. and finally the red bay below the great grey slab taken by VIA VALENCIANOS.

The routes are described as approached on this path, that is right to left.

El Traversa Nautilus (650m 22 pitches)

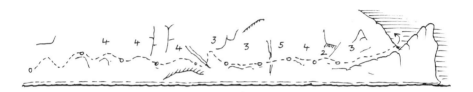

Descent

From the top of the hill a good footpath zigzags down the north east face (or take the shorter, rougher, direct route halfway round the first zigzag) to a tunnel which pops out under the north west face a short distance above the town. About 30 minutes is adequate to get back down. Because of the complex structure and large size of the south face, abseil descents are a very bad idea, except in a total all out emergency.

The Climbs

There is a girdle of the sea cliff section of the Peñon starting at the end of the dirt track, EL TRAVERSA NAUTICO. This is reputed to be about HVS but the first pitch at least looks like a full blown aid extravaganza with lots of old rusty bolts and tatty bits of rope (pendulum points?) littering the wall up to 40ft above the sea. On a hot calm day it may repay a visit by anyone with a panache for horizontal soloing as long as they don't mind a wetting. The topo from the definitive guide to the Peñon is included here for any adventurous spirits.

The great right-hand buttress of the Peñon is criss-crossed with a network of a dozen or so intricate climbs, many of which still require considerable amounts of aid. I have not climbed on this part of the face but for completeness a diagram and the grades of the best climbs is offered here. Adventures guaranteed.

South face Right side

1. NUEVA DIMENSIONS 7b, 7a, 6b+, 6c, 5, 5+, 5, 6b, 6c 360m
The right-hand line, fully bolted, some chipped holds and with a couple of moves of A0 early on.

2. REVELACION 6a&A0, 5+&A1, 3, 5+, 6a, 6b&A0, 6a, 5+, 5+, 4+ 300m
A strong natural line with only a small amount of aid, probably the one to go for! Take a rack of wires and a set of Friends.

3. SUPER DIRECTA A3&6a, A1&5+,?, ?, A2&6a, A2&5, 6c, A2&5 300m
A spectacular climb up the centre of the face, carry a dozen pegs, a rack of wires and a set of large Hexes.

4. DIRECTA RUSA 6b, 5+, A2&6a, A3&5+, 4+, A2&6b, 5+, 4 300m
A direct route largely free though with some short sections of aid climbing.

Peñon de Ifach
South Face, Right Side

1. NUEVA DIMENSIONS   7b, 7a, 6b+, 6c, 5, 5+, 5, 6b, 6c   360m
2. REVELACION   6a&A0, 5+&A1, 3, 5+, 6a, 6b&A0, 6a, 5+, 5+, 4+   300m
3. SUPER DIRECTA   A3&6a, A1&5+, ?, ?, A2&6a, A2&5, 6c, A2&5   300m
4. DIRECTA RUSA   6b, 5+, A2&6a, A3&5+, 4+, A2&6b, 5+, 4   300m
5. DIRECTA MANFRED   5+&A2, A2, 6b, 5, 4, A0&6b, 6b, 4, 6a, A1&4   310m

5. DIRECTA MANFRED 5+&A2, A2, 6b, 5, 4, A0&6b, 6b, 4, 6a, A1&4 310m
A direct line on which some of the fixed gear is antique.

South Face Left Side

The first fully described route is:

1. VIA ANGALADA-GALLEGO 6b 255m
An old classic that climbs the centre of the face. It passes to the left of the central cave system and finishes in the notch between the twin summits of the Peñon. Most of the difficult climbing is on the lower section of the route with things easing as height is gained. Unfortunately the rock on the crucial lower pitches is generally not good and despite the fact that the Spanish guide rates the route highly, it cannot really be recommended unless you like that kind of thing! The upper section of the climb is reportedly on excellent rock.

Start a short distance down the slope from the foot of the conspicuous rightward rising crack line taken by 2. VIA GOMEZ-CANO. The name is painted on the rock in faded lettering.

1. 35m 6b Climb straight up the wall on Gogarth like rock to gain the crack line about 20m up. Follow this out to the right with difficulty to gain an uncomfortable hanging stance with an array of belays.
2. 35m 6b/6c Either continue rightward until forced to climb straight up the wall following the pegs, or climb straight up from the stance then traverse right. Both ways reunite at a traverse to the right leading into a corner, a short distance up which is a good stance and the end of the major difficulties.
3. 20m 4 Follow the corner easily to gain the base of the great cave system.
4. 20m 5 Move left in to a corner system which is rather strenuous. Belay in a recess at the top of the corner.
5. 25m 6a Climb left across the wall to a stance below overhangs.
6. 35m 5+ Traverse right to get into a long corner system. This is taken directly and gives pleasant climbing until it rears up. A few steep moves out to the right lead to a good stance at the foot of the final easy gully

line.
7. 45m 4 Plod up the groove.
8. 40m 3 Continue to the col. The summit lies 5 minutes away to the left, otherwise scramble down the back to join the descent path.

2. VIA GOMEZ-CANO ♦ 6a & A1 (or 7b) 295m
An excellent expedition climbing the cliff at its highest point. The climbing is varied, on good rock and follows a strong natural line. The small amount of aid required by most mortals on pitch 3 adds to rather than detracts from the experience. It can be done using a couple of slings for foot-loops. One well known Scottish climber rated this as the best limestone route he had done anywhere!

Start at the foot of the most obvious rightward rising crack line.

1. 40m 6a Climb the crack up to the right strenuously to an easing in the angle then follow the flake system that trends back to the left by undercutting jamming and bridging. Eventually a big new bolt in the right wall is reached, either finger traverse past this (safe but a move of 6a+), or climb a little higher and stride out right (easier but a little bolder). Both ways lead to a sloping stance and a selection of belays.
2. 15m 5+ Climb the groove above the stance past an awkward bulge (big bolt on the right) to another sloping ledge.
3. 40m 5 & A1. Gain the groove awkwardly and climb it past a couple of old pegs until it is possible to trend right up the wall by sustained and occasional blind moves. Steeper climbing straight up the wall leads to the bottom of a slanting crack sprouting a row of pegs. Aid up these (all very traditional) or free climb at 7b, until it is possible to pull into the base of the giant cave system. Thread and high bolt belay.
4. 20m 4 Climb up to the right then traverse to the left towards the arete of the cave. Ascend this on fossiliferous dinosaur dongo to a stance in a bay.
5. 35m 4 Step left and climb the very exposed rib to a major change in atmosphere. Amble

159

up the rough grey slabs to a belay in a dusty hollow.

6. 40m Continue up and left on easy ground to the apex of the cave system to a belay below a corner crack.

8. 30m 6a Climb the corner groove to a pedestal (possible belay on the right) then make awkward moves to get into the bulging crack above. This eases with height until it is possible to swing left to gain a comfortable ledge.

9. 40m 6a Get back into the crack system and wriggle up into the chimney above. This leads to more open climbing up cracks and grooves on the left. As the rock steepens a niche is reached, exit right from this in a position of some exposure, and follow the ramp up and right to gain a superbly situated (and rather small) stance below the final obstacle.

10. 40m 6a Climb left up slabby rock to get into the large red corner which leads with the occasional tricky move to a well pegged bulge. Undercuts enable better holds to be reached then the still steep corner is followed until a crack leads out to the left above all difficulties. The top lies 30m above, up easy rock.

3. LINEA MAGICA ✦ 6c 235m

A superb and well named outing following a dramatic line straight up the face, the rock is good and protection is perfect, take a sport rack and a single rack of wires for the two pitches of GOMEZ-CANO. The one very hard move on pitch 5 can be bypassed by a quick pull on a bolt reducing the overall grade to sustained 6b (about E3 5c).

Start a short distance left of the base of the GOMEZ-CANO flake where a line of newish bolts runs up the steep red wall.

1. 40m 6b Climb the wall, sustained and quite delicate in places until it becomes necessary to step into GOMEZ-CANO, up this to the stance.

2&3. 5+&A1 (or 7b) 55m
As for GOMEZ-CANO 2 & 3 into the cave system.

4. 35m 6b Move right and layback up the long corner to get into a small cave, compose yourself then pull out through the crack that splits the lip of the overhangs - exposed or what? Continue to a small but comfortable stance on VIA MANUEL (see below).

5. 40m 6a Follow the bolts rightwards up the wall then pull strenuously back left through the bulges to reach a crack line. Where this splits follow the right-hand branch (loose directly above) out right to a stance on the rib.

6. 35m 6c Climb the wall to a bulge and make a couple of baffling moves (UK 6b) through this before continuing more easily to a small stance.

7. 30m 5 Weave up short awkward walls and ledges to bolt belay 20m below the cliff top, magic.

4. VIA MANUEL 6b 280m

A character building directissima up the centre of the giant buttress between the two biggest cave systems. Some of the rock on the lower section is rather dubious and, except for on the first pitch, the fixed gear is both thinly spread and often in a laughable condition. Devotees of 'Gordale adventure routes' should love it, though it been largely superseded by MAGIC LINE!

Start to the left of the prominent diagonal crack of GOMEZ-CANO below a flowstone wall which sprouts an array of old bolts and pegs. The first pitch is often done as a worthwhile climb in its own right (bottom end 6b ☺).

1. 40m 6b Climb straight up the butch wall following the line of old aid gear. As height is gained the protection becomes a little more spaced but the climbing gradually eases, until it is possible to move right to a groove. Up this past a large loose looking 'tooth' to a restricted stance and multiple belays.

Toix East: Colin Binks high on the well named SOL Y BON TEMPS 6b+

2. 20m 5+ or A0 Climb straight up of the stance via an awkward crack until it is possible to swing right into a groove containing a line of bolts. These provide a direct aid variation that should be avoided in case you get struck down by a thunder bolt from on high. Swing right again to reach the stance above pitch two of GOMEZ-CANO.

3. 40m 6a Go up the rib above the belay or straight up the easier groove to its right. Both ways lead to the tip of a rather fragile flake from which committing and scary moves can be made up and left to a ledge. Optional stance with poor belays. Continue up and right heading for the obvious corner crack which is followed steeply to reach the start of the cave system at the bolt and thread belays of GOMEZ-CANO.

4. 45m 4 Follow Pitch 4 of GOMEZ-CANO then continue up Pitch 5 to the major change in angle. Move right into a chimney, through an arch and round a rib to bolt belays just beyond a groove.

5. 40m 5+ Ignore the bolts of LINEA MAGICA on the right and climb the rib right of the groove up to the bulges which are crossed leftward in spectacular fashion, or alternatively climb the rib to the left of the groove. Both ways lead to an area of slabs from which trend up and left to reach an unexpected haven, a spot to hide for a while.

6. 30m 5+ Plod up the easy chimney to its closure then make difficult undercutting moves out to the right. Possible stance. Above the point of arrival is a crack sprouting a couple of old pegs (tent pegs that is). Up this then leftwards to a thread belay below a corner blocked by a big roof.

7. 30m 5 For the truly keen the impressive corner is the direct finish A1 & 5+, but for those who are long overdue for a cold beer the crack on the right leads to the arête above which another crack leads to easier ground.

8. 35m 4 Wend your way up the rough rock between the sweet smelling herbs all the way to the top.

5. EL NAVEGANTE ♦ 6c 252m

A long climb that was put up in May 1991 and is fully equipped with 10mm bolts. The rock is mostly good and the situations are superb. The only equipment that is required is a dozen or so quick draws. Although about E4 6a all free, pulling on a couple of the bolts on pitches 5 and 7 would reduce the grade to about 6a (E2 5c). Start as for DIEDRO U.B.S.A.

1. 15m 3 Pitch one of DIEDRO U.B.S.A. Slant right on easy rock to a two bolt belay on a good ledge to the left of the groove.

2. 30m 5 Pitch two of DIEDRO U.B.S.A. Step right and climb the steep groove on good holds and with odd pieces of fixed kit to a stance where the groove deepens to form a chimney.

3. 25m 5+ Step right and climb the wall on 'stuck on' holds until it is possible to step left back into the chimney. Continue up easier rock (this far as for DIEDRO U.B.S.A) until a brown ramp runs awkwardly right to an uncomfortable stance and three bolt belay below a wall of alarming looking rock.

4. 30m 6b Climb the vertical, well cemented?? rubble on good holds and while holding your breath until the rock improves and flowstone is climbed rightwards. Steep and difficult moves gain a groove at the top of which a traverse left gains a good stance.

5. 35m 6b Trend easily left then right with greater difficulty until a couple of thin moves gain an area of flowstone. This is climbed on massive holds (easy unless it is seeping) to gain flake crack and a little higher a rather grovelly corner. A good belay ledge is reached at the top of the corner.

6. 22m 6c Climb up and left to gain the foot of a steep scooped arete. This is climbed by difficult laybacking (no grovelling up the groove around the corner!), until a steep pull gains a niche. Exit right from this to reach a

---

Peñon de Ifach: a view of the final section of the great slab of the classic VIA VALENCIANOS 5+

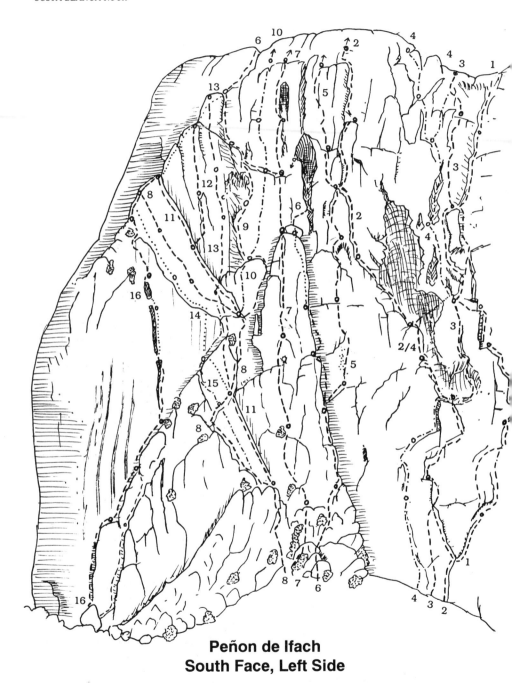

**Peñon de Ifach
South Face, Left Side**

1. VIA ANGALADA-GALLEGO   6b, 6b, 4, 5, 6a, 5+, 4, 3   255m
2. VIA GOMEZ-CANO   &   6a, 5+, 5&A1(7b), 4, 4,-, 6a, 6a, 6a   295m
3. LINEA MAGICA   &   6b, 5+, 5&A1(7b), 6b, 6a, 6c, 5   235m
4. VIA MANUEL   6b, 5+, 6a, 4, 5+, 5, 4   280m
5. EL NAVEGANTE   &   3, 5, 5+, 6b, 6b, 6c, 6a, 6c   252m
6. DIEDRO U.B.S.A.   &   3, 5, 5+, 5, 4, 5, 3, 4, 4+   245m
7. VIA COSTA BLANCA   &   4, 6b, 6b, 6a, 6b+, 6b, 6c   222m
8. VIA VALENCIANOS   ☺   3, 3, 5+, 4, 4, 4, -, -   250m
9. PIRATAS   ☺   3, 3 ,5+, 4+, 4+5, 4, 4+   210m
10. LOS MISERABLES   ☺   6b ,6c+, 6b, 6b   100m
11. POLVOS MAGICOS   ☺   3, 5+, 5+, 5, 5+, 4, -, -   207m
12. VIRGINIA DIEZ   ☺   5, 6b+   45m
13. PILAR LOPEZ DE SANCHO   &   6b, 6c, 5+, 6b+   140m
14. SENSATION DE VIVRE   &   3, 5+, 6b+, 6b+, 6a+   125m
15. DIRECT DE U.B.S.A.   ☺   4, 5, 5+, 5   100/230m
16. VIA SAME   ☺   5, 5+, (6b,4) 5, 3, 5+5, 4+   205/280m

---

good ledge below Pitch 8 of GOMEZ-CANO.

7. 30m 6a Step left and make a couple of awkward moves to gain a steep corner. Follow this until it is possible to swing into a steep crack in the left wall of the corner, which is best attacked forcefully and leads past a ledge to a good stance below the final obstacle.

8. 35m 6c Above the stance is a short bolt ladder which can be climbed at A0 according to the Spanish topo. The short diagonal crack just to the right gives a free alternative with a couple of hard moves before jugs are reached. Trend right then up a steep crack before hand traversing left and pulling into a niche. Exit awkwardly right from this, climb a corner and then a final slab gained by a difficult pull in from the left.

9. 30m Trend easily right to gain the ridge.

6. DIEDRO U.B.S.A.   &   5+   245m

A classic climb of its type taking the continuous flake/groove line up the left side of the main face. The climbing is varied and not overly exposed except for one pitch, any difficulties are well protected. If you feel competent at HVS 5a go for it!

The stances are good throughout and have recently been re-equipped with big belay bolts.

Start below the impressive groove at an apron of easier angled and rather scrappy rock by a large cactus bush.

1. 15m 3 Take any one of a variety of lines, easiest on the left, leading to a stance below the groove proper.

2. 30m 5 Step right into the groove and follow it steeply but on good holds past a poor stance to a better one where the groove becomes a chimney.

3. 30m 5+ The right wall of the chimney is climbed steeply on a rather odd mixture of 'stuck on' holds. This is the crux of the route and is best done quickly. As soon as it is possible to bridge across to the opposite wall things become easier. Continue to another well sheltered stance.

4   25m 5 Keep on trucking up the corner system until it becomes blocked.

5. 30m 4 Move right to gain the slab, then traverse back left to gain the line which has now become a deep gully. Amble up this to a shady belay behind a pinnacle.

6. 25m 4+/5+ or somewhere in between depending on stature.

Climb to a block jammed behind the top of the pinnacle then make a difficult move (or an easy move) up the wall above. Fine climbing now leads up and right across the wall to gain a chimney which is reached all too soon. Up this to a belay.

7. 25m 3 Continue up into the huge cave from which all exits look closed. Scramble left to a massive bunch of tat.

8. 20m Abseil or get lowered (how good is your mate's belaying anyway?) down the wall to reach the right end of the ledge that runs left into a long corner. The far end of the ledge contains several stout anchors, from which point you can discuss methods of getting the second man across.

9. 25m 4 Move left and climb the groove to a shrubby stance, below a steeper section of corner.

10. 20m 4+ The rather impressive final obstacle can be bypassed by a bit of wide bridging, the climbing then eases rapidly to arrive at a notch in the ridge, twin bolt belay.

From here the summit ridge lies a short distance above and is reached by the easy angled corner on the left.

7. VIA COSTA BLANCA ✿ 6c+ 222m

The final one of the trio of recently fully bolted outings on the main section of the wall. This is a great climb up the front of the U.B.S.A. pillar and then on through the cave systems above. The difficulties are limited to a couple of delicate moves on pitch 6 and a couple of strenuous ones on pitch 8. The route is fully equipped, take 15 quick-draws.

Start to the left of the fall-line from the groove of DIEDRO U.B.S.A.

1. 20m 2 Solo up broken rock from the base of VALENCIANOS, or from further right (easy but loose), to a stance and bolt belay on top of the initial pillar where things steepen up.

2. 34m 6b Climb the thin slab on the left (hardest move on the route??) trending left, then follow flakes leftwards before moving back right to a small stance.

3. 44m 6b Trend right up the rough grey slab then step back left and follow the fine steep corner to a band of dubious rock. Trend right through this then pull through bulges to reach a comfortable stance.

4. 32m 6a Climb the slab above following the

bolts, then step left and climb the orange pocketed rock more steeply to a final loose section up a wide crack (directly above the flat area at the foot of VALENCIANOS where the crowds gather to sunbathe and banter) to arrive on the left corner of the DIEDRO U.B.S.A. flake.

5. 10m 3 Traverse left away from the drop and into the cool chimney behind the tower.

6. 33m 6b+ Traverse left along a ramp and then pull over a bulge and climb straight up the bulging wall on a continually surprising set of holds (especially surprising on the one move where there aren't any) to arrive at the ledge at the bottom end of the famous DIEDRO U.B.S.A. abseil.

7. 28m 6b Pull onto the hanging tufa on the right then climb the wall above on good holds until easier climbing leads to a stance in the left side of a comfortable cave.

8. 32m 6c+ Climb the juggy leaning left edge of the cave to its apex then make difficult moves up and left to more good holds. Easier climbing leads to a final steepening and one more difficult move to gain the final crack and a bolt belay just above. Twenty metres of easy rock leads to the summit ridge.

To the left the large slabby buttress projects from the main face of the cliff. This and the tower that hangs over it are home to an excellent selection of climbs, mostly well equipped and on excellent rock. The first to be described of these is the ever popular:

8. VIA VALENCIANOS ☺ 5+ (VS 5a) 250m

A classic climb taking the easiest line up an impressive face. Technical difficulties are not excessive except for a couple of well protected but slippery moves on pitch three. In the event of unforeseen difficulties abseil retreat is straight forward as the stances lie in a straight line even though the climbing wanders a bit. Carry a few medium to large Rocks to supplement the in situ protection.

Start in a red bay below the right corner of the great grey buttress that abuts the left side of the main face. The name is painted on the left wall of the bay.

1. 3 30m Climb up and right then back left (all a bit loose) before going straight up to reach a smooth slab with a peg in it. Step awkwardly right and continue up easier rock to a good ledge and three bolt belay below a big smooth corner (don't worry, it doesn't go up there).

2. 3 35m Traverse to the left, passing an optional stance then climb up to gain a slanting herbaceous border. Graze your way up this then climb the short arete and a blocky crack above to reach a ledge which is followed back to the right to a stance directly above the previous one.

3. 5+ 30m Climb easily up into the corner and follow it (passing an optional stance) until it steepens. The slabby crack in the right wall of the main corner above is the crux; it gives a couple of difficult and polished bridging moves which are fortunately well protected and easily friggable. Once a jug on the right wall is grasped things ease. Continue up the corner until it is possible to traverse left to a stance below the great slab.

4. 4 20m A tricky start leads to easier climbing, trending left to a small stance and single bolt belay with a thread or a bush for a back up.

5. 4 45m Cruise up the slab. There is an option stance by a bush at 22m (nut belays). Otherwise run it out to a stance sat astride the ridge. Superb views in all directions.

6. 4 30m Walk (or crawl?) along the ridge back to the mountain then traverse left along a ledge until just short of a bush. Climb the flaky crack in the grey slab (peg) and pass the bulge on good holds. Slightly easier but rather inferior variations exist to the left. Belay a little higher on a nail!

7. 20m Up rightwards keeping to the clean rock to a 2 bolt belay in a notch (the top of U.B.S.A. - impressive views downwards).

8. 30m Amble up the easy groove on the left to arrive, well chuffed, on the summit ridge a short distance below the top.

9. PIRATAS ☺ 5 210m
A more direct finish to VALENCIANOS up the large corner above the base of the big slab. It misses out the 'great slab' and eventually joins the final section of DIEDRO U.B.S.A. to which it offers an easier alternative way up the cliff. Carry a full rack. Follow VALENCIANOS (or POLVOS MAGICOS see below) to the stance above the crux pitch, 95m 5+.

4. 25m 4+ Head up the corner until after 10m a ramp runs up to the right. Follow this passing pegs and threads to a move round the arete. Bolt belays.

5. 25m 4+ Climb the corner passing a solitary in situ peg to reach a sculptured cave. Thread and nut belays.

6. 20m 5 Climb out of the right side of the cave (high thread) and move right into a crack. Up this to pedestal with a small cave to its right, thread and bolt belay.

7. 25m 4 Climb the groove moving left through bushes and back right to a shrubby stance, below a steeper section of corner.

8. 20m 4+ The rather impressive final obstacle can be bypassed by a bit of wide bridging, or some unpleasant grovelling. After this the climbing then eases rapidly to arrive at a notch in the ridge, twin bolt belay.

From here the summit ridge lies a short distance above and is reached by the easy angled groove on the left.

10. LOS MISERABLES ☺ 6b,6c+,6b,6b 100m
The wall between VIA COSTA BLANCA and PIRATAS gives a sustained route which increases in quality as height is gained. The first pitch takes the pillar to between the corner of POLVOS MAGICOS and the ramp of PIRATAS and after that it trends right onto the face then blasts straight up this, passing the traverse of DIEDRO U.B.S.A. then tackling the bulging wall above in two more pitches.

11. POLVOS MAGICOS ☺ 5+ 207m
A fine route which is worth seeking out. It follows the big corner system right of the slab of VALENCIANOS, with which it shares several stances. A good direct line with optional escape

routes leftwards. Take a light rack. The first pitch is now polished and slippery, though well bolted.

1. 3 30m As for Valencianos pitch 1.
2. 5+ 25m Straight up the smooth corner, with bolts, pegs and as many nuts as you want, a fine sustained pitch with the crux just below the top.
3. 5+ 30m As for Valencianos P3, the difficulties are short and slippery.
4. 5 22m Start as for Valencianos P4 but continue straight up into the corner system. Follow this to a belay in a niche.
5. 5+ 25m Straight on up the corner via varied climbing and the odd bit of dubious rock to a bolt belay on the ridge.
6. 4 20m Up the groove above the end of the ridge to reach bulges that are passed on the left in an exposed position, this leading to easy ground.
7/8. 55m Finish easily as for VALENCIANOS.

12. VIRGINIA DIEZ ☺ 5,6b+ 45m

An excellent exposed finish up the steep wall, crack and superb groove that hangs over the stance below pitch five of POLVOS MAGICOS. Pity is so hard to get at. Doing one of the routes on the slab to the left and then abseiling down the top pitch of the parent route might be a logical way to get at it!

13. PILAR LOPEZ DE SANCHO ♦ 6b,6c,5+,6b+ 140m

Another fine route. Carry a small rack of wires for the first two pitches. Follow POLVOS MAGICOS for 2 pitches then climb the steep crack immediately to the left of the crucial corner of VALENCIANOS to a belay on the easier slab above. Move right and climb a hanging groove to gain a stance on the steep slab above then continue up the stunning arete that hangs over the whole area in two more great pitches. Exposed in the extreme!

14. SENSATION DE VIVRE ☺ 6b+ 215m

A good direct line up the left edge of the great slab and the steep walls below. Start as for VALENCIANOS. Carry a small rack of wires for the first two pitches.

1. 3 30m As for VALENCIANOS pitch 1.
2. 5+ 25m Straight up the smooth corner, with bolts, pegs and as many nuts as you want, a pleasant pitch with the crux just below the top.
3. 3 10m Move up and right to a belay below a steep bolted crack.
4. 6b+ 25m The leftmost bolt protected crack in the steep wall gives strenuous exercise until the angle drops back and generally easier angled climbing trending left leads to a bolt belay.
5. 6a+ 50m Continue in the same line by sustained slab climbing to a final steepening stance on the ridge. A pitch that neatly avoids the vegetated sections of the slab.
6. 4 75m Finish as for POLVOS MAGICOS.

Another good route in this area is:

15. DIRECT DE U.B.S.A. ☺ 5+ 100/230m

1. 30m 4 Follow the first pitch of VIA VALENCIANOS but move left to a bolt belay below the centre of the slab.
2. 15m 5 Climb directly up the slab with plenty of protection to a small stance and belays below a short wall in the middle of the easy traverse on VIA VALENCIANOS.
3. 20m 5+ Climb steeply (crux) to gain another fine slab that is followed to belays.
4. 35m 5 Trend right, climb the right-hand bolt line up the steep wall passing occasional fixed gear to gain the 'great slab'. Climb directly up this to a bolt belay on VALENCIANOS. Either continue up this, 130m with moves of 4, or make three abseils to the ground, or finish up one of the routes on the head wall to the right.

The final route on the south side of the Peñon takes the prominent chimney crack in the right side of the barrel shaped buttress to the left of the main face.

16. VIA SAME ☺ 5+ (6b) 205/280m

An interesting and worthwhile route that visits some rather strange places. Unfortunately the climbing is rather unbalanced, with two tough sections and a long easier middle part. Recently bolts have been added to all the crucial sections, carry a light rack.

Start at the foot of the great barrel shaped buttress that forms the right side of the cliff, behind a large pointed block and below a long straight crack line. There are two alternative starts to the climb.

For those after a quick tick:

1. 5 20m Trend right up a ramp to enter a crack and climb this steeply to a good ledge on the right.
2. 5+ 35m Continue up the awkward wide crack above then pull over a tricky bulge. Step right then continue up the continuation crack to easier rock and a stance below a wide crack.

For those after some 'real' climbing:

1a. 6b 30m Gain the main corner crack steeply and follow it strenuously passing many fixed pegs to a stance and belay at a tree where the angle becomes much more amenable, a good butch pitch.
2a. 4 20m Continue up the slabby corner (occasional threads and pegs) to the stance below the wide crack.
3. 5 20m Climb the wide crack above (easiest facing right) to a stance on easy ground.
4. 3 30m Follow the ramp to the right easily to a stance and belay at the foot of a crack and scoop leading to an imposing chimney line. Those who have a fear of enclosed spaces can and should escape to the right from here onto VIA VALENCIANOS.
4. 5+ 40m Climb the steep and awkward scoop until it develops into a crack then follow this into the base of a chimney. Head up into the blackness to a stance and twin bolt belay in the bowels of the Earth just short of daylight.
5. 5 15m Head for daylight where the chimney narrows and where awkward exposed climbing leads to a stance on the right.
6. 4+ 50m Up the slabbier rock above the stance or (easier) out left to reach a belay on the ridge in common with VIA VALENCIANOS.

From here either finish easily up VALENCIANOS pitches 6, 7 and 8 (75m) or abseil down the lower part of the same route in 3 or 4 rope lengths, always giving due consideration to those having the epic of their lives on the way up.

North West Face
Character
This is the large dome shaped white face that faces north towards the Playa de Levante. There are a variety of routes here that are in the shade for most of the day. From Easter onwards the face gets the sun in the evenings, so later in the year an option exists depending on weather conditions. Compared to the south face the rock is strangely smooth and covered with a white dusty lichen. These two factors combine to make the climbing here an altogether more delicate exercise than is found on most of the other crags in this guide, a nice contrast that should be sampled if the chance arises.

The routes can be divided into two types, longer affairs on the higher right side of the face that require a selection of nuts, and shorter bolt protected routes centred around the fine white wall 50m right of the tunnel entrance.

- **Note 1** The face is closed because of nesting birds between May and September; that shouldn't worry many of us!
- **Note 2** Unfortunately climbing on the left-hand wall is banned at present because of its proximity to the path. Brief notes are included on the four fine climbs here in the hope that the situation will change.

Approaches
Follow the normal walking route for the Penon from the harbour, starting at some broad steps opposite the Bar Gaviota. This takes about 20 minutes. It is also possible to park further up the hill at an isolated small car park by an odd small square tower, cutting about 5 minutes off the walk, but ensure that you will be back to the car by dusk or there is a good chance you will have been 'done over'. The path zigzags gently up

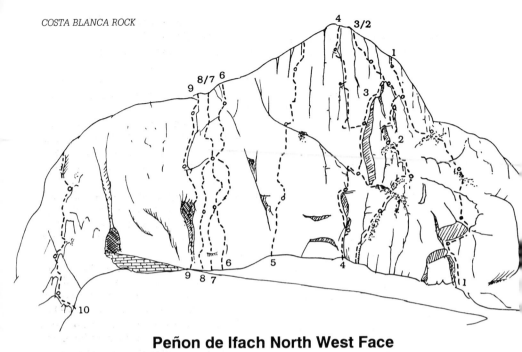

Peñon de Ifach North West Face

1. PERE CABREA   4, 5+, 3, 3, 4, 4, 4+   250m
2. VIA PANY   ☺   4, 3, 3, 4, 4, 4+, 4+   260m
3. DIEDRO BOTELLA   ☺   4, 3, 5+, 5, 4+, 4+, 3   185m
4. VIA ROXY   ☺   5, 5, 5, 5+, 6b, 6a, 6a   205m
5. LA SINFONIA DE LA GAVIOTAS   5+, 6a+, 6b+, 5   160m
6. VAMPIRO   ☺   6b+, 6c, 6c+   90m
7. ASIGNATURA PENDIENTE   ♦   6b, 6b, 5+   80m
8. TABERNA DEL PUERTO   ♦   6b+, 6c, 5+   80m
9. VERDE ESMERALDA   ☺   4+, 6a, 5, 4   95m
10. ROLLO   3, 4, 4+, 4   80m

the hillside (more direct versions should be avoided) and then passes below all of the route on the final 'zag' up to the tunnel entrance.

From this final bend there are impressive views across the largely undeveloped alternating slabs and bulges of the west shoulder of the Penon. The most prominent feature here is a huge roof. Climbing under this and on up the buttress to the right of VIA PANY is PERE CABREA, a 250m route, seven pitches long. Passing the lip of the roof on pitch 2 is 5+ and the rest of the climbing is 3 & 4. It looks worthwhile.

Descent

For the routes on the right side of the face scramble the short distance to the summit and descend by the regular path. For the climbs on the left side either abseil back down the line of the climb or top out on to the ridge and scramble down the back to reach the uphill end of the tunnel, 10 minutes back to the base of the climbs.

The climbs are described as approached on the footpath on the way up the hill, that is from right to left. The first route starts a short distance above the path at the left side of the big buttress dropping from the summit, at a narrow chimney with 'AMA' painted in large letters on its right side. This is reached by a thin track branching right off the main path.

2. VIA PANY ☺ 4 (UK Hard Severe 4a) 260m
An interesting climb at a very reasonable standard up an imposing part of the Penon. Perhaps not of the calibre of VALENCIANOS but well worthwhile (and it is usually in the shade). The climbing is rather vegetated in the lower part but improves as height is gained to give a grand upper section. Carry a light rack and a few slings.

1. 25m 4 Climb the steep awkward chimney on polished pockets passing several threads (not all in situ) and a peg to a thread on a jammed block. Move out right to a thread belay at a good ledge.
2. 55m 3 Easy scrambling and the odd awkward move leads up right through shrubbery to a fat bolt belay on top of the first buttress.
3. 40m 3 Follow the broken rib above the belay, through an awkward groove (avoidable on the right) to a peg and tatty threads. Traverse left to a belay on another fat bolt in a niche below a corner on the right side of a huge block.
4. 22m 4 Up the interesting corner moving right by a bolt into a second corner. Go up this then step right to a stance on top of a rib, bolt and old peg belays.
5. 28m 4 Move slightly left and follow an easy ramp into deepening cracks to a belay on (yet another) fat bolt on top of the buttress and below a sweep of slabs.
6. 30m 4+ Above the stance a slab leads slightly left (not well protected) to reach a large crack falling from the summit. Follow this in a fine position to a stance and belay about 15m up the crack system.
7. 30m 4+ Follow the crack, it is awkward low down but the angle and the difficulties ease as height is gained. Where it becomes vegetated pull out left onto the rib (bolt), and follow this eventually moving left into another groove that leads to the cliff top and a belay on easy ground. The summit lies a little higher.

3. DIEDRO BOTELLA ☺ 5+ 185m
An interesting outing that links the start and finish of VIA PANY with the central groove of VIA ROXY to produce a good direct line up the face. Start at the chimney of VIA PANY (see above) and carry a rack.

1. 25m 4 Climb the chimney on polished pockets passing several threads (not all in situ) and a peg to a thread on a jammed block. Move out right to a thread belay at a good ledge.
2. 45m 3 Easy scrambling and the odd awkward move leads up right through shrubbery until it is possible to follow a ledge leftwards to a stance at the foot of the imposing corner.
3. 30m 5+ Climb past the palm tree on the right then move right to a corner. Climb this past big pegs to a steeper corner which is bridged past a monolithic wooden wedge. A short distance above is a ledge and bolt belay, with peg back-ups around the corner.
4. 25m 5 Continue up the groove which gradually eases, eventually arriving on top of a tower. Cross this and the next one and descend slightly to a stance at the foot of the final slab.
5. 30m 4+ Climb the slab slightly leftwards to reach a crack falling from the summit. Follow this in a fine position to a stance and belay about 15m up the crack system.
6. 30m 4+ Follow the crack. It is awkward low down but the angle and the difficulties ease as height is gained. Where it becomes vegetated pull out left onto the rib (bolt), and follow this eventually moving left into another groove that leads to the cliff top and a belay on easy ground. The summit lies a little higher.

4. VIA ROXY ☺ 6b 205m
A rather indifferent lower section leads to impressive climbing up the great crack system that falls from the left side of the summit dome. The crux is hard but very well protected and eminently frigable. Carry a standard rack, with a few extra large hexes or Friends.
Start as for the previous route.

1. 30m 5 From the chimney at the foot of PANY slant left up rock and two veg. to reach the prominent jamming crack, bridge this(!) to a ledge (bolt) and make a couple of awkward moves around to the left to a stance and nut belays below a wider crack.
2. 20m 5 Bridge elegantly up the corner past threads (or get an arm and leg in and give it some grunting), to a stance on a good ledge a little higher, nut belays.
3. 35m 5 Climb the wall above the stance for 8m then slant up to the right over flakes and blocks to reach the huge ramp that crosses the face at a pair of bolts. Descend for 8m to a good stance at two old bolts.
4. 30m 5+ Climb over (or up) the palm tree on the right then move right to a corner. Climb this past big pegs to a steeper corner which is bridged past a monolithic wooden wedge. A short distance above is a ledge and bolt belay, with peg back-ups around the corner. Escape is possible here up to the right to join PANY at the end of pitch 4.
5. 30m 6b Follow the line of threads across the left wall (great photos) and up to a ledge. Move back right and make a difficult but well protected mantleshelf to reach the break, shuffle right and make more difficult moves to gain the crack above. This leads more easily to a restricted stance.
6. 25m 6a Up the steep crack above, a bit of a thrash to start with and then excellent bridging and jamming leads to a stance on a pedestal on the left.
7. 25m 6a Continue up the groove and crack line to arrive at a twin bolt belay, the best fixed gear on the route. The top lies 50m above and is most easily reached on the right.

To the left are a vast series of steep walls and soaring grooves, containing the odd relic of aid attempts. One route climbs the left side of this starting at the foot of the prominent left trending ramp:

5. LA SINFONIA DE LAS GAVIOTAS 5+,6a+,6b+,5 160m looks good but how much fixed kit it contains and how good it really is

remains open to question.

The next routes lie 100m further up the main track where a fine clean white wall descends within a couple of metres of the path. Unfortunately, as mentioned in the introduction climbing on this wall is banned at present because of its proximity to the path. Brief notes are included on the four fine climbs here in the hope that the situation will change.

The right side of the face has a shrubby groove running up into steeper rock, from this a left slanting crack, containing a prominent thread, heads towards the centre of the face.
Starting under this groove is:
6. VAMPIRO ☺ 6c+ 90m
A taxing series of pitches especially if the easier variations are shunned.

1. 30m 6b+ Climb the groove then move left to gain the slanting crack. Up this until it is possible to head straight up the wall on good but spaced holds and pockets. A few rather more difficult moves lead to easier rock trending left to the stance in the centre.
2. 30m 6c Climb up to the right to gain the right-hand bolt line running up the crest of a blunt rib. Continue straight up following this with great difficulty to a small stance and five(!) bolt belay.
3. 30m 6c+ Step right and follow yet another line of bolts with more difficulty to eventually gain a slab and very substantial tree belay.

Descent
Either abseil back down the face in two rope lengths, 25m first then 50m, or scramble left (3) to get over the ridge then walk down the back to the tunnel.

7. ASIGNATURA PENDIENTE ♦ 6b 80m
A great route following the centre of the wall giving three contrasting pitches. Start behind a bush just above the path, below the right end of an overlap 4m up.

1. 25m 6b Gain and cross the overlap then climb up to the left to reach a crack that slants to the right crossing a series of bulges. Up this strenuously until an awkward pull

gains the easy groove leading to a good stance and multiple belays.

2. 30m 6b Move right to reach the leftmost of a pair of bolt lines. These are followed over a bulge and up a shallow groove until difficult moves lead up and left to better holds. Continue up and left to a long flake crack that leads to a small stance and the five bolt belay.

3. 25m 5+ Climb up above the stance until forced left into the chimney. This has an awkward exit and leads to easier crack climbing with the odd tricky move to reach a big tree belay.

Descent as for the previous route.

8. TABERNA DEL PUERTO ✎ 6c 80m
A difficult and sustained second pitch is the highlight of this route although the initial slab is not without interest.
Start just off the footpath at the left side of the slab where a steep wall bars access to a line of bolts.

1. 25m 6b+ A problem start gains the slab, then some difficult smearing leads to the overlap, which is crossed rightwards. A barrier of steeper rock is passed on good holds to a small stance with a selection of belays.

2. 30m 6c Move up the ramp on the right then follow the bolts straight up the wall via superb sustained climbing. Difficult moves into a shallow niche provide the crux and are followed by some tough laybacking up a flake system to better holds. Move right to the five bolt stance.

3. 25m 5+ Plod up the top pitch of ASIGNATURA PENDIENTE or bail out.

The final route ascends the great twisting groove system that bounds the smooth white face on the left. Its base is recognised by having a short flight of stone steps leading to a tiny cave. This is also covered by the ban.

9. VERDE ESMERALDA ☺ 6a 95m
An interesting trip through some weird and wonderful rock.

1. 30m 4+ Climb through the bushes to gain the groove. A variety of routes lead up, over and through the rock to a comfortable grotto.

2. 20m 6a Move to the right edge of the cave and grapple with the bulges above fixed threads, good holds lead rapidly to easier ground (or even more rapidly back in to the cave). Move left below the bulges to a good stance.

3. 35m 5 The crack and corner system above are followed throughout with the odd moment of interest to a stance a short distance from the ridge.

4. 10m 4 Finish easily.

Descent
The back entrance to the tunnel lies 5 minutes down to the left.

Round to the left of and below the lower end of the tunnel a rounded buttress that is home to

10. ROLLO 3, 4, 4+, 4 80m, a four pitch outing that may be worth checking out if you are after lower grade routes in the shade, take a rack. Down and left again is an impressive undeveloped cliff. Any takers?

MORAIRA SEA CLIFF

Crag Facts

Star rating: *** now, ***** in the fullness of time

Aspect: south east

Height: Up to 60 metres

Spread of grades:

4	5	5+	6a	6b	6c	7a	7b	7c	8
3	2	2	4	2	/	/	/	/	/

Introduction

A superbly situated cliff of high quality (and as usual very rough) rock with, at present, a handful of quality climbs. A 50m rope is a bare minimum here unless you want to walk round and back down the approach gully at the end of each climb. The cliffs stretch either side of the sparsely developed area as far as the eye can see and feature some of the most impressive bits of rock on the Costa Blanca. Have no doubts, this place is going to be big!

Access

From Calpe follow the rather tortuous coastal road eastwards to Moraira (c12km). Pass through the town and continue in the same direction following the one sign for the port (and heading for the hill with the fortification on top). Less than 50m short of the end of the road and the very inviting beach is a left turn signed 'parking'. Drive steeply up this to parking on the right in an extensive field, at least until they build on it! From the top right corner of this, a line of rough earth steps leads to a road running horizontally rightwards. Follow this then turn left up the Calle de Alcudia before turning left again by the sign Calle Puerto de Andraitx. Continue steeply up this to its termination at a turning circle (no parking available here) by a couple of villas one of which is decorated with a couple of rather ostentatious stone eagles. Take the path that starts here (red spots) and zigzags up the hillside

to the crest of the ridge and the first signs of what is to come. Turn right and follow the track as it heads for the hill top tower to reach a col, drop over this and tack down an old fisherman's path that heads down a steep gully until it is possible to branch left below a rounded buttress and climb back up a short distance to a flat area just to the right of a cave containing a solitary bolt. This is situated a couple of hundred metres right of the fisherman's path and 20 sweaty minutes from the car. The routes are described from left to right.

1. ESPUMA DE MAR ☺ 6a 24m
Start just right of the cave with the solitary bolt and climb up a flake and grey slabs to reach the foot of a yellow wall of steeper rock. Climb this on pockets (crux) then continue up easier rock until a short traverse right leads to a lower-off shared with the first pitch of the next route. 13 bolts.

2. ARCOIRIS EN EL MAR ☺ 5, 4+ 50m
Start right of the bushes at an embedded block. Climb the sustained grey rib on excellent rock with tricky moves at three-quarters height to reach a small stance, 24m, 12 bolts. Climb the rib on the left to reach the base of a left trending ramp and follow this keeping right to avoid the dirty rock to a belay on the cliff top, 26m, 10 bolts.

3. CHULLA ♦ 4+, 5+, 5 58m
A great route, probably the best here at the moment. Start right of a grassy corner/groove that runs up to a large 'fang' sticking out of the base of a deep narrow chimney. Climb an awkward slabby groove to easier rock and a 4 bolt belay, 15m, 4 bolts. Step left and climb the steep slab on great rock to final tricky moves rightwards leading to a good stance and low three bolt belay, 25m, 10 bolts. Continue up the

172

Moraira

1. ESPUMA DE MAR ☺ 6a
2. ARCOIRIS EN EL MAR ☺ 5,4+
3. CHULLA ♠ 4+, 5+, 5
4. SOL SAL ☺ 6a+, 4+
5. RIPPER ☺ 6a+
6. MELLIZO BOMBA ♠ 5+,6b
7. EL PENULTIMO MOICAN ☺ 6b+
8. SE NACE Y SE MATA 6a
9. ? ? ?
10. ? ? ?

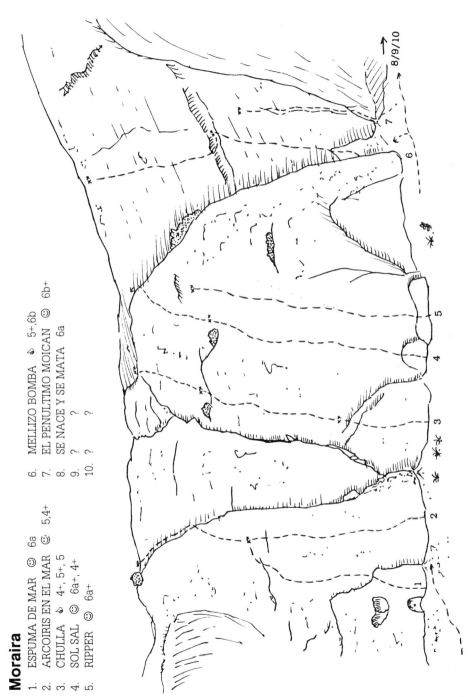

rib above and then a short section of steeper rock before finishing up an easy groove, 18m, 7 bolts.

Ten metres to the right is a steeper section of rock with two bolt lines up it. The first route starts behind a flowering bush below a brown wall:

4. SOL SAL ☺ 6a+, 4+ 55m

Climb onto the ledge then press on up the wall on small sharp holds until things ease and climb the steep slab on better holds trending slightly right to a belay/lower-off, 30m, 15 bolts. A second pitch is available up the rib and easy rock above, though most folk don't bother as it is so much easier than the lower one, 25m, 6 bolts.

5. RIPPER ☺ 6a+ 34m

The right-hand line again starts between a diagonal crack and some blocks and climbing on to a (different) ledge then heads up the steep thin wall (easier on the right) before more straightforward climbing leads to a final steeping. A couple more thin moves lead through a bulge and just a little higher is the lower-off below orange overhangs at the top of the cliff. There is also a separate lower-off at 10m offering the possibility of a short and not very satisfying 5+.

To the right is an area of undeveloped rock and then a long vegetated ramp that cuts leftwards up the face. A short scramble up this is a rough grey triangular slab on the right. Starting on ledges below this is:

6. MELLIZO BOMBA ☙ 5+, 6b 48m

Climb the slab to reach the first bolt in the steeper rock then climb the wall directly above (avoiding some loose rock out left) to an overhung ledge and twin bolt belay, 26m, 6 bolts. Move left and pull through the overhangs to reach the first bolt. Trend left then right to a resting place then climb the excellent leaning wall on 'flatties' to better holds. Step right and climb spiky rock to a twin bolt and karabiner lower-off, 6b, 22m, 8 bolts.

Around to the right is an 'impossible' groove leading to an attractive hanging crack:

7. EL PENULTIMO MOICAN ☺ 6b+ 22m

Use the first two bolts to reach the bird's nest then climb the steep crack to pockets and marginally easier angled rock. Head up this on good holds to reach a twin bolt abseil point (no chains here at present so it may be worth considering leaving a karabiner).

Around to the right is a huge black chimney and in the left wall of this is a long sinuous crack line:

8. SE NACE Y SE MATA 6a 30m

Carrying that full rack you brought from the UK enter the crack from the base of the big chimney and followed with sustained moves and a dearth of fixed kit to a stance and twin bolt belay. Add your own second pitch or abseil off.

To the right is a huge leaning Kilnsey Crag of a cliff that will doubtless become home to some world class desperates and beyond this is a long corner and then a cave with two bolt lines near it. The left-hand one climbs the smooth wall above the cave and the right-hand one, the easier rib to the right, both routes reuniting at twin ring bolts situated above a protruding block. An excellent looking very long (or maybe even two short) extension pitch leads up the steep wall to a point just below the cliff top, though no grades are known.

To the right are miles of rock, running as far as the distant lighthouse on the Cabo de Nao (the true geographical end of the Costa Blanca) and beyond. On a clear day you can see the glittering cliffs of Ibiza and on a very clear day the mythical island of Majorca, but that's another story and of course another guidebook!

MARINA ALTA

1. Peña Roja
2. Alcalali
3. L'Ocaive
4. Font d'Axia
5. Covatelles
6. Coves Rojes

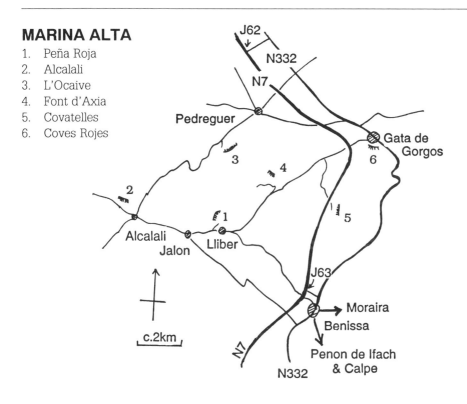

PEÑA ROJA

Crag Facts

Star rating: **
Aspect: south east facing
Height: Up to 25 metres
Spread of grades:

4	5	5+	6a	6b	6c	7a	7b	7c	8
/	1	4	2	1	6	4	5	2	/

Introduction

A pleasant cliff in a quiet setting, with a good collection of mainly tough wall climbs, though there are a few routes of lesser grade for climbers with lower aspirations and several unclimbed crack lines that will eventually make reasonable lower grade climbs. The bowl shape of the cliff means that it can be hot though it goes into the shade at about mid afternoon.

Access

Drive west through Lliber (English tea room on the left if you are feeling at all homesick) towards Jalon and immediately upon leaving the town turn right into a concrete 'canal' (honest). Drive

175

down this, bump across the river bed and follow the track through the local 'el dumpo' to park at the start of the almond groves. Do the local farmers a favour and don't try to get any nearer the cliff which is only three minutes walk away!

The routes are described from left to right, starting with the pleasant grey slab that bounds the left side of the wall and which is home to three climbs.

1. ROUTE ONE 5+ 12m
The left side of the slab through a bulge low down.

2. SANSON SIN PIELT ☺ 5+ 15m
The pleasantly sustained centre of the slab initially keeping left of an incipient flake and trending right to join the next route.

3. COMO UN LOCO 5 14m
The right hand line starts up a left facing flake and can be as hard as 6a+ if you are totally blinkered about it, though weaving a bit eases matters.

4. SANSON Y DALILA 6a+ 12m
Climb the right edge of the slab and cross the bulge rightwards on sharp holds. A direct start just to the right is harder pulling through a bulge at a tough 6b+.

To the right the rounded buttress has three closely packed climbs:
5. AGARRATE COMO PUEDAS 6c 14m
The first line starts at its own painted name, passes a big broken tufa pillar and presses on through the bulges above.

6. PUTA MICI 6c+ 16m
The next line just to the right up the blunt rib, starting from a small cave and on particularly sharp rock.

7. HALL 9000 6c 14m
Right again on the right side of the same broad rib and with paired second bolts is a route requiring more powerful pulls on vicious rock.

To the right beyond a chunky olive tree is:
8. TORO SALVAGE 7a 15m
Tackle the red scoop just to the right again.

The scoop and crack to the right are:
9. EL PAS DE LA DENTS 5+ 20m
The corner crack and butch roof (5+?) lead to herbal ramblings above.

Around to the right past a tree standing close to the rock is a grey ramp with two routes up its right side.
10. THROUGH THE MAGIC DOOR 5+ 22m
The left-hand line starts from a big boulder, has spaced bolts in the lower section, a rather totty bulge and a slab to finish. Marked by an interesting name though not a great route.

11. SOC UNA AGUILETA 6a+ 22m
The right hand line on the steep grey slab has some tenuous moves and the odd bit of loose rock. Trend left to finish as for the previous route.

To the right and up one level is a flat wall running into an open corner which bounds the left side of the main wall of the cliff. There are four tough and closely packed routes here starting behind a large tree 2m out from the wall. The first route climbs the wall and a substantial roof, it may be 7a+ though I have no name for it.

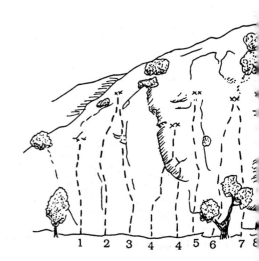

13. TARZAN DE LOS MONODEDOS ☺ 7b 17m
The second outing from the left, climbing directly up the grey wall to the right is both tough and sustained.

14. LA BELLA ☺ 7b 16m
The best route on the side wall. Reach the prominent large pocket and continue to the

small overlap via the crux moves. Climb more easily rightwards to reach the lower-off.

15. LA BESTIA 7b+ 16m
This vicious beast proves to be too close to the corner to be of any real value. Alternatively make the first ascent of the corner and keep leaning out to the left to clip the bolts.

Peña Roja

1. ROUTE ONE 5+ 12m
2. SANSON SIN PIELT ☺ 5+ 15m
3. COMO UN LOCO 5 14m
4. SANSON Y DALILA 6a+ 12m
5. AGARRATE COMO PUEDAS 6c 14m
6. PUTA MICI 6c+ 16m
7. HALL 9000 6c 14m
8. TORO SALVAGE 7a 15m
9. EL PAS DE LA DENTS 5+ 20m
10. THROUGH THE MAGIC DOOR 5+ 22m
11. SOC UNA AGUILETA 6a+ 22m
12. ? 7a+ 16m
13. TARZAN DE LOS MONODEDOS ☺ 7b 17m
14. LA BELLA ☺ 7b 16m
15. LA BESTIA 7b+ 16m
16. SULACCO 7a 18m
17. CABELLO LOCO ☺ 7b 18m
18. MUERTE COMO UN HURACAN ☺ 6c+ 18m
19. SIEMPRE EL ALGUNA PORTE 6c+ 18m
20. LLIBERPOOL ☙ 6b 18m
21. ? ☺ 7a+ 18m
22. ? 7c+? 18m
23. ? ☺ 7b 18m
24. ? ☺ 7a 18m
25. ? ☺ 7c 18m
26. ? 6c 18m

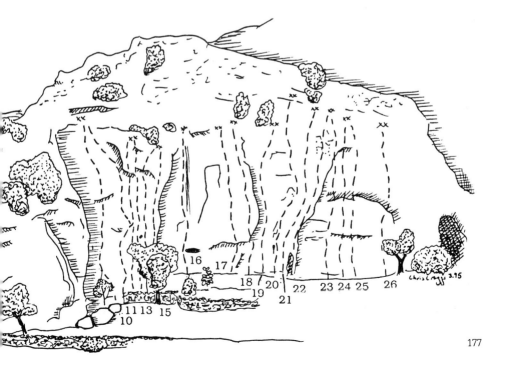

To the right is the high red wall that is the main attraction of the cliff with almost a dozen excellent steep pitches. Just right of the obvious and unclimbed corner is:

16. SULACCO 7a 18m
Climb the wall via a grey streak 2m out from the corner keeping to the left of a tall orange perched flake.

17. CABELLO LOCO ☺ 7b 18m
The crinkly red wall starting behind a diminutive prickly pear is climbed via a tough strenuous start, a technical mid section and a good finish on pockets.

18. MUERTE COMO UN HURACAN ☺ 6c+ 18m
The bulging left arete of the shallow central corner has a steep start and fine climbing above. Trend left to finish.

19. SIEMPRE EL ALGUNA PORTE 6c+ 18m
The route immediately right of the central (unclimbed) corner is OK but the temptation to keep stepping back into the corner is overwhelming.

20. LLIBERPOOL ☙ 6b 18m
The central line of the wall gives a fine and continuously surprising climb, the route of the cliff! Start below a floral pocket and climb the steep wall before moving right to jugs in a niche. Pull left onto the wall and finish direct.

To the right are 6 more climbs for which I have no names. The first route parallels LLIBERPOOL, it is ☺ 7a+, has a tough sequence below a 'blob' and is easier above.
Around to the right is a very steep bulging arete, just left of a cave and this may be 7c+.
Right again are three closely packed routes up a leaning tufa encrusted white wall. The left hand climb starts up a groove and continues up the leaning rib above, this is ☺ 7b. The next line right had been advertised as a juggy ☙ 6b though a thuggy ☺ 7a is nearer the mark. Right again through the centre of the bulges is a ☺ 7c, and the line up the right side of the bay is 6c.

Peña Segurea (Alcalali): Graham Parkes involved with classic pocket pulling on unnamed 6b

PEÑA SEGUREA
(ALCALALI)

Crag Facts

Star rating: ** (with a potential ****)
Aspect: south facing
Height: Up to 30 metres
Spread of grades:

4	5	5+	6a	6b	6c	7a	7b	7c	8
/	1	4	2	1	6	4	5	2	/

Alcalali

A1. 🔥 7b+ 30m
A2. 🔥 7b 30m
A3. ☺ 7a+ 26m
A4. ☺ 6b 16m
A5. 6b+ 14m
A6. ☺ 7b 25m

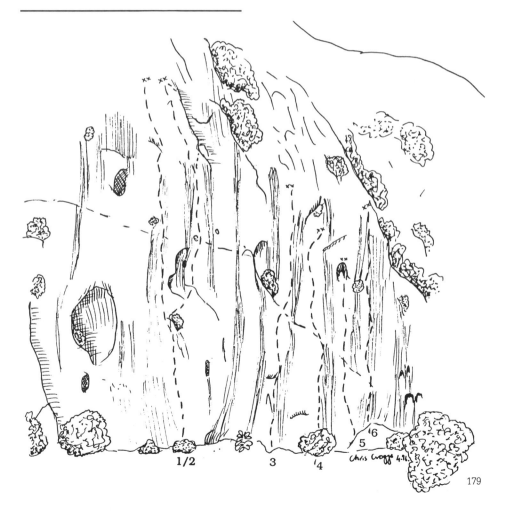

Chris Craggs 4.96

179

Introduction

A recently developed cliff with a clutch of exciting climbs and scope for many more on great rock. Pockets and tufas predominate and this could become one of the most important cliffs in the area in the fullness of time.

Access

Drive west from the town of the same name (signed Pego) and shortly after leaving it a major crag appears on the right. There is parking for 3 or 4 cars on the bend at the developed sector which is two minutes away up to the right by beehives.

To the left of the developed area are two other bolted climbs. On the far left of the large bay (150m left of the other routes) is a climb up a rib, starting behind a solitary prickly pear and to the right of some faded white graffiti, leading to a home-made lower-off. 100 metres to the right, and to the right of the back of the bay, is a two pitch climb slanting left up a clean section of rock. No grades are known but they don't look too desperate.

On the left of the developed area is a 'project' though the first completed routes start 2m left of a low section of drystone walling with a beehive behind it and 'FN' painted on the rock. Unfortunately both these routes were occupied by a very active bee community at Easter 1996.

A1 🐝 7b+ 30m
Climb the grey lower wall to ledges, continue up a black tufa and then on up a long white streak by sustained climbing.

A2 🐝 7b 30m
Follow the previous route for the first three clips and then move right to a parallel line up a rust coloured groove and elongated pockets and up the final crucial rib. Apparently it is possible to swing around the corner to the right on this upper section and lower the grade of the route to 6c, but I bet the first ascensionists didn't plan it that way!

Starting just to the right of the small enclosure is

A3 ☺ 7a+ 26m
Up a tufa and a hanging chandelier, to ledges. Step right and attack a rather soft cruxy tufa (fat pinch grips) then stacks of excellent climbing to the lower-offs.

A4 ☺ 6b 16m
To the right climb the line of big holes, strenuously to start and then more delicately to the lower-off in the groove above.

A5 6b+ 14m
Just to the right where the bank starts to rise up climb the strenuous rib right of a groove to a lower-off on the lip of a prominent cave.

A6 ☺ 7b 25m
Up the slope again, just before private gardens, is large pitch straight up the wall ending just short of the bushes.

L'OCAIVE

Crag Facts

Star rating: ***

Aspect: northwestish

Height: Up to 45 metres

Spread of grades:

4	5	5+	6a	6b
6c	7a	7b	7c	8
/	2	/	12	2
2	1	1	/	/

Introduction

A fine northwest facing tower off crag that is in the shade until mid afternoon and thus is an ideal venue on hot days. The cliff contains a good collection of mid-grade face climbs on rock that is quite superb. Sections of the face look quite vegetated from below but prove to be clean when you actually get stuck into the routes.

Access

From the N332 take signs to Pedreguer. On the outskirts of the town is a Y junction containing a small roundabout. Take the right fork then follow signs for Llos de Camacho and the crag soon appears on the left. Pass a 'fancy' entrance on the right then turn up a steep dirt road as far as you dare, reaching a flat quarried area if successful with the full ascent. Take a good track that slants away to the right and then tack up and left across prickly overgrown terraces to arrive below the centre of the cliff.

The routes are described from far left to high right.

On the far left side of the cliff is HIDDEN ROCK, a monumental fallen flake that leans against the cliff. The steeply tilted underside of this is walled off as an animal enclosure and has an impressive looking route running up it and a lot of goat turds under it. Start from a block and use the in-situ stick clip, about 9 bolts. On the

front of the flake are three much more minute offerings.

1. LAGARTO CACHAS 7b+ 8m
Start at the painted name to the right of the cave entrance and follow the line of 4 bolts to a lower-off.

2. SINS OF LIFE 6c 10m
Eight metres up the slope is this short line up a black tufa right of rib. Wire cable lower-off.

3. THE FLY 6a 8m
Two metres to the right and just left of some drystone walling, head up passing pockets to a smooth slab then pull right over bulge to the lower-off used by the previous route.

200 metres up the slope to the right and 50m to the left of the clumps of trees standing in front of the cliff is the section of developed rock known as the PLACAS TOCHAS. This is situated to the left of the centre of the crag. On the far left a scratched arrow and a couple of old bolts are pointers to a route that looks as if it is best forgotten. To the left of a 3m high mushroom shaped block is the minuscule:

4. EL BORDILLO DE LISTILLO 4 12m
A short pitch (3 bolts) to a good stance at the base of more impressive rock, and the foot of the next two routes. 22/2/98   L KT

5. CUERPO DE MUJER ♦ 6a 18m
The excellent left-hand line off the stance, tricky early on then again approaching the chain and keyhole karabiner. 9 bolts. 22/2/98   L KT
Excellent.   S KT

6. LA ESQUINA ASESINA ♦ 6a+ 18m
Step right and then follow the long rib with the crux moves reaching the chains, superb rock.

181

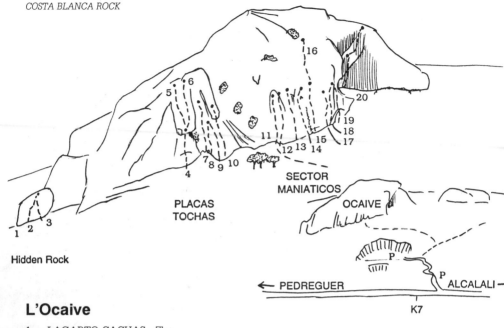

Hidden Rock

PLACAS
TOCHAS

SECTOR
MANIATICOS

OCAIVE

← PEDREGUER

P

P ALCALALI →

K7

L'Ocaive

1. LAGARTO CACHAS   7b+
2. SINS OF LIFE   6c
3. THE FLY   6a
4. EL BORDILLO DE LISTILLO   4
5. CUERPO DE MUJER   ☙ 6a
6. LA ESQUINA ASESINA   ☙ 6a+
7. ALUCINA CON LE ESQUINA   ☙ 5
8. SI TA CAIS TA CODES   6a
9. NO M'ALCARA   ☺ 6a
10. EL GRAJO DE CARAJO   ☺ 6b
11. PLACMANIA   6b+

12. NO T'AS VARES   ☺ 6a+
13. AMPARITO, NO ME TOQUES EL PITO   ☺ 6a+
14. LOS HOMBRES DE PAPEL   ☺ 6a+
15. PIEL DE GATO   ☺ 6a+
16. 96 OCTANOS   ☺ 6a
17. EL INCREDULO   ☺ 6a
18. CORAZON SALADA   ☺ 6a
19. ELLA, LA ARANA   5
20. LOS PRIMOS   ☙ 7a,6c

To the right is a left slanting ramp/gully containing a large tree and on the right of this is a left slanting rib.

7. ALUCINA CON LE ESQUINA ☙ 5 20m
Climb the rib (old bolts) then the steep juggy wall (nice new bolts) to a substantial lower-off. 11 bolts. 22/2/98   L RST, S KT
L KST 5/3/00   Good route

To the right are three shorter routes all with their names painted on the rock

8. SI TA CAIS TA CODES 6a 12m
Start at the top of the ramp reached by a scramble and follow the line of ring bolts.
L EST 5/3/00

9. NO M'ALCARA ☺ 6a 15m
The pleasant sustained rib to the right is reached via tricky start (first bolt missing April 96), and followed with interest.   L EST 5/3/00

10. EL GRAJO DE CARAJO ☺ 6b 18m
To the right follow the ring bolts up the grey rib and through the bulges above to the lower-off.

The next developed area to the right is MANIATICOS, situated just to the right of the trees stood in front of the cliff. This is presently the best developed area of the cliff with most routes having their names painted at the base of the wall, though those on the right have neat white squares and no painted names as yet.

11. PLACMANIA 6b+ 20m
Start at a gap in the bushes and trend left up the pocketed wall and past a smoother section to a lower-off just above a ledge. Eight (old) bolts.

12. NO T'AS VARES ☺ 6a+ 16m
Immediately to the right is this line trending slightly right following twisting cracks up the smooth wall, good climbing.

13. AMPARITO, NO ME TOQUES EL PITO ☺ 6a+ 17m
Up a step to the right, climb crozzly rock to start with then smoother scoopy stuff, more excellent sport. 7 clips.

14. LOS HOMBRES DE PAPEL ☺ 6a+ 18m
Right again behind some trees and below an orange scar high up. 11 clips are followed to a lower-off above and right of a cave. Excellent just for a change!

To the right is prominent vegetated gully and climbing the rib on the right of this is:
15. PIEL DE GATO ☺ 6a+ 20m
Follow the long sustained and excellent rib, 12 clips. Lower-off from here or call up the big guns and go for:

16. 96 OCTANOS ☺ 6a 20m
The extension pitch up bubbly rock, a tufa, then a series of holes is very good and very undergraded.

17. EL INCREDULO ☺ 6a 15m
Start right of a large fallen block, climb past a rock scar and bush then on up a white rib before stepping back left to lower-off in a bay. L BST 5/3/00

Final two routes start just left of the arête of this part of the cliff. L 22/2/98
18. CORAZON SALADA ☺ 6a 18m
Up a pillar, then a long ramp and finally a crack line before moving right to the belay. L BST 5/3/r8

19. ELLA, LA ARANA 5 18m 22/2/98 LIST S KT
A pleasant low grade route with six bolt runners and one manky old thread. Start at a boulder at Crap the base of a groove. Climb over the boulder and on up the groove before swinging left at the top to reach the lower-off of the previous route.

Up to the right is the impressive and undeveloped sector of LA ARANA. This is only home to one route at present but if you climb at the grade the cliff is worth a visit for this alone.

20. LOS PRIMOS ♦ 7a,6c 45m
Scramble up into the cave on the right side of the cliff to find a bolt ladder on the right wall. A two pitch mega-classic, the first pitch is a bit of a one move wonder (a quick layback) and the second pitch a long sustained and exposed outing up the very edge of the wall. Lower-offs are located in the groove just around the lip, clip into the 'up' rope on the way down or you might spend the rest of your life swinging in space.

183

COVATELLES

Crag Facts

Star rating: **

Aspect: west facing

Height: Up to 20 metres

Spread of grades:

4	5	5+	6a	6b	6c	7a	7b	7c	8
/	2	1	5	4	1	1	/	/	/

Introduction

A long low outcrop of limestone that can be seen from the motorway (on the right when travelling north) between Benissa and Gata de Gorgos. Despite this it has a secluded feel about it and is worth a visit (perhaps combined with Font d'Axia which is only 15 minutes away) if you fancy somewhere different. The crag looks quite scrappy from a distance, but the locals have had the bright idea of only developing the best bits of rock on the escarpment.

Access

From Gata de Gorgos take the Lliber road for 3km, passing under the motorway then just after the 3km marker post across a bridge. 200m further on turn left onto a narrow tarmacked road, signed Cami dels Gorgos. Drive down this to a river bed and turn right at the T junction. Swing left through the left-hand storm drain(!) under the motorway (danger of flooding signs!!) and park where the road heads up and right back out of the river bed, 0.7km from the tunnel. From the parking walk along the stream bed for a hundred metres or so, passing a 'tile graveyard', looking out for a red arrow on a rock pointing leftwards into the bushes. Follow a series of these arrows until number 12 (also C16 painted on the rock) and scramble just another 10m or so before heading left along a terrace for a couple of hundred metres to a small stand of pine trees. Climb up one level then walk back right to the start of the climbing. Heading straight up the gully from the last red arrow is possible for thick skinned and well clad individuals. All others are strongly advised to follow the route as described above.

The routes are described from left to right and many of them have their names painted on the rock.

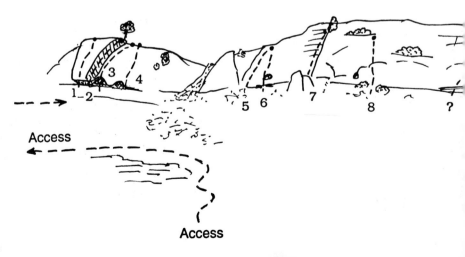

Sector Coloso

The first buttress on the left is easily recognised by a prominent white wall and a large left to right slanting overlap. The routes start from a pleasantly situated terrace that is most easily approached from the right and forms a good sunbathing/bivi platform.

1. LA PRIME ☺ 6a+ 12m
The first offering climbs the front of the buttress pulling over the substantial roof and then stepping right to pass a small overlap to reach a chain and karabiner lower-off. Five bolt runners and rock that is not Spain's best.

2. DEDOS DE METAL 7a+ 12m
The leaning wall is tackled initially by using a large bolted on lump of rock and then sprinting for the chains. Avoiding bridging into the corner on the right is a major problem.

3. EL COLOSO ☺ 5+ 12m
The main red streaked slanting corner gives a pleasant pitch trending right all the way to the top before leaning out left to clip the lower-off of the previous climb.

4. EL BESO DE LA MUERTA ☺ 6c 12m
The grey tilted wall around to the right is harder than it looks and it looks blank. The climbing is sustained and fingery, five bolts protect very well.

Sector Dolmen

Across the gully to the right is a rather scrappy looking wall with a huge fallen block in front of it, and to the right of this is a long low cave.

5. JABON SERRANO ☺ 5 12m
The clean slab on the extreme left is well bolted.

6. THE JUMP KILL ☺ 6b+ 14m
A killer of a jump to start (leap for the orange pocket) or a large cairn for aid, then press on up the sustained wall. 6 bolts.

20 metres further right and behind some huge blocks is a shrubby slab with a pedestal at its foot, and containing only a solitary bolt.

7. GOLPE DE GRACIA 5 16m
Climb the right rib of the slab on good rock to a lower-off just below a tree at the top of the cliff.

8. TRIKI, EL MONSTRUO DE LA CHAPAS ☺ 6a+ 15m
Perhaps the best routes on the cliff, starting at the name painted on a tufa pillar and climbing straight up the pleasantly sustained pocketed wall, six bolt runners.

9 10 11 12

Covatelles

DERECHA 6a
EST 9/3/00

1. LA PRIME ☺ 6a+
2. DEDOS DE METAL 7a+
3. EL COLOSO ☺ 5+
4. EL BESO DE LA MUERTA ☺ 6c
5. JABON SERRANO ☺ 5 KST 9/3/00
6. THE JUMP KILL ☺ 6b+
7. GOLPE DE GRACIA 5
8. TRIKI, EL MONSTRUO DE LA CHAPAS ☺ 6a+ EST 9/3/00
9. EL GUSANO FRANCISCANO 6a
10. BODIDO BABE ☺ 6a EST 9/3/00
11. CHICO LISTO 6b+
12. SAMURAY ☺ 6b+

Up the ramp to the right past a hole are two newer routes up a wall at the back of a flat rocky ledge:

IZQUIERDA ☺ 6b+ 15m
The left-hand line has a tough sustained lower wall, trending rightwards through a small niche to a halfway ledge, and a much easier upper section.

DERECHA ☺ 6a 15m
A direct line to the upper section of the previous route has a couple of tricky moves up the initial wall and then gives pleasant climbing to the shared lower-off.

Sector Gran Buzon

Towards the right side of the cliff are a series of large caves. Starting to the left of these is:
9. EL GUSANO FRANCISCANO 6a 15m
Climb the white wall via a shallow groove (name on the rock) to a lower-off above a big broken flake, six bolts.

10. BODIDO BABE ☺ 6a 18m
Ten metres right head up a steep juggy wall, through a bulge then up a slab to a lower-off at the top of the cliff. Quality rock.

11. CHICO LISTO 6b+ 18m
A much harder right-hand start to the above.

12. SAMURAY ☺ 6b+ 16m
To the left of the large cave are smaller twin caves. This route starts at a belay bolt on the ledge below these. Pull rightwards out of the right-hand cave then swing back left to climb the wall above.

The large roofs and caves to the right are home to at least one project: LA BABOSA MUSCULOSA, though after gluing the first three blobs on the locals appear to have lost interest!

FONT D'AXIA

Crag Facts

Star rating: **

Aspect: southwest facing

Height: Up to 20 metres

Spread of grades:

4	5	5+	6a	6b	6c	7a	7b	7c	8
4	1	1	1	2	2	/	/	/	

Introduction

A small but pleasant crag in an exceptionally remote-feeling and idyllic setting, despite only being a short walk from the road. There are only a small number of climbs here but as a good percentage of them are in the lower grades and are well bolted, the place is perhaps ideally suited to the newcomer to sport climbing who wants to get the feel of the game without being too closely scrutinised. There are a couple of 'mid-grade' offerings for any lost hotshots, though the active bees' nest in the caves at the centre of the cliff can make access to these difficult! The place can conveniently combined with a visit to Covatelles which is only 15 minutes away.

Access

From the minor road between Lliber and Gata de Gorgos, and 200m west of the 5km stone, is a track that runs north, opposite a large white house. Follow this as it bends right then crosses a dry river bed. Continue up this (dirt and concrete in various proportions) keeping left at the only significant junction to a point where a dirt track branches back hard right at a seasonal yellow and white sign 'A Pedruguer'. This is opposite a parking area in the bushes (ideal for keeping the car cool), and is 2km from the road. Follow the track out onto a plateau (it would be conceivable but pointless to drive the car this far) until it is possible to climb up a couple of terraces and cross over to the base of the cliff.

The right side the crag is 100m away, less than 10 minutes from the car park. The routes are described from right to left.

On the right side of the cliff is a low undeveloped wall bound on its left by a scruffy groove. To the left is a route up the back of a bay.

1. FRIZER SE TRANSFORMA ☺ 6c 18m
Climb the right side of the bay following black bolts up a broad fingery rib and into a hollow then pull over a roof on finger pockets, 10 bolts protect.

2. LES ZAPATELLES DEL PASTOR ☺ 6a 24m
The left trending groove is followed, protected by 'plain', bolts up scoops and then an orange streaked groove passing a large semi-detached (and well attached?) flake, before trending left to a lower-off, 12 bolts.

3. EL DRAK ☺ 5 24m
This route starts just to the left, by a ground level niche and is perhaps the best route on the cliff. Trend slightly left to a potential lower-off after 12m (nice beginners' route, 4+) then back right up the wall following pink spotted bolts to join and finish as for the previous climb, 12 bolts. If the final section is climbed rigorously past the bolts award yourself a 6a.

4. LA LEY DEL CANTEO ☺ 6c 20m
Start at the name and arrow pointing the way up a scoop. The lower section is straightforward then 7 bolts protect the climbing up the steepening final wall, generally keeping left of the bolts.

5. LA MALA PATATA 6b+ 20m
Starting in the same place and following the same easy lower section but then trending left up the final wall is this route that is barely independent of the previous one.

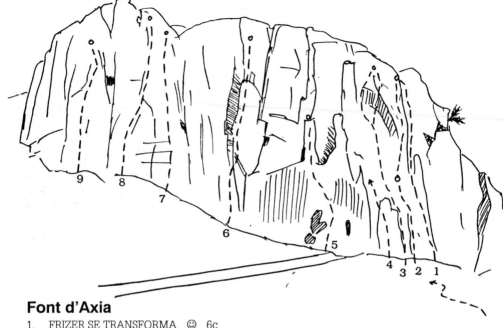

Font d'Axia

1. FRIZER SE TRANSFORMA ☺ 6c
2. LES ZAPATELLES DEL PASTOR ☺ 6a
3. EL DRAK ☺ 5
4. LA LEY DEL CANTEO ☺ 6c
5. LA MALA PATATA 6b+

6. PERELLO EL CACAOLAT ☺ 5+
7. SAVINA ☺ 4
8. EL PAVAL ☺ 4
9. IZQUIERDA RUTA ☺ 4-

To the left a bush grows in front of the cliff and behind this is a cave containing a very active bees' nest. Moving rapidly on is a small fire circle with a cave to its right. Starting here is a short line:
INOMINATA 6b 15m
Pull over a bulge (hard for the short) and climb the crinkly wall to ledges and a solitary bolt lower-off with a maillon.

Left past an area of undeveloped red rock, and behind some old tree stumps, is a patch of bushes and a clean pillar of rock climbed by:
6. PERELLO EL CACAOLAT 5+ 16m
A route with good climbing but protected by six rather antiquated iron men. The final section is easier but run-out, carry a few wires.

Left of some unclimbed grassy cracks (any takers) is:
7. SAVINA ☺ 4 18m
Start at the painted out name and follow clean rock directly before trending away to the left. At least 8 clips.

Six metres left below a long grassy crack is the start of:
8. EL PAVAL ☺ 4 18m
8 bolts protect another good low-grade climb.

Left of a clean pillar and starting at some stepped ledges is the last route on the cliff.

IZQUIERDA RUTA ☺ 4- 14m
6 bolts protect what is very straightforward (and not unpleasant) climbing.

COVES ROJES

Introduction

Included for completeness this cliff has the distinction of being the only "no star" crag in the guide. Using the definitions at the front of the book I guess that means it's not worth visiting even if you live on top of the place! However if you enjoy climbing in the local tip, being pestered by scabby dogs and street urchins this place may be your bag!

Access

From Gata de Gorgos take the Lliber road and turn left opposite the Restaurante El Corral del Pato, follow the road as it bears left then take a right turn and park on the left overlooking the dry river. The crag is below you (honest) and is reached by a steep descent over to the left, looking out.

The Routes

There are about thirty routes here but in general they are very poor. To the left of centre is the best rock here, some steeply leaning walls in the form of an open cave, peppered with large pockets. There are three good (or at least better) climbs here that may be worth calling in for. On the right is a the 'jugfest' (excuse my Americanism) of PAJARO DE HIERRO 6b+, climbing directly out of the cave is SIN MAS NI MENOS 6b+, left of the cave is a line of pockets, L'OBILA 5+ and left again is an orange streak, VIGIN ASESINA 7b+.

GANDIA REGION

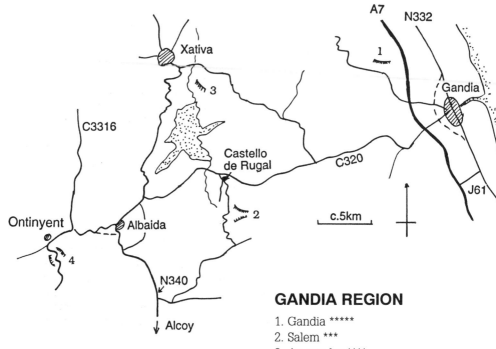

GANDIA REGION

1. Gandia *****
2. Salem ***
3. Aventador ****
4. Barranc de l'Avern ****

NOTE: Once north of the Cabo de Nao the coastline is technically the Costa del Azahar (coast of the orange blossom) though it has long been popular with climbers stopping on 'the Blanca'.

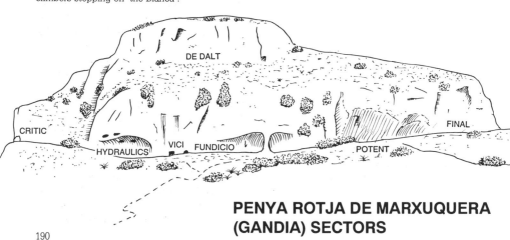

PENYA ROTJA DE MARXUQUERA (GANDIA) SECTORS

PENYA ROTJA DE MARXUQUERA
(GANDIA)

Crag Facts

Star rating: *****
Aspect: south facing
Height: Generally up to 25 metres though there is a handful of longer pitches.

Spread of grades:

4	5	5+	6a	6b	6c	7a	7b	7c	8
9	10	9	23	29	17	23	11	4	1

Note: For some years now this crag has been known simply as 'GANDIA', the reason being obvious.

Introduction

A superbly situated cliff in a quiet valley a few kilometres to the west of the large town of Gandia. The routes are generally short, up to 22m, and are very well bolted almost without exception. There are invariably lowering stations consisting of large bolts with steel rings, installed where the angle relents. There is a variety of styles of climbing varying from the brutish overhangs of the SECTORS HYDRAULICS and FINAL, on to the open more delicate fare of the SECTOR CRITIC or the UPPER TIER, and with lots in between.

The crag faces due south and is in the sun all day but with shelter provided by the larger roofs for those who have already seen too much of it. The outward view over the orange orchards is superb; it is little wonder the locals call the place 'paradise'. Since my 1990 guide the whole of the cliff has been developed with many new routes of the highest quality established. The cliff is now well worth an extended visit.

Crag Geography

The cliff consists of a lower tier, split towards its left side by an open gully. To the right of this the crag is divided into four Sectors: HIDRAULICS, VICI, FUNDICIO, and FINAL. To the left of the gully is the SECTOR CRITIC. Above the left side of the lower tier of cliff is an UPPER TIER reached via the open gully.

Access

Note: At spring 1996 a Gandia ring road was under construction. When completed this will simplify the approach to the cliff considerably and knock 15-20 minutes off the approach time from Calpe. The junction is to be situated at the point where the minor road from the town of Gandia to the crag runs under the motorway.

From Calpe follow the N332 northwards to Benisa. It is possible to continue along the N332 all the way to Gandia but this is very slow due to the narrow roads through the towns and the heavy traffic avoiding the motorway tolls. Therefore just to the north of Benisa get on to the N7 toll motorway and follow it north, towards Valencia. After 30km leave the motorway following the signs for Oliva, Alquera and Gandia. At the N332 turn left and follow the road towards Gandia (about 8km). The ring road will begin just after Bellreguard. Just before entering the main town is a left turn just beyond a conspicuous blue and yellow warehouse which is set back from the road. Turn left here and then take the first right. This crosses the river after a short distance. Immediately on the other side of the bridge turn right into a large car park (honest). Leaving the opposite corner of this is the start of the Passies des Germains, the unmistakable dual carriageway with pedestrian precinct and lines of trees running down its centre. Go straight down this road passing several roundabouts and dozens of double parked cars, until the buildings end and the road bends right and appears to dwindle into a minor track. Follow this small road under the motorway (ring road junction) and up into the valley. After only a couple of kilometres there is a minor right turn signed Raco de Tomba Marxuquera Alta. This is taken until it is possible to park just beyond a dried up river bed directly below the crag. The path up to the cliff is reached by crossing the river bed and cutting leftwards in front of the orange bushes (follow the painted arrows on the path) to a short steep scramble. The path arrives at the main (right-hand) crag, the left-hand crag is at the same level along a terrace two minutes to the left, and the UPPER TIER is reached via the steep gully that divides the two lower cliffs.

THE CLIMBS are described briefly: on the Main Crag first from left to right throughout then on the left-hand cliff from left to right, and finally on the UPPER TIER. The first area is known as the SECTOR HYDRAULICS for obvious reasons.

Sector Hydraulics

This is the section of rock stretching from the open gully that splits the cliff to the rounded rib just right of the biggest overhangs.

1. PRIMERA 3+ 12m
A short distance up the gully that bounds the left side of the cliff is this pleasant though unremarkable offering.

2. SECRETITOS ☺ 4 17m
An untypically pleasant route up the grey rounded rib on the left edge of the cliff. Start just behind a tree and climb the grey slab and the groove above.

3. FE RA ☺ 3+ 17m
Another pleasant climb. Start just right of the tree and climb the steeper slab passing to the right of a small bush.

4. CORAL BAJILLA 4 12m
Start at the left edge of the cave and head straight up the rib passing right of bush and lowering off from beneath another.

5. ERUPCIO 4+ 25m
An odd route that traverses rightwards above lip of caves to the belay above BLANIULUS GUTTULATUS. Some nuts may be required.

6. PEQUENO SALTAMONTES 6a+ 12m
A short and unsatisfying route that starts at the left rim of the arches and makes steep fingery moves up and right past three closely spaced old bolts before romping on to the substantial belay bolt.

To the right a peculiar tube runs up through the cliff. Right again is a line of bolts leading to a small cave over the lip of the overhang.
7. MONSTER OF ROCK ☺ 7a 12m
Start right of the tube (and 4m right of edge) at a 'love heart' scratched on the rock. Use well chalked pockets and follow the big bolts leftwards to a lower-off on the head wall.

8. ASSASSI DE VAMPIRS ☺ 7a 12m
Follow the line of bolts straight up the wall and through the bulges to the sanctuary of the cave with lower-off hanging from it.

9. MEGU GORRIAK 7c+ 15m
Next line just to the right may be a project.

Right again the overhangs become even bigger and contain two small caves. The next route climbs to the left of the largest of these.
10. PHYTHOPTHORA CITROPHTHORA 7b 15m
Start by bush on the floor and climb broad blunt rib with a stubborn 'bloc' move early on, and jug hauling beyond.

Gandia: Dave Spencer on the juggy PEPESTROIKA 6b

11. QUIEN MALONDA, MAL ACABA ❧ 7a
15m
Gain the biggest cave from below using slippery holds then head out left onto the head wall. Step right and finish 'with gusto'.

12. PARABOLICA/SPHERIQUE VOICE ☺ 7b+/7a 15m
Follow the previous route into the cave (7b+) but exit to the right from this and finish across the roof (7a).

Just to the right is a line of small (artificial?) finger holds heading leftwards up the wall, these are the start of
13. KORTATU ☺ 7b+ 15m
Start just to the right of the fall line from the cave and climb direct to the finish of previous climb using drilled pockets and some pretty poor tufas.

14. VIATJE A CUBA ☺ 7b 15m
Start at right end of a large hole (polished rock and red paint and the name 'SOSTRE' on rock) at ground level. Straight up the leaning wall.

To the right is a line of old bolts and right again another cave at 10m.

15. BLANIULUS GUTTULATUS ❧ 7a 18m
Gain the right hand cave from the left or the right, then make difficult moves to reach the jugs that lurk just around the lip. Easier moves on 'biffos' lead to the lower-off.

Starting from the belay above the last route are two easier offerings. These are most logically reached by the traverse of ERUPCIO 4+ (see above) to which they make logical extensions.

16. PAGARAS AMB COSTA 6a 20m
The left-hand line above the lower-off.

17. S'ESTRENA EN LA TRENA 5+ 22m
The line just to the right and trending to the right.

To the right is a large unclimbed tufas and then

a couple of the hardest routes on this section of cliff:
18. PATATAS A LO PROBRE ❧ 7b+ 22m
The steeply tilted wall is climbed initially on tufas and then on pockets above. Finish up the easier wall above.

19. ASAMBLEA DE MAJARAS ☺ 7c+ 15m
Thin tufas lead up leaning white wall with extreme difficulty, the lip can be tackled on the left or the right with no change in grade.

20. OSTIA COQUETA 7a+ 15m
Start just to the left of right trending groove and climb the wall just to the left of the deep pockets of ZUCARICIDA.

The next feature to the right is a slabby groove that forms the right edge of the severely leaning wall. Starting up this is:
21. ZUCARICIDA ❧ 6c 22m
Up the ramp for a couple of moves then swing left on to the bulging wall. Follow the line of pockets until they end then either move right off or continue direct to easier climbing. Continue up the wall to a high lowering point.

22. LA LLEI DEL PERRERO 6c 22m
Effectively a direct start to the right-hand exit of previous climb up the leaning wall immediately left of the slanting groove.

23. FISSURA TAL TRAVERSE PASQUAL ☺ 5+ 22m
The open groove is entered steeply and climbed on jams and layaways. At the top of the crack the climb traverses away to the left, though it is better and more logical to step right onto the wall and continue passing a tricky bulge (6a+) to reach the lower-off of the next route.

24. PASTOR I PORRET 6c 22m
An eliminate up the bulges and rib immediately to the right of the crack of the previous climb. A blinkered approach is needed up the lower section.

Aventador: Colin Binks on JORGE NEGRETE 6a+, typical of the many fine face climbs on this neglected cliff

Penya Rotja de Marxuquera - Gandia

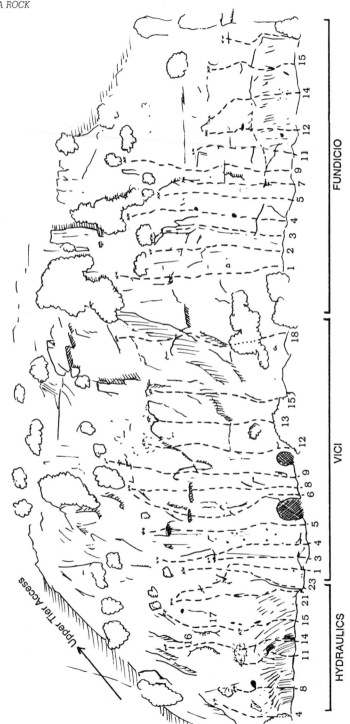

Sector Hydraulics

1. PRIMERA 3+
2. SECRETITOS ☺ 4
3. FE RA ☺ 3+
4. CORAL BAJLLA 4
5. ERUPCIO 4+
6. PEQUENO SALTAMONTES 6a+
7. MONSTER OF ROCK ☺ 7a
8. ASSASSI DE VAMPIRS ☺ 7a
9. MEGU GORRIAK 7c+
10. PHYTHOPTHORA CITROPHTHORA 7b
11. QUIEN MALONDA, MAL ACABA ♦ 7a
12. PARABOLICA/SPHERIQUE VOICE ☺ 7b+/7a
13. KORTATU ☺ 7b+
14. VIATJE A CUBA ☺ 7b
15. BLANIULUS GUTTULATUS ♦ 7a
16. PAGARAS AMB COSTA 6a
17. S'ESTRENA EN LA TRENA 5+
18. PATATAS A LO PROBRE ♦ 7b+
19. ASAMBLEA DE MAJARAS ☺ 7c+
20. OSTIA COQUETA 7a+
21. ZUCARICIDA ♦ 6c
22. LA LLEI DEL PERRERO 6c
23. FISSURA TAL TRAVERSE PASQUAL ☺ 5+
24. PASTOR I PORRET 6c

Sector Vici

1. NINA DE PORCELANA ☺ 6a+
2. GOR E.T.A. 6c+
3. PA ROIG ♠ 6a+
4. ASQUEROSA COINCIDENCIA ♦ 6a+/6b+
5. EL SOL ♦ 6b+
6. ESCORREGUDA PRECOC ☺ 6c
7. KIN MAL D'OUS 7a+
8. PEIOTE DE BOTE ☺ 6a+
9. VALENTET DE VALENCIA ♦ 6a+
10. PLACA DE ULACA ☺ 6b
11. MURCIANA ☺ 6a+
12. NASIO ☺ 6b+
13. MADARIKATUAK 6c
14. CHIQUI 6c
15. FES-TE-HO 6b
16. EN FALLES NO ELLES ☺ 6a+
17. CAPITAN MANCHEGO ☺ 6a
18. KAYA 6b+

Sector Fundicio

1. SENSE OPCIO 6b
2. NUPCIES ☺ 6a+
3. MILAN KUNDERA 6a+
4. CHITIRI CHITIR ♦ 5+
5. LA INSOPORTABLE 6a+
6. LA LEVEDAD ☺ 6a
7. EL SER 5+
8. BOMBEROS GORLERO 5+
9. TAMBOURINAES 93 ☺ 6a
10. PUNTIN D'ERNESTIN 7a/6b+
11. EL RIGIO ☺ 6b+
12. PEPESTROIKA ♦ 6b
13. ULTIMA ALERTENICA ☺ 6b+
14. AMORRADA AL PILO ♦ 6b
15. PERE ♦ 6c+
16. A MI NO M'AFECTA 6b
17. S'AMBOSSA 6b
18. ESPANYA NO M'APANYA ☺ 7a
19. EN MEDIUM ?
20. DIA DE BORATXERA ☺ 7a+
21. JOC DE MANS ☺ 6c

Gandia:Mike Appleton on the steep strenuous classic of ZUCARICIDA 6c

Sector Vici

To the right the wall steps forward and is a much more reasonable angle (only vertical). It contains a fine selection of pitches. This is the SECTOR VICI, and it covers the fine grey and orange walls that form the centre of the lower section of the cliff. The first route starting at the left side of the wall below some pocketed bulges and just left of a line dropping from the conspicuous tree.

1. NINA DE PORCELANA ☺ 6a+ 15/22m
Make steep moves to the first bolt then continue on an odd mixture of holds with both delicate and strenuous manoeuvres to reach lowering bolts to the right. To extend the trip and convert it into a ♦ step left to join top section of previous climb. Originally a tough 5+ it now gets it true grade.

2. GORA E.T.A. 6c+ 15/22m
Difficult climbing though rather 'eliminatish' in nature climbing the rib a short distance to the left of the thin crack that is the substance of PA ROIG. Either lower off the tree or move right to have a crack at the top pitch of ASQUEROSA COINCIDENCIA 6b+.

3. PA ROIG ♦ 6a+ 15m
The thin pocketed crack line gives classical pocket pulling with the crux moves at one third height where the crack closes and some smaller pockets are used for progress. Romp on.

4. ASQUEROSA COINCIDENCIA ♦ 6a+/6b+ 15/25m
The wall to the right of the thin crack of PA ROIG contains many inviting pockets. Steep moves on big jugs then a couple of difficult moves gain more excellent pockets and a lowering point. An excellent though harder extension lies up the rib and small roof above the chains.

The next feature to the right is one of the major ones of the wall a broad red streak dropping from a roof 22m up, and left of large hole at ground level. This is the line of:

5. EL SOL ♦ 6b+ 25m
A great pitch sustained and interesting. Start at the left edge of a small cave where a few steep

moves gain the first bolt. Then follow the sustained line up the streak to eventually reach a poor rest below the roof. A big undercut pinch grip on the lip allows a bolt above to be clipped and finger jugs to be gained for a quick pull over, with the lower-offs just above.

6. ESCORREGUDA PRECOC ☺ 6c 22m
Start as for the previous climb and move right to a prominent lower-off at 10m. Climb the wall and then bulge above this. The route can also be started from the right at no change in grade.

7. KIN MAL D'OUS 7a+ 10m
Start in the cave and cross the roof with difficulty, then continue up the wall above the lip to reach the lowering point. Short and 'ard.

To the right is a section of cliff that contains a whole selection of fine wall climbs at a 'not-too-tough' grade. The rock is sharp.

8. PEIOTE DE BOTE ☺ 6a+ 23m
Above the right edge of the cave is a shallow groove containing a collection of old and new bolts. Climb the groove delicately until a large hole is reached (blue thread in situ). Better holds lead up the wall above to the prominent 3m wide horizontal roof which is crossed centrally with difficulty, there are holds and a lower-off above - honestly.

To the right is a leaning red wall and below it a small bay 5m up the crag containing a tree. The red wall is taken by:
9. VALENTET DE VALENCIA ♦ 6a+ 25m
An excellent pocket-pulling pitch that is easier than appearances might suggest. Gain the tree in the recess and then head up the rather imposing wall. The pockets are generally excellent and more than make up for the angle. As the climbing eases move to the right to gain a recess then battle with the bulge above this left then right to reach a lower-off just above.

10. PLACA DE ULACA ☺ 6b 23m
This fine fingery pitch climbs the grey wall to the right of the previous route. Climb up to the right

edge of the hollow with the tree to gain the steep wall. This is well bolted but the holds are small and the difficulties sustained. Press on until forced rightwards and then back left to reach the belays.

To the right is another cave, 2m high and 2m deep, at the foot of the cliff.
11. MURCIANA ☺ 6a+ 25m
Climb left edge of cave and step right onto the wall. Power through the central bulges on sharp holds, before a small zigzag is required to reach the chains.

12. NASIO ☺ 6b+ 23m
Just to the right of the cave the right edge of this section of wall is climbed past a set of conspicuous holes and up streaky rock, 9 clips required.

Just to right is 4m high flake and a bush at 6m.
13. MADARIKATUAK 6c 14m.
Start right of the flake and climb the wall to a series of large bulges which are passed on their left side.

Starting to the right and behind bushes are four newish climbs;
14. CHIQUI 6c 15m
Start where a diagonal crack reaches the ground and climb slabby rock to an alcove and then steeper rock above passing a broken flake 'en route'.

15. FES-TE-HO 6b 15m
Begin 3m farther right and below an orange alcove at 10m. Head up a shrubby slab and then rather broken rock above to reach the bright golden lower-offs.

Just to the right are two climbs that tackle the steep rock, and both share the same approach up shrubby rock.
16. EN FALLES NO ELLES ☺ 6a+ 30m
The left-hand line from where the routes split climbing the grey wall and eventually a small roof. Lower off if you are in possession of a 60m rope or top out.

17. CAPITAN MANCHEGO ☺ 6a 20/30m
The right-hand line has an optional lower-off at two thirds height. Alternatively join and finish as for the previous route.

To right the lower section of cliff is slabby and shrubby and there is a wide white rock platform at its base. Left of a chimney flake with a tree growing behind it is:
18. KAYA 6b+ 25m
Starting at the left end of the rock platform, pass between bushes then climb slightly rightwards up the steep wall above.

To the right is an open bay with a tree covered ledge and some steep walls behind it. These are difficult of access and are largely undeveloped at present. To the right of the bay is an attractive area of rock, grey in colour and not too steep, trending rightwards into a gently leaning tufa encrusted wall. The whole area is the SECTOR FUNDICIO. In front of this area are open white ledges that make a good picnic or sun-bathing venue.

Sector Fundicio
On the left side of this area is a left trending groove heading for bulges above. To the left of this in the back of the shrubby bay is:
1. SENSE OPCIO 6b 22m
Easy rock leads to steeper things and a substantial roof is the main meat of the pitch.

The left trending groove is:
2. NUPCIES ☺ 6a+ 20m
After a slabby start follow the long open groove to below steep bulges which are climbed leftwards on good pockets (apart from at the start).

3. MILAN KUNDERA 6a+ 20m
Start behind a carob bush, and climb either of two lines up easy slabs then a groove with a flake in the back and a bulging crack, avoiding a tendency to move right if at all possible.

4. CHITIRI CHITIR ♦ 5+ 23m L KST G/3/00
The central line here with a conspicuous bolt on

a bulge low down and open groove full of holes above. Very pleasant and one of the best easy routes on the cliff.

To the right is a steep clean slab with two lines that share a mutual belay
5. LA INSOPORTABLE 6a+ 15m
The left-hand line is quite taxing if tackled direct though the hardest moves are easily avoided.

6. LA LEVEDAD ☺ 6a 15m
The central line is tough for a couple of moves.

7. EL SER 5+ 14m
A short route just to the right, and left of the fall line from a tree at 12m, with a steep start and on some rather odd rock.

8. BOMBEROS GORILERO 5+ 14m
Start just to the right and climb the steep wall which eases rapidly. Move left to the lower-off of the previous climbs. L EST 6/3/00

9. TAMBOURINAES 93 ☺ 6a 22m
A longer and better route just right again, and just to the left of where the cliff becomes untenably steep. A strenuous start passes bulges then continue across a groove and up a rib to a blind pull over a bulge high up. L EST 6/3/00

Around to the right the rock begins to overhang again, and here is an excellent selection of mildly strenuous climbs, a kind of mini-hydraulics for those who thought the real thing all rather too much.

10. PUNTIN D'ERNESTIN 7a/6b+ 15m
The first line of bolts gives a challenging route if they are followed direct up a pillar and flat face. Unfortunately though it is rather too easy to keep escaping rightwards onto the next route.

11. EL RIGIO ☺ 6b+ 15m
From a recess with a hole at head height bridge up right passing a bush at 3m then swing back left rapidly to big holds and easier angled rock.

12. PEPESTROIKA ❧ 6b 15m
Climb up to the hanging 'dong' at 4m, layback up this and then press on to reach easier angled rock. The lower-offs are most easily reached by climbing up to the left and leaning back right to clip them.

13. ULTIMA ALERTENICA ☺ 6b+ 15m
Climb the orange streak to a hole, then the pocketed wall above to a rest before finishing up the bulging wall above. Hard for the grade.

14. AMORRADA AL PILO ❧ 6b 20m
Follow a series of large and usually well chalked pockets, left then right then back left with a tricky move just where you don't want it, right at the top. Continue up the slab to a new set of lower-offs

15. PERE ❧ 6c+ 15m
The big white tooth of a tufa is reached awkwardly, shin up it to pass the bulges, then step right and then make a huge reach over a roof to easier ground.

A new route up the steepest part of the bay is of unknown (but considerable) difficulty.

To the right is an hourglass shaped pillar that bounds the right edge of the steepest section of the wall. There are two routes on the front of this and three more round to the right.
16. A MI NO M'AFECTA 6b 12m
The left edge of the pillar; short, sharp and hard for the grade.

17. S'AMBOSSA 6b 12m
A right-hand finish to the previous route with the same comments applying.

18. ESPANYA NO M'APANYA ☺ 7a 12m
The right side of the pillar is steep, strenuous and technical, great if you like that kind of thing!

19. EN MEDIUM ? 12m
Right again where is this unknown quantity where the rock is at its very steepest.

20. DIA DE BORATXERA ☺ 7a+ 15m
Up the back of the bay to a hole and then on with greater difficulty over the roof and up the 'smooth' wall above.

21. JOC DE MANS ☺ 6c 12m
The very overhanging line on the right side of the bay is tackled on a generous set of 'biffo's.

To the right is an easy way up to the UPPER TIER via gully through the centre of some broken rock. The crag continues to the right for a considerable distance, initially rather scrappy and then as the impressive:

Sector Potent
An extensive sector with many fine climbs, a goodly number of which are very hard. The rather tough nature of the grades here compounds this, though as the sign by the parking says, if you find the climbs hard then get some more training done.

The sector is bounded on its left side by a shrubby gully with oak trees. On the right side of this and rising behind the bushes is a smart grey wall.

1. NOVATILLOS ☺ 5+ 22m
Start behind the bushes then climb the centre of the slabby grey wall by pleasantly sustained climbing. Worth seeking out if you climb at the grade. L BST 6/3/00

To the right again is a large open corner with an attractive grey wall high on its right-hand side, just before the cliff becomes very steep. The rock to the left of the corner is home to two climbs:
2. MAQUI, POPEYE Y LA SIRLA 6b 28m
Start from a big flake/block and climb directly up the wall, slightly artificial in places, then on up the rib above into the trees.

3. DONDE HASTIAS PUTAS VAS JAVI? ☺ 6c 25m
The wall immediately to the left of the (unclimbed) corner is quite tough and gets gradually harder as height is gained.

To the right of the corner the wall juts forward and there is a cave at its base.

4. JOPUTA ☺ 6b 22m
From the cave climb steeply up the wall then cross bulges to get around onto the fine grey wall. Up the centre of this on 'surprising' holds to a thin move right at the very top.

To the left the path steps down to reach the start of the 'real climbing'. The first four routes follow closely squeezed in lines up the severely leaning wall. Some mixing and matching is possible, indeed the routes are so close together it may be inevitable.

5. STAR FORT 7a+
Up the pillar following the left-hand of the three/four bolt lines to eventually gain the hanging rib on the right of the previous climb.

6. TERCER ULT ☺ 7a+ 22m
Start as for the previous climb but where this goes straight up, step out right then climb straight up the leaning wall and easier rock to a lower-off on the right.

7. MULUK EL TARQUI ☺ 7a+ 22m
Start around to the right of the pillar and climb the centre of the bulging wall with a very long crucial reach, before romping onto the lower-offs of the previous climb.

8. URBALU RURAN 7b 24m
Start as for the previous climb but keep to the right to pass the bulges with great difficulty to reach much easier terrain above on the grey face above.

To the right the cliff becomes continuously steep, festooned in bizarre tufas and is home to a collection of superb and hard climbs. After prolonged rain many of these tufas weep for a considerable time.

9. SUGAR GLASS ♦ 7b+ 22m
The steep wall to the right has some conspicuous large ring bolts and some excellent climbing. Head up the steep wall passing a hole with a bush and then press on up the front of the hanging pillar above.

To the right is a large right-facing flake starting 12m up and right again are two tufa systems about 2m apart, both offering superb climbs.

10. BOTOIA SAKATU ♦ 7c 25m
Steeply up the large black left-hand tufa system and then crosses a roof high up the crag.

11. ENYA ♦ 7b+ 22m
The right-hand tufa system starting at a small cave then trending right up the fine sustained and steep wall above.

12. BAILA AL ALBA ☺ 7c+ 24m
Another tufa system and with two sets of roofs thrown in for good measure. As an aid to identification the 4th bolts are paired. The crux is a bizarre move to get stood on a good ledge just below half height.

13. A LA BABALA ♦ 7a 22m
Start just left a bush growing from the crag at head height climb up passing through a 'love heart' at 8m and then on weaving up the cliff. Superb.

To the right is the biggest tufa on this part of the cliff, with a vague resemblance to an elephant wearing a ceremonial head dress!

14. L'OS ♦ 7a 24m
Start just right of the elephant-like tufa and press on up the pocketed seam above and juggy wall above. Yet another superb route.

15. DOS SUPER CARROEAS ☺ 7a+ 18m
To the right this climb starts from a cave. Battle out of the cave with difficulty then press on then still steep territory to lower-off situated just below a tree.

On the right side of the bay are several thin white tufas

16. DON DIEGO ☺ 7a+ 18m
Follow silver bolts trending to the left then to right. All the pockets are good though some are rather spaced!

Gandia: Sectors Potent and Final

1. NOVATILLOS ☺ 5+
2. MAQUI, POPEYE Y LA SIRLA 6b
3. DONDE HASTIAS PUTAS VAS JAVI? ☺ 6c
4. JOPUTA ☺ 6b
5. STAR FORT 7a+
6. TERCER ULT ☺ 7a+
7. MULUK EL TARQUI ☺ 7a+
8. URBALU RURAN 7b
9. SUGAR GLASS ♠ 7b+

10. BOTOIA SAKATU ♠ 7c
11. ENYA ♠ 7b+
12. BAILA AL ALBA ☺ 7c+
13. A LA BABALA ♠ 7a
14. L'OS ♠ 7a
15. DOS SUPER CARROEAS ☺ 7a+
16. DON DIEGO ☺ 7a+
17. JAQUE MATE 8a?
18. SOLTA EL MOS ☺ 7a
19. GALLO DE LA SUSAN ☺ 6c

20. GROCERIES ☺ 6c+
21. ANDREU I PAPANDREU 6b+/7a+
22. A MANO 6c
23. BUM BUM IPANIME ☺ 5 '24/2/93 ∠ EST
24. BEATO ANDRES HIBERNON ☺ 6a
25. LLEONES ☺ 5
26. FETICHE 6c
27. ABU ABD ALLAH MUHAMMAD BEN
    HUDAYAL AL AZARKH ☺ 6b
28. SENSE GOMA NO HI HA CONILL
    ☺ 6a+
29. 3/4 D'HORA ☺ 6a
30. VERGONYA ☺ 5

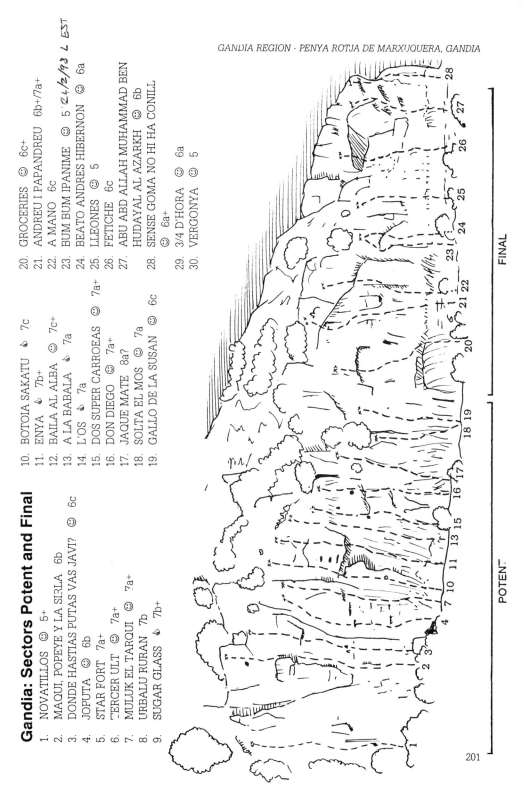

FINAL

POTENT

17. JAQUE MATE 8a? 18m
Starting in the same place and trending slightly to the right to a large pocket above tree and then on up wall is this innocuous looking unknown quantity.

To the right are some grey slabs and right again is a cave with a bush growing in the back. Above the grey slabs are two climbs:
18. SOLTA EL MOS ☺ 7a 15m
Head slightly left up grey rock, then climb straight up the wall, more glorious pocket pulling.

19. GALLO DE LA SUSAN ☺ 6c 15m
Starting in the same place but trending right up red streaked rock is a similar but slightly easier offering.

Sector Final
Running away to the very end of the cliff is this final sector that still has some undeveloped rock, though don't tell anybody.
20. GROCERIES ☺ 6c+ 15m
Right of the cave with the bush mentioned above is this line trending leftwards up scoops and over a bulge. A tough cookie for the grade.

21. ANDREU I PAPANDREU 6b+/7a+ 25m
Four metres to the right is an orange streaked wall, climb the centre of this passing one bulge early on to reach more bulges then, depending how easy you found the lower section, make a choice.

22. A MANO 6c 20m
Just right again is a protruding buttress with this route up its up left edge, protected by different generations of bolts. It is steep at the start and then continues up a flat wall above to a lower-off by tree.

To the right is a small collection of easier climbs worth seeking out by the lower grade climber. The first of these runs up a shallow corner.
23. BUM BUM IPANIME ☺ 5 14m
The shallow corner gives a pleasant pitch with a delicate move passing the second bolt and

with the roof outflanked by a juggy left to right traverse.

24. BEATO ANDRES HIBERNON ☺ 6a 14m
The wall just to the right is a touch harder, proving to quite sustained and having a strenuous finale.

25. LLEONES ☺ 5 15m
Four metres right is an engaging grey slab climbed directly above the point where a diagonal break reaches the ground.

To the right are some good sunbathing ledges well away from the crowds who gather at the other end of the cliff. Above these is:
26. FETICHE 6c 18m
Five metres right again climb a scruffy slab up to a bay with large roof and then through the left side of this with considerable difficulty.

27. ABU ABD ALLAH MUHAMMAD BEN HUDAYAL AL AZARKH ☺ 6b 15m
10m right is this route starting from an area of orange rock by climbing out of a cave and pressing on over roof at 10m. Surely the locals could have found a longer name!

The right arete of the cliff is:
28. SENSE GOMA NO HI HA CONILL ☺ 6a+ 14m
Climb pleasant grey rock up the rounded rib in the lower section then the bulging arete above to chains on the lip of the roof (hint: these are most easily reached from the left).

Finally the crag swings round overlooking Gandia
29. 3/4 D' HORA ☺ 6a 12m
The wall 3m right of the arête passing, unusual 'stuck' on flake at 3m, up a bubbly rib and an overhanging groove.

30. VERGONYA 5 12m
2m right climb up a scoop then trend left to the lower-offs of the previous climb. The Spanish grade as far as the first clip is not very accurate, you have been warned!

Sector Critic

The final part of the LOWER TIER to be described is the SECTOR CRITIC. This is the area of rock that lies 150m to the left of the SECTOR HYDRAULICS and is reached by crossing the gully to the left of the main crag and following a faint path along a narrow terrace. The main feature of this part of the cliff is a big red corner (GRAN DIEDRE) and to its right a fine grey slab of perfect rock with some amenably graded climbs on it. To left and right of the central corner the rock dwindles in height.

For consistency the routes are described from left to right, although this is opposite to the direction of the approach.

The short leaning arête on the far left of the cliff is:

1. MARGARITA 6a+ 8m
Short, sharp and safe with no route finding problems.

The left wall of the big red corner has three lines of bolts running up it. The mixing and matching of the upper sections actually gives five routes.

2. ESPERO GROC 6b 15m
Start behind the big tree and climb the white wall to large pockets, then sharp grey rock above.

3. DIAGNOSIS SUPERFICIAL ☺ 6b 15m
Start as for the previous climb to the level of a large flake on the right. Step onto this then climb the wall and thin crack above.

4. PASANDO DEL POLI ☺ 7b+ 15m
Start on the right of the tree and climb up to a flake with a bush on its right side. Climb up the wall crossing a small overlap, and on very thinly to the top.

VOLDRIA MORIR 7a 15m
Follow the previous climb to the overlap then avoid the crux by moving right to join the final section of the next route.

5. JA ESTIC MORT ☺ 7a+ 15m
The smooth wall just to the left of the big red corner is tackled direct. It is good and tough.

6. GRAN DIEDRE ♦ 5+ 18m
The ledge at the base of the steep section of big corner is approached from the left or the right via a big hole. The upper section is probably best laybacked, though those with big fists and a high pain resistance can jam it. Move left at the top to lowering bolts, or finish out into the hanging groove in the right arête.

To the right of the corner is a steep arete that forms the substance of two routes. Holds on the arête itself are shared by the routes so tandem ascents could prove interesting.

SELECTIVA ☺ 6c 18m
Start under the arete at an large vertical pocket which is climbed followed by the bulges above. Continue passing a substantial thread in to a shallow corner until it is possible to exit round to the right to a lowering point.

7. ESPOLON "WHY" ☺ 6b+ 18m
From below the right side of the arete climb the leaning wall on spaced spiky pockets until the angle eases. Continue up the face close to the arete passing a good thread and an archaic peg to more difficult moves until things ease just below the belay bolts.

8. MEGALOCERAS ☺ 7a 18m
A route with perfect protection but a desperate crux sequence. Start as for the previous route and step right to a flake. Interesting moves lead up the centre of the face until things turn nasty. A thin undercut allows access to the crux, a pull on some miserable sloping pockets ("a 7c move on a 6b route") to reach jugs and then the belays on the left.

To the right is a sheet of grey rock with two prominent flake cracks and an excellent collection of mid-grade routes. The left-hand flake crack is:

9. AGUILES ♦ 5 18m
A fine route that is something of an anomaly as it contains no fixed gear. Several medium sized

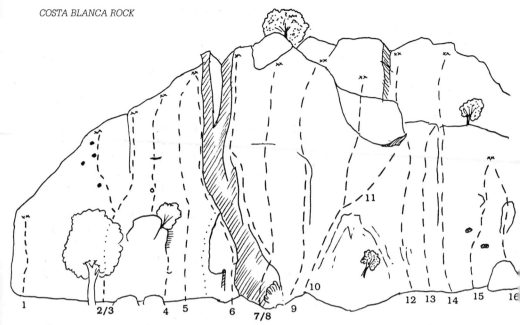

Sector Critic

1. MARGARITA 6a+
2. ESPERO GROC 6b
3. DIAGNOSIS SUPERFICIAL ☺ 6b
4. PASANDO DEL POLI ☺ 7b+
5. JA ESTIC MORT ☺ 7a+
6. GRAN DIEDRE ♠ 5+
7. ESPOLON "WHY" ☺ 6b+
8. MEGALOCERAS ☺ 7a

9. AGUILES ♠ 5
10. PICCOLISSIMA ☺ 6a
11. TERRA LLIURE ☺ 5
12. P.S.A.N. 6b
13. BENIARRES NO EM DIU RES ☺ 4+2⅟₂/9
14. TALLA ☺ 4+ 2⅟₂/98 LEST
15. GARBANSITO 5+
16. STICK FLUISH 5

Rocks are required. Gain the base of the flake easily and follow it steeply on jugs and finger jams. Protection is perfect, unless you don't put any in. At the top of the flake move up to a belay on a higher ledge.

10. PICCOLISSIMA ☺ 6a 18m
The centre of the face between the two flakes contains a prominent bolt. This is gained via a ramp or from directly below and passed via tricky moves (unless you are very tall when it is only 5+), better holds lead to another bolt in the short face and a little higher the belay of the previous route.

The right side of the face has a rising flake

crossing it:
11. TERRA LLIURE ☺ 5 18m
The base of the flake is reached over easy rock as for the previous climb and is followed pleasantly into a corner. Belays are located on the left of the finish or better, in the right wall of the continuation corner.

12. P.S.A.N. 6b 15m
To the right of the previous routes is a grey rib with a bush sticking out of it and then a smooth wall at 10m sprouting a prominent bolt. Gain this from below and improvise past it to reach another bolt then move left to the belays of the previous climb.

Immediately to the right is a line of new bolts:
BENIARRES NO EM DIU RES ☺ 4+ 20m
Pleasant climbing up the wall, starting at the left
side of an alcove/groove and then continuing up
the engaging corner above the ledges.

14. TALLA ☺ 4+ 20m
The open groove with bolts in the right wall is
followed throughout, then continue up the wall
above, very pleasant.

15. GARBANSITO 5+ 10m
Start just left of a fallen block and pass a small
overlap with an orange hole in it to reach the
pocketed wall.

16. STICK FLUISH 5 10m
From the tip of the large fallen block climb
leftwards through an overlap and white scar
where the flake used to live then continue
trending left to the lower-off of the previous
route.

CAP DE LLEO 3+ 20m
Start of the block but trend right to reach a short
crack then press on up the groove above to the
cliff top. Gear required.

PLACA SIMOND 3
15m right of the fallen block is a clean rib with
half a dozen bolts in it.

PETITE DIEDRE SPAR 5
The short groove right again. Not very edifying,
gear required.

Sector de Dalt (a.k.a. The Upper Tier)
The UPPER TIER at Gandia has seen considerable
development in recent years and is now well
worth a visit, especially if you have done
everything on the LOWER TIER or want to
escape the crowds that sometimes gather down
there. It is most easily reached by a steep
scramble up the gully to the left of the SECTOR
HYDRAULICS initially up the bed of the gully
and then by trending out to the right along
ledges at its top. The approach takes a steep

20 minutes from the road.

Alternatives are the rocky gully between the
SECTORS FUNDICIO and POTENT or an easy
scramble around the right edge of the cliff. The
upper crag has a more open aspect than the
LOWER TIER, and it can be pleasantly breezy
up here when it is stiflingly hot down below. The
routes are described briefly from left to right.

On the far left and directly above the upper
section of the normal approach gully is a pleasant
looking rib, about 15m long. No grade has come
to light though it looks like a worthwhile 4/5.

1. PEP CAMARENA 5 30m
On the far left edge of the face is a fine grey slab
running to an overlap with orange staining
below it. Climb this and pull through the overlap
on its right side. Continue steeply to the cliff top.
No fixed gear.

2. GOLONDRINAS 5 30m
Another route with no fixed kit, passing to the
right of a large spiky bush early on, then taking
a direct line to the top of the cliff.

To the right is a fine grey slab with a diagonal
line of overlaps rising across it from left to right.
Five routes climb this section of cliff.

3. EVA LLUNA ☺ 6c 18m
Start off some blocks, step left onto the slab and
climb it keeping to the right of a ragged crack
line. Cross the bulges and press on slightly
rightwards to chains below the final overlap.

4. DERRIBOS ARIAS ☺ 6b 22m
Two metres right is an almost parallel line
tackling the bulges from right to left via a scoop.

5. SANDBAG 7a 20m
Just right of the centre of the slab is a large hole
at 4m, climb past this and then up some small
tufas to the bulges before moving left through
these with difficulty. The lower-off is on ledges
near the cliff top.

6. BOCA DE GRIMPAU ☺ 6b+ 20m
Start as for SANDBAG but avoid its main

Gandia Upper Tier

1. PEP CAMARENA 5
2. GOLONDRINAS 5
3. EVA LLUNA ☺ 6c
4. DERRIBOS ARIAS ☺ 6b
5. SANDBAG 7a
6. BOCA DE GRIMPAU ☺ 6b+
7. GUALETA ☺ 6c
8. QUEFEROSET ☺ 6b+
9. ROSARITO ☺ 6b
10. ESFINTER DILATAT ☺ 5+ ⌐ 24/7/98 ⌐ BST Superb
11. SARCOFAGO 7b+

12. ANATEMA MARANATA 7b
13. CELTAS CORTOS ☺ 6a+
14. GUIRIGAY ☺ 6a
15. TRANQUILIZED ☺ 7a
16. DESCARA ☺ 6b+
17. BOLTXEVIQUE ☺ 6b+
18. VULCANO ☺ 6b+
19. LO QUE SIQUI ☺ 6a+
20. MAL DEL TORD ☺ 5+
21. KAMARI ☺ 6a
22. COTO-EN-PELS ☺ 5 24/7/98 ⌐ BST

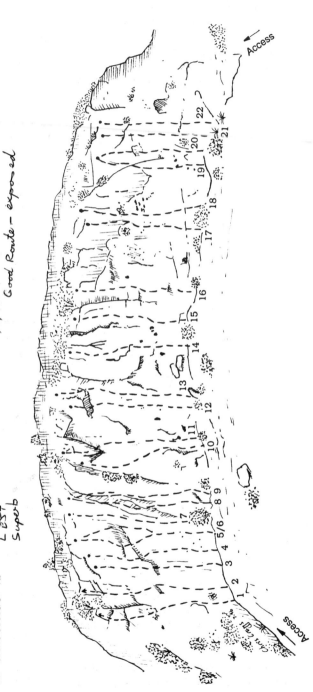

Good Route - exposed

206

difficulties by climbing the bulges just to the right, in a much more sensible fashion.

7. GUALETA ☺ 6c 20m
The right-hand line on the slab starts up a vegetated ramp and then gives sharp and sustained climbing up steepening rock via a ragged crack line.

To the right is an unclimbed corner (better looking than most UK limestone routes) and right again is a narrow pillar with two bolt lines.

8. QUEFEROSET ☺ 6b+ 18m
Start behind a big tree and climb up the rib and press on through an overlap.

9. ROSARITO ☺ 6b 18m
Just to the right is a parallel line starting up a yellow groove and sharing the same lower-off.

To the right is some easier undeveloped rock and then an impressive hanging 'boss'. Starting right under this is:
10. ESFINTER DILATAT ☺ 5+ 20m
Begin at a cave and follow a line leftwards up pleasantly sustained and perfect rock.

11. SARCOFAGO 7b+ 20m
The impressive block overhang is approached direct and then battled with. An even harder left-hand finish is also rumoured to have been done.

To the right of the 'boss' is a fine looking, well-pocketed orange wall just crying out to be developed. On its right edge is:
12. ANATEMA MARANATA 7b 20m
The steep wall and flat roof above.

13. CELTAS CORTOS ☺ 6a+ 22m
Just to the right thin dribbly tufas and finger pockets lead to the roof which is skirted at its right edge, with the lower-offs some distance above. A fine sustained pitch.

To the right is another unclimbed corner and then an extensive and attractive bulging wall.

At the right side of this is:
14. GUIRIGAY ☺ 6a 22m
Start 3m to the right of the base the prominent right-to-left rising diagonal flake/overlap. Climb through a bulge and on up a pocketed white wall. Good climbing but no gift at the grade.

15. TRANQUILIZED ☺ 7a 20m
Start from some holes at ground level climb to and through a tough bulge at three-quarters height.

16. DESCARA ☺ 6b+ 22m
The right wall of the deep (unclimbed!) corner is climbed trending rightwards crossing the bulge with gusto.

To the right is an orange bay vegetated low down and capped by bulges. Two routes penetrate the steep centre of these. Passing just to the right of a tree growing in a hole is:
17. BOLTXEVIQUE ☺ 6b+ 18m
Climb the grey streak in the back of the bay passing right of a tree in a hole and continuing steeply.

18. VULCANO ☺ 6b+ 20m
Start to the right and climb a slab with a prominent bolt then cross a large red overhang explosively before following grey rock to the top.

The final four routes are clustered around the fine grey slabby pillar that forms the right edge of the cliff. They are worth seeking out if you enjoy well protected climbing on perfect rock in the 5 to 6a+ grades. The first two of these start behind bushes and below a small tree sprouting from a diagonal crack.

19. LO QUE SIGUI ☺ 6a+ 20m
Pass to left of the tree and follow the diagonal crack before heading straight for the cliff top.

20. MAL DEL TORD ☺ 5+ 20m
Climb the low angle apron passing to the left of a bush, then continue straight up the wall passing to the right of the tree sprouting from

the diagonal crack. The lower-offs are located where the angle drops back.

The final two routes start in a little hollow at a well trampled area behind a spiky 'palm bush'
21. KAMARI ☺ 6a 20m
The left-hand line climbs past an orange scar

trending slightly to the right via a central steepening then gives easier climbing above.

22. COTO-EN-PELS ☺ 5 22m
Climb the steepening slab past horizontal breaks and on up the wall above. Very pleasant.

*Gandia Sector Fundicio: An unknown Brit. enjoying EL SER 5+
one of the good lower grade climbs on this superb cliff*

GANDIA: SECTOR LA CUEVA

A recently developed area of rock adds a little something extra to the climbing in the Gandia region: very long, very steep, very hard routes. Brief notes are presented here on this new area in topo format.

Approaches

From the minor road that branches right to the main areas at Gandia continue along the main road for 900m to a tarmacked left turn signed (amongst other things) to the Bar Carril. Follow this narrow walled road for a further 900m to a left turn with a 'mountain biking' sign. Drive along this past buildings for 450m to another left turn and drive up a track to limited parking at its end, don't block the turning space. Follow the track that leaves the turning circle and runs across the hillside for 800m to reach the cliff.

Geography

The cliff features a large central cave with a walled animal pen in its base and with impressive walls to both left and right.

The Routes

Below is a topo of the main section of the cliff. The grades are thought to be accurate with the possible exception of the routes to the immediate left of the cave, and feed-back would be welcome.

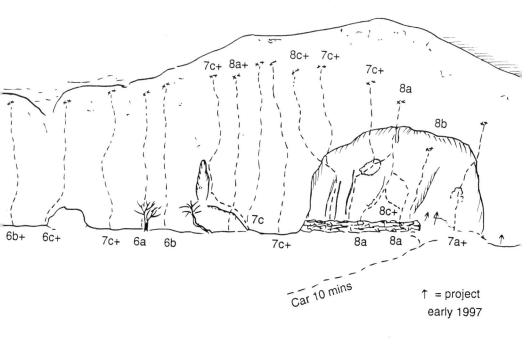

↑ = project
early 1997

SALEM

Crag Facts

Star rating: ***
Aspect: Most directions but especially southwest and north.
Height: Up to 40 metres, though most of the routes are 25 metres or less.

Spread of grades:

4	5	5+	6a	6b	6c	7a	7b	7c	8+
9	8	9	24	25	15	15	10	3	3

Introduction

Here is collection over well over a hundred well bolted routes sprayed around a secluded valley in the lower slopes of the Sierra Marchalets, close to the small town of Salem. Some of the rock is not perfect, and some climbs are rather dusty. On the plus side there are always climbs in both shade and sun, and the best of the routes here are very good indeed. There are climbs on four main faces, and these are described briefly in turn. Be warned - many of the grades here are on the tough side!

Access

Follow the C320 southwest from Gandia for about 20km to the new section by-passing Montichelvo and the prominent town and hilltop church of Castello de Rugat. Just past the latter turn off the by-pass and drive back into the town. Take the second right turn in the town (not the first signed 'Rafot de Salem'). Drive straight up this ignoring an early right turn signed Salem, and follow the twisting road to

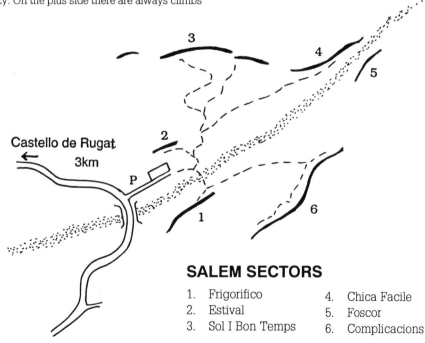

SALEM SECTORS

1. Frigorifico
2. Estival
3. Sol I Bon Temps
4. Chica Facile
5. Foscor
6. Complicacions

suddenly arrive at the crag after 3.4km. Park on the left by a concrete water tank. The nearest rock is one minute away.

> **Note:** the information here comes from a variety of sources, most notably a 1994 edition of the Barcelona based magazine *Extrem*. In some cases it has been difficult to decipher the closely packed topos, especially as new routes may have been added since they were drawn. I apologise in advance if you are looking for classic 6b+ routes and end up on a 7c!

Sector Frigorifico
A misnamed Sector if ever there was one, usually offering a pleasantly warm escape from the searing heat on the two cliffs opposite. The routes are described from left to right and in many cases are very, very close together. No approach notes should be needed for this crag!

1. EL KIKI 6c 12m
The left side of the small buttress is sketchy in the extreme, three bolt runners and single bolt lower-off.

2. EL GRO 6b 12/15m
Start at a bolt splashed with red paint and climb the centre of the small buttress via a tough start to jugs and a tough finish on continuously disappointing pockets. Lower-off as for the previous route or trend right and join the next one.

3. ALAXUPLALA 6a+ 15m
The wall just to the right has an old small bolt to protect the start of a surprisingly tough wall. When things ease trend up to the right to finish.

4. SUC D'AVESPA 5 15m
May be a route just to the right again.

5. XUPLA POLEN ☺ 5+ 15m
Start just to the right at a scratch number 14. A vague scoop and tricky bulging wall leads more directly to the lower-off of the previous routes.

6. MIKEL I ALTRES BROSES ☺ 5 14m
The well pocketed wall (initial bolt is painted pink) just left of the prominent diagonal crack gives a pleasant outing which is easier for the tall, trend right to the belay.

7. MIKEL CAGA FLORS ☺ 5 15m
Start from scrubby ledges (first bolt is of the bean-tin-lid variety) then climb the left slanting crack which gives another satisfying romp. The four bolts runners are in the right wall and lower-off is on the right at the top.

To the right is a an odd rounded rib protruding from the cliff. Immediately to the left of this is:
8. GEROLA QUE VOLA A LA CASOLA ☺ 5 15m
Climb up left of the rib passing a large rusty home-made first bolt, trend left with final difficult moves to large single bolt lower-off.

9. CAMALOT ☺ 5 15m
Climb up to the base of the rib, then follow the groove on its right or if you really must 'a cheval' directly up it! You won't need the piece of gear the route is named after.

10. EL GRADUADO ☺ 5+ 15m
The slab to the right of the protruding rib and left of a shrubby bush has pleasant moves. Continue up the rib above, to a choice of lower-offs.

11. PLACA NUEVO 6a 15m
Climb to a ledge with a bush then up rather grubby slab the slab (using the groove on the left initially) to enter the final groove with difficulty. New bolts but old lower-off.

12. NA HAY PELAS ☺ 6a+ 17m
The slippery slab to the right (and left of a blank groove) leads to a juggy bulge. Swing out right and sprint up the final wall pocketed.

13. BAJAME UNA ESTRELLA ☺ 7a 17m
Climb up the blank left slanting groove then swing out right onto the steep buttress and climb this on finger flakes and well spaced pockets.

14. FORT BATTLE ☺ 7b+ 15m
The right side of the buttress it a tough and well named challenge following the pocketed white streak and using a 'stuck-on' hold.

Sector Frigorifico

1. EL KIKI 6c
2. EL GRO 6b
3. ALAXUPLALA 6a+
4. SUC D'AVESPA 5
5. XUPLA POLEN ☺ 5+
6. MIKEL I ALTRES BROSES ☺ 5
7. MIKEL CAGA FLORS ☺ 5
8. GEROLA QUE VOLA A LA CASOLA ☺ 5
9. CAMALOT ☺ 5
10. EL GRADUADO ☺ 5+
11. PLACA NUEVO 6a

12. NA HAY PELAS ☺ 6a+
13. BAJAME UNA ESTRELLA ☺ 7a
14. FORT BATTLE ☺ 7b+
15. LA PELUSA DE LA PARRUSA ☺ 6b
16. AHORA CORRE LA SANGRE 7b+
17. CUIDADO, CUIDAO ☺ 6b
18. NO ES LOLO TODO LO QUE RELUCE 8a
19. SAS BARA 6c+

20. EAU DANSISSAM ☺ 6c
21. TEMPS AL TEMPS ☺ 7a+
22. QVO VADIS TRONI 8a
23. I DE MAJOR SERE UN OCTAU 7b
24. CANA DULCE 7b
25. SOMNIS DE TARDOR ☺ 5+
26. MAI RIBE A TEMPS 6a+
27. SFINTERMAN EL HOMBRE
    KARANA 5

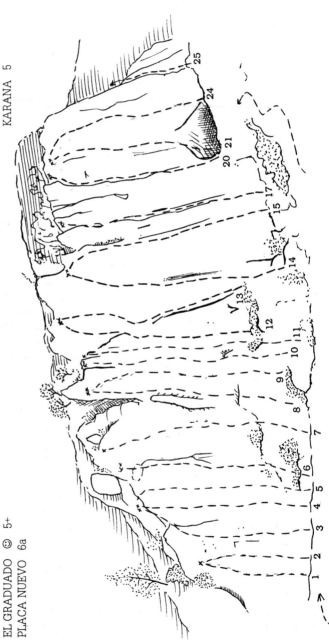

15. LA PELUSA DE LA PARRUSA ☺ 6b 15m
The left-hand of the three pocketed grooves that split the central section of the cliff gives a sustained juggy pitch. Enter the groove from the left and finish out to the left.

16. AHORA CORRE LA SANGRE 7b+ 17m
The narrow buttress to the right is another tough one though it is barely independent.

17. CUIDAO, CUIDAO ☺ 6b 16m
The central yellow/orange groove has a tough exit round a bulge where the crack closes and stiff pulls are needed to reach easy ground.

18. NO ES LOLO TODO LO QUE RELUCE 8a 16m
The near impossible smooth pillar just to the right.

Up a ramp on the right is a deep (snake infested!) cave and to its left an undercut groove where three routes are based:
19. SAS BARA 6c+ 14m
The bulging left wall of the right hand groove is short, rather artificial and tough.

20. EAU DANSISSAM ☺ 6c 14m
The right hand groove enters strenuously from the cave on the right and is more amenable once entered. Pass the detached flake with care.

21. TEMPS AL TEMPS ☺ 7a+ 15m
From the left side of the cave enter and follow the shallow seam in the right wall of the deep groove.

22. QVO VADIS TRONI 8b 15m
The leaning left wall of the cave is climbed past golden bolts and without deviation or you forfeit the grade.

23. I DE MAJOR SERE UN OCTAU 7b 15m
The left wall of the cave passing to the right of a banana shaped pocket early on. A bulging crack above sustains the interest.

24. CANA DULCE 7b 16m
The right arete of the cave and smooth sustained wall above.

25. SOMNIS DE TARDOR ☺ 5+ 17m
The incut corner around to the right of the cave is steep and sustained. At its top swing out right and follow the flake to a lower-off.

26. MAI RIBE A TEMPS 6a+ 17m
The right arete of the deep corner has a thin start using undercuts and a tiny pocket (avoidable on the right if it proves too much). It is much easier and more pleasant above.

27. SFINTERMAN EL HOMBRE KARANA 5 17m
The last route on this cliff climbs a groove and then the juggy slab above. At the top trend left to the lower-off.

Sector Estival
Behind the white sub/pumping station and opposite the SECTOR FRIGORIFICO is this small, and it has to be admitted rather scruffy cliff, two minutes from the car. It has almost a dozen well bolted and sunny lower grade climbs, most of which are ideal for timid beginners or instructional purposes. From left to right these are:
1. ACCESS DENEGAT 5+ 12m
Scramble left across ledges and climb the flat wall, starting in a bay, and finish over a bulge. Three bolt runners.

2. R2 DEDOS 3+ 12m
Start in a hollow directly behind the substation and climb a short steep rib which soon lies back. Four bolt runners.

3. C3 PEDOS 4+ 10m
Start right of a bush and climb a juggy crack and the slab above. Four bolt runners.

4. BOULDER ROC 6c 10m
Just right of a ground level cave and with a move early on that is uncharacteristic for the sector. If successful trend left up easy rock.

5. XEROKI ☺ 4 15m
Start at a 'crozzly' head height crack, then trend right, six bolts.

6. U2 ☺ 4+ 15m
Start in the back of the bay, climb to a ledge then on up the clean rib above. Perhaps the best here, featuring six bolt runners.

7. MOSCATACA 3+ 16m
Starting in the same place but step right and climbing the right side of some grey bubbly rock with a short diversion into the gully when needed, seven bolt runners.

8. PASSEIG DOMINICAL 3+ 16m
Just to the right climbing the low angled gully/groove directly, seven bolt runners.

On the right side of the bay is a clean white slab:
9. LA BRUIXA DE SALEM ☺ 4+ 12m
Step right onto the slab then pass to the right of an orange scar, trending right at the top, seven bolt runners.

10. NEGRA NEUS I ELS SET GIGANTS 4 12m
Climb past cleaned ledges and up the pleasant blunt rib above, five bolt runners.

11. NAXCUDA EN LLIURE 3 14m
Start right of the bushes close to the footpath, trend left up low angled rock passing an orange hole. Six bolt runners.

Sector Sol I Bon Temps
The showpiece of the cliff with some fine climbs on great rock and a name that is oh so apt. The cliff is visible high on the left running down the hill to the right to finish at a buttress with a prominent horizontal roof. The best area is the far left side of the main section cliff where there are some excellent long face routes. The first of these is reached by a strenuous 10-15 minute

Sector Estival
1. ACCESS DEGEGAT 5+
2. R2 DENOS 3+
3. C3 PEDOS 4+
4. BOULDER ROCK 6c
5. XEROKI 4
6. U2 J 4+
7. MOSCATACA 3+
8. PASSEIG DOMINICAL 3+
9. LA BRUIXA DE SALEM 4+
10. NEGRA NEULS ELS SET GIGANTES 4
11. NAXUDA EN LLIURE 3

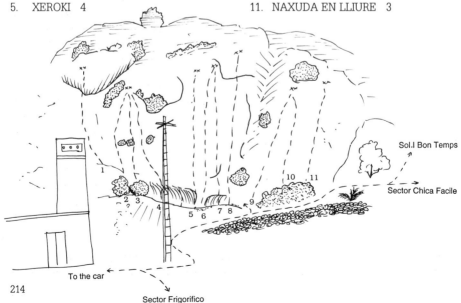

Sol.I Bon Temps

Sector Chica Facile

To the car

Sector Frigorifico

scramble. Pass to the right of the SECTOR ESTIVAL and follow a terrace out to the right. Leave this at a 2m high carob bush for a steeply ascending track and either loop out to the right or head straight up the hill. Neither way is especially pleasant. The cliff is in the sun from mid morning onwards and the routes are described from left to right.

One hundred metres left of the main cliff and across a floral gully are some orange caves much used for pooping. The right-hand of these has two climbs:

1. AKELARRE 6a+ 12m
Climb the left side of the cave using pockets aplenty, four clips.

2. EL HOMBRE DE HUMO 7c 15m
Climb through the centre of the caves, where leaning tufas and a tough bulge lead a to spiky wall, eight clips protect this very well.

Across the gully to the right is the main section of the face. On its left side is a small buttress with two uninspiring bolt lines.

3. EL LOBO VELOZ 6a+ 15m
The left side of the buttress is climbed past a large scar then continue trending right up shrubby rock.

4. SAMURAI 6b 15m
Just left of the groove climb the rib over a couple of bulges then up the slab above. Hard for the grade.

5. A TOT OSTIA ☺ 6a 25m
The corner groove is rather hacked around and is rather tough at the start. It gives a long pitch which ultimately proves worthwhile, take plenty of quick-draws.

6. OFERTA EXPLOSIVA 6b+ 25m
Parallel the groove up a crinkley wall then pass a hole and a small roof before trending left to join the previous climb.

7. SUPER NOVA ☺ 6a+ 24m
The first of the 'really good' routes that you

flogged up here for. Start at small flowstone pillar at foot level and climb up the intricate wall passing an area of white rock before trending slightly leftwards up easier angled terrain.

8. CHINAHAUK ☺ 7a 22m
Start just right of a hole at ground level and climb past an area of white rock, sharp and thin. It is steep but easier above. Recommended if you like the style of climbing.

9. PARABOLES LEJANOS ☺ 7a 22m
Start just left of a small vertical 'seam' at ground level, climb up a white streak and the rib above. The same comment applies as for the previous route.

The next three climbs are excellent sustained 6b+ routes, reported by one party as 'the best wall climbs' they had done in Spain. In keeping with the rest of the crag they are quite hard for the grade.

10. SINIESTRO TOTAL ☺ 6b+ 28m
Start at some low relief tufas and climb the bulging wall and sustained grey scoop above, excellent.

11. TIRANT DE ROC ☺ 6b+ 28m
Just to the right (and just left of the cave) the rock is steeper but the holds are better. Press on up the wall through a hole and up the scoop above. Another excellent offering.

12. SEGUIX L'ANIMAL ☺ 6b+ 28m
Right again and starting on the left edge (or just possibly two bolt lines to the right!) of the cave is another cracker passing a diagonal cave/hole at one third height.

13. AZUL MARCIA ILUSION ☺ 7a+ 28m
Climb out of the right side of the shrubby cave (steeply) following a line of gold bolts until it is possible to step left and join the easier upper section of the previous climb.

14. REPOS CELESTIAL ☺ 6c+ 28m
Start at a tufa with a prominent line of silver bolts

Sector Sol I Bon Temps

Sector Chica Facile

24. TOVARICH 6c+
25. TULIKREMLIN 6c
26. CON IBERIA YA HABRIAS VOLADO 5
27. PELUT I PELAT 6b
28. SINDROME DE SOLETAT ☺ 7a+
29. UN MONTON DE OSTIAS 7a+
30. SARVACHOF 5c
31. CULO FLOJO 5a+

1. AKELARRE 6a+
2. EL HOMBRE DE HUMO 7c
3. EL LOBO VELOZ 6a+
4. SAMURAI 6b
5. A TOT OSTIA ☺ 6a
6. OFERTA EXPLOSIVA 6b+
7. SUPER NOVA ☺ 6a+
8. CHINAHAUK ☺ 7a
9. PARABOLES LEJANOS ☺ 7a
10. SINIESTRO TOTAL ☺ 6b+
11. TIRANT DE ROC ☺ 6b+
12. SEGUIX L'ANIMAL ☺ 6b+

13. AZUL MARCIA ILUSION ☺ 7a+
14. REPOS CELESTIAL ☺ 6c+
15. LA BOLA DEL NAS Z ☺ 7a
16. REUNION TUMULTOSA ☺ 6a+
17. LA MOLLAS DE RIGIO 6a
18. PLAN DE CHOQUE ☺ 6b
19. PAQUETE DE MEDIDAS ☺ 6c+
20. QUE SE MUERAN LOS FEOS ☺ 6c
21. TARUGO 6b+
22. MABLE'S 6a
23. EL CEDRO TORRE 5+

216

and climb the red streak past two holes to a lower-off on the rim.

15. LA BOLA DEL NAS Z ☺ 7a 28m
Start in the shallower cave to the right and climb out of the right side of this and follow the sustained (and in the winter rather floral) crack and pocketed seam passing the left edge of a deep horizontal slot high on the wall.

16. REUNION TUMULTOSA ☺ 6a+ 30m
To the right of the cave climb orange pocketed rock and a vague crack to and through a bulge (easier to the left) then on up a sharp grey rib to lower-offs near the cliff top.

17. LA MOLLAS DE RIGIO 6a 30m
The final route on this section of the wall with a poor start and better finish. A grey rib leads into a grotty cave, escape upwards to find better climbing on quality rock.

To the right are some bushes growing against the cliff and beyond these and slightly down the slope are six routes based around a wall with a prominent scoop in it.

18. PLAN DE CHOQUE ☺ 6b 35m
Climb the floral rib passing between two bushes growing on the face, then trend left passing left of a white tufa, following the left-hand bolt line in the head wall.

19. PAQUETE DE MEDIDAS ☺ 6c+ 35m
Follow the previous route to the headwall where the bolt line splits then climb straight up the sharp rib directly above.

20. QUE SE MUERAN LOS FEOS ☺ 6c 33m
Right of the bush on the lower rib climb steeply then pass a small tree growing out of a hole in the head wall.

21. TARUGO 6b+ 32m
Climb passing to the right of a large spiky palm plant, then trend left up a slab before pressing on through a series of bulges on the left side of the large scoop.

22. MABLE'S 6a 32m
Plough up the rather grotty groove that bounds this section on the right to reach the smart scoop then press on in the same direction passing tufas.

23. EL CEDRO TORRE 5+ 32m
Start as for the previous route but then move right and climb the right edge of the scoop.

Fifty metres down the slope to the right is a tufa encrusted power-blue wall with a prominent large horizontal roof on its right side. On the left there are three routes that share a common lower-off.

24. TOVARICH 6c+ 15m
Climb out of the right side of a cave past three small 'stal' pillars and various flowstone features to a lower-off below a roof at the top of the cliff.

25. TULIKREMLIN 6c 16m
Start at a second small cave (at ground level) and climb straight up the centre of the wall passing a heavily 'adulterated' block to reach the same lower-off.

26. CON IBERIA YA HABRIAS VOLADO 5 16m
Starting just left of a nasty white scar and climbing the rib before stepping left to join the previous climbs.

27. PELUT I PELAT 6b 18m
Start from the ledge and scramble right passing the rock scar to encounter gradually increasing difficulties. Not very edifying.

28. SINDROME DE SOLETAT ☺ 7a+ 30m
Start at a head height hole and climb to the left side of the flat roof and pull over it. Continue up the rib above. The longest and best route on this sector (by quite a margin!).

The right side of the wall has three more climbs
29. UN MONTON DE OSTIAS 7a+ 15m
Climb the centre of the wall between the orange and blue rock to a lower-off right under the roof.

30. SARVACHOF 6c 15m
The rib on the right where the cliff starts to swing round.

31. CULO FLOJO 6a+ 15m
The left wall of the corner gives almost the easiest and definitely the poorest route on the wall.

Sector Chica Facile
This is the natural continuation of the SECTOR SOL Y BON TEMPS as it runs down the slope and swings round above the dry river valley. Here are some long routes in a very sunny setting. It can be reached by descending awkwardly from the routes just described, passing a cave entrance or more directly from the car parking. Follow the path up past the SECTOR ESTIVAL on to a terrace as far as a 2m high carob bush and then follow the terrace horizontally past a slab, a small drystone wall holding up a boulder and a rocky rib to arrive below the Sector. The most obvious approach to the base of the cliff is via the stream bed but this is not recommended because of snakes, scorpions and spiky plants.

The routes are described from left to right. The first three routes start out of an orange cave, containing bushes, on the left edge of the sector.

ASTISORES PERILLOSES/DOLCHE VITTA ☺ 5+,5+ 40m
Climb the left rib of the cave and the wall above to ledges. Continue up the left side of the upper wall, over a roof to the chains. A good sustained route though hard for the grade.

ATMOSFERA O/BITACO ENTRE LAS PIERNAS ☺ 7b+,6a 40m
Power through the centre of the large roof with difficulty then climb the wall to reach the same ledge as the previous route. Continue up the centre of the wall above on excellent rock to reach bushes then trend left to join the previous climb. Good climbing but unbalanced pitches.

HONNEY MOON/PASODOBLES ☺ 6b+,6b+ 40m
Climb the flake crack that runs through the right side of the roof to reach the central ledge again. Climb the upper wall trending slightly right to a lower-off at the top of the cliff. Another excellent combo.

The next routes are to the right of the orange cave where there is a wall with left and right rising ramp lines that form a 'V'. The first three routes share a lower-off above which rises a short single extension pitch

TORRENTE DE MISERIAS 5+ 25m
Climb past a big hole early on then up to shrubby break and then on up slabbier rock.

LA FUEZA DEL VIENTO ☺ 6a+ 25m
Start at the lowest point of a 'V' feature and climb straight up the centre of the wall on pockets then on up the slab above.

DESPEDIDA DE SOLTERO ☺ 6a,6b 35m
The lower wall starts left of a yellow corner then straight up the rib above to a belay. Continue up the bulging scoopy wall above the belay to get the full tick.

CHICA FACIL 6a 25/40m
Start just left of the tree and climb the slightly loose yellow corner, a steep wall and then on up better, easier angled rock. This route may have a second pitch.

Around to the right is a large cave with two holes in its roof. There are five routes based around this feature

CAZA DE BRUJAS 6b+ 20m
Start at the left edge of the cave close to a bush and head up the wall, following a groove and finishing over a bulge.

EL GORDO DE MI MESOTA 6c+ 15m
Jug pulling out of the centre of the cave passing a series of small overlaps and on up a grey groove.

SOLO PARA ABOYADOS ☺ 6c 20m
Climb the right side of the cave passing some big holes early on then up a grey streak.

ESTRENO DURO ☺ 6b 20m
Just right again up tufas, then the wall and through some substantial bulges, ending up at the same lower-off as the last climb.

NO ME TOQUES QUE ME ROMPO 6a 20m
A bubbly rib just to the right of the cave and pleasant scoopy rock above.

EL DEMONO DOJO ☺ 6b+ 30m
Around to the right is an easy shrubby slab, up this then on up the much better rib above.

EL PRINCIPO DEL FIN 5+ 30m
Reportedly an easier right-hand finish to the last route though it looks unlikely at the grade.

Sector Foscor
Opposite the area just described is the diminutive and fairly grotty SECTOR FOSCOR where the route names are almost longer than the climbs. The one advantage the place has is that it is in perpetual shade and thus may be worth visiting when the heat is on. The routes are described briefly from right to left.

LA MEJOR ECOLOGIA MATAR EL PICHI CADA DIA 6b 10m
Start on the right behind a tree and climb across scruffy ledges and up a short wall.

EL NARANJO DE BRINES 5 10m
Start just to the left and climb the same lower-off.

TIERRA TRAGAME 6a+ 14m
Start left again and climb trending left to a belay on a hanging rib.

DE ROMO A ROMO Y SI CAIGO ME LA COMO 6b 14m
Around to the left in the gloomy canyon start up thin crack and climb the wall, the best of the bunch.

AL RUS CON LECHE 7a+
Pull through the roofs just to the left and climb past a hole to a shared lower-off.

Sector Complicacions
This is the extensive north facing cliff that runs diagonally up the hillside behind the SECTOR FRIGORIFICO. This is the least popular of the Sectors, and the name says it all. Some of the rock is dusty and/or loose and the steeply sloping nature of the foot of the cliff makes gearing up (and lounging around) an awkward proposition, such complications. The routes are listed here briefly for completeness. See diagram to further aid identification.

The base of the cliff is reached by following a gradually ascending path that runs leftwards up the hill from the left side of the SECTOR FRIGORIFICO. The first half a dozen climbs start at an apron of slab on the left, at the lowest point of the face.

1. JESUITA BIM BAM 6a+ 25m
Up the slab then branch left along ledges to reach and climb the leftmost line on the wall.

2. ESTOY FRITO TRES DELICIAS 6b+ 25m
Up the slab then left passing the left side of a tall orange cave/hollow finishing up an orange scoop.

3. TBO NEGRO 7b 25m
The same start as above then the wall right of the cave.

4. NO MOLA PORTAR ELS COLLONS A LA GOLA ☺ 6b+ 25m
Climb the slab to grass ledges at its top then step left at the ledge and climb the wall above.

The next four routes start from a grassy ledge with a deep cave on its left side. They can be done in one pitch from the ground though it perhaps makes sense to split them at the ledge system.

5. CHIPANGALI 6b+ 20/10m
Climb directly up the slab to a gassy ledge with caves (or approach the same from the right) then move right and climb a crack that bounds the left side of a pillar.

6. VIUDA NEGRA 6a 20/10m
As for the previous climb then up the front of the pillar.

7. EXPOLON 6a 20/10m
Take the next line up the lower slab starting by a tongue of rock, then at the level of the ledges move left to the left-hand line off the ledge.

8. SEMILLA NEGRA 7a+ 20/10m
As for the previous route but follow the bulging orange wall off the ledge.

CALVOROTAS ☺ 6a 22m
Start as for the previous route at the right side of the slabby apron but head straight up the pleasantly sustained hourglass shaped pillar.

9. MONOMAKINA ☺ 6c 22m
Start as for the previous route but follow a parallel line up an orange streak to the right.

Around to the right of the hourglass shaped pillar is a steep orange and white streaked wall with a flat rock ledge at its base.

1. JESUITA BIM BAM 6a+
2. ESTOY FRITO TRES DELICIAS 6b+
3. TBO NEGRO 7b
4. NO MOLA PORTAR ELS COLLONS A LA GOLA ☺ 6b+
5. CHIPANGALI 6b+
6. VIUDA NEGRA 6a
7. EXPOLON 6a
8. SEMILLA NEGRA 7a+
9. MONOMAKINA ☺ 6c
10. CHUBE PACHI ☺ 7a+
11. BAJA CHOCHO 7b
12. DROGA DURA 8a
13. A MICHES ☺ 6a+
14. LLUVIA ACIDA 7a
15. MARKA PASOS 7b
16. TU ET PUNXES TIO ☺ 6c+
17. PELAS PA LAS PILAS ☺ 7c+
18. MELODIA DE SEDUCCION project
19. TEMBLORES project
20. TOMATE UN RESPIRO 7a
21. PEDROMINA LA PIRULETA ☺ 7b
22. EL SILENCIO DE LOS BORREGOS 7c
23. CON AGUA ME CLOROFORMO ☺ 6b

Sector Complicacions

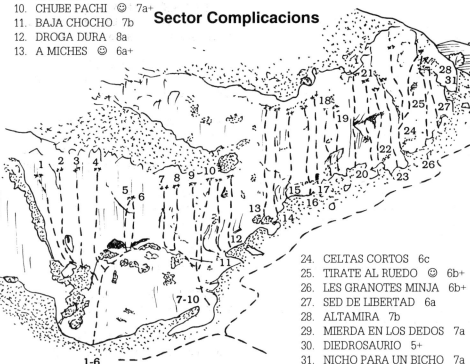

24. CELTAS CORTOS 6c
25. TIRATE AL RUEDO ☺ 6b+
26. LES GRANOTES MINJA 6b+
27. SED DE LIBERTAD 6a
28. ALTAMIRA 7b
29. MIERDA EN LOS DEDOS 7a
30. DIEDROSAURIO 5+
31. NICHO PARA UN BICHO 7a

10. CHUBE PACHI ☺ 7a+ 12m
The left side of the leaning wall is supposed to be 'fun'.

11. BAJA CHOCHO 7b 12m
The line to the right and passing left of a bush half-way up the wall is apparently a sandbag.

12. DROGA DURA 8a 14m
A tough line passing to the right of the bush.

To the right is rounded rib with a small but prominent white patch, left of this is:
13. A MICHES ☺ 6a+ 25m
A tough start over a bulge leads to easier climbing above.

14. LLUVIA ACIDA 7a 25m
Climb past the scar and on up the pillar above.

15. MARKA PASOS 7b 20m
Start in the recess around to the right where a tough start leads to easier rock above.

To the right is a smart smooth grey wall with a deep hole on its left and an orange backed recess to its right

16. TU ET PUNXES TIO ☺ 6c+ 20m
The pocket wall to the left of the hole.

17. PELAS PA LAS PILAS ☺ 7c+ 20m
The smooth looking wall directly above the hole is just that.

To the right are two projects that pull through the bulge above the orange recess and then climb (or don't!) up the smooth wall above. These are 18. MELODIA DE SEDUCCION and 19. TEMBLORES.

Up the slope to the right are some large orange bulges containing two caves
20. TOMATE UN RESPIRO 7a 20m
The line up the left side of the orange rock is another of those sand-bags.

21. PEDROMINA LA PIRULETA ☺ 7b 18m
The roof direct is a spectacular 'gorilla-thrilla'.

22. EL SILENCIO DE LOS BORREGOS 7c 16m
A tougher right-hand version of the above.

23. CON AGUA ME CLOROFORMO ☺ 6b 20m
The rib to the right of the orange overhangs is more sensible in every way.

To the right a grassy diagonal break runs leftwards up the cliff face fizzling out about 5m off the ground.
24. CELTAS CORTOS 6c 22m
Climb to the base of the diagonal break then climb the steep slab on the right.

25. TIRATE AL RUEDO ☺ 6b+ 22m
Start as for the previous route but take a marginally easier line up the slab to the right, finishing at above an orange hollow. The best hereabouts.

26. LES GRANOTES MINJA 6b+ 22m
The slab to the right is climbed direct sketchily to a steeper finish looping through bulges.

27. SED DE LIBERTAD 6a 22m
The last route on the main section of the face is not really worth the walk up.

Around to the right is a small cave with a collection of short routes. These can be approached more easily from a track around to the right rather flogging all the way up the steep bank.
28. ALTAMIRA 7h 12m
At the left edge of the cave, short and hard despite not being a Whillans' route.

29. MIERDA EN LOS DEDOS 7a 12m
Through the right side of the cave.

30. DIEDROSAURIO 5+ 12m
The groove on the right has three bolt runners.

31. NICHO PARA UN BICHO 7a 10m
The short bulging arete on the far right.

PENYA DE L'AVENTADOR

Crag Facts

Star Rating: ****
Aspect: south west facing
Height: Up to 50 metres
Spread of grades:

4	5	5+	6a	6b	6c	7a	7b	7c	8
1	6	9	32	22	6	4	1	1	

Introduction

A high quality cliff, with a sunny aspect and with over 70 routes, pleasantly situated in a secluded valley just to the east of the town of Xativa (pronounced as a rapid cha-tee-va). Unfortunately the locals have bolted the crag with such fervour that the actual identification of individual routes is rather difficult because of their close packed nature! In some cases it is almost possible to get two ticks at once. There are occasional scratched letters at the foot of the face, to aid location, but the crag could really do with the names of all the routes painting at their foot, and individual bolt lines colour coded. The topos and brief notes included here are taken from my original photographs and explorations. I hope they prove adequate at sorting out the geography of this extensive face.

Note: Our last two visits to Aventador have been at Easter time and the place has been infested with unpleasant small black (non-biting) flies. This may be associated to the proximity of the river, and it has never been a problem at other times of the year.

Crag Geography

The cliff is basically a broad wall, lowest on the right and increasing in height the further left you climb. On the far right the cliff is 20m high and relatively easy angled, consequently the climbs are in the lower grades and can be done to the lower-off and back to the ground easily. Further to the left the cliff becomes higher and steeper, with an impressive cave and routes of 45m in length, many of them as two pitches. An abseil descent (in one rope length with double ropes or in two with a single rope) using any one of the anchors on the cliff top is the easiest way back down from these longer climbs. Alternatively it is possible to walk off the right side of the cliff where eventually an easy gully leads through a short rock band. The latter takes about 10 minutes.

AVENTADOR

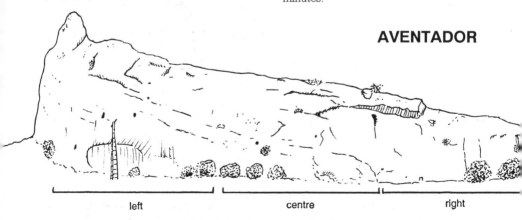

left   centre   right

Access

Follow the C320 road from Gandia towards Albaida, and then turn right towards Xativa on the C332 after 15km. Immediately after the sign for leaving Genoves (35km from Gandia and 5km before Xativa) is a minor left turn, between two stumpy palm trees and to the right of a white factory (ENVASES ORDINANA S.L.). Follow the narrow road for 1.9km to the 'one horse' settlement of Alboy and turn left down its very unimpressive 'one way system'. Pass the grandiose railway station and on reaching the foot of the hill turn left. From here there are two alternatives. Either park by the bar and camping area on the bend (closed in winter) and follow the track for a couple of hundred metres to where a newly concreted road forks down to the right. Scramble up to the left here onto the railway track and walk through the tunnel (shades of El Chorro, torch useful) to arrive unexpectedly at the crag, 10-15 minutes from the car. Or continue driving along the track until it passes close to the river opposite a barred cave entrance and then swings round to the left and heads uphill. Follow this (rough!) to the second parking place on the right from where a good track leads over the ridge to arrive below the left side of the face, 10 minutes from the car.

The routes are described from right to left as most visits start at the right side of the cliff.

Almost at the lowest point of the cliff is a large, white, square block. Eleven metres right of this is a clump of multiple-trunked trees and around to the right of this is a sheltered bay containing the first routes.

1. DIT 5 18m
Start at the toe of a short ramp (71 and an arrow arc scratched faintly on the rock). A rather vegetated lower section leads straight up the slab passing nice new bolts and passes left of two holly bushes and up a long flake to a wire cable lower-off.

2. VIA PEPE ☺ 6a 18m
One and a half metres left the name PEPE is scratched on the rock. Climb the clean slab (new bolts) eventually trending right to the lower-off of the previous route. Done direct the route is

quite tough but this can be eased with some lateral thinking.

3. ????? 5 20m
Start just left of a grey bubbly crack line and climb straight up the slab to a lower-off on the left arete of a corner near the top of the cliff.

4. IDEFIX 5+ 20m
Start off the flake/ramp at head height, and head straight up slab passing a bolt in a scar and pulling over the right edge of an overlap.

5. OBELIX ☺ 6a 22m
From just right of the tip of the flake climb up passing a black bolt early on, head up the smooth grey slab and finish over a substantial bulge just below the top of the cliff.

6. ASTERIX ☺ 6a 22m
Start from the tip of the flake again and climb through a small bulge and follow a pale streak to climb over the left edge of the overhang at the top of the cliff.

7. NAVARRO 6a 24m
Start to the left of the flake and immediately right of the bushes. Step left to follow grassy cracks (new bolts, one of which is situated prominently in patch of white rock) to a lower-off on the left.

Moving around to the left of the multiple-trunked bushes the first line is:
8. PEPET ☺ 6b+ 24m
The fine sustained and fingery white rib directly above the bushes is reached from the left. A bulge near the top proves problematical.

9. VENT ♦ 5 24m
The long bubbly crack line is one of the main features of this section of the wall. It would be tough to protect back home but here it offers excellent sustained climbing and with any description proving superfluous.

10. ARCADIA ☺ 5 24m
Start just left of the pocketed crack line where there is a white scar at the base of the cliff. Climb

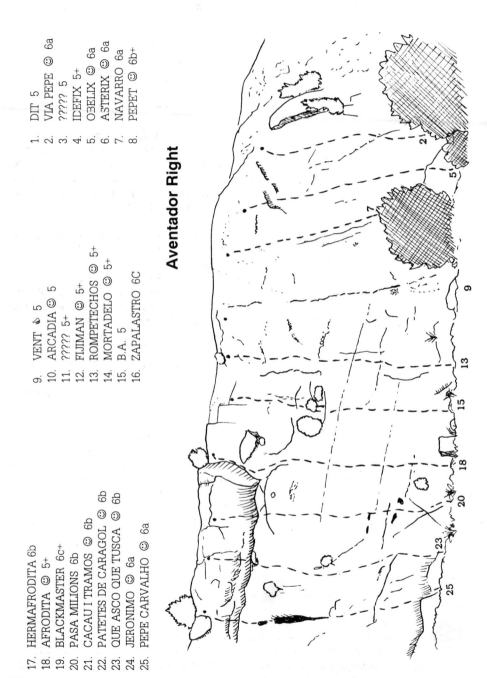

Aventador Right

1. DIT 5
2. VIA PEPE ☺ 6a
3. ????? 5
4. IDEFIX 5+
5. OBELIX ☺ 6a
6. ASTERIX ☺ 6a
7. NAVARRO 6a
8. PEPET ☺ 6b+

9. VENT ⬖ 5
10. ARCADIA ☺ 5
11. ????? 5+
12. FIJIMAN ☺ 5+
13. ROMPETECHOS ☺ 5+
14. MORTADELO ☺ 5+
15. B.A. 5
16. ZAPALASTRO 6C

17. HERMAFRODITA 6b
18. AFRODITA ☺ 5+
19. BLACKMASTER 6c+
20. PASA MILIONS 6b
21. CACAU I TRAMOS ☺ 6b
22. PATETES DE CARAGOL ☺ 6b
23. QUE ASCO QUE TUSCA ☺ 6b
24. JERONIMO ☺ 6a
25. PEPE CARVALHO ☺ 6a

the bubbly grey face and bulging headwall to the lower-off of the previous climb. Rather easier than VENT and a good intro. to the cliff.

To the left is an arrow scratched on the rock and to the left of this is:

11. ????? 5+ 24m
A line straight up grey streaks with a move of UK 5b, and passing a vegetated zone at two thirds height and again lowering off as for the last two routes.

12. FIJIMAN ☺ 5+ 25m
Another scratched arrow marks the start of this climb that passes just left of twinned brown tufas. Climb directly up the slab to a flake crack. Up this then lean left to reach lower-off on the head wall just below a bush. Seven bolt runners protect.

13. ROMPETECHOS ☺ 5+ 24m
Start at a small right-facing corner at 3m with a prominent white scar at the base of it. Climb out of the corner and on up the brown and then white slab. The crux is passing the first bolt and it might just be worth UK 5c.

14. MORTADELO ☺ 5+ 24m
Start right of a tall flake that runs up to a ledge with bushes on it. Head straight up the slab from a hole with sustained 5b moves above the second bolt. Continue passing to the right of the bushes, and on past a cave near the top.

15. B.A. 5 24m
Initially follow the scarred flake system (2m right of a large block at the foot of the cliff) and then take a direct line passing through a gap in the bushes and on to the lower-off. Be warned - the final wall is tough at the grade.

Note: From here leftwards lowering back to the ground with a 50m rope requires great care.

16. ZAPALASTRO 6c 25m
Start at the rounded rib to the left of the flake crack and directly behind the square block on the ground where a vague 'Z' is scratched on the

rock. Climb to the bushes and pass through them as for previous route and then parallel it up the top wall.

17. HERMAFRODITA 6b 26m
Start left of the square block and climb straight up slab, passing to the left of the bushes. Finish up the right wall of corner at the top of the cliff passing the right edge of a huge perched flake.

18. AFRODITA ☺ 5+ 26m
Start just right of some blobs of metal hammered into the cliff and climb up into the base of the prominent hanging corner high above. Bridge up this passing a huge perched flake early on to reach a lower-off on the right.

The next ten routes all cross the overhang that runs across the crest of the wall to the left.

19. BLACKMASTER 6c+ 25m
Start at the hammered bits of lead, climb leftward to and then up the crucial hanging left arete of the corner climbed by the previous route.

20. PASA MILIONS 6b 25m
Start at a 4m long, left slanting crack. 'PM' is scratched on the rock. Climb the wall (old spaced bolts) and cross the roof at a series of deep holes, poor.

21. CACAU I TRAMOS ☺ 6b 26m
Left of the crack mentioned above start off a little flat ledge. The first bolt is above a diagonal crack and right of a large perched flake. Climb straight up pale streaks situated directly below the lower-off then at the roofs move left 1.5m then pull up and swing back right to reach the lower-off. Nine bolt runners.

22. PATETES DE CARAGOL ☺ 6b 26m
Start at a scratched arrow just right of a bush 2m up the cliff. Climb straight up the wall and then pull through roof at large holes before stepping right to the lower-off of previous climb.

23. QUE ASCO QUE TUSCA ☺ 6b 26m
Begin at a small orange tipped flake 2m off the

ground. Climb straight up the wall passing to the left of bushes at 12m and climbing the final bulges via a ragged crack.

24. JERONIMO ☺ 6a 26m
Start just left of the orange tipped flake at pockets with the first bolt above a short white streak. Head straight up the wall past a couple of ledges and passing under a bush at 20m. Finish as for the previous route.

25. PEPE CARVALHO ☺ 6a 26m
Start at a 45 degree left slanting flake and climb to the large vertical cave/slot two thirds of the way up the cliff. Up this then through the roof

directly above.

26. TOT ES MANEO ☺ 6a 26m
Begin at vague rounded rib with 'PX' scratched on the rock. Climb the fine wall to the left of the cave/slot of the previous route on pockets then make delicate moves to reach the roof. Pull rightwards through the roof and use PEPE's lower-off. Eight bolt runners.

27. HAS COBRAT? ☺ 6a 28m
To the left of 'PX' is a rounded rib with pockets, down and right of a ramp with bushes. Climb passing a peg to ledges where there is some large red writing and continue directly to a

26. TOT ES MANEO ☺ 6a
27. HAS COBRAT? 6a
28. ALA ANEM 6a
29. PEGAME EN TO EL MEDIO ☺ 6a+
30. AMADEUS ☺ 6a
31. MESINFOTELES 6a
32. COLLO QUE GUAI ☺ 6a+

33. LUIS MARIANO 6a+
34. CONEIXIMENT DE MOSQUIT 6b
35. O.V. ☺ 6a+
36. JORGE NEGRETE ☺ 6a+
37. COCONUTS ☺ 6a
38. CEFALOGRAMA ☺ 5+
39. ALBOMINA ☺ 5+
40. PEPSIMAN ☺ 6a
41. GUELES 6a+
42. TRIMOMIA 6a+

43. MILI ☺ 4+
44. CALLA PIXORRO 6b
45. CRISTAL PARDO 6b+
46. ACI EM PEGARAS ☺ 6b
47. ASTROKANGRENA BUCOLICA ♦ 6a+
48. ASGARRAMENTA LUMBAR ☺ 6c+

Aventador Centre

lower-off hanging over the top of the cliff. Quite mild at the grade.

28. ALA ANEM 6b 30m
Twelve metres right of the next large tree at the foot of the wall is a 2m high, grey tufa 'slug' with a hole in its top. Start right of this and climb up past the left side of a small overlap and continue to pass to the left of the red writing half-way up the wall.

29. PEGAME EN TO EL MEDIO ☺ 6a+ 32m
Climb past the tufa into the deep right-facing groove that is the most noticeable feature of this part of the face. Continue up this then on up the wall above.

The next three routes share a common lower-off above a smooth white slab at the top of the cliff. Reaching the lower-off is probably the crux on all three routes!

30. AMADEUS ☺ 6a 32m
Climb the shrubby slab and then the left arête of the right facing corner mentioned above, before trending left up the wall eventually pulling through the overlap high on the face just to the right of a prominent yellow patch.

31. MESINFOTELES 6a 32m
Just to the left climb left of a large hole at 15m and pass the final overlap at the distinct yellow patch.

32. COLLO QUE GUAI ☺ 6a+ 32m
Climb leftwards up the lower slab to reach diagonal ledges then head up the steeper wall above (crux) rightwards before climbing behind a bush and out right to the lower-offs.

33. LUIS MARIANO 6a+ 30m
Start just right of the tree and climb leftwards up the lower slabs to a prominent white triangular flake halfway up the cliff. Step back right and continue directly up the wall above.

To the left are three clumpy bushes. These help locate the starts of the next routes. The first

three routes start to the left of the right-hand of the three bushy trees.

34. CONEIXIMENT DE MOSQUIT 6b 30m
Climb the slab to the white triangular flake with a tree growing out of its left side (almost joining the previous climb) then climb straight up the wall above to the lower-off of the previous route.

35. O.V. ☺ 6a+ 30m
Start as for the last climb but at the level of the flake step left and climb past a hole then head straight up the smooth white wall via difficult final moves and then pull over an overlap to reach a wire cable lower-off near the top of the face.

36. JORGE NEGRETE ☺ 6a+ 30m
Starting at the left side of the gap in the trees and trend left up the slab passing a horizontal break and on up clean white rock. Pass left of a bush and pull over a small overlap to finish just left of the corner that forms the exit for MILI (see below).

37. COCONUTS ☺ 6a 30m
Start between the left-hand of the two bushes and climb the floral slab slightly leftwards passing a bulge at 10m and then on directly up the grey slab to finish just left of the previous climb.

38. CEFALOGRAMA ☺ 5+ 30/35m
An excellent long pitch at a reasonable grade. Again start between the two left-hand bushes and trend leftwards to the climb the right side of a broken white flake (possible stance on the left) before climbing the wall directly above to a lower-off on the right. Use this or top out (no belays).

To the left is a prominent ledge halfway up the cliff, which is used as a stance by several routes, and to its left is a steepening slab. In this area there are half a dozen routes that all suffer from having grotty lower sections, though if you can cope with the 'rock and two veg' things improve dramatically above half height.

39. ALBOMINA ☺ 5+ 30m
Start left of the three bushes and climb straight up the wall keeping right of further shrubbery, passing pegs and bolts to a good stance on a ledge. Take the left-hand line of fixed gear (peg, bolt, bolt) to a substantial chain.

40. PEPSIMAN ☺ 6a 30m
Follow the previous route to the stance then follow the right-hand line of fixed gear (bolt, peg, bolt) to the same lower-off. The short upper pitches of both routes can easily be done from the stance, rapidly earning two ticks.

41. GUELES MARXOSES 6a+ 30m
Start below the left edge of the mid-height ledge. The lower slab is rather floral (thread and old bolts), pass a bulge (peg) and then things improve on the upper wall.

42. TRIMOMIA 6a+ 30m
A scrappy start behind a bush leads through loose rock and then past a horizontal break onto the much better upper section. This is the second line left of the stance on top of the central flake and it is protected by rather old bolts. It uses the same lower-off as the previous climb.

43. MILI ☺ 4+ 45m
A worthwhile easy route with a scrappy first pitch and much better second one. Start behind the tree and climb the poorly protected and shrubby slab (or the easier and poorer crack on the left) to a horizontal break. Follow this rightwards and climb a short corner to a good stance and variety of belays on top of a flake. Step off the right end of the ledge and climb the fine slab on surprising holds diagonally rightwards before finishing up the left facing flake crack.

44. CALLA PIXORRO 6b 32m
Start up a left slanting ramp behind a tree and climb over grotty terrain passing the right edge of a ledge and continuing up better rock above.

45. CRISTAL PARDO 6b+ 30m
Start at the diagonal ramp of the previous route

but trend left following a line of bolts that run right behind a large stand of bushes growing close to the wall. Follow these passing a white flake on a ledge then on up steeper rock to a lower-off below the rim of the wall.

Around to the left of the bushes the quality of the routes begins to improve again though they are still closely packed.

46. ACI EM PEGARAS ☺ 6b 30m
Begin on the left side of the bushes at a block behind them and climb the slab (new bolts) passing close to the previous route before climbing a solitary tufa and then the wall rightwards.

47. ASTROKANGRENA BUCOLICA ♦ 6a+ 30m
Start at the name scratched faintly on the rock and head directly up the lower slab passing a weathered black thread at 8m. Continue passing old and then new bolts to some red holes then step right and climb the superb pocketed wall up to a lower-off below a small overhang near the top of the cliff.

48. ASGARRAMENTA LUMBAR ☺ 6c+ 30m
Start at the name, as for the previous route and follow it to the red holes then move left and climb the smooth wall to the lower-off used by the next climb.

The next half dozen routes start up a broad apron of easy slabs running leftwards to steeper rock ending at the right edge of the cave. The locals obviously realised that this is the best bit of rock on the cliff and have bolted it accordingly! Identifying the correct starts to individual routes is difficult except where names have been scratched on the rock, and the addition of a series of unnamed variations on the regular climbs does not help things! One of the most useful identification features here is a small ledge halfway up the cliff with prominent large wire cable belays at both ends.

Aventador: The author on the first pitch of the devious but excellent CARBONO 14 5+ 6a

Aventador: Sherri Davy follows in the pleasant second pitch of Mili 4+

49. VOMITERA OPTICA ☺ 6c+ 30m
Start at the scratched name behind a bush and climb straight up the slab passing to the right of a white broken flake, up smoother wall between two red streaks and then rightwards to the lower-off of the previous route.

50. VAMPIRO ☺ 7a 35m
This is a tough left-hand finish to the previous route (possible stance on the left at half height if needed) and it features some fierce pocket pulling on the upper wall and finishes over a bulge at the top of the cliff.

51. CARBONO 14 ♦ 5+,6a 45m
An excellent route finding the easiest way up this part of the cliff. Start midway between two bushes at the foot of the face and climb the steepening slab, passing a bulge with a small patch of orange rock in it, to the wire cable belay at the right end of the ledge. Traverse left passing another substantial belay then climb in a loop out left and then back right to get into the yellow right slanting corner, finishing up its right wall.

52. EXTRAMAUNCION ☺ 6a,7a 35m
Start just right of the left-hand bush and climb the steepening slab keeping just left of the previous climb, and right of the steeper rock, to the right-hand stance. Attack the wall directly behind aiming for the notch at the top of the cliff.

53. CARUSO ☺ 6a,7a 35m
Follow the previous climb to its stance then climb the smooth wall behind, initially trending slightly leftwards and then more directly.

54. ASTOLFO HINKEL ☺ 6a+, 6c 45m
A good climb with a long first pitch. Start behind the tree and climb up the slab that runs up to the steep wall with a prominent orange tufa. Climb up to the right of this then trend away passing below the left-hand lower-off on the ledge to eventually reach a belay below and left of the final groove of CARBONO 14. Finish up the smooth rib up and left from the stance.

Following the initial line of the first pitch and continuing directly to the stance at the right end of the mid-way ledge is 54a. an unnamed ☺ 6b 20m variant.

55. EISENKOUEN ☺ 6b 15/45m
An easier right-hand finish to the previous route up the wall and shallow groove above the stance.

56. TREMOLANDO ESTOY ☺ 6b 22m
A good direct line up the large red tufa and on directly up superb pocketed rock to the belay at the left end of the midway ledge system.

57. ANTROPIA AFONICA ♦ 6a+,6a 45m
Another very worthwhile route, again with a long first pitch. Start at the name scratched on the rock and climb the pillar left of the prominent red tufa then trend left following good holds and deep holes above steeper rock, passing some lower-offs, to eventually reach a stance at the right edge of a good ledge. The second pitch trends left to enter the prominent right slanting corner that runs all the way to the cliff top (not to be confused with the smaller slanting corner of CARBONO 14 away to the right).

From the stance it is possible to traverse left along the ledge system to finish up the last pitch of ALTO BRONX. This variation is 57a. known as FUGA DEL BRONX 6a 24m.

Climbing the right edge of the cave and then stepping right to eventually pass the belay on the left edge of the midway ledge and then continuing directly to the cliff top is yet another of the 'variations' on this section of wall. It is known simply as:
58. 'D', ☺ 6b 40m.

Starting in the same place and taking a direct line ignoring all topographical features and finishing just right of the final corner of CARBONO 14 is another variation:
59. MESCLAILLOS GUEROLA ☺ 6b 33m.

The next climbs are tough offerings that start in the cave that is the main feature of the left side of the face. They involve steep climbing on tufas and pockets and are well worth seeking out if you are into upside-down climbing.

60. MAYEUTICA ☺ 7c 20m
The smooth right edge of the cave is home to the hardest route on the cliff. Judging by some of the other grades here it must be pretty tough.

61. LA RIENA DE AFRICA ☺ 7b+ 20m
Start at the neatly painted name in the back of the cave and climb through the bulges left then right to a lower-off around the final lip.

62. DALE CANA AL MONO ☺ 7a+ 22m
Start by a spidery bush and following the largest tufas in the cave and finish by a large hole.

---

49. VOMITERA OPTICA ☺ 6c+
50. VAMPIRO ☺ 7a
51. CARBONO 14 ♦ 5+, 6a
52. EXTRAMAUNCION ☺ 6a, 7a
53. CARUSO ☺ 6a,7a
54. ASTOLFO HINKEL ☺ 6a+,6c
55. EISENKOUEN ☺ 6b
56. TREMOLANDO ESTOY ☺ 6b
57. ANTROPIA AFONICA ♦ 6a+, 6a
58. 'D' ☺ 6b
59. MESCLAILLOS GUEROLA ☺ 6b

60. MAYEUTICA ☺ 7c
61. LA RIENA DE AFRICA ☺ 7b+
62. DALE CANA AL MONO ☺ 7a+
63. ALTO BRONX A2,6a+
64. PEDOS DE COLORES ☺ 6c+
65. ALTERFILIA COPENAGUENS ☺ 6b+, 6a
66. PANINI DI BOTIFARRATO ☺ 6b, 6b+
67. FLASOS BRUTALS ☺ 6b+
68. MORTUS EST ☺ 6a+, 5
69. FERMIN APOLITO 6b, 5
70. SPECTRUM 6b, 6a+
71. PLACA COSMICA 6b+
72. CRUS DIABLO 6a+, 6a

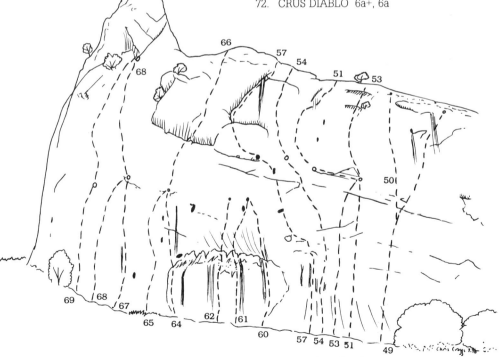

Aventador Left

Just left is a hard looking new route (or project), no name known. It climbs through the cave to arrive at the stance at the end of the first long pitch of ANTROPIA AFONICA. The second pitch lies directly above.

63. ALTO BRONX A2,6a+ 40m
Start at the name on the rock by a spiky bush and aid(!!) up a red streak up the leaning wall to a belay in a cave. The second pitch trends left up the wall passing bulges at half height.

To the left are the rusty remains of an old bolt ladder and just before the left edge of the cave is:
64. PEDOS DE COLORES ☺ 6c+ 20m
A good pitch up large holds and steep rock trending left to the first belay of PANINI DI BOTIFARRATO (see below).

65. ALTERFILIA COPENAGUENS ☺ 6b+,6a+ 45m
Start on the left rib of the cave and climb straight up steep rock, passing deep pockets, before trending left (crossing the next route) to a belay in a hollow. From here climb the steep wall trending right to pass a horizontal break then continue up the fine clean slab to the cliff top.

66. PANINI DI BOTIFARRATO ☺ 6b,6b+ 45m
Begin at some white rock and climb the wall directly before trending to the right (crossing the previous route) to reach the belay at the top of PEDOS DE COLORES. The second pitch heads straight up the bulging wall to a break and then follows discontinuous cracks to the cliff top.

67. FLASOS BRUTALS ☺ 6b+ 22m
Climb directly to the stance at the top of the first pitch of ALTERFILIA COPENAGUENS via a series of pale tufas and the occasional good pocket. Lower off.

68. MORTUS EST ☺ 6a+,5 45m
To the left is a tree. Follow the second bolt ladder to the right of this until it bears away to the right to the belay used by the last route. The second pitch climbs directly up the wall behind, keeping left of the obvious shrubby groove, to arrive at a ledge near the cliff top.

69. FERMIN APOLITO 6b,5
Start immediately to the right of the tree growing close to the rock and climb the bubbly wall trending slightly leftwards to a stance after 20m. The second pitch climbs slightly left and then straight up the wall to the ledge at the top of the previous route.

The final three routes are around to the left of the tree growing close to the rock. I have not done any of these and they don't appear to be of the quality of the routes to the right as the cliff is rather vegetated and broken. Mind you, appearances can be deceptive! From right to left these are

70. SPECTRUM 6b,6a+ 45m
Starting just left of the tree.

71. PLACA COSMICA 6b+ 25m
A single pitch to the belay of the previous climb.

72. CRUS DIABLO 6a+,6a 45m
The last route on the cliff with a short first pitch and long second one.

BARRANC DE L'AVERN: ONTINYENT

Crag Facts

Star rating: ****

Aspect: mostly 'southish'

Height: up to 30 metres, though most of the routes are half this height

Spread of grades:

4	5	5+	6a	6b	6c	7a	7b	7c	8
4	3	3	29	23	21	21	9	/	/

Introduction

An impressive deep-cut ravine with a great deal of exposed rock and a very busy and noisy road running through it. There have been several areas of rock developed in the gorge and the most important of these are described briefly here. In 1995 the road in the gorge bed was widened and a major fire damaged many of the area's trees. Fortunately neither of these events appear to have significantly affected the best of the climbing.

Driving up the gorge the first rock passed is the PARED DE GEGANT high on the left (see map). As the next long left-hand bend is rounded the narrow valley on the right is home to the SECTORS DEL DEPOSIT and VISERA. Across from the road at this point is the extensive SECTOR CAGALLO DE GEGANT, often with a prominently displayed flag, and 1.4km further up the gorge on the same side and rising above an impressive railway embankment is the PARED DE LA VIA. Access to each cliff is described individually.

Access (See map p234)

The gorge runs north from the town of Ontinyent, and is reached by following the newly constructed ring road passing several impressive roundabouts. Take the C3316 (signed Bocarient and Villena) for just less than a kilometre from the last roundabout (the one with a Villena 35km sign) to a parking place on the right immediately before the second bridge in the gorge. This is the parking place for the PARED DE GEGANT and CAGALLO DE GEGANT, and is also the start of the road that runs up to the SECTORS DEL DEPOSIT and VISERA.

Pared De Gegant

This is the spectacular grey sheet of rock high on the left above the lower reaches of the gorge. It offers some fine face routes in an impressive setting, though some of the climbs could do with being rebolted. From the parking place follow the track under the bridge, cross the dry river bed and scramble up onto the rim of the water conduit. Follow this leftwards, crossing it at the first opportunity. A direct ascent to the foot of the main face from this point is best avoided because of the steep unstable nature of the slope, so scramble straight up the bank passing to the left of the obvious pinnacle (the top of the CAGALLO DE GEGANT, see below) to the two prominent trees on the ridge. Behind and to the right of these a low rocky band is passed via an awkward 3m chimney/flake to the second pylon on the ridge and just above this a ramp leads back down to the left to the foot of the face, a steep 10 minutes from the car.

Below and left of the main cliff is a diagonal wall of rock SECTOR LA CEQUIA with about twenty lower grade climbs 10-12m in length. The steep slope below the cliff makes climbing here slightly problematical and as the climbs are not very well bolted they are not described here.

The central section of the crag is 30m high, a 55m rope is bare minimum for most climbs, otherwise use double ropes and make an abseil descent.

On the far left of the base of the wall is a rounded rib which is most easily reached by a short traverse, though it is also possible to start lower down the slope in a small bay.

1. SATIRO 5+ 30m
Follow the rib passing old bolts and threads, and placing your own gear when required. Lower-off as for the next route.

2. MILOTXO ☺ 5+ 30m
The left edge of the main face sports new bolts for the first 15m then older specimens above. Again it is reached by a short traverse out from the end of the ledge and the lower-offs are on the right at the top.

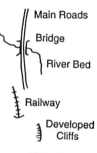

Main Roads

Bridge

River Bed

Railway

Developed Cliffs

Buildings

BARRANC DE L'AVERN, ONTINYENT

1. Pared de Gegant
2. Cagallo de Gegant
3. Sector del Deposit
4. Sector la Visera
5. Pared de la Via

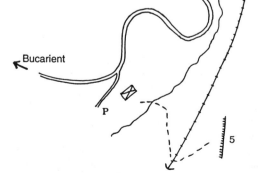

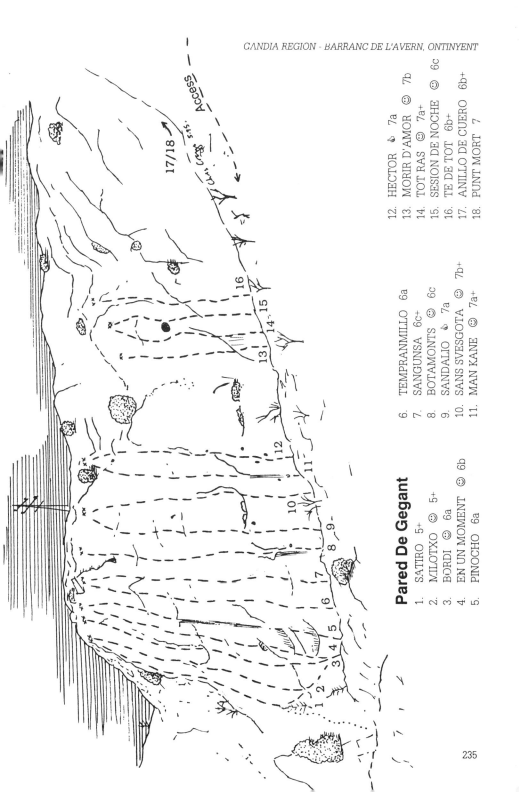

17/18 →

Class Cross 5.15.

Access

Pared De Gegant

1. SATIRO 5+
2. MLOTXO ☺ 5+
3. BORDI ☺ 6a
4. EN UN MOMENT ☺ 6b
5. PINOCHO 6a

6. TEMPRANMILLO 6a
7. SANGUNSA 6c+
8. BOTAMONTS ☺ 6c
9. SANDALIO ⚷ 7a
10. SANS SVESGOTA ☺ 7b+
11. MAN KANE ☺ 7a+

12. HECTOR ⚷ 7a
13. MORIR D'AMOR ☺ 7b
14. TOT RAS ☺ 7a+
15. SESION DE NOCHE ☺ 6c
16. TE DE TOT 6b+
17. ANILLO DE CUERO 6b+
18. PUNT MORT 7

235

3. BORDI ☺ 6b 28m
From the left end of the ledge trend slightly left to climb the rib and prominent thin crack. Above this follow flakes to the lower-off.

4. EN UN MOMENT ☺ 6b 28m
Start in the same place as the previous route and keep just to its right following the line of new bolts all the way up the wall.

5. PINOCHO 6a 28m
Starting just to the right again and trending rightwards to follow a line of older bolts that runs up a long black streak.

6. TEMPRANMILLO 6a 28m
Climb the yellow streak marked by a line of old bolts.

7. SANGUNSA 6c+ 28m
Climb the fine pillar of grey rock, unfortunately it is protected by a mixture of old bolts and threads.

8. BOTAMONTS ☺ 6c 28m
Climb to a wriggling crack at 10m with a black drainage streak issuing from its base and continue in the same line.

9. SANDALIO ♠ 7a 28m
Take the tricky lower wall and pass the left edge of a vegetated ledge at 12m. The upper wall offers superb sustained climbing via scoops and bulges.

10. SANS SVESGOTA ☺ 7b+ 28m
The next climb passes to the right side of the ledge and has a very tough finale with the lower-off just left of a bush on the crest of the wall.

11. MAN KANE ☺ 7a+ 28m
More fine sustained climbing following the new bolts, passing to the right of a large flowering shrub one third of the way up the face.

12. HECTOR ♠ 7a 28m
The last route on the main section of the wall is protected by a line of nice new blue bolts, and sports a tough upper rib.

20m further right on a prominent steep orange wall are four pitches.
13. MORIR D'AMOR ☺ 7b 20m
The left-hand line up the wall.

14. TOT RAS ☺ 7a + 20m
The climb passing to the left of the deep hole.

15. SESION DE NOCHE ☺ 6c 20m
Climb through the deep hole on slightly crunchy rock.

16. TE DE TOT 6b+ 20m
The right-hand line.

A further 50m to the right are two more shorter climbs, 17. ANILLO DE CUERO 6b+ 15m on the left and 18. PUNT MORT 7 14m on the right.

Cagallo De Gegant

Impolitely called the Giant's Turd, the section of rock above the water channel is south facing and has some good though very closely packed climbs up to 20m in length. The diagrams and brief notes below should be adequate to locate the climbs which are generally better than they look. Approach as for the previous cliff but turn right and walk along the rim of the conduit until a plank can be crossed to the foot of the wall.

The climbs are listed from left to right, starting to the left of the footbridge.

1. S'HAS GOLO 7a+ 18m
Four metres left of the plank bridge, the bulge is passed by harsh pocket pulling. Pass smaller bulges and a bush to reach a lower-off on the rim.

2. BARRUFETS ☺ 6c 18m
Start one metre left of the plank bridge and pocket pull around the right edge of the smooth bulges and then head up the easier rib above, the lower-off is rather antiquated.

3. PITUFOS ☺ 6a 18m
Start opposite the plank bridge at a bush. Climb the rib immediately right of the bulges which proves to be sustained and fingery, with particularly thin moves to enter the final crack. The route shares the old lower-off of the previous climb.

4. PELAWATIOS ☺ 6a 18m
Climb left of a yellow scar at 6m then through a bulge (first three bolts are old) and up the final steep wall to a new lower-off up on the right.

5. ESPERO BOXERINI ☺ 6a 18m
The wall directly below the arete high on the cliff has one awkward move to gain the cleaned crack. The arete is pleasantly juggy and is climbed on layaways. At the top move left to the lower-off used by the previous climb.

6. DOLORES ☺ 6a 18m
The wall to the right has a line of new bolts and some quality rock. At the top step left and bridge the corner to a discreet lower-off in the left wall.

7. CARAGOL 5 16m
Start up a short rib above the narrowest part of the path and climb the wall passing a couple of tricky moves at two thirds height to a lower-off by a small tree at the top of the cliff.

8. TIRALI CALCETI 6a+ 15m
Starting at a cave at the base of the cliff and climb direct up a narrowing slab, an orange groove and a short leaning wall.

To the right are four closely packed lines up the wall. All are pleasant but unremarkable.
9. CAP DE CAIXO 6a 14m
The first route right of the cave with a prominent large bolt early on. Climb left of a yellow flake up two short leaning walls.

10. DOLORES CON PIANO 6a 14m
Follow the line of new bolts over an overlap and straight up the orange wall.

11. FLAMINGO 6a 14m
An older bolt above the initial overhang marks the start of this route that climbs grey bubbly rock and a left-trending shallow groove.

12. TORTUGO 6a 12m
The face just left of an easy groove is reached over a couple of overhangs and climbed via a broken flake.

13. L'ORATGE 4 10m
The left-hand flake on the right side of the buttress is quite hard for the grade.

14. OBRI LLAUNES 4 10m
The odd wide yet shallow chimney feature is bridged or jammed to a selection of lower-offs.

To the right is an easy left-slanting ramp and then another buttress with the prominent flake crack of VA QUE'S PER HUI towards its left side.
15. SOPA DE GANSO 6a+ 20m
The left-facing orange crack on the left side of the wall is followed to difficult moves out right to reach the lower-off.

16. VA QUE'S PER HUI ☺ 6a 20m
Start immediately right of the large flake and reach the thin hanging crack via a block overhang and some left trending grooves. Once gained it gives excellent sustained climbing to a lower-off on the left.

17. ROCABOLA ☺ 6a+ 20m
Just to the right with a steep start up a rusty-red flake and grey wall, then the left side of the broad bulging rib. The route features plenty of unhelpful holds and a traverse out right to reach the lower-off.

18. PANXA VERDA ☺ 7b 20m
A line of green bolts up the 'blank' rib is hideously hard.

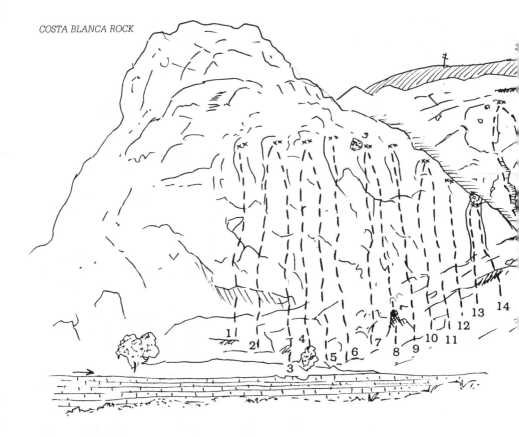

Cagallo De Gegant

1. S'HAS GOLO 7a+
2. BARRUFETS ☺ 6c
3. PITUFOS ☺ 6a
4. PELAWATIOS ☺ 6a
5. ESPERO BOXERINI ☺ 6a
6. DOLORES ☺ 6a
7. CARAGOL 5
8. TIRALI CALCETI 6a+
9. CAP DE CAIXO 6a
10. DOLORES CON PIANO 6a
11. FLAMINGO 6a
12. TORTUGO 6a
13. L'ORATGE 4
14. OBRI LLAUNES 4
15. SOPA DE GANSO 6a+
16. VA QUE'S PER HUI ☺ 6a
17. ROCABOLA ☺ 6a+
18. PANXA VERDA ☺ 7b
19. MITJA VIA 6c+

20. MAN FOTUT ☺ 7a+
21. BON TACTE 7a+
22. SI HAY SIROCO NO COMAS EL COCO 6c+
23. ARA NO BAILO 6b+
24. MARTI TIRALI ☺ 6b
25. LA PENYA DELS BOTIFARRES ☺ 6a+
26. PABLITO CLAVO UN CLAVITO ☺ 6b
27. DE REPENT UN PARAPENT 6c+
28. SECCIO HOMOS 6c
29. DESASTRE PER UN A SASTRE 6b+
30. XE QUIN BOLET 6a
31. QUE CONTEN QU'ESTIC 6c
32. RELAJACIO 6c
33. OPA OSTIL 7a
34. CAP FINET 6b+
35. MANO GUARRA 7a+
36. LA TRAMPA 6a

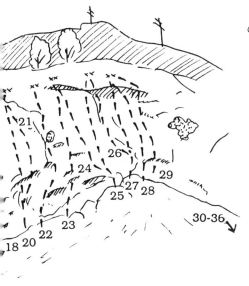

then pass the left side of the final overhang.

Scramble up and right to where there are two low bolts close together at the base of the wall.
24. MARTI TIRALI ☺ 6b 18m
Pull over the right side of the lower bulge then trend left up the fine grey wall to the lower-off of the previous climb.

25. LA PEÑYA DELS BOTIFARRES ☺ 6a+ 18m
A direct line above the start of the previous climb up the wall left then right via a flake before crossing the roof at the top of the top of the cliff.

26. PABLITO CLAVO UN CLAVITO ☺ 6b 18m
Start from a flat ledge and climb past a big bolt into a scoop then follow a left-trending white rib to the lower-off used by the previous climb.

27. DE REPENT UN PARAPENT 6c+ 18m
A line directly above the start of the previous climb up a tough shallow groove.

28. SECCIO HOMOS 6c 18m
The wall just to the right leads to the large roof at the cliff top.

29. DESASTRE PER A UN SASTRE 6b+ 18m
The last line on this part of the wall starts up shattered bubbly rock and eventually tackles the upper roof at its widest point.

Further to the right there is some impressively smooth rock that is undeveloped at present. On the far right is a small tower above a dam, with five short climbs and just to the left are two longer offerings. Start from a high ledge (most easily reached by the next route) is 30. XE QUIN BOLET 6a, up a right trending flake crack and on the left of the lower wall is the longest route in this area 31. QUE CONTEN QU'ESTIC 6c, reached by crossing the canal, climbing scruffy rock passing two bolts and then better climbing up the rib above.

On the small tower the five routes are:
32. RELAJACIO 6c 10m
The short left-hand line up a rib.

---

19. MITJA VIA ☺ 6c+ 20m
The line through the smooth scoop starts as for the last route then steps out right to give thin fingery climbing up the left side of the open shallow scoop.

20. MAN FOTUT ☺ 7a+ 18m
The right side of the scoop gives another fierce and sharp pitch.

21. BON TACTE 7a+ 20m
A right-hand variant start to the previous climb.

Up the slope to the right the cliff bulges to its lower section and is capped by a long narrow roof. The routes offer good climbing on solid rock but the steep rock and loose ledges at the foot of the cliff are a real pain!

22. SI HAY SIROCO NO COMAS EL COCO 6c+ 18m
A line up tilted grey rock passing below the large tree growing from a niche, and then trending left to the lower-offs.

23. ARA NO BAILO 6b+ 18m
The lower bulges are tackled direct via a hanging ramp (directly below a tree at the top of the cliff),

33. OPA OSTIL 7a 10m
The first route on the main part of the wall on very smooth rock and then the bulges above tackled rightwards.

34. CAP FINET 6b+ 10m
The central line passing a hole.

35. MANO GUARRA 7a+ 10m
The centre of the orange wall directly above the dam.

36. LA TRAMPA 6a
The right-hand line starts up the brick work and then follows the rib above.

Sector Del Deposit
A short (15m) wall with 22 very well bolted routes on rock that is vertical or gently overhanging. The wall faces south west and so is usually in the sun and is ideal for climbers with short ropes who want to do a lot of routes!
ACCESS. Turn up the track by the parking for the PARED DE GEGANT and drive up this for 200m to parking by the water pumping station. Do not block access or restrict the turning of other vehicles. The crag is 5 minutes walk up the valley to the right of the buildings.
The routes are listed from right to left.

1. NUI D'AMOUR 6a 15m
Start on the far right just left of where the rock turns scruffy and climb a grey rib, some bulges and 'odd' rock above. Entering the niche above the third bolt is tricky if done direct.

2. TARAMBANA ☺ 6b 15m
Two metres left start by a block embedded in the ground and climb red rock through a hollow and over bulges, the first of which is the crux.

3. PATIRAS ☺ 6b+ 15m
Start just to the left and climb the wall via precarious moves and then press on more strenuously up the leaning wall above. A superb sustained pitch on which the drilled 'mono' is easily avoided!

To the left is an undeveloped area which includes a large hanging flake.

4. PATOMAS ☺ 7b 15m
Left of the lowest point of the cliff and a grey tufa streak is this steeply bulging arete.

5. ARACNIDO 6b+ 15m
Start up the slope to the left and pass the right edge of an overlap then press on up the right edge of the bay above.

6. PEPE TROLA 7a 15m
The first bolt is below a stal/tufa, pull over the centre of the roof and then climb the steep back wall of the bay above.

7. BOMBERS ☺ 6c+ 15m
Green bolts protect this line that weaves up the wall.

8. EL SOMNI ☺ 7a+ 15m
Pass tufas, a couple of roofs and finish up the crinkly red wall above.

9. LINXO DE BOLINXO ☺ 6c+ 15m
Black bolts protect a tough start through stacked roofs. Higher up the climbing is easier but also sharper.

10. MAULETS ☺ 6c 15m
Start to the left where the roofs are broader, cross these and the wall above.

11. CAMARON ☺ 7a 15m
Tackle the roof at its widest part and press on to a lower-off below a bush at the top of the cliff.

12. TATACHAM ☺ 6a+ 15m
Rather older looking (but still very substantial) bolts protect a tough move over the lower roof and the sustained shallow groove above. The easiest pitch on the cliff.

13. RATAMPLAN ☺ 6b 15m
The sustained wall left of the shallow groove with the crux right at the very top.

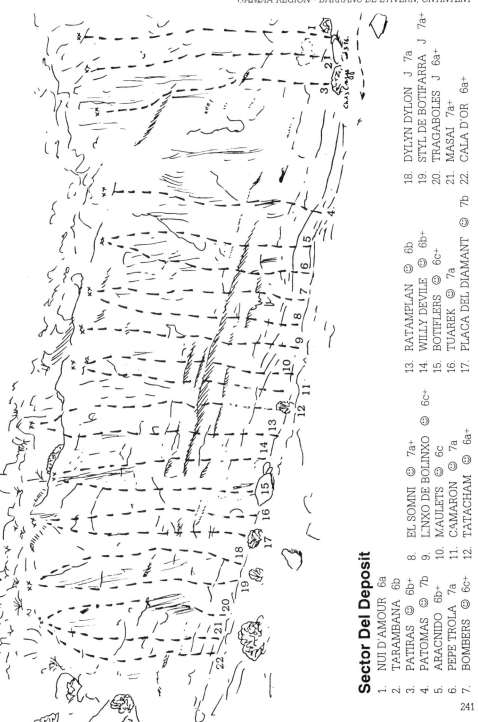

Sector Del Deposit

1. NUI D'AMOUR 6a
2. TARAMBANA 6b
3. PATIRAS ☺ 6b+
4. PATOMAS ☺ 7b
5. ARACNIDO 6b+
6. PEPE TROLA 7a
7. BOMBERS ☺ 6c+

8. EL SOMNI ☺ 7a+
9. LNXO DE BOLINXO ☺ 6c+
10. MAULETS ☺ 6c
11. CAMARON ☺ 7a
12. TATACHAM ☺ 6a+

13. RATAMPLAN ☺ 6b
14. WILLY DEVILE ☺ 6b+
15. BOTIFLERS ☺ 6c+
16. TUAREK ☺ 7a
17. PLACA DEL DIAMANT ☺ 7b

18. DYLYN DYLON J 7a
19. STYL DE BOTIFARRA J 7a+
20. TRAGABOLES J 6a+
21. MASAI 7a+
22. CALA D'OR 6a+

Sector La Visera

1. SU UNA ROSA ES UNA ROSA 4
2. TEORIA EN LA PRACTICA 4
3. PELAILLA 5
4. MATA CASTELLANS 6b+
5. TECNOLOGIA PUTA 7a
6. FRAUDE MILLONARIO 6a+
7. TOT MON TESOR 7a+
8. LA CARA AL VENT ☺ 7a+
9. POLIVALENT ☺ 7b
10. PREMATURO ☺ 7a
11. ALTAIR ☺ 6b+
12. ANTROPOMORFO ☺ 6b+
13. ETERNA ☺ 6c+
14. CALLO LARGO ☺ 7b
15. MISION IMPOSIBLE ?

14. WILLY DEVILE ☺ 6b+ 15m
Start at a big block on the ground and head for the top!

15. BOTIFLERS ☺ 6c+ 15m
Start at some white rock and cross the bulges at an orange streak. Blue bolts protect.

16. TUAREK ☺ 7a 15m
The gently leaning wall is climbed following the right edge of an orange streak. Wire cable belay.

17. PLACA DEL DIAMANT ☺ 7b 15m
The left side of the orange streak.

18. DYLYN DYLON ☺ 7a 15m
Straight up the brown streak.

19. STYL DE BOTIFARRA ☺ 7a+ 15m
The line just to the right of the prominent tufa systems.

20. TRAGABOLES ☺ 6a+ 15m
The tufa systems are climbed on large spaced holds with a hard move at the top. Shorties might question the grade.

21. MASAI 7a+ 15m
Just left climb directly up the wall.

22. CALA D'OR 6a+ 12m
The final offering is perhaps the least worthwhile on the whole cliff.

Sector La Visera
A steeply tilted wall with some excellent 'gorilla thrillers' just across the gully from the SECTOR DEL DEPOSIT. Approach as for the previous area and scramble left along ledges. The angle of the cliff coupled with its more easterly aspect means that it goes into the shade earlier than its immediate neighbour.

On the right edge of the cliff is a rather scrubby slab. Three routes climb this and share a common lower-off.
1. SU UNA ROSA ES UNA ROSA 4 12m
A rib and slab on the far right.

2. TEORIA EN LA PRACTICA 4 12m
Immediately to the left, more of the same.

9. POLIVALENT ☺ 7b 15m
The right side of the hanging red rib, tufa climbing near the bottom then pocket pulling above.

10. PREMATURO ☺ 7a 15m
A leaning wall is climbed on finger pockets via an orange streak passing a hole with a bush in it. Finish up the rib.

11. ALTAIR ☺ 6b+ 15m
Steep jug pulling leads into a cave, then climb the steep pocketed rock to a lower-off on the rim of the wall.

12. ANTROPOMORFO ☺ 6b+ 15m
Tackle the smart left-slanting orange ramp that narrows as it rises.

13. ETERNA ☺ 6c+ 15m
The grey and black tufa, and constricted and severely overhanging groove above.

14. CALLO LARGO ☺ 7b 15m
Four metres left get into the big hole at 4m then swing left on to the leaning rib.

15. MISION IMPOSIBLE ? 15m
4m left again, the last route on the face is listed as a project in the latest guide to the area, any takers?

3. PELAILLA 5 12m
Steeply up a yellow streak for 4m then easier above.

4. MATA CASTELLANS 6b+ 14m
Up a short sharp leaning wall, then more straightforward climbing above.

5. TECNOLOGIA PUTA 7a 14m
Green bolts protect this line on the right side of the arete.

6. FRAUDE MILLONARIO 6a+ 14m
The first line on the left side of the arete, with a bulging start, then easier above.

7. TOT MON TESOR 7a+ 14m
Viciously up the leaning wall just to the left.

8. LA CARA AL VENT ☺ 7a+ 15m
The diagonal break that is main feature of the right side of the face is climbed by this route with a tough finish up a rib.

Pared De La Via

This section of developed rock is situated highest up the valley (2km from the start of the gorge and 1.4km from the main parking area) and rises above a railway embankment of impressive dimensions. The cliff is the most extensive in the valley and despite a good selection of routes there are also some wide sections of undeveloped rock. The cliff is reached from an extensive tarmacked parking area amongst ruined buildings directly below the face. This is accessed via a short steep track that starts at a narrow entrance on the outside of the long right-hand bend in the road directly opposite the cliff. This section of road is fast and GREAT CARE is needed when turning off here to avoid problems with traffic that really flies down the gorge. From the parking area descend to and cross the river via a log, then take a steep track that diagonals up to the right following the base of the impressive embankment to reach the railway line. Walk back left 50m then scramble up to the foot of the face. The routes are listed from right to left as this is the usual point of arrival. 10 minutes from the car.

Note: Climbers who are using a 50m rope will have difficulties here, take care when lowering off.

The first five routes are clustered around a hollow bay at the far right side of the cliff.

1. QUE FACILE ☺ 5 20m

Climb the easy rib to the right of the bay, then continue up a short bulging wall before following a ramp up to the right and then climbing the right edge of the slab to a lower-off just short of the gully.

2. CAP AMUNT 5+ 20m

Follow the easy rib and bulging wall of the previous route but then climb straight up the slab above until a couple of moves left lead to the new lower-off of the next climb.

3. PIPIOLO ☺ 6a 20m

Bridge up the back of the groove then swing left and mantleshelf onto a cleaned ledge. The slab gives sustained and delicate climbing, that slowly eases.

4. SI, QUE ☺ 6a 20m

2m to the left is a right facing corner. Climb steeply into the corner and continue passing some rock scars then continue up the slab to the last bolt, at which point a short traverse right to the lower-off of the previous climb is possible.

5. CINQ-ZERO ☺ 6a+ 20m

Climb the rib that forms the left edge of the right facing flake passing a couple of ledges then continue up the scoop to a lower-off just below the rim of the wall.

To the left are two new routes that share a common and prominent lower-off at 12m. The right-hand one climbs the smooth bulging rib and looks about 6c and the left-hand one passes just right of a tufa and looks easier. Down the slope to the left are three blocks standing in front of the face. Just left of these are some white cleaned ledges sprouting bits of shrubbery.

8. QUE PALLISSA ☺ 6a 20m

Climb through some scoops then up a steep pocketed wall before finishing up a short rib with conspicuous wire cable lower-off on holds that keep appearing.

9. MOLLERUNGA ✤ 6b 28m

A tough pitch at the grade but well worthwhile. Start in the same place as the last route but move left and make hard moves to reach a large hole and harder moves to leave it. If successful continue on up the pumpy wall to eventually reach easier climbing, ledges and then the lower-off.

10. LLUM ARTIFICIAL ☺ 6c 28m

To the left again climb easy slabs between

Pared DeLa Via (right side)

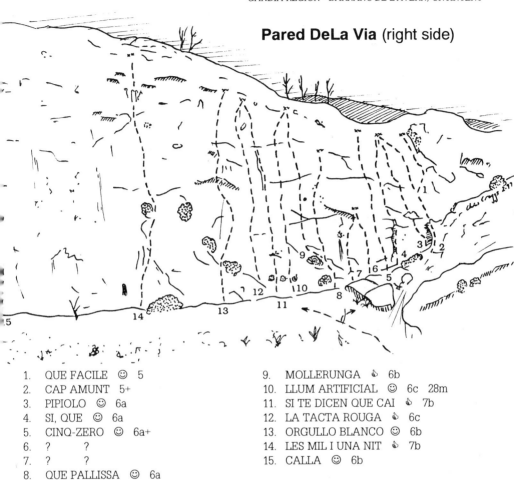

1.	QUE FACILE ☺	5
2.	CAP AMUNT	5+
3.	PIPIOLO ☺	6a
4.	SI, QUE ☺	6a
5.	CINQ-ZERO ☺	6a+
6.	?	?
7.	?	?
8.	QUE PALLISSA ☺	6a

9.	MOLLERUNGA 🌢	6b
10.	LLUM ARTIFICIAL ☺	6c 28m
11.	SI TE DICEN QUE CAI 🌢	7b
12.	LA TACTA ROUGA 🌢	6c
13.	ORGULLO BLANCO ☺	6b
14.	LES MIL I UNA NIT 🌢	7b
15.	CALLA ☺	6b

bushes to reach a couple of old bolts. Above this new ones protect difficult moves up the steep wall to reach a diagonal break and the even steeper wall above this point.

11. SI TE DICEN QUE CAI 🌢 7b 30m
Start at the flat base of the cliff and climb easy rock to reach the first bolt at 10m, passing a hole then on up smooth powder grey streak, and bulging wall to a hole and on through more bulges above, 11 bolt runners protect this majestic pitch.

12. LA TACTA ROUGA 🌢 6c 30m
Start to the left and climb to a bolt on the lower lip of a hole 10m up then head through the centre of big patch of yellow rock riddled with holes before crossing an overhang and finishing up grey rock above.

13. ORGULLO BLANCO ☺ 6b 30m
Climb the hard black lower slab on crinkley holds then pull over an overlap and pass to the right of a tree on up much better holds above keeping to the right of the bolt line.

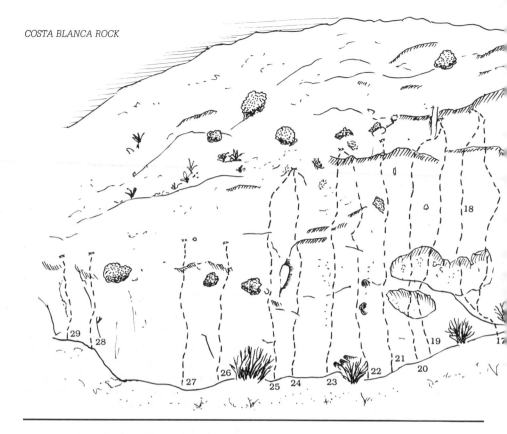

8m further left is the longest route on the cliff:

14. LES MIL I UNA NIT 🔊 7b 35m
Perhaps the showpiece of the cliff staring up a grey slab behind some prickly bushes then following a direct line straight up the face pulling through bulges and finishing close to the top of the wall.

Past a 25m wide strip of undeveloped rock and a small tree growing from the face is a solitary route with the lower-off situated between twin tufas at 18m:

15. CALLA ☺ 6b 18m
Short lived but excellent climbing. Climb the grey pocketed rib on sharp rock gradually steeping as it rises to a position below the prominent tufa system. Make tough move on small sharp holds to grasp the tufa and sprint smartly onto the lower-off.

10m to the left is a bolt line up a rib then through

some 'cheesy' caves before trending to pull through bulges and up tufas eventually reach a chain lower-off that hangs from the centre of the large roof high on the cliff. This looks at least as good as the superb LES MIL I UNA NIT (see above), is 35m long and appears to be in the 6c-7a range.

Towards the left side of the cliff there a large, shallow, oval-shaped cave/hollow 10m up the face. There are four routes that pass through this feature.

17. MOCADOR BLAU ☺ 6b 30m
Climb an easy rib/ramp to get into the cave then step right climb through the juggy bulges before heading up the grey wall, right and then left, to reach a lower-off set in a white streak.

18. BAIXADA 41 ☺ 6c 30m
This climb attacks the centre of the leaning back

Pared De La Via
(left side)

16. ?   ?
17. MOCADOR BLAU ☺
    6b 30m
18. BAIXADA 41 ☺ 6c
19. EL CERDO VOLADOR
    ☺ 6c
20. NO TALLES EL TEIX
    ☺ 6b+
21. CAXIPOLLA ☺ 6c
22. LA LEY DEL AGARRE
    ☺ 6b+
23. JHONY MENDIETA
    ♦ 6a+
24. ORELLES LLARGUES
    ☺ 6c
25. ORELLES CURTES ☺
    7a
26. ALEX ?
27. EL PRINCIPE ?
28. BRIMONSTER 6b+
29. CAPOLL 6a+

and then the lower-off of the previous climb.

To the left of the small bush and the caves is a steep grey slab up which the next three worthwhile climbs all start.

21. CAXIPOLLA ☺ 6c 30m
Climb the right edge of the grey slab up smooth rock and then on through a series of overlaps to a lower-off hanging from the overhangs above, sharp and sustained.

22. LA LEY DEL AGARRE ☺ 6b+ 28m
The central line on the grey slabs good and is hard for the grade, especially if the 'true line' is adhered to. Pass left of a hole at 10m then climb up the slab (easier to the left) and on through a series of bulges.

23. JHONY MENDIETA ♦ 6a+ 28m
Just left again and just right of a cave at the base of the wall this excellent route climbs the left side of the slab on more user friendly rock than its near neighbour, through a small overlap, up a yellow streak and over a juggy bulge to the lower-off of the previous climb.

The next feature left is a protruding hanging flake halfway up the cliff. The next two routes pass either side of this prominent feature.

24. ORELLES LLARGUES ☺ 6c 26m
Start up a yellow wall, climb over a small overhang then keep just right of the flake passing through a large bulge and finish up a leaning yellow 'crusty' wall.

25. ORELLES CURTES ☺ 7a 26m
Start up a grey apron of slabs and climb the wall passing between the flake and a bush growing out of a hole, through a bulge (crux) before trending left to reach the lower-off.

The next two lines are located to the left just past a section of slabby rock. The local guide suggests these are both projects and although no grades are known they don't look especially tough.

wall of the wide shallow cave and then climbs up the sharp grey wall above to reach the belay of the previous climb by slanting left.

Left of the grey slabby ramp is a smaller deeper cave set below the large shallow oval one.

19. EL CERDO VOLADOR ☺ 6c 30m
Climb through the centre of the lower cave, juggy, then up the back wall of the large cave passing close to a large prickly bush. Continue up the grey rock above to reach a big hole in the final roof with the chains up and left of this point.

20. NO TALLES EL TEIX ☺ 6b+ 30m
The next route left climbs just right of a small bush on the wall to reach a large area of yellow rock, through some big holes and then a more broken area. From here climb rightwards until just below a bulging prow and make a finger wrecking move out right the reach final section

26. ALEX ? 18m
Climb a grey slab and yellow streak passing right of bush on a ledge below an overhang and on up a short leaning wall to a lower-off located on the rim of the wall.

27. EL PRINCIPE ? 18m
The second 'project' passes left of the bush and climbs a white rib and then a thin wriggly crack line.

The final two climbs are a couple of short and uninspiring offerings close to the very left edge of the cliff.

28. BRIMONSTER 6b+ 12m
The right-hand route climbs a ragged overhanging crack starting from a bay with a bush in it and is reached past a hacked flake and a tree stump.

29. CAPOLL 6a+ 12m
3m left the short line up a white awkward leaning crack is the final route on the cliff.

Barranc de l'Avern: The author on the well bolted
TATACHAM 6a+ on the Sector del Deposit

NOTES

CICERONE CLIMBING & SCRAMBLING GUIDES

SCRAMBLES IN THE LAKE DISTRICT
R.B. Evans
ISBN 0 902363 39 5   192pp   PVC cover   £9.99
MORE SCRAMBLES IN THE LAKE DISTRICT
R.B.Evans
ISBN 1 85284 042 0   200 pp   PVC cover   £9.99
Exciting rock scrambles in gills or easy angled craglets, to thrill the mountaineer.

WINTER CLIMBS IN THE LAKE DISTRICT   Bob
Bennett , Bill Birkett , and Brian Davison
A new edition packed with the latest routes which confirm the area as a major winter climbing venue.
ISBN 1 85284 246 6   200pp   £14.99

CLWYD ROCK *Gary Dickinson.*
Rock climbs on the Welsh Border, around Wrexham and Llangollen. *ISBN 1 85284 094 3 232pp PVC cover £14.99*

SCRAMBLES IN SNOWDONIA   *Steve Ashton*
The classic rock ridges and other adventurous routes up challenging rocky faces. Second edition. *ISBN 1 85284 088 9 168pp PVC cover £9.99*

WELSH WINTER CLIMBS *Malcolm Campbell &Andy Newton* The snow and ice climbs of North Wales. Superb diagrams and colour photos.   *ISBN 1 85284 001 3   256pp   PVC cover   £14.99*

WEST MIDLANDS ROCK *Doug Kerr*
The latest guide to the popular crags. *ISBN 1 85284 200 8   168pp   £7.99*

CORNISH ROCK *Rowland Edwards & Tim Dennell*
A superb photo topo guide to West Penwith, the most popular climbing in Cornwall, by the area's leading activists. *ISBN 1 85284 208 3   272pp   A5 size Casebound   £18.99*

CAIRNGORMS Winter Climbs   *Allen Fyffe*
Covers the classic winter climbs in the Cairngorms, Lochnagar and Creag Meaghaidh.
ISBN 0 902363 99 9   120pp   PVC cover   £7.99

THE ISLAND OF RHUM - A Guide for Walkers, Climbers and Visitors *Hamish M.Brown*
The complete companion for any visitor to the island, owned by the Nature Conservancy.
ISBN 1 85284 002 1   100pp   £5.99

SCRAMBLES IN LOCHABER *Noel Williams*
Some of the best scrambling in Britain around Glencoe and Ben Nevis and much of the Western Highlands around of Fort William. *ISBN 1 85284 234 2 Revised edition   192pp   £9.99*

SCRAMBLES IN SKYE *J.W.Parker* The Cuillins is a paradise for scrambling. A unique large scale 4-colour map accompanies the book to facilitate route finding in this complex area. *ISBN 0 902363 38 7 144pp   PVC cover   £9.99*

WINTER CLIMBS BEN NEVIS & GLENCOE
Alan Kimber   Britain's finest winter climbing area.
ISBN 1 85284 179 6 232pp   PVC cover   £14.99

FRENCH ROCK *Bill Birkett*
THE guide to many exciting French crags! Masses of photo topos, with selected hit-routes in detail. *ISBN 1 85284 113 3.   332pp   A5 size. £14.99*

Selected ROCK CLIMBS IN BELGIUM & LUXEMBOURG *Chris Craggs*
Perfect rock, good protection and not too hot to climb in summer. *ISBN 1 85284 155 9   188p   A5 £12.99*

ROCK CLIMBS IN THE VERDON. An Introduction   *Rick Newcombe*   An English-style guide, which makes for easier identification of the routes and descents. *ISBN 1 85284 015 3   72pp   £5.50*

ROCK CLIMBS IN THE PYRENEES *Derek Walker*
The first English guide to these impressive climbs. Includes Pic du Midi d'Ossau and the Vignemale in France, and the Ordesa Canyon and Riglos in Spain. *ISBN 1 85284 039 0   168pp   PVC cover   £9.99*

ANDALUSIAN ROCK CLIMBS *Chris Craggs*
El Chorro and El Torcal are world famous. Includes Tenerife. *ISBN 1 85284 109 5 168pp £6.99*

COSTA BLANCA ROCK *Chris Craggs* Over 1500 routes on over 40 crags,some described for the first time in English. The most comprehensive guide to the area. *ISBN 1 85284 241 5 256pp   £12.99*

ROCK CLIMBS IN MAJORCA, IBIZA & TENERIFE *Chris Craggs*
Holiday island cragging at its best. *ISBN 1 85284 189 3 240pp   £10.99*

WALKS & CLIMBS IN THE PICOS DE EUROPA

Robin Walker A definitive guide to these unique mountains. Walks and rock climbs of all grades. *ISBN 1 85284 033 1 232pp PVC cover £10.99*

KLETTERSTEIG Scrambles in the Northern Limestone Alps

Paul Werner Translated by Dieter Pevsner Protected climbing paths similar to the Via Ferrata of the Dolomites. *ISBN 0 902363 46 8 184pp PVC cover £7.99*

THE CENTRAL APENNINES OF ITALY Walks, Scrambles and Climbs

Stephen Fox The mountainous spine of Italy, with secluded walks, rock climbs and scrambles on the Gran Sasso d'Italia, and some of Italy's finest sport climbing crags. *ISBN 1 85284 219 9*

ITALIAN ROCK. Selected Climbs in Northern Italy

Al Churcher. Val d'Orco and Mello, Lecco and Finale etc. *ISBN 0 902363 93 X 200pp PVC cover £8.99*

VIA FERRATA SCRAMBLES IN THE DOLOMITES

Höfler/Werner Translated by Cecil Davies. The most exciting walks in the world. Wires, stemples and ladders enable the 'walker' to enter the climber's vertical environment. *ISBN 1 85284 089 7 248pp PVC cover £10.99*

THE MOUNTAINS OF TURKEY

Karl Smith Over 100 treks and scrambles with detailed route descriptions of all the popular peaks. Includes Ararat. *ISBN 1 85284 161 3 184pp PVC cover £14.99*

TREKS AND CLIMBS in WADI RUM, JORDAN

Tony Howard. The world's foremost desert climbing and trekking venue. Masses of fantastic climbing. *ISBN 1 85284 254 7 252pp A5 Card cover £17.00*

THE ALA DAG, Climbs and Treks in Turkey's Crimson Mountains

O.B.Tüzel The best mountaineering area in Turkey. Destined to be one of the in-places. *ISBN 1 85284 112 5 296pp PVC cover £14.99*

TREKKING IN THE CAUCAUSUS

Yuri Kolomiets & Aleksey Solovyev The great mountains hidden until recently behind the Iron Curtain. 62 walks of which half demand basic climbing skills. Included are the walks to the highest tops in Europe, the summits of Mt Elbrus. *ISBN 1 85284 129 X 224pp PVC cover £14.99*

ROCK CLIMBING IN HONG KONG

Brian J.Heard Great climbing for both locals and travellers. *ISBN 1 85284 167 2 136pp A5 size £12.99*

OZ ROCK A Rock Climber's Guide to Australian Crags

Alastair Lee An overall view of climbing in Australia with details of each crag and how to get there. From 10m sport climbs to 800m adventure climbs the choice and quality is exceptional *ISBN 1 85284 237 7 184pp A5 size £10.99*

TECHNIQUES

ROPE TECHNIQUES *Bill March* Best selling handbook for experienced climbers, includes self-rescue techniques. *ISBN 1 85284 120 6 200pp £5.99*

SNOW & ICE TECHNIQUES *Bill March* Essential reading for all ice climbers. Emphasis on self-arrest. A best seller for many years. Updated by Bill Birkett. *ISBN 1 85284 238 5 96pp £5.99*

THE HILLWALKERS MANUAL *Bill Birkett* Everything the hillwalker needs to know from safety to photography. *ISBN 1 85284 111 7 152pp £7.99*

THE TREKKER'S HANDBOOK *Thomas R. Gilchrist* Everything a trekker needs to know, from gear to health. *ISBN 1 85284 205 9 A5 A5 size £10.99*

TREKKING

ANNAPURNA - A Trekker's Guide *Kev Reynolds* Includes Annapurna Circuit, the Annapurna Sanctuary and the Pilgrim's Trail, with lots of good advice. *ISBN 1 85284 132 X 184pp £8.99*

EVEREST - A Trekker's Guide *Kev Reynolds* The most popular trekking region in the Himalaya. Lodges, tea-house, permits, health - all are dealt with in this indispensible guide. *ISBN 1 85284 187 7 £8.99*

LANGTANG, GOSAINKUND & HELAMBU - A Trekker's Guide *Kev Reynolds* Popular area, easily accessible from Kathmandu. *ISBN 1 85284 207 5 £8.99*

ADVENTURE TREKS IN NEPAL *Bill O'Connor* *ISBN 1 85223 306 0 160pp large format £9.99*

ADVENTURE TREKS WESTERN NORTH AMERICA

Chris Townsend   ISBN 1 85223 317 6 160pp large format   £9.99

CLASSIC TRAMPS IN NEW ZEALAND *Constance Roos* The 14 best long distance walks in both South and North Islands. *ISBN 1 85284 118 4   208pp PVC cover   £14.99*

FAR HORIZONS Adventure Travel for All!

Walt Unsworth "These are adventures to dream abouty! From the glories of Samarkand to the thrills of the Dolomites' airy paths; from the jungles of Borneo to crossing the Grand Canyon and sleeping under the stars - it's all here. This exciting and informative book makes you want to pack your bags immediately and get going!" Sir Christian Bonington

Base on the author's wide experience of this growing form of holiday travel - there are over 250 specialist firms in Great Britain alone. *ISBN 1 85284 228 8 160pp A5 size   £8.99*

PRICES SUBJECT TO ALTERATION - SEE
CURRENT PRICE LIST

PVC BOOK PROTECTORS to fit all Cicerone standard pocket sized card cover Guide Books are available from many book shops. Ask for size 176mm. For A5 ask for size 210

Send for complete Price List of over 280 books - Long Distance walks, day walks, short family walks, canal walks, bike guides, canoeing, trekking, climbing etc.

Available from all good outdoor shops, bookshops or direct (include P&P) from
**Cicerone Press, 2 Police Square, Milnthorpe, Cumbria LA7 7PY.
Tel: 015395 62069**

TEXT PRINTED AND BOUND BY
WBC BOOK MANUFACTURERS LTD, BRIDGEND, MID GLAMORGAN